FIFTH EDITION

THE STRUCTURE OF SOCIAL STRATIFICATION IN THE UNITED STATES

LEONARD BEEGHLEY

University of Florida

Boston ▪ New York ▪ San Francisco ▪ Mexico City ▪ Montreal
Toronto ▪ London ▪ Madrid ▪ Munich ▪ Paris ▪ Hong Kong
Singapore ▪ Tokyo ▪ Cape Town ▪ Sydney

Executive Editor: *Jeff Lasser*
Series Editorial Assistant: *Lauren Houlihan*
Senior Marketing Manager: *Kelly May*
Production Editor: *Claudine Bellanton*
Editorial Production Service: *Connie Strassburg*
Composition Buyer: *Linda Cox*
Manufacturing Buyer: *Debbie Rossi*
Composition Full-Service Project Management: *GGS Book Services*
Cover Administrator: *Joel Gendron*

For related titles and support materials, visit our online catalog at www.ablongman.com.

Between the time website information is gathered and then published, it is not unusual for some sites to have closed. Also, the transcription of URLs can result in errors. The publisher would appreciate notification where these errors occur so that they may be corrected in subsequent editions.

ISBN-13: 978-0-205-53052-6   ISBN-10: 0-205-53052-4

Library of Congress Cataloging-in-Publication Data

Beeghley, Leonard.
    The structure of social stratification in the
United States / Leonard Beeghley.—5th ed.
        p.   cm.
    Includes bibliographical references and index.
    ISBN-13: 978-0-205-53052-6
    ISBN-10: 0-205-53052-4
        1. Social classes—United States.
    2. Social stratification—United States.
    3. Social structure—United States.
    I. Title.
    HN90.S6B44 2007
    305.50973—dc22

                                    2007002621

Printed in the United States of America

10 9 8 7 6 5 4 3 2   11 10 09

This book is dedicated to
Mary Anna
who remains my best friend after all these years.

Thank you
for the many nights of conversation,
for sharing your hopes and dreams,
for listening to mine,
and for your trust and love every day of the year.

CONTENTS

CHAPTER SIX

Political Participation and Power   145

PREFACE

In this book, I have tried to distill out of the rich vein of sociological research some of what is known about the *structure of stratification* in the United States. The term refers to the distribution of resources in society, such as income, prestige, and power. The structure of stratification affects every aspect of life: where (and whether) one lives, who one marries, how (and whether) one earns a living, who one's friends are, and much more. In revising the book, my objective has been to make each chapter factually accurate, interesting to read, and relevant to readers' lives. In the process, the book has been completely reorganized, updated, and rewritten for this fifth edition.

In making these revisions, I have tried to keep in mind that science is the art of asking questions. But questions are always asked in light of an intellectual framework—which needs to be explicit. In Chapter 1, the ideas of the most important theorists of stratification are reviewed, and a coherent strategy for studying stratification is developed and used throughout the book. This strategy has three elements: First, as often as possible, I place data in a historical and cross-national context. This information leads to important questions. For example, if the rate of poverty has fallen in all Western societies (and it has), one wants to know why. But if, even given the historical decline, the rate of poverty in the United States is much higher than in Western Europe (and it is), one again wants to know why. Second, I distinguish between social psychological explanations of individual actions and structural explanations of rates of behavior. Just as one obtains different insights from examining a painting up close and afar, these two levels of analysis provide complementary but different insights into social life. For example, the reasons why individuals become poor (for example, they lack skills) have nothing whatsoever to do with why so many people are poor (for example, macroeconomic policy restricts the number of jobs that are available whenever it is necessary to control inflation). There is an enduring insight here: Regardless of the topic, the variables explaining why individuals act differ from those explaining why rates of behavior vary. This fact will be illustrated throughout the book. This distinction aids in understanding issues as diverse as poverty, mobility, voting, gender stratification, and racial/ethnic stratification. Third, I emphasize the importance of power for understanding the structure of stratification. The story of the last century is one of increasing control over human affairs. As just one example, nations now control how much inequality and poverty exist. Hence, the periodic use of macroeconomic policy to restrict the number of jobs provides one example (there are others) of how poverty is created and maintained in this country. More generally, I argue that the level of inequality in the United States reflects the power of the rich and middle class to protect their lifestyles. Again, there is an enduring insight here: *The higher the social class, the greater the influence over the distribution of resources in the society.*

This statement is called the *Political Power Hypothesis* in Chapter 1. It is just one of many hypotheses and findings presented in the book. The importance of hypothesis testing is emphasized throughout. This is, in part, a pedagogical device. It illustrates for students (rather than merely asserting) the possibilities of scientific sociology by showing both how much we know and, by implication, how much remains to be learned. Most hypotheses and empirical generalizations (stable findings) are phrased as statements of covariance. This tactic shows students how a change in one phenomenon is associated with change in another. This point is typically made in methods and (less often) theory courses, but neglected elsewhere. Too frequently, I think, text writers give the impression that sociological knowledge depends upon the assumptions observers make. Nothing could be further from the truth. In part, however, the emphasis on hypothesis testing is also a statement about the nature of social science. If science is the art of asking questions, then our answers must reflect knowledge based on observation.

Yet how observations are to be interpreted remains a vexing issue. In the study of stratification, for example, the relationship among class, race, and gender as systems of domination has become controversial in recent years. Throughout this book, I try to show how they are interrelated. Minorities remain unequal to Whites; women remain unequal to men. This inequality reflects the historical legacy and continuing impact of prejudice and discrimination. Yet these forms of inequality have declined in recent years. In considering these issues, the larger question is the degree to which people's location in the stratification structure is determined by birth or achievement. One of the paradoxes of modernity is that our very concern with gender and racial/ethnic stratification reflects a degree of movement (I would say progress) toward class-based stratification structures. When societies are stratified by class, unlike medieval estates, there is an increased emphasis on achievement. This historical transformation is one example of what I meant earlier in saying that people and, indeed, entire societies, now have greater control over how they organize themselves.

The book is written primarily for students, but also for general readers who want to know more about how the distribution of resources occurs. I have tried to write simply and clearly. Although some jargon is unavoidable, I have kept it to a minimum. When technical terms are necessary, they are introduced, defined, and illustrated. Even so, most textbooks are boring. Having taught social stratification for over thirty years, I have found that the use of metaphors, vignettes, even nursery rhymes, can be useful pedagogical devices. So I sometimes invent people, families, and situations in order to introduce or describe sociological findings. Occasionally, these episodes are (I hope) mildly humorous. Underlying such efforts at relieving the tedium, however, is a serious issue: The great world trend has been movement in the direction of more democracy and less inequality (the two are connected). The United States is thus part of a great historical process. I am convinced that sociology can and should inform public debate about it.

Leonard Beeghley
University of Florida

ACKNOWLEDGMENTS

No author works alone. I would like to take this opportunity to thank those individuals who helped in the process of revising this book. My most enduring debts are to George Wilson of the University of Miami and Marion Willetts of Illinois State University. As they have before, each took time out of their busy lives to read much of the manuscript and made valuable suggestions. Their comments and criticisms were extremely useful, often at crucial times. In addition, my students Christine Armstrong and Katie Schubert read much of the manuscript and helped me clarify the prose. Jane Dominguez and Jeff Stevens translated my crude drawings into several of the figures. As in the past, my editor at Allyn & Bacon, Jeff Lasser, has been very helpful throughout the project. In addition, both the copy editor, Terry Lane, and the production editor, Connie Strassburg, did an excellent job finding my mistakes and improving the presentation. Finally, the support of colleagues and friends is one of the joys of academic life. This book is better as a result and probably would be better yet if I had just had the good sense to take more of the advice offered. The usual caveat applies: Any errors that remain are my responsibility.

CHAPTER ONE

SOCIOLOGY AND STRATIFICATION

THEORETICAL PERSPECTIVES ON STRATIFICATION
Karl Marx
Max Weber
Kingsley Davis and Wilbert Moore
Ralf Dahrendorf
Gerhard Lenski

MODERNITY, THE AMERICAN DREAM, AND ANOMIE

A STRATEGY FOR THE STUDY OF STRATIFICATION
Historical and Cross-National Dimensions of Stratification
Levels of Analysis and Stratification
Power and Stratification

All societies display stratification. The term conveys an image of geological strata, of layers stacked one upon the other. Like geological strata, societies also display interconnected layers with what appear to be a ranked structure. The **structure of social stratification** can be defined as the distribution of resources in society, such as income, wealth, occupation, education, and power. In every society, these resources are allocated unequally.

Unequal possession of resources affects people's **life chances:** their ability to share in the available goods and services.[1] To visualize the practical way unequal resources affect life chances in modern societies, consider the long-term possibilities of two twenty-year-old young adults: George and Peter. George's parents are, respectively, a college professor and a clinical psychologist. In the (imperfect) classification schemes used by sociologists, they are middle class. Peter's parents are, respectively, a janitor and a secretary. They are working class. George is more likely to become a physician than Peter, simply because George's parents possess more resources. For example, because they have higher prestige occupations, more education, and higher incomes they can more easily provide advantages to George as he grows up. And this process will continue in the next generation as well. George's children are more likely to become physicians than Peter's children. The example illustrates a well-known observation: In all societies, parents pass on whatever advantages and disadvantages they have to their children.

Unequal distribution of resources also affects people's **lifestyle:** the way people choose to live, as indicated by their consumption habits, use of leisure time, and fundamental values. For example, people differ in whether (and what) they smoke, the kinds of alcohol they consume, the location and size of their housing, their level of health and whether they have health insurance, whether they have a pension and its amount, and myriad other ways. They also differ in attitudes about abortion, guns, how unequal our society should be, and other important social problems. The ability to choose a lifestyle, however, constitutes a new historical phenomenon. People's lifestyles were relatively homogeneous in preindustrial societies; in contrast, people's lifestyles display wide variability in modern societies.

Although geological strata may appear to be static and unchanging, this is misleading. In reality, dynamic processes shape the formation of the earth, which means that understanding the geological record requires looking at both stability and change. This orientation is also necessary when studying the structure of stratification.

Inequality in the distribution of resources does not arise by chance. Conflict occurs as individuals and groups struggle to keep and expand their share (of income and wealth, for example). Levels of inequality change over time as a result. Imagine that all the goods and services available in a society are like a pie. Everyone competes, both as individuals and as members of groups, for a piece of the pie. And no one wants to diet; everyone wants a bigger piece, at least so long as it is obtained fairly (and sometimes even if it is not). People want to improve their life chances—with health insurance, for example. They want better opportunities for their children compared to themselves—to become physicians, for example. And they want better lifestyles, too, as signified (perhaps) by moving into bigger houses in nicer neighborhoods. The outcome of the struggle over resources and variations in the level of inequality that result can be expressed by a simple question: Who gets what and why?[2]

The answer is reflected in the three systems of domination that characterize modern societies. Think of them as like geological strata, convoluted and crosscutting one another. Unlike geological strata, however, social systems of domination reflect the exercise of power and authority.[3] Thus, the arrangement of these ranked structures indicates the ongoing struggle over the structure of stratification in the United States.

The first is by class.[4] People in the same **class** tend to be equal to one another in terms of the distribution of resources. For example, those with similar levels of occupational prestige display roughly similar levels of income and education. People in different classes tend to be unequal in these same terms. Such variations affect people's life chances and lifestyles. For example, because their occupations differ, they also differ in access to health insurance, access to first-rate schools for their children, and many other goods and services.

As a system of domination, class is rather new in history. It arose along with economic development and democracy (the two are related) over the last few centuries. Power and authority in democratic societies are based on "the will of the people" expressed in procedurally correct ways—by elections, for example. In such contexts, while individuals' initial class placement reflects their family background (based on such factors as their parents' education and occupation), their own educational and occupational achievements become more important over time as they compete against others. This tension between the effects of family background and one's own achievement is unique to class systems, unique to modern societies. At the same time, even though they may not be formally organized, classes struggle for greater shares of the available resources (pieces of the pie). For example, laws providing huge tax breaks for the very rich, thereby increasing the level of inequality, reflect the class struggle: The rich have a greater ability to affect public policies to their benefit than do other social classes. Similarly, the system of employer-provided health insurance benefits the middle class, making it resistant to change even though millions of people go without health insurance, endure more health problems, and die younger as a result. The latter are mostly working class and poor. Generally, the most powerful classes benefit the most from public policies in every society, which is another way of saying they obtain more resources and have better life chances.

The second system of domination is by race and ethnicity. Members of racial and ethnic groups are often unequal to one another in terms of civil rights, infant mortality, income, occupational prestige, and other resources. For example, due to prejudice and discrimination, fewer minority group members are middle class than Whites. But even within the middle class, members of minority groups are often unequal to Whites. For example, given similar incomes, African Americans often pay higher interest rates for mortgages and auto loans, thus restricting their life chances and lifestyles. Such differences reflect the enduring impact of prejudice and discrimination, which function as mechanisms of domination by the more powerful racial and ethnic groups (Whites). Even so, racial and ethnic inequality has declined over the last two centuries as achievement-related criteria have become more important. This change results from the struggle for equal opportunity by racial and ethnic minorities, which is unique to modern societies.

The third system of domination is by gender. Women and men are unequal to one another in terms of income, occupational prestige, and other resources. Historically, discrimination in the form of traditional gender norms meant that women have not only had less access to resources than men but less autonomy in shaping their lives. Their life chances differed, and differ today as well. Such differences reflect the power and authority of men over women. But gender inequality has declined over time as both women and men are increasingly evaluated by their educational and occupational achievements. Again, this change results from struggle for equal opportunity by women, which is also unique to modern societies.

These ongoing conflicts over the structure of stratification raise important questions: How much opportunity is there to share in the available goods and services? And how do life chances vary across societies, especially in economically developed nations like the United States? In terms of the example used earlier, how much opportunity exists for Peter (who came from a working-class background) to become a physician if he is talented and works hard? And what about someone named Jane, Tamika, Julio, or Rashad? Would their opportunities be better or worse if they lived in, say, the United Kingdom or France?

One way sociologists answer these questions is by distinguishing between ascription and achievement. **Ascription** refers to the use of nonperformance-related criteria in evaluating a person, such as class of origin, race/ethnicity, or gender. This is a complicated way of saying that people obtain positions based on birth. For example, to the extent that certain types of people—say, white males—have advantages in seeking to become physicians indicates an emphasis on ascription. In societies emphasizing ascription, opportunity is relatively low and status (in the sense of prestige in the community) is often inherited. **Achievement** refers to the use of performance-related criteria that are equally applied to all persons, such as grade point averages, college degrees, or skill requirements. This is a complicated way of saying that people compete to obtain positions (such as occupations) and status based on hard work and ability. To the extent that anyone—regardless of class of origin, race/ethnicity, or gender—can become a physician based on grades and other skills indicates an emphasis on achievement. In societies emphasizing achievement, opportunity is greater.

In no society, of course, does either ascription or achievement constitute the sole basis for evaluating people. Seen as two ends of a continuum, they constitute **ideal types,** to use a phrase of Max Weber's.[5] Ideal types identify the characteristics of a social phenomenon in the purest form possible and observations reveal the degree to which societies resemble the "pure form." As illustrated in Figure 1.1, history reveals a pattern: In many societies today, a long term movement from ascription toward achievement has occurred.

As suggested by the figure, ascriptive criteria were of much greater importance than achievement in the past. As a result, the structure of stratification in all societies was relatively rigid, displaying high levels of inequality and low mobility rates, because almost everyone obtained positions based on birth. In such contexts, of course, most people's life chances and lifestyles were also determined at birth.

The situation differs a great deal today in that people's positions are determined by a combination of achievement and ascription. On the one hand, economic development, democracy, and other changes that occurred over the last few centuries have lead to an increasing emphasis on achievement via competition with others. One result is that stratification structures are now less rigid, displaying varying levels of inequality from one nation to another and higher mobility rates. Increased opportunity exists in class-based systems of domination. People can now advance compared to their parents, occupationally and in other ways, based on their effort and abilities. This change means their life chances can improve and lifestyles become more varied. On the other hand, ascription remains significant. Note that in Figure 1.1, the arrow indicating "present" is located, for illustrative purposes, only halfway across the continuum. Family background in the form of class of origin, race/ethnicity, and gender all affect access to resources and, hence, people's life chances, regardless of how much ability they have or how hard they work. Even in class-based systems of domination, it makes a difference if one is born rich or poor, white or brown, male or female. The built-in, uneasy tension between achievement and ascription in modern societies can never be resolved.

The existence of this tension, however, indicates the new historical possibilities characteristic of modern societies, with their lower levels of inequality, greater mobility,

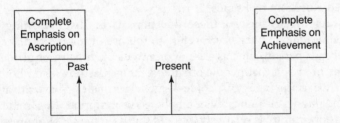

FIGURE 1.1   The Changing Importance of Ascription and Achievement

and considerable variation across nations. Where did these changes come from? How can they be understood? Theorists have tried to answer these questions.

THEORETICAL PERSPECTIVES ON STRATIFICATION

Economic development, capitalism, democracy, the rule of law, and other changes coalesced in the nineteenth century and shaped the modern world, including the structure of stratification. The first generation of sociologists appeared at that time as scholars sought to understand the great transformation that was occurring.[6] In terms of the pie metaphor used earlier, with this transformation, the size of the economic pie increased—radically. There are now more resources available to everyone and most people are better off than in the past.

Karl Marx

Karl Marx (b: 1818; d: 1883), like many others, saw that inequality increased with the rise of capitalism, industrialization, and the other changes that were taking place during the first half of the nineteenth century. In this context, he believed, capitalist social relationships are inherently exploitive and alienating, and that a communist revolution was certain to occur. From his point of view, the trick was to explain how and why.

In developing his explanation, Marx saw himself as both a revolutionary and a social scientist, an unfortunate methodological linkage. Marx the revolutionary sought to stimulate the masses to overthrow capitalism. In its place, he said, the communists would substitute collective control of society by the people. They would act cooperatively to reduce the level of inequality so that everyone's needs could be met and everyone could develop their full potential as human beings. Marx the social scientist developed a theory that appeared to show such collective control is historically inevitable. The result, he wrote in the *Communist Manifesto*, would be a new kind of society, one in which "the free development of each is the condition for the free development of all."[7] In this new social order, Marx believed, the few would no longer exploit the many.

Marx's revolutionary goal was based on an accurate initial observation: Capitalism in its early stages does produce increasing inequality, then and now. This relationship is expressed by the solid diagonal line in Figure 1.2, labeled "what Marx observed." The result was a paradox in the middle of the nineteenth century: Although technological advancements associated with the early stages of industrialization meant huge increases in productivity only a few people seemed to benefit: the very rich who owned capital (income-producing assets). He observed that the capitalists, whom he called the bourgeoisie, were the most powerful class and they exploited the masses, who lived in great misery and depravity. On that basis, he extrapolated a simple argument: *The greater the economic development, the greater the inequality*. This is Marx's master hypothesis, expressed by the dashed diagonal line in Figure 1.2. Marx, of course, wanted to indict "capitalism." He would have used that term rather than the more generalizable **economic development,** which refers to increases in productivity. In any case, he recognized that the observed relationship between economic development and

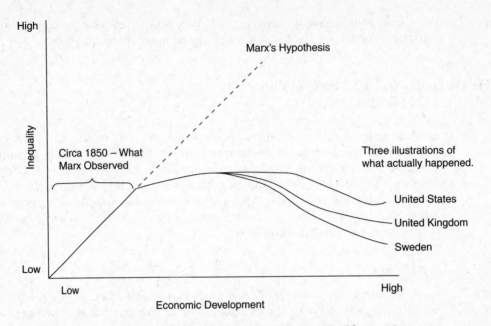

High

Inequality

Low

Marx's Hypothesis

Circa 1850 – What
Marx Observed

Three illustrations of
what actually happened.

United States

United Kingdom

Sweden

Low   High

Economic Development

FIGURE 1.2   Marx's Hypothesis Compared to Illustrative Observations

inequality would be unsustainable over time—if it continued. Marx, like other scholars during this period, assumed that it would continue and that revolutionary change to some form of communist society was historically inevitable. The only issue was when.

In developing his explanation for the inevitability of revolutionary change, Marx began by recognizing that conflict over the distribution of resources occurs in every society. As he put it in the famous opening lines of the *Communist Manifesto:* "The history of all hitherto existing society is the history of class struggles."[8] But capitalist societies, Marx wrote in the *Manifesto,* were unique in history. Wherever capitalism and industrialization combine, huge bursts in productivity occur:[9]

> The bourgeoisie . . . has created more massive and more colossal productive forces than have all preceding generations together. Subjection of nature's forces to man, machinery, application of chemistry to industry and agriculture, steam navigation, railways, electric telegraphs, clearing of whole continents to cultivation, canalization of rivers, whole populations conjured out of the ground—what earlier century had even a presentiment that such productive forces slumbered in the lap of social labor?

In this new historical context, Marx continued, not only has inequality increased steadily (as shown in Figure 1.2), but this process would continue and the stratification structure would remain rigid, without much opportunity for advancement based on achievement. Rather, a small class of capitalists would control the distribution of resources (in his words, they owned the means of production). Moreover, they would protect their wealth by dominating the government and controlling public policies. As Marx put it, "the executive of the modern state is but a committee for managing the common affairs of the whole bourgeoisie."[10]

When he looked at social arrangements, Marx always asked a simple question, one that modern sociologists also ask: Who benefits? For example, in his greatest work, *Capital*, he used British government data to show (correctly) that the capitalists' attempts at lengthening the working day and raising productivity in order to secure greater profit for themselves also increased workers' exploitation.[11] In every arena, at home, at work, in court, at church, and in the doctor's office, Marx argued, it is useful to ask who benefits from current social arrangements. The answer usually suggests which classes are the most powerful in a society.

It also suggests which classes are relatively powerless; that is, its members usually find it hard to overcome the disadvantages with which they are born. Because they do not own capital, most people must sell their ability to work (what Marx called their "labor power") in order to survive. This necessity means they continually recreate their own exploitation. For example, because employees at Ford, Wal-Mart, Bank of America, and other companies, need cars in which to get to work, food for sustenance, and mortgages for their homes, they continually return their wages to these companies and their stockholders (most of whom are rich and powerful). And this is a generalized process: Their life chances are limited because as they go about obtaining goods and services, working people return nearly all their income to the capitalists. The latter, in turn, reinvest their profits to make still more money. As Marx explained in *Capital*, "the circle in which simple reproduction moves alters its form and . . . changes into a spiral."[12] He meant that the exploitation of working people by capitalists is a self-perpetuating social structure.

Strangely, however, even though their interest lies in change, most working people accept the prevailing structure of inequality. According to Marx, this acceptance occurs because the schools, the media, government, and even religion teach them that their exploitation is right and proper. For example, he argued that "religion is the sigh of the oppressed creature—the opium of the masses."[13] He meant that religion diverts people's attention from their exploitation in this world by promising an illusion: happiness in the next world. Thus, he asserted, the nonobvious impact of religious teaching is to make the masses blind to their interest in overthrowing capitalism, thereby benefiting those who desire to maintain it: the capitalists. In this context, Marx said, alienation is widespread. That is, most people see themselves as powerless, unable to control their own lives, and they do not know why. They do not understand either that they are being exploited or how it is accomplished. They lose the class struggle without knowing it is occurring. The pervasiveness of alienation is a dominant theme in Marx's work. It constitutes the standard by which he judged societies. In a nonalienated world, inequality would be less and the stratification structure would be relatively open so that people could move up based on achievement. But such opportunities, Marx believed (incorrectly) could not occur in capitalist societies.

In order to emphasize the significance of class struggle, Marx divided the stratification structure into two parts—the bourgeoisie (or capitalists) and proletarians (or working class). This division is an ideal type, of course, although Marx did not use this phrase. It allowed him to stress (correctly) that classes always have competing interests and that conflict over the distribution of resources occurs in all societies. For Marx, however, class conflict constitutes the mechanism for historical change, the vehicle that would lead to a communist revolution. Historically, industrialization and capitalism stimulated an unprecedented social transformation: a mass movement of people from the farm to the city where they worked as employees for others. Marx called these working men and women proletarians; today, we would call them the working class (see Chapter 9). Thus, he believed, the transition from capitalism to communism was inevitable because capitalists created both the productive forces necessary for a communist society and the people capable of making a revolution: proletarians. As inequality steadily increased, he predicted, the proletarians (now the great mass of the population) would become poorer and more alienated. Living in an urban environment, they were in close contact with one another; they were becoming more educated in order to operate the machines, and a leadership cadre was emerging among them. In this context, Marx claimed, ever-worsening economic crises caused by overproduction would lead proletarians to become class conscious: They would now understand how they were being exploited and be willing to revolt.

The proletarians, Marx said in the *Manifesto*, would begin by seizing control of the state, taking all capital from its owners, and centralizing the means of production. Although Marx's goal was human freedom, these measures lead inevitably to totalitarianism. Marx, in fact, forecasted a temporary "dictatorship of the proletariat."[14] Nonetheless, Marx was an optimist about the future. The *Manifesto* ends with some of the most famous lines ever written: "Let the ruling classes tremble at a Communist revolution. The Proletarians have nothing to lose but their chains. They have a world to win. WORKING MEN OF ALL COUNTRIES, UNITE!"[15] Marx's words would live on today had he written nothing else but this little political pamphlet.

But Marx was wrong. Inequality did not continuously increase with economic development. Rather, as illustrated in Figure 1.2, what really occurred is that inequality stabilized and then declined, although with much variation across nations. The lines in the figure showing what happened are arbitrarily arranged to suggest some of the observed variations (which will be described in more detail in later chapters): Inequality today is lower in Sweden than in the United Kingdom and lower in the United Kingdom than in the United States. Note also that Figure 1.2 suggests increasing inequality in the United States in recent years (another issue to be described later). In modern democratic societies, the level of inequality varies a great deal, depending on the political choices their citizens make.

Even so, Marx was, perhaps, the greatest student of capitalism in history.[16] He saw the *centrality of economic development* in modern societies. When observers point out, for example, that the former Soviet Union collapsed because it couldn't match the efficiency, productivity, or wealth-creating power of capitalist societies, they are implicitly adopting Marx's argument that the economy is the driving force in history. He saw the *global spread of capitalism*. The world, Marx said, is being transformed into a single market, a process called globalization today. He saw the *revolutionary dynamic* inherent to capitalism. As capitalism becomes worldwide, it destroys traditional cultures and ways of life. Protests against McDonald's in France provide an easy example. He saw capitalism's *economic dynamism*. In his words, it stimulates an "uninterrupted disturbance of social conditions." For example, small trades' people sometimes lose out as large companies undercut them (as when Wal-Mart enters a community or Amazon makes purchasing books so easy). He saw that industrialization could *liberate women* from the home (although he was against this), since all could run the machines. Finally, he saw the *social psychological impact* of capitalism. The mass production of consumer goods in a cash-based economy makes human beings into creatures of avarice. There is now, he said, "no other nexus between man and man than naked self-interest, than callous cash payment."[17] As the italicized phrases suggest, Marx, writing in the mid-nineteenth century, understood many of the inherent qualities of capitalism.

His evaluation of these qualities, however, was always negative—which is misleading from today's vantage point. Although Marx offered a reasonable hypothesis based on the data available to him, capitalist societies have proven to be much more humane than he believed possible. They better insure that "the free development of each is the condition for the free development of all." Consider: Modern capitalist societies display less inequality and more mobility than ever before in history. Most people, even the poorest, are healthier and live longer than ever before. Although Marx's indictment of globalization has merit—as production moves around the world, wherever labor costs are less, some people lose their jobs and their life chances decline—globalization has positive consequences as well. For example, within a few days of publication of each Harry Potter book in London and New York, consumers could find it on the shelves in Prague, Cairo, and Hong Kong. This mundane example illustrates a more general point: with globalization, jobs are created and prices of many goods decline—which benefits most people. Moreover, the economic dynamism of capitalism leads to new products (computers, cell phones, iPods) that become available, often at cheaper prices. Again, jobs are created and people's lives improved as a result. Finally, although human relationships based on "callous cash payment" may sound harsh (as Marx intended it to), they also allow individuals greater personal freedom and autonomy, fundamental values in all modern societies.

In addition to his analysis of the nature of capitalism, Marx's writings also contain important themes that contributed to the development of sociological inquiry. These themes are especially relevant for understanding stratification.

The first is the *emphasis on social structure*. Marx was a structuralist, although he did not use that word. For example, his analysis in the *Manifesto* of the context under which proletarians transform themselves into a class-conscious revolutionary group does not deal with social psychological issues, such as the decision-making processes of individuals. Rather, he tries to show that increasing urbanity, education, political sophistication, and other factors can lead large numbers of oppressed people to recognize their common condition and revolt. But they do not revolt, at least in capitalist societies. While capitalism (more generally, economic development) does generate greater inequality initially, he failed to see that it is not permanent and usually declines over time. This decline is one reason why mass movements of oppressed persons in capitalist societies (not just the working class, but women and racial and ethnic minorities as well) have responded by seeking to get into the class system rather than overthrow it. Nonetheless, a structural approach is implicit in his work; that is, a focus on showing how the historical context in which people act affects rates of behavior.

The second theme is the *degree of opportunity* built into the stratification structure. Marx believed that it was becoming more rigid and that as the proletariat (working class) became ever larger and poorer its members would recognize their situation and overthrow capitalism. Implicit, here, is the idea that ascription would remain—as it always has throughout history—the main determinant of people's access to valued resources. But he was wrong: The stratification structure in modern capitalist societies is much more open than in the past. A relatively high rate of mobility based on achievement occurs in class-based societies. This mobility, both upward and (less often) downward, indicates that ability and hard work are becoming more important for people's life chances. As mentioned earlier, a tension exists between ascription and achievement. What should the proper balance be? How much opportunity should be allowed? There is, of course, no answer to these questions; they can only be resolved politically. Marx, however, saw their importance for understanding modernity.

The third theme is the *significance of class conflict*. Marx believed that class conflict would be the historical mechanism by which a new, communal society would emerge. Although this grandiose view of history proved incorrect, he was right to emphasize that classes have different and usually opposing interests. And he was also right in noting that these differences are often hidden by a set of ideological beliefs that seem reasonable on the surface. A key question is thus how values lead to and sometimes veil exploitation, another way of recognizing that social facts are not always what they seem to be. This essential sociological orientation can be applied to the other dimensions of stratification as well: One might wonder, for example, how traditional gender norms hide (or justify) the exploitation of women by men.

The fourth theme is *the emphasis on power*. For Marx, power was redemptive in the sense that it was a means to a positive end, a society in which people would be free to develop their human potential. But in those societies that subsequently became communist, the Communist Party justified its total rule by invoking the common good. This invocation was an ideological veil, however, as the Party functioned much like a feudal aristocracy: The few exploited the many.[18] Despite revolutionary rhetoric, the practical issue is not whether the ends justify the means. It is, rather, can the means produce the ends desired; that is, can power unfettered by accountability produce individual freedom? The answer is no. History shows that capitalist, not communist, societies display less exploitation and alienation. This is mainly because capitalist societies are democratic: Those exercising power are (more or less) held accountable for their decisions by voters. The flippant parenthetical comment is deliberate. Marx's assertion that governments often protect the interests of the rich and powerful ("a committee for managing the common affairs of the . . . bourgeoisie") remains true today. This orientation occurs partly because citizens may not accurately perceive their economic and political interests; in fact, they may be persuaded to vote against these interests. And it occurs partly because the role of money in the form of campaign contributions affects the political process, allowing the rich to achieve their goals at the expense of the other classes. Thus, Marx's emphasis on power constitutes an enduring legacy, one that Gerhard Lenski would build upon.

The final theme is the *importance of alienation*. If, as Marx suggested, alienation ought to be the criterion by which societies are judged, then he had it wrong: Modern capitalist societies display much less alienation than those in the past. But less, even much less, does not mean there is no alienation in capitalist societies. Parts of the population (the poor, some members of minority groups) are indeed relatively powerless and unable to control their lives. Yet their alienation is often hidden behind an ideological veil.

Karl Marx believed he had discovered the pattern of history, that a communist revolution and the destruction of capitalism were inevitable historical events. The result, he thought, would be a society without classes in which people acted cooperatively for the common good and, in so doing, realized their human potential. It is a utopian vision, not of the sorcerer but the sorcerer's apprentice. Yet even though he was wrong in some important ways, his writings anticipated and framed many of the issues that continue to be relevant in the study of stratification. One does not have to be a Marxist to see inequality, class conflict, alienation, and exploitation in modern societies.

Max Weber

Max Weber (b: 1864; d: 1920) helped establish sociology as a social scientific discipline in the first two decades of the twentieth century. In *Economy and Society: An Outline of Interpretive Sociology,* he analyzed the significance of religion on social life, the types of domination, and the structure of stratification, among many other topics.[19] Like Marx, Weber was trying to understand the great transformation that was taking place with economic development, the rise of democracy, and other historical changes. In so doing, however, he rejected Marx's apocalyptic vision of capitalism's demise. Thus, while recognizing and agreeing with many of Marx's insights, Weber analyzed the unequal distribution of resources in modern capitalist societies rather differently.

Underlying Weber's analysis was an explicit and (at that time) unique methodological approach: Unlike Marx, Weber insisted that sociologists should not infuse scholarly analyses with their personal values, economic interests, or political agendas. As he put it, the research process should be *value free*, as unbiased and objective as possible. He thus distinguished between "what ought to be," the sphere of values, and "what is," the sphere of science.[20]

In order to obtain objective knowledge about "what is," Weber argued that sociologists should apply a "rational method" to their work; that is, they should use clear concepts and systematic observations, and then make logical inferences.[21] But this task is very difficult. After all, researchers participate in social life. One might be, say, a white male from a middle-class background. Another might be a Hispanic woman born of immigrant parents. These different characteristics imply different life experiences, which inevitably generate preconceived opinions about social issues. Moreover, any specific research project usually provides only a partial picture, which can imply taking sides about the topic being studied.[22] For example, an analysis of the troubles impoverished people face in maintaining their eligibility for Medicaid (the federal health insurance program for the poor) may generate sympathy for their plight. No matter how objective the presentation, it seems to take the side of the potential recipients. The solution to these difficulties is for scholars to critically evaluate and replicate research. Although this practice is imperfect (since human beings are imperfect), it leads to a self-correcting process that produces research findings that are as objective as possible over time. They are called empirical generalizations.

In sociology and the other social sciences, however, even empirical generalizations are subject to change.[23] Findings vary over time and across societies because human beings rebel, subvert the established order, enact new laws, and in other ways change society. They make history. Here is a simple example: In the past, cigarette smoking was so widespread that this behavior was unrelated to social class. Today, however, cigarette smoking has declined a great deal and is now negatively related to social class; that is, the lower the social class, the higher the rate of cigarette smoking.[24] Such changes rarely occur in the natural sciences, which is why technology works. This difference means that no matter how objective the research, the social sciences carry a special burden because scholars can never be sure that what they find today will be true in coming years or decades. Weber observed, however, that this burden carries with it an unexpected benefit: The social sciences are granted eternal youth because findings must be revisited.[25]

Given this qualification, Weber argued that accurate and objective social scientific knowledge can provide the information necessary for political decisions by citizens and policy makers. Even further, sociologists can sometimes suggest strategies for achieving policy goals and possible consequences.[26] But when the problem becomes what is to be done ("what ought to be"), values intrude. Weber addressed this issue in a famous essay titled "Politics as a Vocation," where he described politics in modern democratic societies as a process by which competing interest groups seek to affect public policies and the state as monopolizing the use of force in implementing them.[27] In this context, political parties become the vehicles by which interest groups, such as classes, compete for a share of the available resources. This process is often indirect, as when occupational associations or unions try to influence public policy to benefit their members. But the outcome is important. Recall, for example, the varying levels of inequality illustrated in Figure 1.2.

Classes, as explained earlier, constitute a new system of domination that appears in modern capitalist societies. They typically display tension between achievement and ascription. Weber described this tension by distinguishing between "class" and "status," although they are interrelated.[28]

According to Weber, a **class** comprises all those sharing similar life chances based on their economic interests, such as their ownership of capital or their occupational positions.[29] Although this definition differs slightly from that presented earlier, the overlap should be apparent. People's class, Weber said, reflects a market situation, as people meet competitively under the rule of law to determine their life chances. This assertion constitutes his way of describing the importance of achievement in modern societies. People strive for economic success (income and wealth) based on their hard work and ability in light of performance-related evaluative criteria. One result of this process, explained in Chapter 5, is that mobility rates increase. But no society is (or can be) totally achievement oriented. Although Weber did not talk about gender and race as systems of domination, he did mention the existence of ethnic segregation based on caste and (as will become clear) emphasized how status concerns limit the impact of class.

Based on the definition above, Weber outlined a model of the class structure in modern societies. Like Marx, Weber began with the recognition that the most fundamental division occurs between those who own capital and those who do not. In his words, "'property' and 'lack of property' are . . . the basic categories of all class situations."[30] He continued, however, by identifying additional classes within these two rubrics. Table 1.1 compares Marx's and Weber's models.

As shown in the table, Weber divided the owners of capital, the very rich, into two subclasses, which he called "rentiers" and "entrepreneurs."[31] "Rentiers" comprise those who live off their investments and pursue a relatively nonacquisitive lifestyle, ranging from public service to indolence. They often inherit their wealth. "Entrepreneurs," in contrast, comprise those who rise to the top of the business world or pursue economic gain in other ways. Often more wealthy than "rentiers," "entrepreneurs" do not inherit their wealth;

TABLE 1.1   The Class Structure as Outlined by Marx and Weber

MARX'S MODEL	WEBER'S MODEL
1. Capitalists	1. Owners of Capital
2. Proletarians	a. Rentiers
	b. Entrepreneurs
	2. Nonowners of Capital
	a. Middle Class
	b. Skilled Workers
	c. Semiskilled Workers
	d. Unskilled Workers

rather, they are typically upwardly mobile persons from the middle class. Regardless of whether they work as an avocation or vocation, the members of both groups are very rich and make up a very small proportion of the population. Taken together, they are distinctive because their ownership of income-producing assets not only allows them to consume expensive amenities but also, more importantly, to influence public policy to their benefit. As Weber pointed out, a capitalist system inevitably "favors the owners."[32] Although he did not use the term class conflict, the ability to use wealth as a means to political power constitutes one of the most important mechanisms by which the rich obtain and expand their share of the resources in a society, thus protecting their life chances.

Writing a half-century after Marx, Weber recognized more clearly than the dead revolutionary that those who do not own capital also possess resources, mainly the worth of their services and skills. Moreover, the importance of these skills increases as economic development occurs. As displayed in Table 1.1, Weber divided these people, the great mass of the population, into two classes, both of which are historically new.

Weber observed that industrialization, capitalism, and scientific advances combined to produce fundamental changes in the occupational structure: White-collar jobs requiring high levels of training and education become increasingly important in modern societies. As a result, a new class appeared comprising those "in the middle," between the rich and the working class. According to Weber, the "middle class" includes those who possess services and skills based on knowledge: public officials, managers of businesses, technicians, members of the professions, and other white-collar workers. As will become clear in subsequent chapters, Weber's classification scheme was pretty accurate. Because their services and skills are in demand in modern societies, persons filling these newly created middle-class jobs usually have higher incomes and more political power than those who work with their hands. Like the rich, middle-class people use their resources to enhance their life chances and lifestyles, influence public policy, and affect others' opportunities—albeit at their level. For example, they try to insure their children attend "good" schools and end up with credentials that allow them to enter the professions (like becoming a physician). More importantly, because they vote at such a high rate, elected decision makers often respond to middle-class interests. As a result, middle-class people protect their life chances and the stratification structure remains stable.

Without explanation, Weber divided people who do manual labor into three groups: skilled, semiskilled, and unskilled workers. It is unclear whether he saw these groups as separate classes or subdivisions within a single working class. In any case, like the rich and middle class, working-class people also try to protect their life chances. Their share in the distribution of resources is less, however, and their lifestyles are more precarious as a result. Nonetheless, because hard work and ability can pay off in economically developed societies, some people from working-class origins are upwardly mobile into the middle class. Even so, the class structure is reproduced over time.

As will be seen in later chapters, the class structure in the United States resembles the model originally sketched by Max Weber many years ago. Although the number of categories making up the class structure may vary (within limits) depending on the purposes of the observers, a simple four-class rubric will be used in this book: the rich, middle class, working class, and poor.[33]

Yet birth (in the form of family background) continues to matter. Weber used the concept "status" to get at the evaluations people make of others' lifestyle, as indicated by their consumption habits, use of leisure time, and fundamental choices and values. Some elements of status reflect moral stances while others constitute aesthetic judgments. For example, one's house and its furnishing as well as selection of wine or entertainment (the ballet versus a college football game) convey lifestyle choices. It is also expressed by the educational goals held for children: public school versus prep school, the state university versus Ivy League college. Finally, status is indicated by people's values and how they organize their lives; for example, such basic choices as gender roles in marriage and attitudes toward abortion. Examples like these illustrate what Weber called "status oriented action." They are "value rational" in the sense that they reflect people's standards of honorable behavior. Note that as Weber uses the term "status," nonperformance-related criteria are used to evaluate people and their way of life. This concept is thus his way of describing the continuing significance of ascription in modern societies.

Weber's emphasis on status is important because people understand their class location and actively maintain it. This is the sense in which class and status are interrelated. Class is maintained by means of a simple mechanism: **discrimination,** the unequal treatment of individuals and groups based on their personal characteristics. In practice, much discrimination results from the fact that lifestyle is rooted in family experience, which influences who people know and what they know about the dominant culture.* As individuals grow up, they participate in their family's claim to social prestige, its occupational subculture, and its educational level. They experience its religiosity, suffer its unemployment, and enjoy its leisure pursuits. Thus, even in the absence of formal organization, families in the same class display similar consumption habits, attitudes, values, and many other characteristics. As a result, people from similar backgrounds need not communicate in order to identify those who are like themselves, to protect their interests, and discriminate against others who are different or who have different interests. They act in concert without being organized to do so.[34]

Although not organized groups, Weber argued that members of each class act to maintain their distinctive lifestyle and pass on their advantages to their children in

---

*Subsequent scholars refer to "who you know" as **social capital** and "what you know" as **cultural capital.** See Chapter 5 for an explanation.

specific ways.[35] (1) Families extend hospitality only to social equals. Thus, they tend to invite into their homes, become friends with, eat with, and socialize with, others who are like themselves. (2) Families restrict potential marriage partners to social equals. Thus, they tend to live in segregated neighborhoods (by class and race) and send their children to school with youngsters of others who are like themselves, with the result that their offspring generally marry someone from a similar background. (3) Families practice unique social conventions and activities. Thus, they tend to join organizations, such as churches and clubs, and spend their leisure time with others who share similar beliefs and ways of living. And, most importantly, (4) families try to obtain and retain "privileged modes of acquisition," and pass them on to their children. Thus, they provide their children with extra educational benefits (tutors, computers) in order to enhance their opportunities to get into better colleges. A college degree constitutes a credential necessary to enter many professions.

Weber observed that the protection of "privileged modes of acquisition" also occurs at a collective level as classes exercise power to protect their interests. Although Marx saw how the rich (the capitalists) engaged in this process, he did not recognize that occupational groups could do the same thing. Weber realized, however, that when "the number of competitors increases . . . the participants become interested in curbing the competition."[36] They organize and try to close off access to the occupation in order to raise their income and obtain other rewards, such as health insurance. For example, educational credentials and licensing requirements are justified in order to prevent "unqualified" persons from participating in a profession. This strategy functions to limit the supply of persons who can offer the service, thereby increasing the incomes of those who do. Physicians, financial advisors, real estate agents, and hairstylists provide some examples. Among working-class people, unionization functions in a similar way. These tactics reveal how class conflict occurs in modern societies.

Max Weber was among the first generation of academic sociologists. He realized that a politically committed discipline, illustrated by Marx's work, would inevitably produce unreliable knowledge and, hence, become politically irrelevant. Thus, Weber redirected (or tried to redirect) the emerging discipline toward the production of objective knowledge, even though this goal will always be achieved imperfectly. His analysis of the structure of stratification in modern societies illustrates how he proceeded.

Kingsley Davis and Wilbert Moore

In the mid-1940s, Kingsley Davis (b: 1908; d: 1997) and Wilbert Moore (b: 1914; d: 1987) wrote an essay, titled "Some Principles of Stratification," that asked a simple question: What is the function of stratification for the society? They answered that its hidden impact is to "insure that the most important positions are conscientiously filled by the most qualified persons."[37] As a result, they argued, stratification functions to insure a society's survival. In so doing, they shifted the discussion away from the dynamic processes shaping the stratification structure, such as class struggle. Not a good move.

In all societies, Davis and Moore said, a division of labor exists in which positions are clustered in four areas necessary for a society's survival: economic, political, technological, and religious. In each sphere people must be motivated to fill positions and enact roles; some, for example, must become janitors and others physicians. Davis and Moore claimed that a few positions in each area are more important for societal survival than others and that they are also more difficult to fill because they require scarce talent, extensive training, or both. Hence, such positions must be more highly rewarded. Their example is from modern medicine. Medical training is so long, costly, and burdensome, they argued, that few persons would become physicians if the position did not carry very high rewards. They concluded that societies use unequal rewards (such resources as income and occupational prestige) to motivate people to obtain functionally important and difficult-to-fill positions in each area identified above.

One result of Max Weber's emphasis on critically evaluating and replicating research is that sociologists are often skeptical of others' ideas and, hence, the Davis–Moore analysis generated much debate over many years.[38] The conclusion is that the argument constitutes an illegitimate teleology and is untestable. A teleological statement imputes inherent purpose to a phenomenon. Thus, the purpose of an automobile is to provide transportation; it is designed and built with that goal in mind. The application of this notion to human societies, however, is dubious. Although a society must decide among priorities, such as cutting taxes or funding the Medicaid program, these decisions reflect the outcome of political competition and the relative ability of classes to protect their interests. The society was not designed for that purpose. Davis and Moore took an empirical generalization, the existence of stratification, and transformed it into a functional necessity. They thus avoided the dynamic issues in the study of inequality, such as the variations in the level of inequality and the increasing emphasis on achievement, and the way these differences reflect the struggle of people, groups (such as physicians), and classes for a greater share of the resources. Such a strategy cannot work. The thesis is untestable because the functionally necessary tasks and most important positions cannot be identified without invoking values. As a result, sociologists have rejected Davis and Moore's analysis.[39]

This same judgment applies to functionalism as a theoretical tradition. Davis and Moore were students of Talcott Parsons (b: 1902; d: 1979), the most well-known functionalist in sociology, whose work reveals both of the flaws outlined above.[40] Hence, functionalism is now passé, mainly for theoretical reasons but also for political ones. Indeed, it is easy to see how Davis and Moore's argument could be used politically to support the status quo in any society: Those obtaining the most resources (and, hence, enjoying the best life chances) would simply argue that their benefits are necessary for the survival of society. Physicians have made this argument very successfully in the United States. The rich have made a similar argument: The benefits of tax cuts to them (supposedly) trickle down to all citizens.

Nonetheless, although functionalism has been rejected, the Davis–Moore essay and the theoretical tradition it illustrates contain two useful themes that remain relevant to the study of stratification structures.

One theme involves the simple act of looking for the functions of a social phenomenon. Although the term is too vague for detailed empirical analyses, attempting to uncover the functions of occupational closure, poverty, and other social facts is sometimes a good way of piercing the veil justifying the status quo, which can be done without the problems afflicting Davis and Moore's analysis.[41] They tried to identify the nonobvious effects of stratification, which is good sociology, only to go wrong by imputing generic needs to society.

In addition, functionalism provides a useful way of identifying the parts of the social structure, a problem Marx and Weber also struggled with. Although Davis and Moore asserted that the tasks they identified—economic, political, technological, and religious—constituted functional necessities for survival, one need not make this assumption. Today, these tasks are termed **social institutions** and they provide a model of the complex division of labor in modern societies; they are the parts of the social structure—seen horizontally. Thus, in studying the distribution of resources observers typically look at how classes differ in terms similar to the institutions identified by Davis and Moore, Parsons, and others. (1) The occupation, amount of income, and source of income are identified, since they indicate peoples' economic and political interests. (2) The rate and type of political participation and power are examined, since they influence the stratification structure. (3) The rate and type of crime is ascertained, since they are affected by class location. (4) The rate and type of religiosity is recognized, since it influences (and is influenced by) class location and values. (5) The level of educational attainment is investigated, since it is related to class location, political interests, and values. (6) Kinship characteristics are sketched, since they affect class location, economic and political interests, and values.

It is not hard to see that these basic tasks are interconnected. Thus, macroeconomic policies affect street crime (offenses some poor and working-class persons commit) by altering people's employment situation. In any science, it is essential to develop a model that identifies the structure of the phenomenon under investigation (for example, the parts of the body or the atom) and shows how they are interrelated. As noted earlier, Weber sketched a model of the class structure, one of the vertical dimensions of the stratification structure. The functionalists added to this analysis by identifying the social institutions that appear characteristic of each society, the horizontal dimension of the stratification structure.

Ralf Dahrendorf

Functionalism constituted the dominant theoretical orientation in the United States from World War II until Ralf Dahrendorf's *Class and Class Conflict in Industrial Society* appeared in 1959. Responding to Marx, Dahrendorf (b: 1929) argued that American sociologists had failed to realize the significance of class conflict in all modern societies. To rectify this problem, he observed, sociological study of stratification must become "an exact social science with precisely formulated postulates, theoretical models, and testable laws."[42] Alas, while Dahrendorf saw the problem accurately, his solution was very flawed.

He began by developing a series of postulates, or assumptions, about the nature of society that contradicted those of Davis and Moore, Parsons, and other functionalists: (1) "Every society is at every point subject to change; social change is ubiquitous." (2) "Every society displays at every point dissensus and conflict; social conflict is ubiquitous." (3) "Every element in a society renders a contribution to its disintegration and change." (4) "Every society is based on the coercion of some of its members by others."[43] The stratification structure is thus riven with class conflict.

Although Dahrendorf's conclusion is correct, these assumptions are empirically unrealistic. After all, if a society were continually subject to change (#1 above), then organized social life would be impossible. More importantly, no science can assume relationships among the phenomena it is attempting to study. The scientific task is to test hypotheses, keeping assumptions to a minimum.

In the next step, Dahrendorf transformed his assumptions into a causal model that sketches how people move into and out of relationships of authority. Not a Marxist, he argued that possession of authority (rather than capital) identifies people's access to resources and their interest in keeping what they have and adding to it. The result is "class conflict." Although the idea of defining all forms of "class conflict" as disputes over authority is interesting (but probably too extreme), its correctness remains unknown because Dahrendorf asserted its truth by assumption. While his causal model displays other flaws, this one is the most serious.

Finally, Dahrendorf developed a testable theory that, he insisted, is derived from the model. This theory focuses on the conditions under which classes organize, the forms of class conflict, and the process of change.[44] While the theory comprises a large number of formal statements, only one example is provided here: In discussing the forms of class conflict Dahrendorf proposed "there is a close positive correlation between the degree of superimposition of [class] conflicts and their intensity." In plainer language: The more several class conflicts overlap with one another, the greater their intensity.

In contrast to the assumptions outlined earlier, this hypothesis is useful. Because it is formally stated and abstract (independent of time and space), it can be applied to many different empirical issues that divide social classes. Nonetheless, neither it nor the other elements of Dahrendorf's theory emerge from his model. Actually, his theory constitutes an extrapolation of work by Marx, Georg Simmel, Lewis Coser, and others.[45] This fact makes it less original than he asserts and calls his strategy for theory construction into question.

Although Dahrendorf's work is flawed, he contributed to the study of stratification in two essential ways. First, more than anyone else, he alerted sociologists in the United States to the fact that class conflict is built into the stratification structure in modern societies. American sociology (unlike European sociology) lacks a vibrant Marxist tradition and, as a result, scholars were relatively insensitive to these issues. Second, in stating his propositions formally, Dahrendorf took theoretical analyses to a new level of sophistication. Theories could no longer be buried in discursive prose, a format that promotes vagueness and makes testing difficult. Dahrendorf is easy to criticize, mainly because he made his assumptions explicit, clearly identified his variables, defined them, and stated how they covary. Thus, while widely and appropriately criticized, his work redirected sociological research.

Gerhard Lenski

Gerhard Lenski's book, *Power and Privilege*, constituted a decisive break with the past because he produced the first truly theoretical explanation of stratification processes.[46] His theory has two parts. First, he explained the basis for stratification in every society and, second, he explained why it has varied historically. In so doing, Lenski (b: 1924) tried to demonstrate "who gets what and why" in all societies over the course of history.

1. In explaining the basis of stratification in all societies, Lenski focused on the distribution of power and privilege. Like Marx, he emphasized the importance of producing goods and services, of the economy as the driving force in history. He distinguished between societies in which people produce only the minimum necessary for subsistence and those where a surplus exists and must be distributed. In the former, Lenski hypothesized, people "will share the product of their labor to the extent required to insure the survival and continued productivity of those others whose actions are necessary or beneficial to themselves."[47] In plainer language, the first hypothesis is: *The more dependent people are on each other for survival, the more they will share the products of their labor with one another.* Lenski reasoned that individuals usually act out of self-interest.

Data show that throughout most of the millions of years of human history, bands of men and women roamed the earth as hunters and gatherers. They were few in number, lived communally, and produced little. Each individual depended on the others and, according to the hypothesis, they shared what they had.

But when a surplus exists, the situation differs a great deal. About 10,000 BC, in what is called the Neolithic Revolution, human beings invented agriculture and began domesticating animals, creating a surplus of food and (a few) other commodities. In such a context, Lenski proposed, "power will determine the distribution of nearly all the surplus possessed by a society."[48] In covariance form, the second hypothesis is: *The greater the economic development, the more power determines the distribution of goods and services.* In short, as Marx, Weber, and Dahrendorf all emphasized, albeit in quite different ways, Lenski argued that power is highly correlated with the distribution of resources—such as income, wealth, education, and occupational prestige—and the improved life chances that follow. In every society where a surplus exists, he shows, power leads to privilege, by which he means improved life chances because some (usually only a few) people possess a greater share of the available resources.

2. In order to explain why the stratification structure varies across societies over time, Lenski focused on two main factors: the level of technology and the nature of the state, ignoring the other transformative changes mentioned earlier. As Lenski phrased the hypothesis: "Variations in technology will be the most important single factor determining variations in distributive [or stratification] systems."[49] In covariance form, the third hypothesis is: *The greater the level of technology, the greater the productivity and inequality.* The term **technology** refers to scientifically verified knowledge about the environment. Improvements in technology, Lenski argued, are applied to the practical task of producing goods and services for people to enjoy (economic development, in other words). The result, following from the second hypothesis (and as Marx suggested), is that those with the greatest power acquire nearly all the surplus, which means they have access to most resources and better life chances as a result. This process leads to great inequality and a rigid stratification structure, without much mobility. As indicated earlier, this situation exists in all preindustrial societies.

With industrialization, however, human history changed forever. Not only did the level of technology and, hence, productivity, increase exponentially, but this process occurred just when democratic societies were emerging. In this new context, Lenski said, where people vote and hold decision makers accountable, the many can combine against the few—leading to less inequality. Lenski's fourth hypothesis follows: *The greater the level of industrialization and the more democratic the state, the less inequality.* Lenski emphasized, however, that this statement only means that the rich possess a lower proportion of the total wealth. They remain, according to the second hypothesis, the most powerful class and they have greater access to valued resources.

In testing the theory, Lenski used archeological, anthropological, and historical data on all the world's known societies. He used evidence skillfully and demonstrated the accuracy of each element of the theory, except the last. As suggested by Figure 1.2, inequality usually declines to varying degrees in industrial (which is to say economically developed) societies. In some contexts, however, as in the United States, inequality can increase (as suggested at the far right of the figure). What is clear, then, is that modern societies can control how much inequality exists. So Lenski's last hypothesis must be modified in light of the evidence: *The greater the industrialization and the more democratic the state, the more inequality will vary in light of political conflict.* Although Lenski does not mention it, class conflict provides one example.

Although their writings are flawed in various ways, the theorists reviewed here merit study, partly because they show how sociology has advanced over the years and partly because they contain enduring lessons. Stripped of its radical millenarianism (a belief in the coming of an ideal, communal society), Marx's work illustrates the usefulness of a structural approach focusing on how class location affects the choices people have. In addition, his emphasis on the significance of class conflict directs modern sociologists to look for the different levels of power, economic interests, and values, displayed by various classes. Further, Marx's stress on alienation suggests the importance of ascertaining who benefits from public policies. Sometimes the answer is not obvious. From Weber, modern sociologists take a recognition of the importance of class and achievement in modern societies, an understanding that people's lifestyle and values (what he called "status") often influence behavior, a model of the class structure, an emphasis on power as a determining factor in social life, and a directive to do research that is as objective as possible. In addition, in their different ways, Marx and Weber both confronted how modern societies have been transformed by industrialization, capitalism, science, freedom and democracy, the rule of law, and (as will be discussed in the next section) the culture of capitalism. These changes mean that modern, class-based societies display an inherent tension between ascription and achievement. Davis and Moore, and functionalists generally, show that social arrangements frequently contain nonobvious dimensions, what Merton called latent functions. In addition, the functionalists offer a model of the division of labor, the horizontal dimension of the stratification structure that remains useful. Dahrendorf reminds sociologists that issues related to class and class conflict can be analyzed outside a Marxist framework and that theories need to be stated formally. Finally, Lenski illustrates how a simple but powerful theory can be used to explain the basis of and historical variation in the structure of stratification. This theory becomes especially useful in understanding modern societies, such as the United States.

MODERNITY, THE AMERICAN DREAM, AND ANOMIE

In the traditional societies that existed before the seventeenth century, behavior was based on custom, often sanctified by religious belief. In this context, inequality was great, poverty was rampant, and the stratification structure was relatively rigid, with most people's life chances determined at birth. Today, sociologists would describe this situation in terms of a high level of ascription. But modern societies differ.

They have been transformed.[50] They are like Prometheus unbound, released from the chains of the past.[51] Although they vary a great deal, modern societies generally display the following characteristics.

First, they are industrialized. With **industrialization** new forms of energy are substituted for muscle power, leading to huge advances in productivity—the indicator of economic development referred to earlier. Although this process is harsh in its early years, bringing with it dislocation and misery, in a relatively short time industrialized nations become wealthy and healthy compared to the past. They also display a high rate of upward mobility and a low rate of poverty. These results occur because, in order to take advantage of new technology, the occupational structure changes in fundamental ways: leading first to the rise of blue-collar jobs (and a working class) and later to the dominance of white-collar jobs (and a middle class). Some observers have argued that the increasing emphasis on professional knowledge in recent years along with the rise of service occupations signify a change to a "postindustrial" society, especially in the United States. But this judgment seems premature. These are long-term trends inherent to the logic of industrialization.[52]

Second, modern societies are **capitalist.** The term refers to the production of goods and services in an open market for the purpose of making a profit. In capitalist societies, supply and demand determine the prices of goods, services, and labor. The means of production are mainly privately owned. The idea is that the economy is self-organized as individuals and companies, acting in self-interest, compete to provide goods and services that people want at a price they are willing to pay. Of course, no society is purely capitalist, as government must intervene for the common good (however defined). Nations like Sweden, the United Kingdom, and the United States illustrate the degree of variation that results (recall Figure 1.2).[53]

Third, modern societies emphasize the use of **science** to solve practical problems. The term refers to the systematic use of observation and reason to understand and explain natural and social life. Scientific knowledge provides the mechanism for rapid technological change that drives industrialization. In addition, a scientific ethos underlies capitalism and permeates modern societies. This spirit reflects a long-term historical process that Max Weber called **rationalization.** All aspects of social life become methodically organized based on the use of reason and observation. Everyone who uses modern technology learns to approach problems (including social problems) systematically, rather than relying on magical thinking. Although the results bring many benefits (straight teeth, longer lives, less poverty), the implications can be disquieting as old ways of thinking prove to be ineffective.[54]

Fourth, modern societies are **democratic.** As mentioned earlier, in democratic societies power and authority are based on the "will of the people" as citizens elect their representatives and hold them accountable for their policy decisions. In such contexts, personal freedom and the innate dignity of every individual become fundamental values. These orientations fit with capitalism, which also requires that people compete in pursuit of their self-interest.[55] As will be described in Chapter 2, democracy has become one of the standards by which societies are judged.

Fifth, modern societies are governed by the **rule of law.** Written laws adopted via established procedures describe the nature and extent of authority, especially government authority. Moreover, those who make and enforce laws are also bound to obey them. The rule of law results not only in a long-term decline in interpersonal violence as a mechanism for solving disputes, it also increases predictability in human interaction. These characteristics not only allow capitalism to flourish, they also make democratic decision making possible.[56]

Finally, while a great deal of variation exists, all modern societies display some sort of **culture of capitalism,** a set of values that emphasize occupational achievement, individualism, universalism (being evaluated based on merit), rationality (dealing with issues methodically), activism (taking direct action to obtain a goal), and making money.[57]

Taken together, these structural changes display what Weber called an "elective affinity" for one another; they came into being gradually over the long span of Western history and coalesced in northwestern Europe in about the seventeenth century. By the nineteenth century, as Marx described so eloquently, they had become an engine for change never before seen in history. Poverty declined as opportunity increased, and this result has a seductive quality that few who experience it can resist. This is why oppressed people, such as the working class, women, or racial and ethnic minorities, do not rebel in economically developed societies.

Max Weber emphasized how these six dynamic processes combined to produce modern societies. He was especially interested in the significance of the last one: the culture of capitalism. He argued that all modern, class-based societies display, in some form, a set of mutually reinforcing values like those described above. These values originated in the West and manifest themselves in extreme form in the United States. Some observers, in fact, refer to them as the **American Dream,** which can be defined as an ideology shared by nearly all citizens that everyone who has ability and works hard will achieve economic success.[58]

Yet the American Dream carries with it an inherent irony, due mainly to the unequal distribution of resources and the continuing impact of ascription, especially in the form of discrimination, which restricts opportunity. Robert K. Merton (b: 1910; d: 2003) captured this irony in his famous essay "Social Structure and Anomie," where **anomie** refers to a lack of connection between cultural values and the legitimate means to achieve them.[59] Anomic societies—which is to say all modern societies—are organized based on a paradox: Opportunity is great and everyone is supposed to keep striving for success, yet built-in restrictions limit the legally approved means for achieving this goal. As a result, the competition for economic success is not really (and cannot be) open or equal.

In a way, an anomic society is a little like a baseball game, albeit one that is perversely organized so as to illustrate the paradox of modernity: Opportunity is far greater today than in the past but also restricted.[60] The actual game was invented in the nineteenth century, perhaps in Cooperstown, New York, but who knows. Before that time, people's place in society was pretty much fixed at birth. Since then, however, people (at least white people) have been able to compete under relatively fair rules for their share of resources. In the metaphorical game presented here, people's score (occupationally and economically) depends on how far they advance around the bases.

The farther they move ahead, the more money they make—which is the mark of achievement in America. The cultural dominance of the American Dream means that everyone grows up believing that hard work and ability will allow them to advance along the economic bases, thereby making loads of money along the way.

The accident of birth, however, means that not everyone begins the baseball game at the same point. Some people, for example, start from the batter's box. Nonetheless, they believe in the American Dream, that they can and will get a hit and, because of their great speed, progress to subsequent bases. In playing the game, all they ask is that they be allowed to make it on their own and be evaluated fairly. A few succeed in that they get to first base and some go even further. Opportunity exists in a competitive environment. But limits also exist because other people clog the bases ahead of them, restricting advancement. In addition, the base paths (at least in this game) become steadily narrower as one advances—one more restriction. The competition, then, allows success for some but cannot be completely fair or equal; it cannot be based only on achievement (recall Figure 1.1). Some of those who begin by going to bat at home plate recognize these limits and become angry when they strike out, whether swinging or based on an unfair call (discrimination). Sometimes they turn this anger inward, blaming themselves for their lack of success. And sometimes, they act aggressively or violently toward one another, even though such behavior will not get them anywhere.

Others have a better chance at succeeding because they begin the baseball game at first base. They also believe fervently in the American Dream, that with hard work they will move on around the bases and make money as they go. Again, all they want is to be fairly evaluated. And some of them make it to second base and even beyond. But, once again, progress is difficult because still others started the game ahead of them—at second and third base—and, of course, the base paths become narrower still. A few people start the game at second and third bases, and because they and all the other players believe in the American Dream, they assume they got there by hitting doubles and triples (by achievement instead of by birth). Although their cumulative wealth is much higher, and advancing to ever-greater riches is easier for them, they believe intensely in the values epitomized by the American Dream: occupational achievement, individualism, universalism, rationality, activism, and making money. They tell themselves and everyone else that the American Dream is real for everyone—anyone can advance. And nearly everyone playing the game believes them.

This metaphorical baseball game illustrates what Robert K. Merton meant by an anomic society. You should keep the metaphor in mind, as it will be used for illustrative purposes in subsequent chapters.

People respond to an anomic social structure in predictable ways. Because opportunity exists, nearly everyone works hard and tries to do the best they can—including those at the bottom of the class structure and those suffering from discrimination. Merton calls this response "conformity." And some people succeed. The increased opportunity for upward mobility is one of the unique features of modern societies. But because everyone believes in the American Dream, those who are less successful also believe that they should just try harder; the only real failure is giving up. But, inevitably, some do. Another predictable response is "ritualistic"; that is, some people reject success goals but continue going through the motions. A third response to anomie is "retreatism," withdrawing from society in some way. For example, a few people find solace in drugs, while others descend into psychopathology (perhaps considering suicide). Paradoxically, others express their withdrawal by acting out, sexually and in other ways (graffiti). Fourth, some people try to get around the structurally based barriers by taking illegal short cuts. In his charming way, Merton calls this response "innovation." He summarizes the anomic character of all modern societies by noting that, this "cardinal American virtue, 'ambition,' promotes a cardinal American vice, 'deviant behavior.'"[61]

Apart from his conceptual scheme, there are, as the examples above illustrate, only a few ways of responding to the disconnect between the values people learn and the built-in inability to obtain them: such as high rates of psychopathology, sexual acting out, drug use, and crime—all of which have structural sources. Again: Such responses occur whenever an anomic social structure exists, which is to say all modern societies. The United States, as is often the case, displays high rates of such behaviors. One of the best examples occurs in Arthur Miller's play, *Death of a Salesman*. In it, the main character, Willy Loman, believes that America is a land of opportunity even though he has consistently failed to succeed (he is the low man) despite a lifetime of futile effort (including some pathetic attempts at "innovation"). Ultimately, he commits suicide.[62] In psychological terms, it is not much of a leap to suggest that when impoverished people or those suffering pervasive discrimination are denied opportunity and engage in self-destructive acts, they are expressing their free-floating alienation and anger in inchoate ways: against themselves or one another.

The last response to an anomic situation described by Professor Merton is "rebellion," which means "efforts to change the existing cultural and social structure rather than to accommodate efforts *within* this structure."[63] Yet, despite Marx, rebellion does not occur in class-based societies. The paradox of modernity is that while opportunity is restricted, it is also far greater than in the past—and people know this. This paradox emerges naturally out of the tension between ascription and achievement described earlier. Economically developed societies, then, become relatively stable as the ability to become successful by means of hard work and ability (with a little luck) increases, mobility rates go up, and inequality usually goes down. In such a context, it becomes useful to analyze the structure of stratification as objectively as possible, using the methods of science.

A STRATEGY FOR THE STUDY OF STRATIFICATION

The material reviewed so far introduces many of the issues that must be confronted in the study of stratification. One way of taking advantage of them is to develop an overall theory, as in Jonathan H. Turner's, *Societal Stratification*.[64] Turner translates the arguments made by Marx, Weber, Davis and Moore, Dahrendorf, and Lenski into a set of formal theoretical statements. He sees this theory as a step toward a larger goal, the identification of the generic theoretical principles underlying all human behavior. Another approach, pursued in this book, involves using previous works as the basis for a middle-range analysis of the stratification structure.[65] This more modest goal requires a method, by which is meant a strategy for explanation rather than a statistical technique. The strategy used here is to (1) assess the historical and cross-national dimensions of stratification, (2) distinguish levels of analysis—individual and structural—necessary for understanding stratification, and (3) describe how the systems of domination (power and authority) affect the distribution of resources in modern societies.

Historical and Cross-National Dimensions of Stratification

Sociology at its best looks at the data along two dimensions: historical and cross-national.[66] Historical data reveal how much change in the level of inequality has occurred over time within one society, such as the United States. For example, in examining changes in racial and gender inequality, poverty, mobility, and other topics, the analysis will usually be extended back 100 to 200 years, or as far as plausible data are available. This is a useful period to examine, since it marks the transition to modernity and the rise of class-based stratification structures. Cross-national data indicate the extent of inequality in several nations. Such information provides a way to place the American experience in perspective. In this book, cross-national comparisons will usually be restricted to Western societies. Since they share a common cultural heritage and display advanced economies, their similarities and differences regarding the issues are especially revealing.

Max Weber pioneered use of such data in his *The Protestant Ethic and the Spirit of Capitalism* and other studies of the relationship between religion and the origin of capitalism.[67] Weber wanted to understand why capitalism as an economic system arose in Western Europe and ushered in modern life. Thus, he performed a "logical experiment" by comparing the West in the seventeenth and eighteenth centuries with India and China at the same time. What distinguished Europe (and the United States) from these other nations was not the level of technology, a free labor force, or other factors. Rather, the West became unique due to the rise of the culture of capitalism as an unintended consequence of the Protestant Reformation. What happened was that behaviors undertaken for purely religious reasons, such as hard work aimed at acquiring wealth, were transformed over time into secular cultural values. These ethical standards, in combination with the other dynamic changes summarized previously, helped to usher in a new kind of society, one never before seen in history, a society based on class with an increasing emphasis on achievement.

Weber's research strategy is significant because it can be used with any topic, not only stratification. As an aside, note that Weber's "logical experiment" differs from the approach usually presented in methodology courses. There, students are taught to form a hypothesis and gather data with which to test it. In contrast, Weber begins by gathering data, which are then explained. This explanation is often multivariate in form, but the variables are related logically rather than mathematically. This strategy is often useful in dealing with structural issues.[68]

The use of historical and cross-national data leads to productive questions. For example, if the rate of poverty in the United States was high in the past (and it was), but is much lower now, one asks what has changed. Individual motives? Perhaps. But if the poverty rate in this country is much higher than in Western European nations, one wonders if structural barriers have been deliberately created that keep so many people impoverished. The strategy, once again, is to look for explanatory factors that differ historically and internationally, and appear logically related to poverty. Science is simply the art of asking questions. The idea is that there are no secrets. The facts of nature, social life, and even people's unconscious motives, can be discovered if one asks the right questions. In sociology, historical and cross-national data provide an empirical basis for such queries. They lead to greater understanding. They also lead to a distinction between levels of analysis.

Levels of Analysis and Stratification

In order to illustrate the importance of distinguishing levels of analysis, imagine you are enrolled in an art history course and must try to understand a painting by the Dutch impressionist, Vincent van Gogh. Let us assume it is "The Café Terrace at Night" (finished in 1888). In looking at the painting, one sees a humble concern where people eat, drink, and talk. Like much great art, "The Café Terrace at Night" can be understood on several levels and each displays different properties. At one level, you might use a spectroscope to inspect the paint's chemical composition. Such an examination is useful because of the bright colors typical of van Gogh's works. At another level, you might use a magnifying glass to study his brushstroke technique. This analysis would be useful because van Gogh used heavy, slashing strokes. At still another level, you might look at the painting from a short distance to see how the images fit together. At a final level, you might move several feet away to get an overall view. These last two levels are useful because distance alters what viewers see. What you should remember with this example is that each level of analysis not only provides different data, the explanatory variables differ as well. Yet explanation at each level is valid. And combining them leads to greater insight about the painting. So it is with the study of stratification.

The initial task is to understand why individuals act, which constitutes the first level of analysis. Only individuals vote or look for jobs. Only individuals justify their actions morally and live with the result. Only individuals give their lives meaning. The basis on which individuals make decisions is their personal experiences (which are not always conscious). Sociologists use the term **socialization** to describe these experiences. It refers to the lifelong process by which individuals learn norms and values, internalize motivations and (unconscious) needs, develop intellectual and social skills, and enact roles as they participate in society.[69] In plainer language, socialization refers to the process of growing up, with the addendum that it continues throughout life. In effect, individuals' personal experiences form a template providing a basis for their behavior. The dimensions of this template can be formally stated: (1) Childhood interactions are usually more influential on individuals than later experiences. (2) Interaction in primary groups (such as family and religion) is usually more influential on individuals than interaction in secondary groups. (3) Interaction with people who are emotionally significant (such as parents, teachers, and friends) is usually more influential on individuals than interaction with more distant persons (such as a crowd). (4) Long-term interaction is usually more influential on individuals than short-term interaction.[70]

Knowledge of these experiences helps observers understand how individuals' backgrounds lead them to act as they do. A person's biography is composed of family, friends, and enemies. It also comprises the schools attended, books read, television programs watched, the religious faith adhered to, the Scout troop joined, and the orgies participated in. Eventually it will include the gang joined, the occupational group entered, the political party identified with, and all other experiences. With this background, then, a person learns what is expected (norms and values), develops personality characteristics (motivations and needs), and understands how to act (knowledge and skills). These are the elements of the socialization process defined above. Note the active verbs: Individuals attend, join, enter, and the like. Even when they are young, people choose. Socialization is an active (not a passive) process. It varies by class, race, and gender.

It was mentioned earlier that socialization continues throughout people's lives. This continuity means that the template through which individuals channel their behavior is not set in childhood and left that way forever. Rather, people periodically change their template—that is, they change their orientations in light of new experiences—as they move through life and adopt a variety of **reference groups** along the way.[71] The phrase refers to collectivities of people whose characteristics (values, norms, tastes, and patterns of action) are significant in the development of one's own attitudes and behavior.

Taken together, knowing how individuals are socialized and their choice of reference groups leads to understanding of their behavior. For example, poor people sometimes find that they have little control over what happens to them or their children. One's job disappears. A child witnesses a murder on the street. Savings stored under a mattress (because no banks are available) are stolen. Marx would say that when such experiences cumulate people become alienated. Merton would say that modern societies are inherently anomic. In any case, most people persevere. Some, however, do not. They lose hope and act out: with drugs. Or they become angry and act out: sexually or violently. Now these reactions do not happen as often as you might think, but they do happen. Although understanding does not excuse such behaviors, it does explain them.

Although the connection may surprise you, one can see alienation as a dominant theme in the *Star Wars* movies. Darth Vader represents all alienated people, acting out in extreme ways. Luke Skywalker represents the redeeming social values Darth has rejected. In the penultimate scene in the third movie (Episode 6), they are fighting to the death and, frankly, Darth is winning. Luke appeals to the goodness hidden inside Darth. Can he reject the seduction of the Emperor, who represents evil (or the devil, depending on your theology)? Ultimately, Darth overcomes his alienation, hurls the Emperor to his death, and, at the end of the movie, is reincarnated as Luke's father and reunited with Obiwan Kenobi and Yoda. The empire is defeated. One reason Americans feel so good after the movie is that it celebrates the triumph of individuals over great odds. Individuals, Americans believe, possess all the will and ability they need. Like Darth and Luke, they need only use it to achieve positive results. This belief may be why public policies in the United States often demand heroic action by exploited and alienated people. Such requirements are often shortsighted, as the following chapters show. Not many people possess either Darth's or Luke's courage.

Understanding why individuals act, however, provides only one kind of information. Just as a painting can be understood at different levels, so can social life. The structure of stratification must be considered—the second level of analysis.

As both Marx and Weber emphasized, the **social structure** provides the context in which people act and thereby affects rates of events, and rates of diverse events characterize a society and can only be explained at that level. Thus, in studying stratification, such issues as rates of occupational mobility, political participation, poverty, job perquisites, voting, gender inequality, and racial and ethnic inequality can be best understood structurally.

Yet this orientation seems backward to many people, primarily because the ethic of individual responsibility is so pervasive in the United States. The origins of this cultural value probably lie in the transformative effect of Puritanism, with its emphasis on each individual's personal relationship with God, along with the myth of the frontier, with its requirement that individuals be self-reliant in order to survive.[72] The long-term impact of these factors has produced in many Americans a preference for focusing on individuals when thinking about social issues. For example, if the rate of occupational mobility is high (and it is), then many people argue (incorrectly) that it reflects each individual's hard work. Similarly, if the rate of voting is low (and it is), then most people believe (again, incorrectly) that nonvoters must be satisfied with the status quo. The underlying assumption in both examples is that the whole, the rate of mobility or voting, is no more than the sum of its parts, the individual actions making up the rate. This assumption, however, is incorrect. Just as water is qualitatively different—in touch, taste, and many other characteristics—than its component parts (hydrogen and oxygen), so the rate of social events is qualitatively different than its component parts (individual behaviors). From this point of view, it makes sense to suggest, by analogy, that the rate of mobility, voting, and other issues reflect the structure of stratification.

Although Marx, Weber, and the other theorists reviewed before were all structuralists, another early sociologist, Emile Durkheim (b: 1858; d: 1917), explained this angle of vision most clearly when he said, that it is "in the nature of the society itself that we must seek the explanation of social life."[73] He meant that structural phenomena exist externally to individuals, guiding their behavior in predictable ways. But guidance is not force and not all individuals react in the same way. His example had to do with suicide. Although this is a solitary act, he showed that even in social contexts where the ties binding individuals to the society are strong—as among employed married people with children who regularly attend church—some suicides would occur. This fact is irrelevant to Durkheim's point, however, which was that the suicide rate would be higher in such contexts than in others, where the bonds tying individuals to the society are less.[74] Thus, if he was correct, it should be possible to show how the social structure produces varying rates of other events, such as the level of mobility or poverty, apart from individual acts.

The reason why social structure affects rates of events is that it determines the range of choices available to people.[75] This is another way of describing anomie, of course. People's location in the stratification structure (high to low) systematically influences their choices and their consequences. This argument can be formally stated as the *Class Structure Hypothesis:* The lower the social class, the fewer choices people have and the less effective they are in solving personal problems. But the impact of social class is interrelated with the other systems of domination described earlier. For example, the *Gender Hypothesis* is that *women at every class level have fewer and less effective choices than do men.* Similarly, the *Minority Group Hypothesis* is that *minority groups at every class level have fewer and less effective choices than do non-Hispanic Whites.* Much of this book consists in demonstrating the usefulness of these hypotheses.

The rationale underlying these hypotheses is the same as Durkheim's: The structure of stratification is external to individuals; it provides the context that affects both people's choices and their effectiveness. Paradoxically, then, while the total number (or rate) of a phenomenon—such as the proportion of people in each class who vote—reflects the sum of individual actions, that information does not explain its level. For example, as described in Chapter 6, understanding the motives for voting does not explain why working-class and poor people go to the polls at lower rates than middle-class and rich persons. Only knowledge of how the social context influences the choices available to individuals in each class can explain these differences. For this reason, Durkheim said, "social facts are things"; they have a reality independent of individuals.

The *Class Structure Hypothesis* is fundamental for understanding modern societies. Although Durkheim and Merton are cited here, each of the theorists reviewed previously also influenced its formulation. Thus, virtually every theme in Marx's writings can be considered in light of this hypothesis, without recourse to his revolutionary millenarianism. Similarly, Weber's analysis of the class structure focuses attention on rates of events. The functionalists contributed by identifying key elements of the social structure that influence the level of poverty, voting, and many other phenomena. Although his work is flawed, Dahrendorf pointed out how class conflict is built into the social structure. Finally, Lenski's emphasis on the significance of power in the distribution of resources in society is obviously consonant with the theory presented here.

The *Class Structure Hypothesis* has many practical implications. For example, one can pick any behavior by individuals—finding a spouse, obtaining an education, getting a job, purchasing a car, recovering from mental stress, any behavior at all—and, if the hypothesis is correct, poor persons will usually have fewer choices and less effectively resolve their personal problems than the members of other social classes, and this fact will be reflected in different rates of behavior by class. Moreover, these differences will exist no matter how hard poor individuals work or their ability. Such insight helps observers to understand why impoverished people sometimes make decisions that appear unwise from a middle-class vantage point.

The *Class Structure Hypothesis* reflects a more general argument that merits repeating: *The social structure sets the context and affects rates of behavior.* Yet, as also emphasized earlier, individuals choose. In sociological jargon, they have **agency.** The relationship between individuals and social structure has been a (needlessly) controversial topic in sociology. The issues are the degree to which individuals can act independently (do they have choices?) and whether the social structure can be changed. And the answers are as follows: First, individuals have a great deal of independence, but in practical terms their choices are not unlimited. You can, for example, choose to use a typewriter rather than a word processor. You can also choose to have several spouses at the same time. Since the first is inefficient and the second illegal, only a few persons make such choices. In this sense, then, the social structure exists externally to individuals and sets boundaries (which are sometimes wide and sometimes narrow) on behavior. Second, people can and do change social structures. How this process might occur and the difficulty involved can be suggested by using college football as an example.

There is a sort of class and race structure to college football and participants make choices within that context. It is like a system of domination. In a game, for example, players operate within a set of rules that affects their behavior: Only ends and backs can catch forward passes, for example. In addition, players, many of whom are African American, often improvise during a play. But, while fans may not wish to recognize it, each game is part of a multimillion dollar industry that provides a context in which some people and organizations make a great deal of money at the expense of others.

The structural question, then, is who organizes the industry and to who's benefit, and how do these issues affect the players? Let us begin with the coaches. They are nearly always white and are relatively well paid (indeed, they make serious money at major universities). Coaches, of course, decide who gets to play and at what positions. They also have a lot of influence over rules adopted by the National Collegiate Athletic Association (NCAA), since its governing body is made up of coaches. So they have power. For example, at their behest, the NCAA decided that when Coach Charisma induces an 18-year-old football player to sign a contract to play at State University, he is bound to the school even if Mr. Charisma moves on to a (better paying) position at another institution. So the players are bound by contract but the coaches (usually) are not. In addition, along with coaches, athletic directors, university presidents, and NCAA administrators determine the rules under which games will be played and eligibility requirements for players, among other things. Like coaches, these people are nearly always white males and they make lots of money.

In this context, if you happen to be an eighteen-year-old male with some football skill, your choices involve whether to take the right courses to become eligible, whether to play or not, and for whom to play. You cannot, however, negotiate about pay. You cannot even ask to be paid the minimum wage for all the hours put into practicing, attending meetings, lifting weights and staying in shape (often all summer), and playing in the games. In effect, you sign a contract to work long hours for room, board, and tuition. As one observer noted, this is an industry where the employees are called amateurs and employee–employer contracts are called scholarships.[76] As a result of this peculiar arrangement, the university obtains a certain degree of publicity and its athletic associations and others make lots of money. At the University of Florida, for example, the head football coach makes (via salary and other income-producing perquisites) more than two million dollars per year. But others do quite well also: announcers, television executives, and stockholders of firms that advertise on football telecasts, to name only a few. Yet most players and fans think this situation is proper. This is so even though many (if not most) players at major universities fail to graduate. So they do not even get an education for their labors. One might say that college football is the sigh of the oppressed creature—the opium of the players.

Perhaps this sarcasm is unfair. But think about who has more choices and how effective they are. The players can choose to play or not. They can choose to attend (real) classes or not. But unless they organize themselves to strike before a big game or unless (until?) someone hires a lawyer to sue the NCAA, they will remain bound by contract even if a coach leaves and they will not be paid for their labors. So changing the structure of college football will be difficult for them. Coaches and administrators, on the other hand, make the rules. They can more easily change the structure of college football. But it would not be in their interests to do so, which means that paying the players (even minimum wage) is unlikely. The point: People at the top have power and authority; hence, they also have greater ability to change the social structure than those at the bottom. This fact is essential to understanding the class structure in modern societies.

Power and Stratification

Max Weber's definition of power as the ability of an individual or group to get things done, to achieve goals, even if opposition occurs, has become standard.[77] And, as Gerhard Lenski showed, power determines the distribution of resources in every society where a surplus exists. It follows that people have power when they can choose to spend or withhold money, prestige, or other resources from others. They have power when, faced with a divorce, lawsuit, or mental stress, they can find the right lawyer or therapist to help them deal with the problem. They have power when companies and governments pay attention to their needs and desires. But power is not confined to individuals. Because the ability to achieve goals is highly correlated with class, race and ethnicity, and gender, people with similar interests often act in concert and discriminate against others, even though they are not formally organized into groups. Hence, it is not possible to understand the structure of stratification without focusing on the class basis of power. In addition, however, as with college football, white males occupy most positions of power in this country. Hence, power is also race and gender based.

As you should recall, a class consists of those persons with similar occupational prestige, education, income, and other characteristics. In every society, power is class based and correlated with race and gender. This fact means that the very rich, both individually and as an aggregate, have more influence over access to valued resources than do middle-class people; that the middle class, in turn, has more influence over access to valued resources than do working-class people; and that the working class has more influence over access to valued resources than do poor people.

This argument has many practical implications. It implies, for example, that rich people usually have a greater variety of choices and they are more effective in solving personal problems. This is, of course, another way of describing their better life chances. Similarly, as subsequent chapters will show, it suggests how to understand the distribution of wealth and poverty, the nature and level of benefits from income transfers, the level and kind of supervision on the job, the characteristics of housing occupied by different classes, the structure of political participation, and certain aspects of racial, ethnic, and gender inequality. In addition, this approach follows from theoretical analyses of stratification. This argument can be stated formally as the *Political Power Hypothesis:* The higher the social class, the greater the influence over the distribution of resources in the society.

Here is a brief example of the political power of the rich, of the way in which class struggle occurs today. One problem such persons face is retaining as much income as possible after taxes. As will be shown in Chapters 6 and 7, over the past few years the rich have persuaded Congress to transfer much of the tax burden from them to the rest of the population. As a result, despite what Lenski thought, income and wealth inequality have increased in recent years and are now at their highest point in

American history (see Chapter 7). Most of the time, tax breaks for the rich are justified by their benefits to "the economy" and to the majority of people through the so-called "trickle-down effect." Such arguments are veils, of course, designed to hide the way in which the tax system channels income up rather than down. In reality, rich persons avoid contributing to the common good and retain most of their income because of their enormous political power. Put differently, rich people (acting collectively, as a class) use their resources to expand the range and effectiveness of their choices. Thus, instead of merely reacting to government policies, the rich decisively affect their formation. This fact provides them with enormous advantages over the members of other classes.

These advantages mean they can often affect how resources are distributed in society. Although it is true, that every society displays stratification, the result of this dynamic process varies considerably. And this result affects people's life chances.

SUMMARY

The structure of social stratification can be defined as the unequal distribution of resources in society. Possession of such resources as income, education, and occupational prestige affects people's life chances and lifestyles. Individuals and groups struggle to keep and expand their share of income, wealth, and other resources. Three systems of domination characterize modern societies: class, race/ethnicity, and gender. People in the same class tend to be relatively equal to one another in terms of occupational category, income, source of income, education, and other resources. People in different classes tend to be unequal in these same terms. The impact of traditional gender roles means that women are often unequal to men. Because of prejudice and discrimination, members of minority groups are often unequal to Whites. Although these differences have declined in recent years, they remain important. Another indicator of the processes shaping stratification is the emphasis on ascription versus achievement. All modern societies display a tension between these two bases of evaluation.

Karl Marx proposed that in all societies people produce goods and that a structure of stratification emerges based on private ownership of the means of production. Capitalist societies display two classes, Marx said, the bourgeoisie and the proletarians. Class conflict is inevitable and will ultimately lead to a communist revolution. Although Marx was wrong, a number of sociological insights permeate his work: the emphasis on social structure, the degree of opportunity built into the stratification structure, the significance of class conflict, the emphasis on power, and the importance of alienation.

Max Weber helped establish sociology as an academic discipline by emphasizing the importance of objectivity. He distinguished between the analysis of "what is" (the sphere of science), and "what ought to be" (the sphere of values). In outlining the class structure, Weber began (like Marx) by distinguishing between those who own capital (property) and those who do not. But Weber saw more clearly than Marx that those who do not own capital possess resources, the worth of their services and skills, which increase in importance with economic development. Weber thus outlined a more complete model of the class structure than did Marx. Weber's emphasis on the difference between class and status was his way of describing the tension between ascription and achievement in modern societies. By discriminating against others who are different, the members of each class use their power to maintain their positions. Classes do not have to be organized in order to pursue their interests.

Kingsley Davis and Wilbert Moore argued that stratification is the means society uses to motivate people to fill difficult and functionally important positions. Their analysis, however, is an illegitimate teleology and untestable. Nonetheless, functionalism contributed to the study of stratification by emphasizing the importance of looking at nonobvious (or latent) aspects of social life and identifying the key elements of the division of labor.

Ralf Dahrendorf argued that sociology should develop a set of assumptions about the nature of society, a model in which variables are linked by assumption, and a set of testable hypotheses. This orientation is very flawed. Nonetheless, Dahrendorf's work remains useful because he taught U.S. sociologists that problems of class and class conflict can be dealt with in a non-Marxist framework and illustrated the importance of formally stating hypotheses.

Gerhard Lenski developed a theory that explains why the distribution of power and privilege varies within and among societies, and tested his idea using historical and comparative data. He found that the more people are dependent on each other for survival, the more they will share the products of their labor. At the same time, however, the greater the surplus of goods and services, the more power determines their distribution. Among preindustrial societies, Lenski found that the greater the level of technology, the greater the productivity and the greater the inequality. Finally, Lenski proposed that the greater the industrialization and the more democratic the state, the less inequality. Empirically, this last hypothesis has to be modified.

Modern societies display specific characteristics: They are industrialized and capitalist. They use science to solve problems. They are democratic and governed by the rule of law. They display (in some form) a culture of capitalism. In the United States, these characteristics result in the American Dream, a belief that hard work and ability will lead to economic success. But modern societies are anomic; that is, while everyone is supposed to keep striving, built-in restrictions limit the legal means to achieve success.

The initial step in developing a strategy for studying stratification is to assess its historical and cross-national dimensions. Historical data reveal how much change has occurred over time within one society, such as the United States. Cross-national data show the extent to which inequality in its various forms occurs at similar rates in other nations. This research strategy, which parallels Max Weber's, constitutes a "logical experiment" that facilitates identifying the structural variables affecting rates of behavior.

The second step is to distinguish levels of analysis. This procedure is important because the psychological variables explaining why individuals act differ from the structural variables explaining why rates of behavior vary.

People act in terms of their personal experiences, which can be described by the socialization process. The term refers to the lifelong process by which individuals learn norms and values, internalize motivations and (unconscious) needs, develop intellectual and social skills, and enact roles as they participate in society. Socialization is an active process. As people move through life, they adopt a variety of reference groups, collectivities whose characteristics are significant to the development of their own attitudes and behavior. Taken together, knowing how individuals are socialized and their choice of reference groups leads to understanding their behavior.

The social structure affects rates of events—such as poverty, occupational mobility, and the like—because it determines the choices available to people. The *Class Structure Hypothesis* follows: *The lower the social class the fewer choices people have and the less effective they are in solving personal problems.* This hypothesis, along with the *Gender* and *Race Hypotheses*, has practical implications. It means that regardless of the problem, poor persons will usually have fewer choices than members of other social classes, and this fact will be reflected in differences in behavior by class.

The third step is to look at how power affects access to valued resources. Power, the ability to achieve goals even if opposition occurs, is not confined to individuals; it is class based and correlated with race and gender. Again, this argument has practical implications. It implies the higher the social class, the greater the influence over access to valued resources in society.

NOTES

1. Max Weber coined the term life chances (1968 [1920]:926).
2. The image of society as like a pie comes from Lieberson (1980). The question comes from Lenski (1984).
3. The term *systems of domination* comes from Max Weber (1968 [1920]:941), but I am using it in a somewhat different way here. On Weber's use, see Turner, Beeghley, and Powers (2006).
4. At a time when inequality is increasing, some observers suggest that the United States is becoming a "classless society"; see Kingston (2000), Grusky and Weeden (2001). For an opposing point of view, see the aptly titled *Class Matters* (Correspondents of the *New York Times*, 2005). Ironically, in light of the argument in Grusky and Weeden (2001), Charles and Grusky (2004) provide a good example of the relevance of classes and class-based analyses.
5. Most of the classical theorists used ideal types in some form. Only Weber explained their use as part of an explicit methodological strategy (1968 [1920]:6). For further explanation, see Turner, Beeghley, and Powers (2006).
6. The following sketches are necessarily brief and I have avoided citing the secondary sources. For more extended commentary on Marx and Weber, see Turner, Beeghley, and Powers (2006). On the modern theorists, see Turner (2003).
7. Marx and Engels (1971 [1848]:112). Although both Marx and Engels' names are on the published version of the *Communist Manifesto*, Marx wrote the final draft (see Turner, Beeghley, and Powers, 2006).
8. Marx and Engels (1971 [1848]:89).
9. Marx and Engels (1971 [1848]:94).
10. Marx and Engels (1971 [1848]:91).
11. Marx (1967 [1867]).
12. Marx (1967 [1867]:581).
13. Marx (1978 [1843]:54).
14. Marx (1956 [1875]:9–11).
15. Marx and Engels (1971 [1848]:125).
16. Cassidy (1997).
17. All the quotations in this paragraph are from Marx and Engels (1971 [1848]:91–92).
18. Djilas (1965), Voslenski (1985).
19. Weber (1968 [1920]).
20. Weber (1949 [1904]:54).
21. Weber (1946a [1920]:143; 1949 [1904]:105).
22. Becker (1967).
23. Lieberson (1992).
24. Lee et al. (2004), Cutler and Glaeser (2006).
25. Weber (1949 [1904]:104).
26. Weber (1949 [1904]:53).
27. Weber (1946b [1918]).
28. Weber (1968 [1920]:302–7, 926–39). As the page numbers suggest, *Economy and Society* contains two essays on stratification. They were written at different times and overlap in content, which means some interpretation is necessary to understand Weber's "true" intention. For further information, see Roth (1968) or Turner, Beeghley, and Powers (2006).
29. Weber (1968 [1920]:302, 927–28).

30. Weber (1968 [1920]:927).
31. Weber (1968 [1920]:303, 928).
32. Weber (1968 [1920]:927).
33. By comparison, see Fussell (1983), Weeden and Gruskey (2005).
34. Controversy exists over whether classes need to be organized in order to discriminate (see Grusky & Sørensen, 1998). Some of the wording in this paragraph comes from Bendix (1974).
35. Weber (1968 [1920]:306, 935).
36. Weber (1968 [1920]:339–48, 926–39). The quotation comes from p. 341. On the issue of occupational closure, see Weeden (2002).
37. Davis and Moore (1945:244).
38. See Tumin (1970), Wallace (1997).
39. International variations in mobility rates provide one context in which a quasi-functionalist hypothesis has been tested and refuted (see Chapter 4).
40. Parsons (1951; 1954).
41. Goode (1973).
42. Dahrendorf (1959:ix).
43. Dahrendorf (1959:162).
44. Dahrendorf (1959:236–40).
45. Simmel (1908), Coser (1956).
46. Lenski (1984).
47. Lenski (1984:44).
48. Lenski (1984:44).
49. Lenski (1984:90).
50. Weber (1958 [1905]). See Kumar (1988) for an excellent chapter-length review of the nature of modernity.
51. In Greek mythology, Prometheus is kept in chains and suffers at the hand of Zeus. He is eventually released and thrives. See Aeschylus (1975), especially the appendix by the translators.
52. See Daniel Bell on post-industrial society (1973). The argument that Bell's judgment is premature comes from Kumar (1988).
53. Adam Smith's, *The Wealth of Nations* (1976 [1776]) is the classic study of the origins and nature of capitalism.
54. Weber (1946a [1920]). See also Turner, Beeghley, and Powers (2006).
55. Berger (1986) argues that capitalism and democracy are linked in that economic development leads to pressure for personal freedom and vice versa.
56. See Beeghley (2003) on Max Weber and the significance of the rule of law.
57. Weber (1958 [1905]). See also Turner, Beeghley, and Powers (2006).
58. For the classic statement of the American Dream as an ideology of success, see Adams (1931). On the argument that the United States manifests these characteristics in extreme form, see Hochschild (1995) and McNamee and Miller (2004).
59. Merton (1968a).
60. An earlier version of this metaphor appeared in Beeghley (2003:85).
61. Merton (1968a:200).
62. Miller (1996).
63. Merton (1968a:194). Italics in original.
64. Turner (1984).
65. Merton (1968).
66. Kohn (1987).
67. Weber (1958 [1905], 1951 [1913], 1952 [1917], 1968 [1920]). For an overview, see Turner, Beeghley, and Powers (2006).
68. Beeghley (1999; 2003).
69. Brim (1966).
70. The elements of socialization theory are rarely stated formally, as here. To see how they can be useful, see Beeghley (2003).
71. Hyman (1942), Merton and Rossi (1968).
72. On Puritanism, see Weber (1958 [1905]). On the significance of the frontier, see F.J. Turner (1920). Note that while Turner's thesis has been severely and correctly criticized (Limerick, 1995), his emphasis on the frontier as myth remains important.
73. Durkheim (1982 [1895]:128).
74. Durkheim (1951 [1897]).
75. Merton (1968).
76. Rhoden (2002).
77. Weber (1968 [1920]).

RACE/ETHNICITY AND STRATIFICATION

This chapter tells the story of Jefferson's Dilemma. In the *Declaration of Independence*, written in 1776, Thomas Jefferson declared: "We hold these truths to be self-evident, that all men are created equal, that they are endowed by their Creator with certain unalienable Rights, that among these are Life, Liberty, and the pursuit of Happiness."[1] Self-evident? In 1776? Nothing like these 32 words had ever been written before. They helped change the course of history. A revolution was fought and a new nation established based on them, with far-reaching implications.[2] First, these few words implied that both African Americans and Whites should have the same civil rights and the same ability to succeed in light of their talent and skills. The struggle by minority groups for equal opportunity follows inexorably. And the value orientation expressed by these words is generalizable to all other ascriptive classifications—by gender or sexual orientation, for example. Second, these words signify the emergence of class-based societies with their movement from an emphasis on ascription to achievement. Any society that values personal freedom and democracy should apply achievement-oriented criteria to all. Finally, the Declaration created an altogether new moral standard for nations to live up to. A government's legitimacy must now reflect the will of the people—all of whom possess inherent dignity and self-worth. In the modern world, both nations and individuals are judged by this standard.

But Jefferson did not live up to it. He was a slave-owner. His only book, *Notes on the State of Virginia*, written in 1785, shows that he believed in the inferiority of those held in bondage.[3] So he and the other founders of the new nation excluded African slaves from its moral promise. They thus created a dilemma: freedom and equality of opportunity for all versus freedom for some and slavery for others. Jefferson recognized the difficulty this dilemma represented. In *Notes*, he forecast the long-term harm to the nation created by a division into free and unfree. Yet he fathered children by one of his slaves, Sally Hemings. He freed only two slaves during his lifetime and only five in his will. Jefferson never resolved his dilemma.[4]

Nor have we. As commonly used, the term **race** refers to groups identifiable in light of their physical traits, such as skin color. Thus, African Americans, Whites, and those of Asian origin are typically defined as races. But these are social constructions; variations in skin pigmentation merely reflect long-term adaptations to climate.[5] Racial distinctions are socially meaningful because people attach meaning to them. The term **ethnic group** refers to aggregates with distinctive social and psychological characteristics, as indicated by their nationality, religious heritage, and other unique elements of their background. Thus, the Irish and Italians are typically defined as ethnic groups. So are persons who came from or whose ancestors came from various Hispanic and Asian nations. Note, however, that few "Hispanic" or "Asian" people see themselves as sharing a common culture. Rather, they usually identify with their ethnic group—for example, as Chinese Americans or Mexican Americans. Moreover, recent immigration from sub-Saharan Africa and the Caribbean has meant a corresponding increase in ethnic group identification among people of African descent, who identify, for example, as Nigerian Americans or Jamaican Americans.[6]

These permutations mean that, in one sense, racial categories serve as an arbitrary way of describing inequality in the distribution of resources, such as education or occupational attainment. Thus, the United States population now approaches 300 million persons. Although some people identify with more than one group, roughly 67 percent of the population is White American, 14 percent Hispanic American, 13 percent African American, 4 percent Asian American, and 1 percent Native American.[7] As a convention, any reference to "Whites" in this book excludes Hispanics, who can be of any race. In another sense, though, these categories are metaphors for the dilemma the founders created at the beginning, the establishment of a system of domination based on the enslavement of dark-skinned people. In 1790, just after the Constitution was adopted, nearly all of the white population was of English origin.[8] Hence, other groups appearing on these shores have not only been forced to adapt to English norms and values, but also to endure their prejudice and discrimination. **Prejudice** refers to people's hostile attitudes toward others in a different group or toward other groups as a whole. **Discrimination** refers to the unequal treatment of individuals and groups due to their personal characteristics, such as race or ethnicity.[9] **Minority groups,** then, are racial and ethnic populations subject to hostile attitudes and unequal treatment by more powerful racial and ethnic groups (Whites in the United States).[10]

The extent of prejudice and discrimination today has become controversial. Some observers argue that America is becoming a "color-blind" society such that minority group members are increasingly integrated into the mainstream of American life and inequality has declined as a result.[11] This is another way of describing the move toward a class-based, achievement-oriented society. Others argue, however, that continuing prejudice and discrimination mean much racial and ethnic inequality remains.[12] This is, of course, another way of describing the continuing importance of ascription. Both interpretations are correct. As a metaphor, consider a 16 oz. cup in which the level of water within has risen to 8 oz. Is the cup as now half full or still half empty?

The gap between attitudes and behavior illustrates the interpretive dilemma. On the one hand, attitudinal surveys show a long-term trend: Most Whites now embrace the value of equality, especially equality of opportunity.[13] For example, in the 1940s about 68 percent of Whites thought that African-American and white children should go to separate schools. Today, this question is not even asked because virtually no one argues for segregated schools. The pattern is similar with other topics, such as access to transportation, jobs, and housing. One of the best indicators of prejudice lies in attitudes toward intermarriage. Thomas Jefferson (said he) opposed unions between Whites and African slaves, and most Whites opposed them until recently. In 1958, 96 percent of Whites disapproved of marriage between the races. By 2002, however, only 10 percent disapproved.

On the other hand, a gap exists between "say" and "do." Many Whites are like Jefferson so long ago in that they oppose policies designed to provide equal opportunity for all.[14] For example, although only 3 percent of Whites object if their children's school has "a few" African-American students, if "more than half" are African American, the proportion of Whites objecting rises to 59 percent. Moreover, 66 percent of Whites oppose busing children to achieve integration. Thus, while the question about separate schools is not asked, schools remain segregated.[15] So do neighborhoods and jobs. And these differences, which reflect discrimination (past and present), have important consequences. Although minority groups now display higher rates of occupational mobility than in the past (see Chapter 5), they still tend to be overrepresented in the lower and working classes. Even though equality has become a widespread value, Whites remain like the founders of the new nation: willing to tolerate discrimination. Jefferson's Dilemma is our dilemma.[16]

DIMENSIONS OF RACIAL AND ETHNIC STRATIFICATION

Racial and Ethnic Stratification in the United States

In order to assess the degree of change in the distribution of resources among racial and ethnic groups it is useful to distinguish between its absolute and relative dimensions. "Absolute change" refers to difference over time. Thus, if the median income of African-American households changed from about $1,900 per year in 1950 to $31,400 per year in 2004 (and it did), then most are better off—even after taking inflation into account. "Relative change" refers to a difference in relationship to some other group, such as Whites (recall that this term excludes Hispanics). Thus, if during the same period the median income among white households changed from about $3,400 per year to $49,000 per year (and it did), then the relative relationship between the two groups has changed—although not by much. In 1950, African-American households earned about 56 percent as much as white households, which increased to 64 percent by 2004.[17] Over the last century, minority groups have improved their situation both absolutely and relatively.

Civil Rights.   **Civil rights** refer to citizens' legally guaranteed opportunity to participate equally in the society. This guarantee constitutes the foundation for a democratic society; it provides a legal basis for achievement. No nation can be considered democratic if some of its people are denied civil rights. For example, those possessing civil rights can vote, sit on juries, buy a house if they have the money, educate their children, obtain a job, and marry whomever they wish. They have access to public accommodations, such as eating in a restaurant, boarding a plane or bus, renting a hotel room or an apartment, or being treated in a hospital. Civil rights guarantee individual freedom and opportunity. Without civil rights, entire groups are evaluated based on nonperformance criteria: ascription. For those without civil rights, the law itself can be and has been used as a mechanism for insuring that racial and ethnic minorities remain subordinate to Whites.

When the Constitution was adopted in 1789, only property owners who paid taxes could vote, which meant only privileged English men enjoyed civil rights. Over time, accompanied by much protest and violence, those who did not own land and various white ethnic groups (German, Scandinavian, Irish, Italian, etc.) obtained a legal guarantee of equal participation.

By contrast, Native Americans were denied civil rights.[18] The independence and personal autonomy displayed by Native Americans amazed the Europeans when they arrived in the "new world." The colonists (and European intellectuals) learned a great deal about liberty and equality based on the example provided by Native American societies. Even so, over time these societies endured massive depopulation in a context of systematic oppression. The Native American population in what would become the continental United States was probably about five million souls, and possibly much more, at the time of contact with Whites in the fifteenth century. The continent was filled with people who had their own governments, territories, and ways of life. By 1900, the population had fallen to about 375,000, mostly due to disease and systematic extermination. Although the population has rebounded since then, a 93 percent decline is a good definition of genocide.

By normal Western standards, the various Native American tribes living in what is now the United States held "compelling legal and moral rights to be treated as fully sovereign nations."[19] And, at least initially, Whites agreed by treaty to deal with them as such. In fact, however, the law was used to take tribal land and deprive Native Americans of their civil rights. A belief in *Manifest Destiny*, that the United States had a divinely inspired mission to extend freedom and democracy throughout continental North America, provided a (hypocritical) justification for taking Native American lands. As only one of many examples, the *Indian Removal Act of 1830* forced thousands of people from at least four nations to cede their land east of the Mississippi River and move west. Many died on the journey. As the nineteenth century progressed, Native Americans became trapped in two ways. First, as citizens of foreign nations by treaty, they could not vote or exercise other civil rights outside their reservations. Second, subject to regulation by the Bureau of Indian Affairs, which was run by Whites, Native Americans could not determine their fate even on the reservations. Since 1976, however, federal law has allowed some Native American nations to gain (actually, regain) legal recognition. Along with the right to vote and other legal changes, Native American people now enjoy greater civil rights.

Those of Asian ancestry were also denied civil rights.[20] By origin, the Asian population today is approximately 24 percent Chinese American, 19 percent Indian American, 18 percent Filipino American, 10 percent Korean American, 11 percent Vietnamese American, and 7 percent Japanese American. Much of this diversity has only developed over the last four decades, but the percentages would vary a little if those with dual ancestry were included. Although Whites usually fail to see the differences, each group displays a distinct language, culture, and pattern of social organization.

The few Chinese and Japanese immigrants who came to the United States in the nineteenth century faced very high levels of prejudice and discrimination.[21] Immigration laws provide an indicator. As only one example, the *Chinese Exclusion Act of 1882* suspended immigration of persons of Chinese origin and prohibited those already residing here from obtaining U.S. citizenship, with all the rights that follow. This law remained in effect until 1943 when Congress substituted a quota system for Chinese immigrants. Another indicator of the denial of civil rights was the confinement of U.S. citizens of Japanese descent to internment camps located east of the Rocky Mountains during World War II. Because they were forced to sell their homes and businesses before being moved, they received only about five cents on the dollar. They lost everything. Their property was never returned. This whole process was deemed vital to American national security at the time and the Supreme Court, in *Korematsu v. United States*, declared it constitutional. By contrast, citizens of German descent neither lost their land nor were jailed. Thus, while nineteenth century European immigrants faced many obstacles, the barriers confronting Asian Americans were more significant. The influx of immigrants from Asian nations over the last 40 years reflects, in part, the impact of the *Immigration Act of 1965* coupled with other legal changes that now protect civil rights.

Hispanic people were denied civil rights as well.[22] By origin, the Hispanic population is about 65 percent Mexican American, 9 percent Puerto Rican American, and 3 percent Cuban American, with the remainder coming from other nations. Again, including those with dual ancestry would produce a little variation in these percentages. Although united by language and Spanish heritage, each group exhibits a distinctive culture and pattern of social organization.

Historically, the early settlers from Mexico displaced the Native Americans and regarded the Southwest as their homeland.[23] In the nineteenth century, then, the United States confronted Mexico on its western border. The belief in *Manifest Destiny* made this situation intolerable and the United States eventually acquired, via war and the Gadsden Purchase (1853), what is now the American Southwest. Although the *Treaty of Guadalupe Hidalgo*, which ended the Mexican War in 1848, guaranteed people of Mexican origin full civil rights, its provisions were ignored in practice. Whites viewed all Mexican Americans, including landholders, as "cheap labor" and denied their civil rights. Historically, the need to import laborers from Mexico during periods of economic expansion and return them to Mexico during economic contractions has affected the lives of Mexican Americans, who are treated as second-class citizens. Wages are depressed. Citizenship is questioned. Education is denied. The right to vote is restricted. Housing is segregated. Although Puerto Rican Americans were granted citizenship when the island was annexed in 1892, immigration to the mainland has also reflected economic cycles. Historically, Puerto Rican Americans have also been kept segregated and denied their rights, partly by custom and partly by law. Recent immigrants from Cuba and other Latin American nations have endured less (but not zero) discrimination due to passage of civil rights laws.

Finally, the Civil War's promise of freedom was empty as African Americans went from slavery to serfdom in the form of sharecropping.[24] For a few years after the war, African Americans began to participate more fully in all aspects of social life. But this period was short-lived. At war's end, white Southerners began an immediate campaign of terror against the former slaves, using lynching as one of several tools. Most African Americans ended up as sharecroppers in a system of debt peonage, unable to pay debts to white landowners (who kept the books). The goal was to keep African Americans poor and uneducated in order to insure the availability of a large and compliant labor force. The success of this strategy hinged on the denial of civil rights. This denial was eventually given the force of law by the Supreme Court in *Plessy v. Ferguson* (1898). In this case, the Court declared "separate but equal" school systems to be constitutional. Its logic, however, served to justify denying African Americans (and all minority groups) the ability to participate in every sphere of society. Separate and very unequal became the law of the land.[25]

In Mississippi in the 1950s, more than half a century after the *Plessy* decision, supposedly free African Americans still toiled for slave wages in the same fields where their enslaved forebears had picked cotton. In some counties, African Americans outnumbered Whites by as much as four to one, yet it was common for not a single African American to be registered to vote, to be part of jury pools, to be served in restaurants, or be treated in a county-funded hospital. "The state kept it that way by sanctioning violence against black people who got above themselves by agitating for the vote, talking back to white folks, or failing to give way on the sidewalk."[26]

One of the most potent symbols of oppression was the denial of access to public accommodations, which affected every aspect of daily life. In the spring of 1946, Jackie Robinson and his new wife, Rachel, boarded a plane in Los Angeles. A three-sport All-American at UCLA and one of the rising stars of the Negro Baseball League, Robinson had recently signed a contract to play for the Brooklyn Dodgers organization. The couple was bound for spring training: overnight from Los Angeles to New Orleans, with connections to Pensacola and Daytona Beach, Florida. After arriving in New Orleans, the Robinsons were "bumped" from their New Orleans-to-Pensacola connection, even though several seats were available. They went to the airport coffee shop for a snack and were refused service. The restrooms and drinking fountains in the airport were marked "White Only" and "Colored Only." They spent the night in one of the few hotels that accepted "Negro" guests and went back to the airport for the next available flight. After boarding this plane, they were forced to give up their seats to a late-arriving white couple. The Robinsons eventually took a 32-hour bus ride from New Orleans to Daytona Beach. (There was no interstate highway system in those days.) Of course, they rode in the back of the bus.[27]

On buses, the system worked like this: The first four rows were reserved for Whites. The rear rows were for African Americans, who often comprised most of the riders. Seats in the middle rows were available to African Americans until needed by Whites. At that point, African Americans had to move to the rear, stand, or (if there was no room) get off the bus. As with the airlines, this process would occur even if African American passengers had paid the fare and were only part way to their destination. On local buses, which had front and rear doors, African Americans would board in front to pay the fare, then disembark, and get back on the bus via the rear door. This kind of daily humiliation was typical of African American life before the Civil Rights revolution.

But the structure of discrimination broke down in the 1950s and 1960s, as court decisions and legislative enactments made most forms of unequal treatment illegal. For example, in 1954, the Supreme Court overturned the *Plessy* decision in *Brown v. Board of Education*, ruling that segregated school systems violated the Constitution. This decision was but one, although a key one, in a series of decisions by which the Court struck down the legal basis for the denial of civil rights, not only to African Americans but to all racial and ethnic minorities and to women as well. In addition, the struggle for civil rights moved to the streets during this same period. Looking back, it is easy to see the battle over civil rights as a simple tale of morality in which a great wrong was made right. But segregation had been maintained for a century or so by means of violence and terror; white Southerners and many (perhaps most) Northerners resisted the call for equality. The bitter fight to overcome this system was chaotic and the outcome uncertain. Only the sustained effort and heroism, not only of leaders such as Dr. Martin Luther King, Jr., but also thousands of activists—mostly unknown today—made the Civil Rights movement successful.[28] Ultimately, Congress passed a series of civil rights acts designed to outlaw all forms of discrimination. As a result, all minority groups obtained the right to vote, access to public accommodations, the right to equal educational opportunity, and the right to purchase housing, among many other changes.

Although brief, this discussion shows that discrimination due to race or ethnicity is now illegal in the United States. African-American, Hispanic, Asian, and Native citizens improved their situation both absolutely and relatively. This change means that inequality is far less today than in the past as people have begun to use their civil rights to seize opportunities. When observers claim that America is becoming "color blind," they refer to this increased opportunity. Even so, while civil rights provide a legal basis for personal freedom and dignity, and thus indicate a transition toward a class-based society, they do not mean equality of opportunity in other areas.

Infant Mortality.   The **infant mortality rate** refers to the number of live babies who die within the first year of life. It indicates life chances because it reflects people's level of nutrition, sanitation, housing, prenatal care, admission to hospitals for birth, and access to other goods and services. As such, it provides a useful measure of overall health differences among racial and ethnic groups. Here are infant mortality rates in 1900 for various white ethnic groups and African Americans. The numbers refer to deaths per 1,000 live births.[29]

Native Whites	142
English Immigrants	149

German Immigrants   159
Italian Immigrants   189
African Americans   297

Thus, white ethnic groups who were immigrants displayed higher rates of infant mortality than did native Whites at the turn of the century. This difference means that immigrants endured lower living standards than natives. Their life chances were unequal. In comparison, however, the African-American infant mortality rate was far higher than immigrants' and more than double that of native Whites. The magnitude of these differences suggests that while the living standards of white immigrants were low, they were far worse for African Americans, who confronted much greater discrimination. Their life chances were far worse, too.

This fact has not changed, even though infant mortality rates declined steadily over time. Here are data for 2002, in deaths per 1,000 live births:[30]

Asian Americans   5
Hispanic Americans   6
White Americans   6
Native Americans   9
African Americans   14

These data illustrate that everyone is healthier today, an important benefit of modernity. People's ability to share in the available goods and services is better. Although historical data on Asian and Hispanic American infant mortality rates are not presented, their situation has improved both absolutely and relatively. The African-American infant mortality rate, however, remains twice that of Whites, just as it was in 1900, which means their life chances are significantly worse as well. In fact, the African-American infant mortality rate today resembles that in many third world nations. By this indicator, African Americans have the poorest health of all racial and ethnic groups. But Whites live in different neighborhoods and rarely notice these differences.

Housing Segregation. Housing segregation also affects life chances.[31] Where people live influences the quality of education available, employment opportunities, the probability of criminal victimization, access to community services (such as libraries and parks), the degree of neighborhood disorganization (exposure to violence and drug markets). It affects every aspect of life. As people succeed, they usually move to better residential environments, which not only provide immediate benefits but also improve future prospects for wealth creation and occupational mobility due to greater access to neighborhood-determined resources. When such opportunities are blocked, however, so that a better job or increase in pay does not translate into better housing, the ability to maintain that success or pass it on to one's children declines.

In 1900, 90 percent of African Americans still lived in the rural South.[32] But after two centuries of confinement to the land (as slaves or sharecroppers), African Americans began moving north in search of opportunity and found instead another trap—the urban ghetto, a context in which people were crowded together in impoverished conditions. As will be discussed later, this location was not accidental. African Americans (and, in the West, Asian Americans) were prevented by law and violence from living in many communities and suburbs. They were called "sundown towns," so named for the signs informing African Americans that they must be out of town by sunset. Trapped in ghettos and unable to find (legal) work except in menial occupations, the American Dream of occupational success proved unattainable for most. Throughout the twentieth century, African Americans endured more housing segregation than any other racial or ethnic group.[33]

Housing segregation remains pervasive today, although the isolation of African Americans has declined in recent years. Table 2.1 displays the level of segregation in American metropolitan areas by racial and ethnic group from 1980 to 2000, the most recent year for which data are available. The table uses the Index of Dissimilarity, the most common measure.[34] Although the method by which it is calculated is complex, that issue is not important here. What you need to remember is that the index varies between zero and one, with zero meaning no segregation and one complete segregation. Essentially, then, the higher the number, the greater the residential segregation. The table shows that Native Americans living in metropolitan areas bear less segregation than other minority groups, with a score of .33. This "low" score, however, occurs because many Native Americans still live in rural areas and on reservations rather than in metropolitan areas. Segregation among Asian Americans is higher, .41, and that of Hispanic Americans is higher still at .51. One reason for the latter is that a significant proportion of Hispanics have dark skin; those who look white can more easily move into white neighborhoods and suburbs. African-Americans, however, endure significantly more housing segregation than any other group, with a score of .64. As will be shown, these scores reflect continuing discrimination. At the same time, however, looking across the bottom row of the table shows that the level of African-American segregation has declined significantly, a relative improvement. These data provide a quantitative indicator of increasing opportunity. As African-American citizens have become more successful in recent years, some have been able to secure better housing and thereby not only improve their life chances but those of their children as well.

These data are averages across metropolitan areas, however, and thus understate the degree of residential segregation in some cities. For example, Asian Americans are much more segregated in San Francisco (.48) and New York City (.51) than in other cities. Similarly, Hispanic Americans are much more segregated in New York City

TABLE 2.1   Trends in Residential Segregation, United States Metropolitan Areas, 1980–2000

	1980	1990	2000
Native American	.37	.37	.33
Asian American	.41	.41	.41
Hispanic American	.50	.50	.51
African American	.73	.68	.64

Notes: The measure used is the Index of Dissimilarity, which varies between zero and 1.0. The higher the number, the greater the segregation.

Source: United States Bureau of the Census (2002:20, 36, 60, 78).

(.67).[35] Again, however, the housing situation of African Americans is much worse. Using the Index of Dissimilarity, the most segregated city in America for African Americans is Detroit, with a score of .85. This high score is not accidental, as Detroit is surrounded by "sundown suburbs."[36] Moreover, thirty metropolitan areas, in which about 40 percent of all African Americans live, are "hypersegregated" such that virtually everyone in their own and adjacent neighborhoods is also African American.[37] Whites live in the suburbs. "Hypersegregation" affects every facet of daily life and, hence, the ability to share in the distribution of goods and services that others (Whites) take for granted.

And the consequences of housing segregation are profound. Many African Americans (poor and not poor) are forced to live in neighborhoods with concentrated poverty, inadequate schools, fewer support facilities (such as hospitals), fewer amenities (such as parks), and other problems. As described in Chapter 1, sociologists describe this situation as **anomic;** that is, a disconnect exists between the goals people learn, such as striving for occupational and economic success, and the ability to obtain those goals (legally).[38]

Poverty, Occupation, and Income. One of the best single indicators of racial and ethnic inequality in the distribution of resources is the level of poverty. Here are poverty rates in 2004:[39]

White Americans	8%
Asian Americans	10
Hispanic Americans	22
African Americans	25

Although some variation occurs year-to-year, the pattern displayed here has been relatively stable over the last 30 years or so. These data provide a rough measure of the impact of discrimination by race and ethnicity, as people are being denied access to education and jobs.

Historically, the United States has been characterized by a rigid pattern of occupational segregation. Whites worked at higher prestige and higher paying jobs than other racial and ethnic groups. But this situation has altered somewhat over the past 30 years, as shown in Table 2.2. The table reveals that only 6 percent of African Americans worked in white-collar jobs in 1940, compared to 53 percent in 2005. This is significant relative change. Similarly, only 19 percent of Hispanics worked in white-collar jobs in 1960, compared to 39 percent in 2005. The lack of change between 1990 and 2005 reflects the impact of immigration among Hispanics. About 70 percent of Asian Americans now work in white-collar jobs, although they tend to work (because of discrimination) in a limited range of professions. In general, these data show that the gap between Whites and others has become smaller over time, as members of minority groups have been upwardly mobile into white-collar jobs.[40] As a result of affirmative action policies, more employers have been willing to hire people with potential, even when their credentials (such as education) are slightly less. Research shows that job performance is no worse and that workforce diversity pays off.[41]

This mobility has important implications because more African Americans have the prestige and income to purchase homes in middle-class neighborhoods. As the

TABLE 2.2 Percentage of Racial and Ethnic Groups in White-Collar Jobs, Selected Years, 1940–2005

	1940	1950	1960	1970	1980	1990	2000	2005
White American	35%		44%	48%	54%	60%	64%	63%
African American	6		13	24	37	44	51	53
Hispanic American			19	22		39	38	39
Asian American						64	67	70

Note: The system of occupational classification changed between 1970 and 1980. Blank cells indicate that data are not available.

Sources: United States Bureau of the Census (1975:381, 2005), United States Bureau of Labor Statistics (2006:191).

occupational structure changes, more African Americans and members of other groups are becoming middle class. This relative change indicates less inequality.

The pattern of declining inequality can also be seen when a few detailed occupations are considered, as shown in Table 2.3, although the change is not as great. In looking at the table, begin by scanning across the rows for African Americans in 1970 and 2004: In most cases, their percentages have increased, which suggests less inequality. Temporal data for other groups are not available over this same time. Despite these changes, job segregation remains. Now look down the columns for the year 2004. Although African Americans comprise about 13 percent of the population and Hispanic Americans 14 percent, they include only 3 percent and 7 percent of architects, and 5 percent and 3 percent of lawyers, respectively. With regard to Asian Americans, the table suggests how they cluster in certain occupations, especially those requiring higher education. These data show continuing absolute inequality. They also indicate that minority groups still have more difficulty obtaining high prestige and, hence, high paying white-collar jobs.[42]

TABLE 2.3 Racial and Ethnic Minorities in Selected Occupations

	AFRICAN AMERICANS		HISPANIC AMERICANS	ASIAN AMERICANS
JOB CATEGORY	*1970*	*2004*	*2004*	*2004*
Architects	2%	3%	7%	6%
Civil Engineers	1	8	5	12
Physicians	2	6	5	17
Lawyers	1	5	3	3
Insurance Underwriters	3	8	5	4
Electricians	3	7	14	1
Firefighters	2	8	9	1
Police	6	16	13	2

Source: United States Bureau of the Census (2006:401).

Data on income reveal continuing relative inequality. As shown below, median household income in 2004 varies by racial and ethnic group and the rank order looks like that displayed in Table 2.1, which deals with housing segregation.[43] This similarity is not accidental. Asian and white American households have the highest incomes, with African and Hispanic Americans lower.

Asian American	$57,500
White American	49,000
Hispanic American	34,200
African American	31,400

The United States is a heterogeneous society, comprising a variety of racial and ethnic groups who continue to be unequal to one another across many dimensions. The differences in access to valued resources portrayed here are not unique. Other nations show a similar pattern.

Racial and Ethnic Stratification in Cross-National Perspective

In comparison to the United States, most of the nations comprising the European Union are relatively homogeneous by race and ethnicity. Although Muslim immigrants from various Asian and African countries have arrived in recent years, their proportion of the population remains very low. Throughout the continent, these immigrants display higher levels of poverty and unemployment than do native-born citizens.[44]

The most heterogeneous nation in the European Union is the United Kingdom, due mainly to its colonial legacy. Its diverse population allows for a comparison to the United States and the focus here is on a crucial issue: unemployment. This indicator of inequality is useful because, as will be shown in more detail in Chapter 9, those without jobs are economically deprived, display a lower self-concept, and are more likely to endure familial disruption, among other problems.

The United Kingdom has a population of about 60 million persons, of whom 2.0 percent are Black from various Caribbean and African nations, 1.7 percent of Indian origin, 2.2 percent of Pakistani or Bangladeshi origin, and 1.7 percent from other nations around the world. Thus, racial and ethnic minorities in the U.K. constitute about 7.6 percent of the total population.[45]

Table 2.4 displays unemployment rates in the United States and the United Kingdom by race and ethnicity, and by gender. It reveals that Whites of both genders in both nations are significantly less likely to be out of work than members of racial and ethnic minorities. In both the United States and the United Kingdom, the table shows, about 5 percent of white men and 4 percent of white women are out of work. By comparison, the unemployment rates for African-American men and women are around 11 percent. In the United Kingdom, unemployment rates among ethnic minorities (with the exception of Indians) are much higher. Other indicators of inequality, such as those used earlier in this section, show that racial and ethnic minorities in the United Kingdom suffer discrimination similar to that in the United States.[46]

If a class of college students were to go back in time to mid-twentieth century America, they would observe a society almost unrecognizable by today's standards.

TABLE 2.4   Unemployment by Racial/Ethnic Group and Gender, United States and United Kingdom

UNITED STATES	2004	
	Men	Women
White American	5%	4%
Asian American	4	4
Hispanic American	6	7
African Americans	12	10

UNITED KINGDOM	2002	
White	5%	4%
Indian	7	7
Black Caribbean	14	9
Black African	15	13
Pakistani	16	16
Bangladeshi	20	24

Note: Data for Whites in the United States include Hispanic Americans.

Sources: United States Bureau of Labor Statistics (2005:187), Office for National Statistics (2005).

"Separate and unequal" remained the law of the land. In both the North and South, prejudice and discrimination were widespread and seen as legitimate by most Whites, who tried to maintain race as a system of domination in every sphere of life. Much has changed, however, as racial and ethnic inequality has declined in both relative and absolute terms in many areas. The United States now comes closer to the moral standard established by the Declaration of Independence. Thus, when observers claim that the United States is becoming "color blind," by which they mean that minority groups have increased opportunity to succeed, they are correct.

Much, however, remains the same. Data on infant mortality, residential segregation, poverty, occupational segregation, and income show that this country remains deeply divided along racial and ethnic lines. Thus, when observers claim that America still displays a huge chasm between Whites and minority groups, they are also correct. Race remains a system of domination in a class-based context. This enduring gap between American values and behavior carries with it enormous consequences.

ANOMIE, THE AMERICAN DREAM, AND THE IMPACT OF RACIAL AND ETHNIC STRATIFICATION

The passage of civil rights laws during the 1960s not only made the United States more democratic and created opportunities for minority groups, they also committed the nation to using achievement-oriented criteria in evaluating people. This new context has allowed some minority group persons to become upwardly mobile (see Chapter 5) and, in a few cases, to become rich. At the same time, recall that all modern societies are **anomic;** that is, there exists a lack of connection between dominant cultural values (such as economic success) and the legitimate means to achieve them (such as hard work).[47]

People respond to built-in restrictions on opportunity in predictable ways, regardless of race or ethnicity.[48] For example, Liverpool, England, resembles many American cities except that its population is almost completely White. As in American cities, manufacturing jobs have left and the rate of unemployment is very high. In fact, long-term unemployment has become normal for many persons, especially young adults. Poverty is rampant. Located outside the economic mainstream, poor people in Liverpool are concentrated together and isolated from the rest of the nation. Most residents work and have stable families. As Merton pointed out, even in an anomic context, they conform to societal expectations. Nonetheless, a foreseeable set of problems appear: high rates of violence, drug use, and sexual acting out. These problems reflect, then, the way in which the level of inequality (in this case in the United Kingdom) restricts opportunity in modern capitalist societies.

This restriction is peculiarly worse in the United States, however, because of the impact of two centuries of slavery followed by a century of systematic discrimination. For African Americans, the baseball metaphor described in Chapter 1 was the literal state of affairs. Major league baseball simply prevented African Americans from participating for many years until Jackie Robinson broke the "color barrier" in 1947. This prohibition symbolizes the larger fact that for most of American history minority group persons have been arbitrarily excluded from trying to achieve the American Dream. Table 2.2, for example, shows that only 6 percent of African Americans were employed in white-collar jobs in 1940. They were unable to go up to bat, let alone run the occupational base paths. Of course, this same (metaphorical) point applies not only to African Americans but to people of color more generally, along with women, immigrants, and others. Yet, despite the anomic character of the game, with its built-in restrictions, members of these groups have always wanted into the game rather than to overthrow it. This desire reflects a recognition that increased opportunity and the possibility of a better life exist when modernization occurs.

Even so, emphasis here is on the long-term impact of the extraordinary situation in which African Americans found themselves for so many years. Thus, people living in hypersegregated environments still learn—at home, at school, and in the media—that hard work is supposed to lead to success. And most, nearly all, struggle on—working steadily, forming stable families, going to church. As one commentator points out, "most Black people [today] are not poor. Most are not criminals. Most are leading productive lives. The Black middle class is larger and more successful than ever."[49] But a significant minority does not obtain success via employment. In such anomic contexts, however, many—especially the young—become disaffected with foreseeable results: (1) high rates of violence and crime, (2) drug selling and use, and (3) sexual acting out.

1. In an anomic context, especially when it is made worse by discrimination, crime and violence become common. Because of the long-term impact of housing and other forms of discrimination, many African Americans reside in neighborhoods characterized by multiple and accumulated disadvantages and there emerges "a racially distinctive ecological niche of violence."[50] A "code of the street" develops, a set of informal but widely known norms governing interpersonal behavior in public places. In this environment, residents see the police as abusing the people they are supposed to protect. Thus, inhabitants believe they must protect themselves. The code of the street constitutes an attempt at regulating the use of violence in a context where the law is viewed as irrelevant to daily life. Such contexts are inherently lethal because everyone is made hostage to the most violent among them.

The norms embodied in the code of the street dictate that people, especially males, should carry themselves in an assertive manner that communicates the willingness and ability to be violent. So they use gait, facial expression, and talk to promote "respect" and deter aggression. For example, people do not make eye contact; it can be taken as a challenge. Seeking "respect" (or honor) in these ways is more than mere vanity; it constitutes a form of **cultural capital** that is designed to help people keep themselves physically safe in public places.[51] One way to protect oneself is to carry a gun because its display can intimidate others and thus provide a means of self-protection. Nationwide, about five percent of all high school students admit to carrying a gun at least once during the last 30 days, a figure that is probably higher in poor inner city neighborhoods where violence is pervasive.[52] As a result of so many people going armed on the street, however, the violence takes on a life of its own. Some people use their guns.

This social context, then, is one in which the norms of civility with which most people are familiar, based on mutual trust and the rule of law (buttressed by police protection) do not apply. It is, rather, a peculiar social niche in which honor can only be established and preserved by the strategic use of violence. From early childhood, individuals growing up in such environments are socialized to fight to protect themselves. In this social context, aggressive and violent behaviors are not aberrant; rather, they constitute a rational response to a hostile environment.

Thus, poor African-American neighborhoods are divided between "decent families" and "street families."[53] Again: Even in the poorest areas, "decent families" comprise the majority of the population. Most work. And when they cannot find jobs "on the books," they work in the informal economy, doing construction, cutting and styling hair, repairing automobiles, repairing appliances, driving cabs and jitneys, peddling goods, selling food from a cart—anything to make a few honest dollars.[54] They show by example the value placed on hard work and self-reliance; they employ strict child-rearing practices; they ally themselves with churches and schools; and they try to teach their children norms of civility. "Street families," by contrast, lack jobs and education, seek "respect" as an indicator of self-esteem, and feel bitter about the pervasive discrimination. They are right about discrimination; it is not rocket science to look around one's impoverished, segregated neighborhood and see racism at work. At the extreme, the most alienated and embittered people show contempt for others, especially anyone representing "the system." They become predators. But this difference between "decent" and "street"-oriented families turns out to be irrelevant in public places in inner-city neighborhoods, where everyone must live by the code of the street; everyone must fight. The carnage is very self-destructive. Murder is now the leading cause of death among African-American men, aged 15 to 24. There are now more African-American men in prison than enrolled in college.[55]

2. In an anomic context, drug markets develop to serve those who turn their anger inward. Like the psychotropic substances middle-class people obtain via prescription (Ridalin, Prozac), alcohol, crack cocaine, heroin, and other drugs help individuals cope with the stress of life.[56] In addition, for the capitalist-minded, selling drugs and engaging in other illegal activities turns an anomic setting to one's favor by combining work-oriented values with unconventional means (what Merton called "innovation"). And the opportunity for such entrepreneurship is great in impoverished environments. One study, for example, shows that independent drug dealers (not gang affiliated) who worked about four hours each day earned an average of $24,000 per year.[57] Although this income seems modest, it is spectacular in neighborhoods bereft of jobs, more than twice what one would earn at the minimum wage working full-time all year long. In some areas, however, gangs dominate the illegal drug market. In one study, gang leaders paid two fees to high-level suppliers, one for the right to distribute crack cocaine and the other for the product itself.[58] They profited a great deal, making between $50,000 and $130,000 annually, thus becoming the Bill Gates (or perhaps the Al Capones) of poor neighborhoods. They organized their employees into teams whose members' income ranged from the minimum wage and up, depending on the level of responsibility. Of course, these activities are not regulated by law but by violence, which is another reason why so many hypersegregated neighborhoods look like war zones.

3. Finally, in an anomic context, some people use sex as an outlet for anger.59 Men and boys make women and girls pregnant. Women and girls desire to become pregnant and give birth. After all, in an anomic setting, making babies is one of the few tasks at which people can be successful. It becomes a mark of their existence in an environment that denies their significance. They fail to see the long-term negative consequences. The percentage of babies born to unmarried women by race and ethnicity indicates how inequality restricts opportunity and leads to conduct. These data, which are for 2003, suggest the degree of discrimination among various minority groups.60

African American	68%
Native American	61
Hispanic American	45
White American	29
Asian American	15

African Americans display the highest rate of unmarried births, followed by Native Americans. Among Hispanics, the rate of unmarried births corresponds to the degree of housing segregation and the proportion whose members look white. These high rates reflect the corrosion of family life in minority communities, with predictable consequences.[61] Such children are more likely to drop out of school, struggle economically, initiate or be victims of violence, and endure poor health, among many other problems.

Minority groups, like everyone else, believe in the American Dream. Historically, however, they have not been allowed to participate in the game due to discrimination. This denial leads to several questions: (1) In what contexts does discrimination against individuals occur and what is its impact? The other questions are structural: (2) Why have members of some racial and ethnic groups succeeded at greater rates than others? (3) What factors maintain the level of racial and ethnic inequality shown here?

THE INDIVIDUAL AND RACIAL AND ETHNIC STRATIFICATION

Everyone likes nursery rhymes. "Humpty Dumpty sat on a wall. Humpty Dumpty had a great fall." Have you ever thought about why Humpty fell? Being an egg and, hence, oval, he probably took precautions to prevent falling. It is thus unlikely that he fell accidentally. Someone pushed Humpty off, which means we have a rhyming whodunit: Who pushed Humpty and why?

Maybe some of the other eggs were not used to seeing someone like him on the wall. Having had little contact with eggs like Humpty, maybe they disliked him because he was different. Maybe their (unexamined) stereotype was that eggs like him ought to remain at the base of the wall. Alternatively, maybe the other eggs resented someone like Humpty for taking up the limited amount of space on the wall, space someone from their own group was entitled to. Maybe they resented eggs like him appearing so high and mighty. So now we have two possible motives for pushing Humpty, either dislike born of unfamiliarity or resentment due to competition for space on the wall. The reason: He was a brown egg and all the others were white. "All the king's horses and all the king's men could not put Humpty Dumpty together again." Whether from dislike or resentment of Humpty, maybe the king's men did not try very hard. They were, after all, white eggs, too. In fact, maybe they were glad to see him fall because a white egg could now replace him. This interpretation may be flawed (!), but it illustrates a sociological point: Minority groups have always been pushed off the wall of opportunity by prejudice and discrimination.

The interpretation suggests, for example, some of the situations under which prejudice and discrimination occur. One situation is the degree of interaction and familiarity, as summarized by the *Contact Hypothesis: The more contact people from dominant and minority groups have with one another, the less likely are members of the dominant group to display prejudice and discriminate.*[62] This hypothesis suggests that prejudice is simply a way of judging members of minority groups without knowing anything about them and that as interaction occurs negative stereotypes dissolve—at least under the right conditions. Empirically, this negative relationship between contact and prejudice (more contact=less prejudice) occurs when people in different groups are not in a competitive situation and thus have nothing to fight about, are interdependent in some way, have roughly equal social status, and the context is conducive to friendly interaction. For example, in one of the classic studies done in 1951, white housewives living in integrated housing projects developed positive views of African Americans.[63] Similarly, recent research confirms that contact in positive circumstances undermines prejudice and discrimination, as when college students have minority roommates.[64] Three venues in which people might become familiar with others in different groups and have egalitarian and cooperative interaction are churches, schools, and neighborhoods. But they remain segregated.

The interpretation of the nursery rhyme also indicates another situation in which prejudice and discrimination occur: when people from different groups compete for the same jobs, land, or other resources (a spot on the wall). The *Resource Hypothesis* summarizes the argument: *The more people from dominant and minority groups compete for scarce resources, the more likely are members of the dominant group to display prejudice and discriminate.*[65] Population size often constitutes an intervening variable in this relationship. For example, as long as the population of a minority group remains small, not much competition for jobs or other resources occurs and, hence, less hostility or unequal treatment. As the minority group population increases, however, the dominant group (Whites) becomes threatened and acts to protect its interests (its spot on the wall).[66] They discriminate, which results in greater racial and ethnic inequality. In the process, members of the dominant group (Whites) develop rationalizations about those at the bottom, which justify keeping them there. Such reasoning justifies practices, such as not hiring others of a different race (or gender), which would otherwise be seen as unjust. (This is why the interpretation of the rhyme suggested that "all the king's horses" might stand by while Humpty lay broken.) Two contexts in which discrimination continues to exist are public places and organizations. Although the following discussion focuses on African Americans, the logic applies to all minority groups.

Public Place Discrimination

Most Whites do not think about how the color of their skin affects their treatment by others.[67] This is a form of "white privilege," an ascriptive advantage due simply to skin color. Most African Americans, however, confront their color and its implications every day. This is because when they are away from family and friends, in public places, they have little protection from discriminatory behavior, regardless of civil rights laws.

One strategy for discrimination is avoidance. Hailing a cab in a large city, for example, can be a difficult process for African Americans—especially men. It is a chance for drivers to discriminate, without being caught. Middle-class African Americans take this behavior as evidence of drivers' true feelings. More subtlely, Whites may cross the street to avoid African Americans or take their children away from play sites (a jungle gym in a park, for example) when joined by dark-skinned children. So it becomes important to make Whites feel safe. Some African-American males apparently whistle classical music while walking down the street as a sign they are not dangerous.[68] Such actions make daily life more stressful for the victims.

A second strategy is rejection.[69] Providing poor quality service is one way. African Americans sometimes find that getting seated in restaurants often takes a long time. While waiting, they may be handed coats to be checked. When seated, it is in the back by the kitchen door (even when other tables are available). Then the meal arrives cold. Harassment while going to work is another example: being frisked on suburban commuter trains and mistaken for a delivery boy when entering the building where one works. Finally, rejection occurs in the office. Clients wonder "Why did I get the black lawyer?" (or accountant, etc.); this concern is manifested in questions about qualifications ("Where did you get your degree?") that would not ordinarily be asked. Such experiences mean that ordinary interaction is often tinged with stress and anger.

Rejection can occur simply while doing one's job. Reginald Pitts, an African-American human resources manager for GAF Materials Corporation, based in Tampa, Florida, went to the local Wal-Mart just before Christmas to pick up gift cards for company employees. The company had purchased these cards annually for several years. He called ahead to verify the purchase and was assured the cards were ready and that there would be no problem. On arriving at the store, he presented a check for $13,600 for the cards. There was a delay and Mr. Pitts was informed there was a problem verifying the check. Other Wal-Mart employees, observing the situation, told Mr. Pitts that other companies' representatives (who were white) had made similar purchases that same day with no trouble. Store officials used the delay to call the police, alleging a possible forged check. On arriving the police appeared ready to arrest Mr. Pitts, frightening him, but after reviewing the situation, they left. Mr. Pitts was left with his anger. As he was leaving, the store manager told him to "have a nice day." GAF chose to purchase its gift cards from Target.[70]

A third strategy is verbal and nonverbal harassment.[71] Racial epithets occur—when it is safe: from passing cars, from across the street, in crowds during athletic events. The targets are both adults and children. The "hate stare" attempts intimidation without overt violence. When shopping, African Americans note that clerks and security guards follow them around the store. Such forms of psychological assault must usually be endured without reply. A response is often either impossible or dangerous. Then parents must explain hate to their children. Stress mounts.

The final strategy is violence in some form. Whites throw cans or bottles from moving cars. Occasionally, when middle-class African Americans find themselves in the wrong area, they are pulled from their cars or accosted on the street. Sometimes they are "merely" threatened. But since the end of the Civil War, homicide has been an important strategy for terrorizing African Americans. As three recent research findings suggest, this tactic continues today: (1) The higher the African-American population in a city, the higher the rate of white-on-black homicide. (2) The more unemployment levels of Whites resemble that of African Americans, the higher the rate of white-on-black homicide. (3) The greater the political influence of African Americans in cities, the higher the rate of white-on-black homicide.[72] Events like these are daily possibilities that make life more difficult.

The constant strain wears people down.[73] Assume for the moment that every person has 100 ergs of emotional energy available each day. The average white person uses 50 percent of them coping with work-a-day issues and problems, leaving the other 50 percent for everything else. An average African American also uses 50 percent of them coping with the same work-a-day issues and problems. In addition, however, each African American must also use 25 percent to deal with being black in a white society, leaving only 25 percent to do everything else. In college classes, white students sometimes say that small slights should be ignored. And they usually are. But the erg metaphor illustrates the cumulative impact of stress on the lives of African Americans. Occupational and other forms of success become harder.

Discrimination by Organizations

Civil rights laws mean that discrimination by people in organizations is now illegal and those wishing to act on their prejudice must be covert. One area in which unequal treatment occurs is in housing and it will be the focus here. Housing is important because where people live affects access to urban amenities and services, good schools, and jobs, all of which are keys to economic success, to realizing the American Dream.

As economic development accelerated during the early years of the twentieth century, African Americans began migrating north. Most sought to settle in large cities (Chicago, Detroit, New York, etc.) where the promise of jobs seemed greater. Typically, however, people also spread out, many ending up in medium and small towns—from which they were often driven out. By means of violence, threat, and intimidation, Whites created "sundown towns" in which no African Americans (or very few) were allowed to reside. This is one reason why African Americans became concentrated in large cities.[74]

This location, however, proved to be a trap as Whites tried to isolate the intruders in rigidly segregated neighborhoods, both as a matter of public policy and by violence. Early twentieth century Chicago illustrates how this process occurred.[75] As African Americans moved into the city between 1900 and 1920, Whites began inserting restrictive covenants in deeds. **Restrictive covenants** are legal obligations built into a deed. They sometimes serve a legitimate public interest, as when a homeowner is forbidden to run a business from the residence. But such provisions were also used throughout the North to discriminate in order to maintain housing segregation. They would state something like this: "No part of said property hereby conveyed shall ever be used, occupied by, sold to, or rented to Negroes or any person of Negro blood." The Supreme Court upheld the legality of such provisions in 1926, in *Corrigan vs. Buckley*. By the 1940s, 80 percent of residential property deeds in Chicago included restrictive covenants. When these denials of civil rights failed to work and African Americans persisted in seeking better housing, Whites turned to violence. Between 1917 and 1921, African-American homes located outside the Chicago ghetto were firebombed about once every twenty days. As a result of processes like these, African Americans became residentially segregated in every large American city.

In addition to the Supreme Court, the executive branch of the federal government joined the effort at trapping African Americans.[76] During the 1930s, the Federal Housing Administration (FHA) developed the modern mortgage, which allowed lower- and middle-income families to become homeowners for the first time. But the FHA encouraged local authorities to discriminate against African-American buyers. In every large city, color-coded maps were drawn indicating the credit-worthiness of neighborhoods. These maps assumed that property values would fall if African Americans moved into a neighborhood. As a result, mortgage lenders were free to refuse loans to African Americans, realtors were free to refuse to show homes to African Americans, and owners were free to refuse to sell to African Americans. All of these forms of discrimination were legal at that time. Moreover, in this context, realtors and financial speculators regulated the size of a ghetto by "blockbusting." They would sell a house to one African-American family or simply encourage African Americans to walk and drive through white neighborhoods adjacent to the ghetto. Speculators (working in tandem with realtors) would then purchase homes from panicky Whites at low prices and resell them to African Americans at high prices and with high-interest mortgages. After World War II, passage of the G.I. Bill meant that the Veterans Administration (VA) joined the FHA in promoting low-cost mortgages—leading to the largest increase in home-ownership in U.S. history: by Whites.[77] African Americans were left out—deliberately.

When these legal mechanisms failed to work, Whites again turned to violence. Once again, Chicago illustrates a common pattern.[78] In the aftermath of World War II, housing was short in this city as in many others. In this context, the Chicago Housing Authority chose to build subsidized housing, a popular move at the time. The first project was integrated without incident. When a few African-American families tried to move into the second project in early 1946, however, mobs of Whites fought with police over several weeks—effectively preventing integration. This became the model: "Whenever integration was attempted, white violence ensued" between 1946 and 1950. As a result, the city simply erected separate projects in white and African American neighborhoods. Chicago, like most American cities, remains segregated to this day.

Most Whites supported these actions, although the percentages have declined over time.[79] In 1942, 84 percent of all Whites agreed that "there should be separate sections in towns and cities for Negroes to live in." Similarly, in 1962, 61 percent of Whites agreed that "white people have a right to keep blacks out of their neighborhoods if they want to and blacks should respect that." In 1984, 28 percent agreed with this same assertion. By 1996, only 13 percent agreed. So the vast majority of Americans now say they oppose housing segregation. Yet, as suggested earlier, a gap often exists between attitudes and actions. Most American cities remain segregated.

Banks and mortgage companies are aware of this gap between attitudes and behavior, and continue to (covertly) discriminate today. There is an old Eddie Murphy sketch (probably from *Saturday Night Live*) that suggests what happens: A perfectly dressed Murphy enters a mortgage office to apply for a home loan. The lenders greet him with a smile, give him the application, and assure him it will be carefully considered. After Murphy leaves, they dissolve in laughter and throw the application away. When a white person then enters and asks for an application, the lenders open the vault and tell him to take what he needs.

The sketch is chilling in its accuracy, especially given the history of the FHA and VA. And such behavior still occurs today. As implied in the sketch, discrimination is often a face-to-face affair. Differences in mortgage approvals provide one clue to discrimination: Regardless of income, credit history, or other relevant characteristics, African and Hispanic Americans are more likely to be denied home loans than Whites. As a result, African and Hispanic Americans have less access to good schools and jobs. Differences in interest rates on loans provide another clue: African and Hispanic Americans often pay higher rates than do Whites with the same income and credit history.[80] (As an aside, African Americans also pay higher interest rates for automobile loans than do Whites with the same income and credit history.)[81] As a result, African and Hispanic Americans spend more of their monthly income on housing, thus reducing their ability to share in other goods and services. They also acquire wealth more slowly than do Whites, a fundamental way in which current generations pass on advantages to future generations. Of course, difference does not automatically mean discrimination. But one study shows that the higher the percentage of African-American loan officers in a lending organization, the less its lending practices vary by race or ethnicity.[82]

Realtors are also aware of the gap between attitudes and behavior; they discriminate covertly because of the perceived prejudice of their white customers.[83] So they also smile and then deny African Americans and Hispanics the ability to rent or buy homes in white neighborhoods. In Worcester, MA, one outfit placed the word "Archie" next to houses not to be shown to African Americans or Hispanics. In Orange County, CA, a realtor simply told minority applicants—falsely—that no apartments were available. But extreme examples like these are rare. More common is the polite brush-off, as shown when housing audits are done. Applicants with matched characteristics approach realtors seeking housing, either to rent or buy.[84]

> A 43-year old white female tester inquired about a 2-bedroom unit advertised for rent at $590 in Billings, MT. The agent informed the tester that the unit was available, gave the tester an application form, a brochure, and a business card. The agent then took the tester to inspect two model units that were similar to the advertised unit.
>
> A 37-year old Native American woman, with equivalent economic characteristics to the white tester, inquired about the same 2-bedroom unit the next day. The agent responded that she was too busy to talk, gave the tester an application form, brochure, and business card, and told her to come back on Monday if she wanted to see the apartment. The agent did not indicate whether or not the advertised apartment was still available.

The frequency of this kind of brush-off can be illustrated quantitatively, as in Table 2.5. Thus, between 1989 and 2000, discriminatory treatment of African-American testers seeking to rent or buy housing declined significantly. Hispanic testers seeking to purchase housing also experienced less discriminatory treatment between 1989 and 2000. There was no change between the two periods, however, when Hispanic testers sought rental housing. With this exception, the data reveal significant relative change. At the same time, the data also reveal that discriminatory treatment occurs for all minority groups about one in five times when they attempt to rent or buy housing. The smiling brush-off includes being told units are not available, being shown fewer units, receiving less encouragement, or being offered less help in obtaining financing or other aspects of the purchasing process (inspections, for example).

The costs of housing discrimination are significant. It is estimated that African- and Hispanic-American households pay a discrimination "tax" of almost $4,000, on average, each time they search for a house to buy.[85] In addition, of course, when cities remain segregated, people's life chances remain unequal. Finally, although minority

TABLE 2.5   Percent of Minority Groups Experiencing Discriminatory Treatment When Looking to Rent or Buy Housing

	RENT		BUY	
	1989	*2000*	*1989*	*2000*
African Americans	26%	22%	29%	17%
Hispanic Americans	25	26	27	20
Asian Americans	—	22	—	22
Native Americans	—	29	—	20

Notes: In all cases, the data represent averages across metropolitan areas. Considerable variation occurs from one metropolitan area to another. Data for African and Hispanic Americans represent 23 large metropolitan areas. Data for Asian Americans are based on 11 metropolitan areas accounting for three-fourths of the Asian American population. Data for Native Americans are for metropolitan areas in three states with high proportions of Native people: Minnesota, Montana, and New Mexico.

Sources: Turner, et al. (2002), Turner and Ross (2003a), Turner and Ross (2003b).

persons seeking housing do not have the quantitative data from Table 2.5 at hand, they know what is going on. They must spend emotional energy (ergs) worrying about and dealing with this possibility.

The data show clearly that housing discrimination has declined over time. This relative change means that opportunities for contact in positive contexts have increased as well. It also implies that the United States is moving closer to the moral standard posed so long ago in the Declaration of Independence. At the same time, however, Americans still discriminate against minority groups, not only in housing but on the job and in schools. The ability to find space on top of the wall remains limited for people of color.

SOCIAL STRUCTURE AND RACIAL AND ETHNIC STRATIFICATION

Historical Differences in Racial and Ethnic Group Mobility

Whites often wonder why so few members of minority groups have succeeded until recently. The numbers are revealing. As mentioned before, only 6 percent of all African Americans were white-collar workers in 1940. Although the gap has closed over the last 60 years (see Table 2.2), African Americans, Hispanics, and Native Americans lag behind Whites. Data on poverty rates show a similar pattern. By contrast, many people point to their forebears (Germans, Irish, Italians, and others) who struggled and eventually thrived in a new society. More recently, in the post-Civil Rights era, many immigrants have done relatively well, suggesting that the United States continues to be a land of opportunity. Everyone gets to bat and can run the bases depending upon their ability. The focus in this section is on African Americans because of the legacy of slavery. At the risk of unduly simplifying a complex process, here is a hypothesis designed to explain these differences: *Until recently, African Americans' relative lack of economic success compared to other immigrant groups reflects historical differences in (1) conditions of settlement, (2) discrimination, and (3) affirmative action.*

Conditions of Settlement.   This factor refers to the circumstances of arrival in this country. That is, some groups came to these shores voluntarily while others arrived involuntarily and remained as slaves.[86] Voluntary immigrants responded to changing conditions in their homeland. For example, the German and Irish people who settled in the Midwest from 1820 to 1840 had been driven off land they had occupied for generations. This was a fairly typical experience. Other immigrants, already urban, had skills or expertise in demand in the United States as it industrialized. In fact, American companies actively recruited skilled immigrants with the promise of a better life. After arrival and with the passage of generations, many of them became successful. In contrast, African people were taken from their homes to this continent as forced labor. Slavery produced profit—for others. In a way that parallels that of free immigrants, many slaves were imported precisely because they possessed needed expertise. For example, rice cultivation required knowledge of specialized techniques and processing skills, so Africans with such know-how were brought to South Carolina for this specific purpose.[87] In addition to agricultural knowledge, other slaves either were or became multilingual or possessed specialized craft skills. Plantation owners, of course, gained directly from owning such persons. But northern ship owners, bankers, and others, also benefited from the trade in cotton and other products. Also, it is often unrecognized that Northerners held slaves as well, in some states right up to the Civil War, who generated wealth for their owners.[88] Forced labor stimulated economic development in eighteenth and nineteenth century America. Generations of captivity passed during which enslaved people could not take advantage of the opportunities available to others.[89]

As this brief description suggests, compared to slaves, the conditions of settlement encountered by various white ethnic groups were relatively advantageous. Over time, these differences led to their assimilation and group success.

Discrimination.   Unequal treatment of persons based on race was legal in the United States in the aftermath of the Civil War and it remained so until passage of civil rights laws in the 1960s.

In 1865, the Thirteenth Amendment to the Constitution abolished slavery. At about the same time, however, President Andrew Johnson pardoned ex-confederate soldiers and allowed them to legally reclaim their land. In this context, southern states codified pre-War Black Codes, laws restricting movement, residence, and other civil rights (such as the ability to testify in court). For example, sharecroppers, supposedly free people, were forced to enter into annual labor contracts and penalized one year's wages if they ran away. Like slaves, fugitives were subject to arrest and taken back to employers.[90] In comparison, during this same period, immigrants from Russia, Scandinavia, Italy, and other places began arriving here. Many built farms on the Western Plains. Others settled in cities and found economic niches. Over time, many became successful.

The Fourteenth Amendment, ratified in 1868, was supposed to overturn the Black Codes by requiring the states to provide equal protection to all persons. Moreover, the Civil Rights Act of 1875 provided that "citizens of every race and color, regardless of any previous condition of servitude" were entitled to full and equal access to public accommodations. But these attempts at protecting the freedom of African Americans failed. In the *Civil Rights Cases* (1883), the Supreme Court ruled that the Fourteenth Amendment did not give the Congress the power to regulate private discrimination and found the Civil Rights Act unconstitutional. In *Plessy vs. Ferguson* (1896), of course, the Court legitimized the separation of the races. These decisions provided the legal justification for racial discrimination that lasted another 70 years.

This discriminatory legal structure did not exist in isolation; Whites used systematic violence to buttress it. After the Confederate surrender at Appomattox Court House in April 1865, Southerners began what amounted to a guerrilla war directed at the now free African Americans. Their goal was to reestablish the pre-War social order of the South under conditions as near to slavery as possible. Their tool was homicide.[91] In a context where law enforcement was minimal, murderous race riots occurred in southern cities, the pre-War night watch (designed to capture slaves off their plantations) evolved into the Ku Klux Klan and other secret societies whose members murdered and lynched, ordinary killings apparently occurred often, and various "militias" practiced their own forms of lethal violence. The murder of individuals (usually men) was designed to cow the entire population of African Americans into submission.

One indicator of the murder rate comes from lynching data, which exist for the years 1880 to 1930. During these years, the estimated number of African Americans murdered in this fashion ranges from about 2,800 to more than 4,700. The lower estimate translates into a murder rate due only to lynching of about 41 per 100,000 African-American residents of ten southern states during this period. This lower estimate, however, is "a serious undercount." The higher one, of course, would translate into a much higher rate. By either figure, the frequency of lynching constituted a veritable *Festival of Violence*.[92] This lower rate—just for lynching—is higher than the estimated homicide rate in Europe during medieval times.[93] Across the European continent, by the way, the homicide rate had dropped to about one per 100,000 in the nineteenth century, where it remains today. And, make no mistake, lynchings comprised a deliberate reign of terror. Most, but hardly all, occurred in the South.

The lynching of Jesse Washington in Waco, Texas, on May 16, 1916, provides an example.[94] During this period Texas stood "at the intersection between the casual violence of the frontier and the mad dog racism of the South." Washington, an illiterate and probably mentally retarded cotton hand, allegedly confessed to raping and killing a farmer's wife, Lucy Fryer. His trial took less than an hour; the jury took four minutes to return a guilty verdict. At that point, the crowd seized Mr. Washington, stripped him naked, and dragged him several blocks to City Hall. There he was chained to a tree and castrated. After that, he was hung and lowered into a fire. The crowd observing this process numbered several thousand. The mayor and police chief watched the proceedings from nearby. As occurred often, the lynching was planned. A photographer had been alerted and recorded the event in a famous photograph that circulated nationwide.[95]

This sordid event was not unique. The lynching process often involved sadistic rituals designed to terrorize African-American people: The victim (or victims) would be tortured, have body parts removed, be hung to death, and then the body would be burned.[96] Whites enjoyed a "social permission to lynch" during these years, not only because law enforcement would not stop the practice, but such events constituted community performances, attended by hundreds and, in some cases, thousands of people, including children. In their aftermath, coroners typically concluded that "parties unknown" performed these acts, even though leading members of the community were often present. In addition, photographers often took pictures of the lynching process, which were then sold widely so that all would know about and learn from what had happened.[97] In this context, African Americans (especially men) could not get through a day, travel, move freely around the community, or even relax at home without fear of arbitrary death.[98]

But lynching did not stand alone; it made up only part of the total rate of African-American homicide victimization in the South. It was during this period that, for the first time, guns became the most popular instrument in homicide. In the South, Whites were determined to rule "by the pistol and rifle."[99] Some data on homicides other than lynching are available for Louisiana, for example, which became one of the most violent states in the nation. Excluding New Orleans, the rural areas of this state displayed a homicide rate higher than that in Medieval Europe: about 52 per 100,000 for the years 1866 to 1876, falling to about 19 in 1877 to 1884. In the northwestern part of Louisiana the rate was 197. In the vast majority of these cases, Whites killed African Americans.[100] Although the data only refer to one state, they suggest the dimensions of the overall campaign of terror that occurred throughout the southern United States. Unreported murders of African Americans were common. For example, "white capping" occurred as African Americans were driven from their homes or land and sometimes murdered in the process. In addition, of course, race riots, massacres, and day-to-day homicides took place every so often that terrorized all who might resist restoration of white power.[101] Finally, southern states clearly used legal executions as part of the campaign to control the black population, a form of legal homicide.[102] After all, going from lynching to discriminatory legal execution is not much of a jump. Everyone—meaning Whites—in the community "knew" the victim was guilty. Of course, African Americans could not vote or sit on juries, even when (especially when) they outnumbered Whites in a county. In *Roughing It*, written in 1870, Mark Twain observed that "ours is 'the land of the free.' Nobody denies that—nobody challenges it." Of course, he continued, "maybe [that] is because we won't let other people testify" and deny them civil rights.[103]

The combined total rate of African-American victimization, then, is unknowable but must have been incredibly high, well above that recorded at any prior period in Western history—including medieval Europe.[104] It suggests, as Norbert Elias put it, a "savagery of feeling," that "fear reigned everywhere; one had to be on one's guard all the time." He was referring to medieval Europe, however, not the American South.[105]

It is not too strong to say that the legal decisions made by the Supreme Court and the systematic violence that supported them, shaped twentieth century America. As the process of economic development accelerated, Whites got better jobs, increasingly, white-collar jobs. They moved into better housing in better neighborhoods. Their children went to college. African Americans and other minority groups were shut out by discrimination.

Affirmative Action. **Affirmative action** refers to public policies giving advantages to members of one group over others.[106] Such policies have become controversial recently because many Whites believe it is unfair to do more than guarantee civil rights to the entire population. Policies designed to increase opportunity for minority groups (and women) because of unequal treatment in the past seem discriminatory. Although this problem can be seen in terms of fairness or morality, the underlying issue is power. Racial and ethnic relations always involve obtaining *A Piece of the Pie*, as Stanley Lieberson titles his study of the topic.[107] The referent is a metaphor for the distribution of resources: jobs, land, education, and other benefits. People will fight, discriminate, and use the law in order to obtain (or retain) their "fair" share. Most groups do not diet; they desire a bigger rather than smaller piece of the pie. Historically, affirmative action has been by Whites, for Whites.

One piece of the pie is land.[108] It was mentioned earlier that German and Irish immigrants settled in the Midwest in the 1820s. Neither the timing nor location was accidental. The Land Act of 1820 provided pieces of the pie. Immigrants obtained 80 acres of land on credit, with payoffs at $1.25 to $2.00 per acre, which made the land essentially free. Similarly, Scandinavian immigrants settled the plains states in the 1860s and 1870s. Again, neither the location nor time was accidental. Because the federal government wished to open up this area, it passed the Homestead Act of 1862.

Under its terms, anyone who farmed 160 acres for five years could purchase them for $10. The land was given away. Coupled with access to eastern markets via the railroads (subsidized by the government), the Scandinavians worked hard for a piece of the pie. This is affirmative action, of course, the provision of opportunity for white immigrants.

In comparison, newly freed African Americans were promised 40 acres and a mule in the aftermath of the Civil War. In fact, under an executive order by General William Tecumseh Sherman, nearly a half-million acres were divided into 40-acre plots and, along with mules, horses, and food, were turned over to former slaves.[109] President Andrew Johnson rescinded the order at the same time he pardoned former Confederate officers and allowed them to reclaim their lands. The "free" slaves were forced into sharecropping. But if this commitment of land and the means to farm it had been kept, millions of second- and third-generation freed African Americans would have been upwardly mobile, like immigrants. Affirmative action policies provided opportunities for Whites while denying it to African Americans.

Another piece of the pie is access to education.[110] In 1862, Congress passed the Morrill Act, which funded land grant colleges in every state. The federal government spent more than $250 million (in the 19th century!) because "every citizen is entitled to receive educational aid from the government." The idea was that the children of farmers should be able to go to college. Yet this massive outlay of money did not go to "every citizen." In fact, it was directed at Whites, especially in the South. The University of Florida, for example, did not admit a single African-American student until 1969. Instead, a few African-American colleges were established, largely due to the efforts of private philanthropic organizations. Donated by Whites, receipt of the little money available depended upon accepting a philosophy of "racial adjustment." (This was a euphemism for knowing one's place and accepting the daily humiliations described earlier.) In 1890, the second Morrill Act led to the creation of separate land grant institutions in the South, such as Florida A & M. Poorly funded, these institutions kept southern states eligible for federal support while providing poor quality college education to very small numbers of African-American youth.

This last statement also summarizes the educational opportunities available to African-American children from the time of the Civil War until recently. There were few schools for African Americans because an educated black labor force would not have wanted to work in the fields or houses of Whites.[111] In 1911, for example, only 64 high schools were available to African-American students in the 18 southern states. There were none in Atlanta and other major cities. In most places, schooling for African-American children stopped in the seventh grade. And elementary schools were underfunded, teachers poorly trained, supplies minimal, and the length of the school year short. For example, in Augusta, Georgia, in the 1940s, the African-American elementary school had 1600 students and thirty teachers. In one first grade class, there were 63 students but only 40 desks. The elementary school dropout rate was very high: from 400 pupils in the first grade to only 100 by the seventh. These examples illustrate the broader pattern of denial of educational opportunity to African Americans. For about a century after the Civil War, then, the United States practiced affirmative action—white children were provided educational opportunity. They were thus prepared to fill the rapidly growing number of the white-collar jobs being created by economic development. African-American children were not.

A third piece of the pie is access to a job. Even without land or education, it can be argued that the absence of job discrimination would have made upward mobility easier for African Americans, especially in the years between 1870 and 1960. But when Congress passed a series of bills in the 1930s designed to allow workers to organize, antidiscrimination (essentially civil rights) clauses were omitted despite the efforts of African-American leaders. The most important of these bills was the National Labor Relations Act (NLRA) of 1935. This initiative placed wages, hiring policies, layoffs, and other issues under the rule of law rather than the "goodwill" of an employer. In addition, worker organization under the NLRA facilitated other benefits: good credit rating, group insurance, group discounts, easier qualification for home mortgages, and the like. Certain working people were thus issued pieces of the pie. But the NLRA left unions free to discriminate, which they did. Over the years, Whites parceled out jobs to kin, friends, and others who looked like themselves.[112] For example, the National Apprenticeship Act of 1937 established government training programs under union control for skilled workers. This program not only covered blue-collar jobs but also training as occupational and physical therapists, librarians, medical technicians, and many others. Over nearly 40 years, virtually all the participants in this program were White. In 1964, the same year as the Civil Rights Act was passed, the federal government paid $4 million in job subsidies. Once again, the historical pattern reveals affirmative action for Whites.

A fourth piece of the pie is access to federal benefits that can lead to upward mobility and economic security.[113] For example, during the 1930s, when most African Americans held agriculture and domestic household jobs, the federal government excluded these occupations from minimum wage protection, Social Security eligibility, unemployment insurance, and workmen's compensation. Another example: The Serviceman's Readjustment Act (the G.I. Bill) provided $95 billion for soldiers returning from World War II to attend college, obtain job training, start a business, and purchase a home. The results were wildly successful—at least for Whites. In Mississippi in 1946, for example, 6,500 former soldiers were placed in nonfarm jobs, 86 percent of the skilled and semiskilled jobs were filled by Whites, 92 percent of the unskilled jobs by African Americans. In New York and New Jersey, about 67,000 homes were purchased by former soldiers, fewer than 100 of whom were African American. Again, these policies provided affirmative action for Whites.

With regard to education, jobs, and federal benefits, African Americans were excluded from the opportunity to succeed in three ways.[114] First, legislative provisions would be written so that African Americans were left out, as when occupations in which they were concentrated were denied minimum wage protection or social security eligibility. Second, legislation would specify that administration would occur at the local level, which allowed hostile local officials (not just in the South) to deprive African Americans of opportunities. The administration of the G.I. Bill provides an example. Third, antidiscrimination provisions were deliberately not attached to legislation, as with the NLRA, but also including community health services, school lunches, and hospital construction grants, among many others. As a result, during the very years when a wide array of public policies was developed that provided most white Americans with valuable tools to better their lives and secure their future—good jobs, education, home ownership, old age insurance, and more—most black Americans were left out. Affirmative action was white.

In sum, the answer to the question with which this section began is that more African Americans have not succeeded because structural impediments created by Whites stacked the odds against them. During the 1960s, however, and continuing for the last 30 years or so, the federal government developed policies designed (very imperfectly) to provide some opportunity for minority groups to increase their share of the pie, especially in terms of access to jobs and education. Such policies have been mildly effective; one example is the increase in the proportion of African, Hispanic, and Asian Americans in white-collar jobs. During the past few years, however, many Whites have begun protesting that such policies are unfair. And this assertion is true. The protest reflects an underlying (albeit inchoate) goal: Whites want to retain their share of the pie.

Racial and Ethnic Stratification Today

In Chapter 1, it was posited that *minority groups at every class level have fewer and less effective choices than do Whites*. Although this argument cannot be tested here, it provides a way to understand racial and ethnic stratification today: *Racial and ethnic stratification today reflects (1) the reproduction of the class structure and (2) institutionalized discrimination*.

Reproduction of the Class Structure.   A great deal of racial and ethnic inequality occurs as the unwitting result of individuals acting normally to raise a family and seek economic success. As they do these things, people from each class use their resources in order to protect their lifestyle and pass it on to their children. This process can occur without anyone overtly discriminating. The result, however, is the reproduction of the class structure; that is, its stability across generations.

Consider the following vignette: A large group of runners enter a race for economic success in the form of jobs and income that began, let us say, in 1865. Some of the runners are White, while others are African American, Hispanic American, and Asian American. All the Whites run in the normal way, with few impediments. Minority group runners, however, must wear backpacks carrying varying amounts of weight: 50 or 100 pounds, depending on the level of discrimination. In this context, of course, it is easy to predict the outcome of the race: Whites will be more successful and so will their children and their children's children. Their income, for example, will be significantly higher, which means their life chances will be better. Disparities in wealth will increase over time. In the 1950s and 1960s, however, the terms of the race changed as courts ruled that discriminatory laws were unconstitutional and the Congress passed civil rights acts. Although the runners then become more or less equal, the legacy of past discrimination means that they are at different spots on the course: Even if no more discrimination occurs, Whites' head start means they will continue to be able to pass their advantages on to their children. This is how the class structure reproduces itself.

Although a great deal of mobility occurs in this country, the mode is for occupational continuity across generations. For example, as will be shown in detail in Chapter 5, parents employed in blue-collar jobs tend to have children who work in blue-collar jobs, while parents employed in white-collar jobs tend to have children who work in white-collar jobs.[115] This continuity reflects class-related differences in opportunity. Think about the data presented earlier in terms of the vignette. At every class level, different levels of infant mortality not only mean that fewer minority children survive, but those that do have inferior life chances. At every class level, housing segregation not only means that minority children are isolated from Whites, but they have less ability to share in the available goods and services. Occupational and income differences have a similar impact. Precisely because members of minority groups have always had less opportunity to succeed due to structural barriers, the odds of occupational mobility are still stacked against them and their children—simply by their class of origin.

Institutionalized Discrimination. A great deal of inequality results from **institutionalized discrimination,** the unequal treatment of people with different physical or social characteristics that is embedded in the social structure. In many cases, such unequal treatment occurs as families try to provide opportunities for their children.

The example used here is the process of finding a job. Most people learn about jobs informally, by word of mouth. They rely on relatives and friends in their social networks as the primary source of information.[116] Who you know thus makes a great deal of difference; it constitutes a form of **social capital** that enhances opportunities for success.

This manner of learning about jobs has enormous implications. Segregation means that members of each racial and ethnic group work at different jobs. Their children go to different schools. They live in different neighborhoods. They also attend different churches.[117] These variations identify the boundaries of the social networks in which people participate. The presence of such boundaries indicates how the social structure affects interaction patterns: contact, friendship formation, and the like. Although daily life may appear integrated, members of each group lead separate lives. As a result, individual Whites, African Americans, Hispanics, Asians, and Native Americans tell their relatives and friends about different job opportunities. Hence, even in the absence of prejudice or discrimination, this process produces a high level of occupational segregation—and, hence, inequality.

One recent study, *Race and the Invisible Hand: How White Networks Exclude Black Men from Blue-Collar Jobs,* by Deirdre Royster, illustrates this process.[118] Comparing graduates of a vocational high school in Baltimore, she found that young white men possessed a wider network of family, teachers, friends, and acquaintances compared to young African-American men. Given comparable levels of ability and motivation, the Whites in her sample were better able to locate and obtain jobs. The Whites were also treated more indulgently (given second and third chances) when they got into trouble with the law or employers.

In addition, people must be physically able to get to a job. This is not always easy, especially for members of minority groups. In the past, cities were centers for the manufacture and distribution of goods. Hence, people without much formal education could find work. These opportunities have declined, however, as suggested by the *Spatial Mismatch Hypothesis: The more employment opportunities move from central cities to the suburbs and greater the housing segregation, then the greater the unemployment among minority workers.*[119] Since about 1970, cities have lost hundreds of thousands of manufacturing jobs. Many are now located in suburban areas. Housing segregation means fewer job opportunities for African Americans and other minority groups because getting to these jobs requires a long and expensive commute by car or, in a more complex way, by public transportation. One study, for example, looked at what happened to the employees of a single company when it relocated from the central business district of Detroit to suburban Dearborn.[120] Detroit, as mentioned earlier, is the most segregated city in the United States for African Americans, nearly all of whom reside in just a few neighborhoods. Suburbs like Dearborn are nearly all white. As in other metropolitan areas, evidence suggests that this result reflects discrimination (they are sundown towns). In this context, when the company moved, many of its white employees had shorter commutes and others were more easily able to relocate to keep their jobs. Many of its African-American employees, by contrast, had longer commutes and were unable to relocate; hence, they were more likely to quit their jobs. Observers can only speculate about why these jobs have moved out of central cities. One reason is probably cheaper land and easier access to transportation (interstate highways and airports). Another reason is corporate aversion to African-American workers.[121] Regardless of the reason, the result is massive unemployment in central cities, concentrated among minority people.

Race is maintained as a system of domination by the reproduction of the class structure and institutionalized discrimination. And these factors, in turn, reflect the conditions of settlement of various groups, the degree of prejudice and discrimination they endured over time, and the history of affirmative action directed toward white ethnic groups. Although modern societies are anomic by definition, the serious and negative impact of racial and ethnic inequality in the United States goes well beyond that in other nations.

It can be argued, however, that the struggle for civil rights during the 1960s is really the story of how the United States moved toward becoming a modern—which is to say, class-based—nation. For example, as one observer points out, Dr. Martin Luther King Jr. "had to overcome the determined resistance of terrorists without conscience, politicians without backbone, rivals without foresight, and an F.B.I. Director [J. Edgar Hoover] so malicious that he would stop at nothing to destroy a man who believed in justice."[122] Put more sociologically (but less evocatively), Dr. King and others strove to replace ascription with achievement as the basis for people's position in society. The task has begun but remains far from complete. We still live with Jefferson's Dilemma.

SUMMARY

The United States has always confronted a dilemma: freedom and equality for all versus freedom for some and slavery or discrimination for others. The historical dimensions of racial and ethnic inequality must be assessed in both absolute and relative terms. African Americans, Hispanics, Asians, and Native Americans were systematically denied civil rights throughout U.S. history until passage of civil rights laws in the 1960s. In other arenas, however, change has not been so great. Although significant absolute improvement has occurred, infant mortality rates of African Americans have always been about double that of Whites. African-American housing segregation has increased over the course of this century (Table 2.1). Although data for Hispanic, Asian, and Native Americans do not go back very far, they are much less segregated. Even though occupational segregation has been the norm in the United States historically, increasing proportions of African Americans, Hispanics, Asians, and Native Americans are employed in white-collar jobs (Table 2.2). In the highest prestige positions, however, far less change has occurred (Table 2.3).

Most western industrial nations are relatively homogeneous compared to the United States. The United Kingdom, however, displays a significant minority population. Comparing unemployment rates in the two nations shows that minority groups fare less well in both (Table 2.4).

In an anomic context buttressed by discrimination, some members of minority groups are left behind, unable to pursue the American Dream. Crime, drug abuse, and sexual acting out are common results. This occurs regardless of race.

Most discrimination against individuals occurs when people lack familiarity with others who are different and when members of different groups compete for scarce resources. Whites who have not had much contact with members of minority groups tend to avoid them in public places, reject them, harass and intimidate them, or subject them to violence. Although discrimination in and by organizations is illegal, it is also easy. Housing provides an example (Table 2.5).

In order to understand why more African Americans have not succeeded, it is useful to examine historical variations in racial and ethnic group mobility. The key issues involve the conditions of settlement, discrimination, and affirmative action. The conditions of settlement refer to voluntary versus involuntary migration, and the opportunities presented by the geographical size of the United States and industrialization. Discrimination has always affected African Americans, Hispanics, Asians, and Native Americans more than Whites. And affirmative action has always benefited Whites more than any other group. At the structural level, the most important factors producing racial and ethnic inequality today are the reproduction of the class structure and institutionalized discrimination. The latter is not always intended, as illustrated by the process of finding out about and getting to jobs.

NOTES

1. The phrase, "Jefferson's Dilemma," comes from Shipler (1993). On the history of the Declaration, see Maier (1997).
2. Lipset (1963).
3. Jefferson (1999).
4. On the DNA evidence, see Foster et al. (1998). Gordon-Reed makes the logical case for Jefferson's paternity (1997). Unlike Jefferson, some eighteenth century men resolved the dilemma by freeing their slaves (see Levy, 2005; Ely, 2005).
5. National Research Council (2004), Bamshad and Olson (2003), Bamshad et al. (2004), Cavalli-Sforza et al. (1995). See also Gans (2006) and Loury (2002) for a thoughtful discussion of the implications of race.
6. Swarns (2004), de la Garza (1992), Takaki (1989).
7. United States Bureau of the Census (2006:15).
8. The white population estimate comes from United States Bureau of the Census (1975:1168). Although the population was mostly English,

they came from varying backgrounds. In *Albion's Seed: Four British Folkways in America*, David Hackett Fischer shows that English immigration occurred in four waves from different regions, and that people from each differed in speech, courtship and marriage customs, religious rituals, attitudes toward education and freedom, and other ways (1989). These differences appeared where they settled—New England, Virginia, the Delaware Valley, and the Colonial backcountry—and the legacy of the original immigrants can still be found in these areas.
9. National Research Council (2004).
10. Aguirre and Turner (2004:5).
11. See Thernstrom & Thernstrom (2002; 1997), Patterson (1997).
12. See Blakeslee (2005), Delgado (1997), Hacker (1992).
13. General Social Survey (2004), Krysan (2002), Bobo (2001). All the data in this paragraph come from these sources.

14. Harper and Reskin (2005:370). All the data in this paragraph are from General Social Survey (2004) and Bobo (2001).
15. Orfield (2001), Kozol (2005).
16. This gap between American values and behavior was Gunnar Myrdal's theme in *An American Dilemma* (1944).
17. United States Bureau of the Census (1975:297; 2005:31). African-American household income declined in comparison to white household income from 65% in 2002 to 62% in 2004.
18. See Mann (2005; 2002), Thornton (2001; 1987).
19. Jaimes (1992:113). On Manifest Destiny, see Hayes and Morris (1997) and the classic study by Weinberg (1935). See also Aguirre and Turner (2004:105–43).
20. See United States Bureau of the Census (2006a), Nakanishi (2001), and Takaki (1989).
21. On immigration law, see Ueda (2006; 1994). On the internment of Japanese-American citizens, see Commission on Wartime Relocation and Internment of Civilians (1982). See also Aguirre and Turner (2004:182–216).
22. United States Bureau of the Census (2006), Camarillo and Bonilla (2001).
23. Acuña (1987). See also Aguirre and Tuner (2004:144–81).
24. Foner (2005; 1988), Oshinsky (1996), Kennedy (1995). On the campaign of terror, see Beeghley (2003). For a case study, see LeMann (2006).
25. Medley (2005).
26. Staples (2003). The phrasing above the quotation parallels Staples' words.
27. Simon (2002).
28. See Arsenault (2006), Branch (2006), Library of America (2003), McWhorter (2001), Garrow (1986).
29. On the usefulness of infant mortality as a measure of inequality, see Collins and Thomasson (2002). The data below are from Lieberson (1980:46).
30. National Center for Health Statistics (2005:155).
31. Echenique and Fryer (2005), Massey (2001).
32. Lemann (1992), Lieberson (1980).
33. On sundown towns, see Loewen (2005). On the history of metropolitan housing segregation, see Massey (2001), Massey and Denton (1993), and Lieberson (1980).
34. See United States Bureau of the Census (2002) for an exceptionally clear explanation of the the various measures of housing segregation.
35. United States Bureau of the Census (2002: 45 & 86).
36. Loewen (2005:116–20).
37. Massey (2001).
38. Merton (1968a).
39. United States Bureau of the Census (2005:46). The way poverty is measured will be discussed in Chapter Ten.
40. G. Wilson (1997), G. Wilson et al. (1999).
41. Holzer and Neumark (2000), Harper and Reskin (2005).
42. G. Wilson (1997), G. Wilson et al. (1999).
43. United States Bureau of the Census (2005:31).
44. Buijs and Rath (2002).
45. Office for National Statistics (2005).
46. Hiro (1991), Skellington (1992).
47. Merton (1968a).
48. Innis (1992).
49. Herbert (2005).
50. The phrase is Massey's (1995). See also Massey & Denton (1993), Massey & Fischer (2000). On the code of the street, see Anderson (1999; 1994). On residents' relationship to the police, see Anderson (1999:320). For an explanation of high American homicide rates, see Beeghley (2003).
51. As will be explained in Chapter 5, the term refers to awareness of the dominant culture. Here it is used to refer to the "code of the streets." See Anderson (1999).
52. Centers for Disease Control (2000:Table 6).
53. Anderson (1999:35–65).
54. Losby et al. (2003). On Hispanics and the informal economy, see Edgcomb and Armington (2003).
55. National Center for Health Statistics (2005a:30), Justice Policy Institute (2004).
56. Hagedorn (1998).
57. Reuter et al. (1990).
58. Levitt and Vankatesh (2000).
59. Anderson (1999:142–78), Patterson (2006).
60. National Center for Health Statistics (2005:142).
61. Herbert (2005). My phrasing parallels Herbert's, who refers to "the corrosion of Black family life."
62. Bramel (2004), Forbes (1997; 2004). The classic analysis is by Allport (1954).
63. Deutsch and Collins (1951).
64. Duncan et al. (2003). See also Miller (2002), Brewer and Gaertner (2001), Pettigrew and Tropp (2000).
65. Aguirre and Turner (2004).
66. Forbes (1997; 2004), Bramel (2004).
67. On "white privilege," see McIntosh (2000), Rothenberg (2004). The forms of discrimination described in the following paragraphs are taken loosely from Allport (1954).
68. Sims (2006), Lueck (1999). On the whistling strategy, see Staples (2003).

69. Graham (1995).
70. Helgeson and Shedden (2005).
71. Meeks (2000), Fifield (2001), Fountain (2002).
72. Jacobs and Wood (1999). See also Beeghley (2003).
73. Clark et al. (1999).
74. Loewen (2005).
75. See Adler (2006:120–25), Farley and Frey (1994).
76. Farley and Frey (1994), Massey and Denton (1993). On blockbusting in Chicago, see Hirsch (1983).
77. United States Bureau of the Census (1994). Ironically, from the point of view of racial discrimination, the title of this report is "Tracking the American Dream—Fifty Years of Housing History."
78. Freedman (2006), Polikoff (2006). See also Choldin (2005). The quotation below comes from Freedman, p. 25.
79. Massey and Denton (1993:49), General Social Survey (2004).
80. Association of Community Organizations for Reform Now (2005), Squires and O'Conner (2001).
81. Cohen (2001).
82. Squires and O'Conner (2001).
83. Galster and Godfrey (2005). On the motives of realtors, see Ondich et al. (2003). The anecdotes are from Herbert (1998).
84. Turner and Ross (2003b).
85. Yinger (1997), Rusk (2001).
86. On the slave trade, see Harms (2001). On the "generations of captivity," see Berlin (2003).
87. Vernon (1993), Carney (2001).
88. Berlin and Harris (2006).
89. Although unable to take advantage of economic opportunity, the enslaved people struggled, surprisingly successfully, to preserve both a degree of personal independence and the survival of their cultures; see Vernon (1993), Morgan (1998).
90. Foner (1988; 2005).
91. The following paragraphs are extrapolated from Beeghley (2003:53–55).
92. *A Festival of Violence* is the title of Tolnay and Beck's study. The lower estimate comes from it (1995:38, 271). The higher estimate comes from Zangrando (1980:6). Steelwater points out the "serious undercount" (2003:267).
93. Beeghley (2003:41–46).
94. Bernstein (2005). The quotation is from p. 14.
95. The picture can be seen in Allan et al. (2000).
96. Steelwater (2003:185).
97. See Vandal (2000:99) and Steelwater (2003:185) on lynching rituals. Allen et al. review the lynching photographs (2000). Gatrell provides a chilling description of the process by which one hangs to death (1994:29–99). Brundage examines the various explanations for the Southern reign of terror (1997).
98. Carrigan (2004).
99. Foner (1988:119).
100. Vandal (2000:47–49).
101. On "whitecapping," see Holmes (1969; 1973). On the terror, see Trelease (1971), Foner (1988; 2005), Williams (1996).
102. Tolnay et al. (1992).
103. Cited in Steelwater (2003:190). She cites Twain (1963:128–29). Twain actually had a different reference in mind, the denial of civil rights to Chinese Americans on the Pacific coast.
104. Kennedy (1995); see also Tolnay & Beck (1995: 4–13), Steelwater (2003:75–85).
105. Elias (1978).
106. This definition is deliberately provocative. See Swain (2001) and Harper and Reskin (2005) for alternatives.
107. Lieberson (1980).
108. Smith (1987).
109. Smith (1987), Foner (1988:70–71). For a particularly good example of the impact of President Johnson's order, see Butterfield (1996:35–37).
110. Smith (1987:115).
111. These examples come from Lieberson (1980) and Butterfield (1996:72–81).
112. Smith (1987).
113. Katznelson (2005).
114. Katznelson (2005:22). The closing sentence of this paragraph parallels Katznelson's conclusion.
115. Blau & Duncan (1967), Featherman and Hauser (1978), G. Wilson (1997), G. Wilson et al. (1999).
116. Granovetter (1995).
117. Beeghley et al. (1981), Gallup Poll (1997:13).
118. Royster (2003).
119. On the spatial mismatch hypothesis, see Kain (1968), Mouw (2000). On the movement of jobs to the suburbs, see Kasarda (1995), Brennan and Hill (1999). On the impact, see W. J. Wilson (1996).
120. Zax and Kain (1996).
121. Williams (1987); Zax and Kain (1996).
122. Wolfe (1998:12).

GENDER AND STRATIFICATION

Historically, men were supposed to focus their lives on producing an income and participating in the community. This emphasis meant that the value placed on achievement has been applied to men, especially White men, and that women were evaluated based on ascriptive criteria. Thus, it is no accident that a woman would be asked, "What does your husband do?" at social gatherings. Men's status in the community depended on what they did for a living, on their productive activity outside the home. It indicated their place in the stratification hierarchy, their ability to share in the distribution of resources. Men were often called breadwinners because their income put food on the table. Women, by contrast, were supposed to reproduce, raise children, and care for the home. This emphasis meant that educational and occupational opportunity was restricted no matter how much ability they had or how hard they worked. Women's position was set by birth; as wives, they were attached to men, accompanied men, and helped men succeed. It would have been odd to ask a man, "What does your wife do?" Although women were not usually called breadservers, that was their role. This rather rigid gender-based system of domination meant that women at every class level had restricted life chances. But the issue goes beyond sharing in the distribution of goods and services: Women have had less autonomy, less freedom to make life choices. The name for these expectations and the basis for gender as a system of domination is **traditional gender norms.**[1]

Until recently, these different rules based on birth seemed right and proper. During the early 1950s, a popular television series called "Father Knows Best" epitomized traditional gender norms. The main character was Jim Anderson. He left each day in the family's only car to sell insurance. His wife, Margaret, stayed home—isolated and dependent. She watched the children, cleaned house, ordered groceries, prepared dinner, and provided any other support services Jim needed. Minor problems occurred in each episode that Jim would resolve, since, of course, "father knows best." Looking back, the popularity of this series suggests women's enormous ability to take a (bad) joke. After all, it was pretty clear that one sex was supposed to be the domestic servant of the other. These television characters mirrored social life at that time.

Despite traditional gender norms, some women worked for pay. But so-called "protective laws" and discrimination forced most into dead-end jobs, ensuring the maintenance of male domination. Such practices enjoyed overwhelming support. A 1945 Gallup poll asked the following question: "Do you approve or disapprove of a married woman earning money in business or industry if she has a husband capable of supporting her?" Only 20 percent of women and 16 percent of men approved. Most people thought women should remain at home, serving bread, like the fictional Margaret Anderson, regardless of talent or motivation.[2]

Gender-based domination can be illustrated by looking at the economic dependence of married women in the past.[3] As economic development occurred and the middle class expanded between 1870 and 1930 or so, wives usually did not work for pay and husbands controlled the family's money. Wives often did not even know how much their husbands earned. Household funds were either given to wives on an as-needed basis or by allowance. But many men opposed allowances because they gave wives too much independence. Thus, middle-class women developed various strategies to acquire more money, strategies that illustrate their restricted opportunities. They went through their husband's pockets for change, had shopkeepers put fake items on bills and took cash instead, kept money from goods and services produced at home (e.g., by renting rooms and sewing), and saved money from housekeeping expenses. Because working-class families had lower and more unstable incomes (see Chapter 9), their situation differed. These husbands often held back some money for their own use and gave the remainder to their wives, who were also generally ignorant of their husbands' earnings. For both middle- and working-class women, this ignorance reflected a legal fact: Family income belonged to husbands. They earned it; they had the right to spend it. Thus, although many men were kind and loving, like the fictional Jim Anderson, they kept their wives economically dependent. Their legal basis means that traditional gender norms were not "merely" informal expectations but built into the social structure.

Gender norms are changing, however, becoming more egalitarian, and both men and women are increasingly evaluated based on achievement. One indicator of this change is that it has become more common for husbands to be asked, "What does your wife do?" The query implies that norms about earning money have changed, a fact reflected in survey data: The last time people were asked the same question about married women working for pay was in 1998: 82 percent of women and 83 percent of men approved a wife's employment.[4] But these high percentages mislead: What people say and what they do often differs. Hence, most analyses of gender inequality find that while much has changed, much remains the same. People's gender still comprises a lens through which all interaction is filtered. This duality—the decline of gender stratification coexisting with its continuation—constitutes the theme of this chapter.

DIMENSIONS OF GENDER STRATIFICATION

Although traditional gender norms are slowly giving way to egalitarian gender norms, this process is not inevitable (nothing in history is) and is fraught with uncertainty (change always is). **Egalitarian gender norms** refer to expectations that women and men should balance their reproductive and productive tasks, and that when women engage in productive tasks they should be evaluated in terms of performance-related criteria that are equally applied to all.

Gender Stratification in the United States

Gender Differences in Labor Force Participation.   When women are not employed, they may have access to resources (such as husband's income) but rarely control over them, which makes them unequal to men and makes their life chances inferior to men. For this reason, the most important change in women's behavior over time has been the steadily increasing proportion participating in the paid labor force. Not only is employment the key to improving life chances, paid work constitutes a rejection of traditional gender norms, a rejection of gender domination. This is so even among those women who state (sometimes passionately) that they are not feminists; employment carries the potential for economic independence. In 1890, about 75 to 80 percent of all adult men were in the labor force, a figure that has remained relatively stable over time. In contrast, in 1890, only 17 percent of all adult women were employed. This latter percentage rose steadily, however, to 70 percent in 2004.[5] Thus, a majority of women now work for pay outside the home.

In terms of traditional gender norms, however, the labor force participation rate of married women, especially with children, is very significant. Figure 3.1 presents these data. It shows that in 1890 only 5 percent of all married women participated in the labor force. They were mainly poor, members of minority groups, and immigrant women who could not, due to poverty and discrimination, live according to traditional gender norms. Most women, if they ever worked for pay, did so only before marriage. But this pattern changed over the twentieth century, as the percentage of employed married women increased steadily. By year 2000, the figure shows that 71 percent worked outside the home. Although the data do not go back so far in time, married women with children also increased their employment rate: those with preschool-age children, from 12 percent to 63 percent in 2000, and those with school-age children, from 28 percent to 77 percent.

A change has occurred in the last few years, however, as the proportion of married women in the labor force dipped slightly. Although this change may signify a long-term trend, it more likely reflects women's and men's dissatisfaction with the difficulties of balancing work and family life under today's conditions.[6] In any case, the fact that most women in the prime earning years are employed suggests the change to egalitarian gender norms. Work is a place where achievement-oriented criteria are (or are supposed to be) applied.

The implications are profound, as can be illustrated by juxtaposing women's labor force participation with the changing divorce rate. Please look back at Figure 3.1, noting the overall pattern of increasing labor force participation. Now imagine a line depicting the divorce rate that rises in a way roughly parallel to the lines in the figure. The divorce rate rose steadily over the last century until about the mid-1970s when it

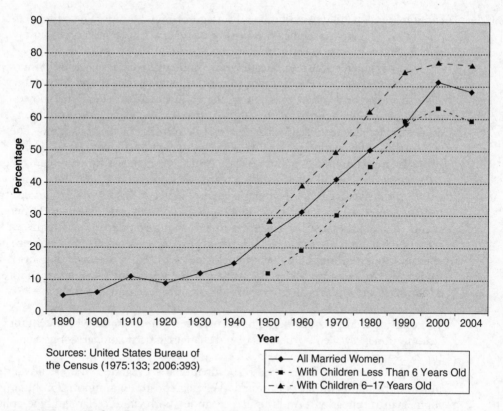

FIGURE 3.1   Labor Force Participation of All Married Women and Those with Children, 1890 to 2004

Sources: United States Bureau of the Census (1975:133; 2006:393)

leveled off at around 50 percent. In covariance form, the finding is: *The higher the rate of women's labor force participation, the higher the rate of divorce.*[7]

In considering this finding, recall Marx's point that the context in which people make decisions is fundamental to understanding rates of behavior. In a social context in which few women are employed, as existed at the turn of the century, a relatively small proportion sought a divorce, simply because they could not be economically independent (since they had no job skills or their skills had eroded during their years as mothers and homemakers) and they did not have much opportunity to meet other adults. Similarly, a small proportion of men sought a divorce because they were obligated to continue supporting, more or less indefinitely, both their former family and any new family they formed. Furthermore, legal and religious sanctions along with the fact that most people lived in rural areas created additional barriers to divorce. In this situation most people had to maintain their marriages even if they had broken down.

The social context, however, has changed in several ways. Because of economic development, advances in medical technology, and other factors to be explained later, women have entered the labor force. This historical process means that a higher proportion of women will end their marriages, simply because they enjoy a modicum of economic independence and take advantage of opportunity. Their life chances have improved. Similarly, a higher proportion of men will seek a divorce, simply because they have fewer economic obligations to their wives.[8]

The rising divorce rate is usually seen as a negative consequence of modernity (it rises with economic development in all modern societies) and it certainly has an adverse impact on many women, men, and children. At the same time, however, it has positive consequences as well: significant declines in wives committing suicide, domestic violence (especially abuse of wives), and the murder of wives.[9] The divorce option thus reflects greater equality between men and women.

But not complete equality. (Recall: Much has changed; much remains the same.) Nearly one-third of all married women are still homemakers and those employed still earn, on the average, far less than do men. Their options are more limited. In addition, women have difficulty obtaining equitable divorce settlements.[10] Differences in earnings mean they usually endure a loss of living standards, with many ending up poor (see Chapter 10). Finally, child custody is nearly always given to women, many of whom manage without help from their former spouses. While child support laws exist in every state, they are not well enforced. Men becoming independent more easily, while wives and children are worse off does not reflect gender equality.

Occupational Segregation.   The dual pattern of continuing yet declining gender stratification is revealed by the level of and changes in occupational segregation. Table 3.1 provides an illustration.

On the one hand, the level of occupational segregation in 2004 illustrates how much segregation continues to exist.[11] Women constitute a minority in high prestige, high paying occupations. And this is true among both white-collar and blue-collar jobs. For example, only 12 percent of civil engineers and 29 percent of physicians are women. Similarly, women comprise only 2 percent of carpenters and electricians. By contrast, women are bunched in several categories: Among white-collar workers, 76 percent of cashiers and 97 percent of secretaries are women; among blue-collar workers, 78 percent of textile machine operators and 90 percent of private household workers are women.

Occupational segregation reflects the system of gender domination. As shown in the table, most women have "women's jobs"; that is, they perform tasks resembling those at home—assisting men, raising children, and picking up after others. Nurses, after all, are subordinate to and appear to assist doctors. Elementary school teachers not only impart knowledge, they also (and just as importantly) socialize the very young, a task traditionally assigned to women who remain at home. Finally, private household workers pick up and clean other people's houses, while police officers and firefighters (dominate and) protect them. By contrast, many men work at "men's jobs"; that is, they perform tasks signifying their power and authority. These differences suggest the degree to which both women and men remain prisoners to traditional gender norms, both at home and work.

Occupational segregation also reinforces the system of gender domination, affecting life chances. In a segregated context, women have fewer job options as they are channeled into stereotypically women's occupations. As a result, they earn less compared to men, get fewer training and promotion opportunities, and become more likely to work part-time. The impact of these differences is passed across generations (as discussed in Chapter 5): Having a mother in a stereotypically "women's job" leads daughters into a similar job.[12]

TABLE 3.1   Women as a Percent of All Workers in Selected
Occupations, 1970 and 2004

OCCUPATION	1970	2004
White-Collar		
Civil Engineer	2	12
Architect	4	24
Marketing Manager	8	40
Engineering Technician	9	20
Physician	10	29
Sales Supervisors	17	43
Computer Programmer	24	27
Accountant	25	31
Cashiers	84	76
Elementary Teacher	84	81*
Bank Teller	87	88
Registered Nurse	97	92
Secretary	98	97
Blue-Collar		
Carpenter	1	2
Electrician	2	2
Truck Driver	2	5
Mechanist	3	4
Protective Service	7	22
Bartender	21	58
Textile Machine	79	78
Private Household	94	90

* Includes middle-school teachers in 2004.

Sources: Rytina & Bianchi (1984), United States Bureau of the Census (2006:401).

Moreover, the data in Table 3.1 understate the level of occupational segregation.[13] For example, women and men in the same job category often work for different companies, with significant economic consequences. Thus, high-priced restaurants employ waiters (men) whose income is relatively high, while low-priced restaurants employ waitresses (women) whose income is relatively low. Moreover, men and women in the same job category work in different industries, again with significant economic consequences. Thus, women are often employed in the textile industry where the pay is low while men work in the petroleum industry where the pay is high. Finally, even when men and women appear to have similar jobs within a company, the former often has more and the latter less income and authority. Just because a person has the title of Manager, does not mean she controls resources or makes fundamental decisions. Much remains the same.

On the other hand, Table 3.1 suggests how much has changed: Occupational segregation is declining and women are increasingly evaluated by achievement-oriented criteria. Comparing the data for 1970 and 2004 shows that the proportion of female civil engineers increased six times, from 2 percent to 12 percent; female physicians almost tripled from 10 percent to 29 percent. Although not as much change occurred in some of the skilled blue-collar jobs, there are exceptions. For example, the proportion of women protective service workers (police officers and fire fighters) rose from 7 percent to 22 percent. Although these data only refer to selected occupations, they illustrate the degree to which women and men are no longer prisoners of traditional gender norms.[14]

Occupational segregation has also declined among African-American and other minority group women, thus enhancing their life chances. In 1940, three-quarters of employed African-American women were doing private household and farming work. Even today, as shown in Table 3.2, disproportionate numbers of African- and Hispanic American women work in service occupations. But overall, the occupational distribution among minority group women now resembles that of white women.[15] Of course, this resemblance means that minority group women are like all women: Due to occupational segregation, they earn less money and are less able to be economically independent.

Income Differences. In the past many people accepted the idea that women should earn less then men. Today, survey data show that nearly everyone agrees that women working at the same jobs as men should receive equal pay.[16] This change means that achievement values are currently viewed as applicable to women, at least with regard to income on the job. Unfortunately, however, this ideal has never been realized in practice, as revealed by Table 3.3. Panel A shows that the estimated median income of

TABLE 3.2 Women in Occupational Categories by Race and Ethnicity, 2004 (16 years of age and older)

CATEGORY	WHITE AMERICAN	AFRICAN AMERICAN	ASIAN AMERICAN	HISPANIC AMERICAN
White-Collar				
Management, business, & financial	13.6%	9.9%	14.6%	7.8%
Professional	25.0	20.7	29.2	14.6
Sales	12.4	10.6	11.5	12.3
Administrative support & office	23.2	22.7	16.7	20.9
Blue-Collar				
Construction & extraction	.4	.3	.1	.4
Installation, maintenance, & repair	.3	.5	.3	.5
Transportation	1.9	2.8	1.1	3.6
Production	4.1	5.4	7.6	8.6
Service	18.8	27.0	18.8	30.3
Farming, forestry, & fishing	.3	.1	.3	1.2
	100.0	100.0	100.2*	100.2*

* Rounding error.

Source: United States Bureau of Labor Statistics (2005a:35).

TABLE 3.3   Women's and Men's Income

PANEL A: WOMEN'S MEDIAN INCOME AS A PERCENTAGE OF MEN'S, 1890–2005 (year-round, full-time workers, 18 years and older)

Year	Women as % of Men
1890	54%
1950	54
1960	61
1970	59
1980	60
1990	72
2000	74
2005	77

PANEL B: MEDIAN INCOME BY GENDER AND EDUCATION, 2005 (year-round, full-time workers, age 25–64)

Education	Men's Median Income	Women's Median Income	Women as % of Men
Elementary (< 9 years)	$ 22,300	$16,200	73%
High School Degree	36,400	26,400	73
College Degree	60,100	42,200	70
Professional Degree	100,000	80,700	81

PANEL C: MEDIAN INCOME BY GENDER AND AGE, 2005 (year-round, full-time workers)

Age	Men	Women	Women as % of Men
25–29	$32,200	$30,400	94%
30–34	39,900	33,500	84
45–49	50,900	36,000	71
50–54	50,900	37,700	74

PANEL D: MEAN INCOME BY RACE AND ETHNICITY, 2005 (year-round, full-time workers)

Race/Ethnicity	Mean Income	Women % of White Men
White American Men	$48,100	—
Asian American Women	36,800	77%
White American Women	34,100	71
African American Women	30,400	63
Hispanic American Women	25,000	52

Note: Hispanic American Women in Panel D can be of any race.

Sources: Goldin (1990:60), United States Bureau of the Census (2006:11; 2006c).

women working full-time was about 54 percent of men's in 1890. More than 60 years later, in 1950, that figure remained unchanged. Since then, the earnings of women employed full-time increased slowly and fitfully. As of 2004, women's median income is still only 77 percent of men's, indicating that a wage gap continues to exist.

Variations in skill level affect income in predictable ways, as displayed in Panel B of Table 3.3. Educational attainment is a typical indicator of skill. At each higher level of education, women who work full-time all year long earn more. At the same time, however, at each level of education, they earn only 64 to 75 percent as much as men. These data can be summarized by two empirical generalizations. *For both genders, the greater the skill level, the higher the income.* This fact means that achievement pays off. However: *At every skill level, men earn significantly more than women.* This fact means that ascription remains a powerful force.

Age also affects income, again in predictable ways. Panel C of Table 3.3 shows that the wage gap between young men and women starting their job lives and working full-time all year is only 6 percent: women earn 94 percent as much as men. Older women increase their incomes as their experience and skill increase, but not as much as do men. In their prime earnings years, women's income is 71 to 74 percent as much as men's. As will be discussed later, this is because women have often left the labor force for extended periods of time and suffered more from discrimination.

Racial and ethnic variations exist, of course, as shown in Panel D. Asian women earn about 77 percent as much as white men. White and African-American women earn much less, on average, 71 percent and 63 percent, respectively, compared to white men. And Hispanic American women earn even less, about 52 percent. The impact of discrimination by race/ethnicity and gender combine to produce a high level of inequality.[17]

Gender Stratification in Cross-National Perspective

Women are also stratified along these same dimensions—labor force participation, occupational segregation, and income—in all economically developed nations. For example, as illustrated in Table 3.4, more than two-thirds of working-age women (15 to 64) participate in the labor force and these figures are typical. One result is that divorce rates go up in all societies as women enter the labor force.[18] Women employed full-time all year long earn three-fourths (or a little more) compared to men. Column (4) of the table illustrates the degree of occupational segregation, using the index of dissimilarity. You should recall from Chapter 2 that it varies from zero to one. In this case, a zero means no segregation, implying an equal number of women in each occupation; a one means complete segregation, implying that all women are in occupations with no men. Thus, a higher number indicates greater segregation. Among the nations compared in Table 3.4, the United States displays the lowest level of occupational segregation. Finally, the table presents data on the proportion of women and men working part-time. In all economically developed nations, far more women than men work part-time, significantly depressing the former's earnings, job security, and pensions.

The information presented in this section suggests the duality mentioned earlier: (1) Gender inequality has declined significantly in recent years and (2) a great deal still exists. The continuity of gender inequality is shown by the many women who remain

TABLE 3.4   Women's Economic Situation, United States and Selected Nations

(1) COUNTRY	(2) % WOMEN IN LABOR FORCE	(3) WOMEN'S INCOME AS % OF MEN'S	(4) OCCUPATIONAL SEGREGATION INDEX	(5) % EMPLOYED PART-TIME	
				WOMEN	MEN
Sweden	75%	83%	.60	25%	8%
United States	70	77	.46	26	11
United Kingdom	69	75	.58	28	7
Netherlands	67	81	na	49	17
Germany	65	na	.51	24	4
France	64	na	.55	17	4

Notes: Column (2) data are for 2003. Column (3) data are for 2002 for Netherlands, 2003 for United Kingdom, and 2004 for United States and Sweden; these data are for those working full-time all year long. Column (4) data are for 1990 for Sweden, 2000 for United States, 1991 for United Kingdom, 1993 for Germany (and apply only to the former West Germany), and 1999 for France. The measure used in column (4) is the index of dissimilarity, as explained in the text. Column 5 data are for 2004. na means data not available.

Sources: Column .(2): United States Bureau of the Census (2006:879). Column (3): Statistics Sweden (2005), United States Bureau of the Census (2005b), Office of National Statistics (2005a), and Statistics Netherlands (2005). Column (4): Anker et al. (2003), Charles and Grusky (2004:71), Elliott (2005). Column (5): Eurostat (2005).

out of the labor force, the high level of occupational segregation, and income inequality. The reduction in gender inequality is revealed by rising female labor force participation along with declining occupational segregation and income inequality. Hypotheses to account for these patterns are offered later. Now, however, it is important to recognize that the difficulty most women have in becoming economically independent, regardless of skill, indicates not only the continued salience of traditional gender norms but also how few women exercise authority and how many are victimized.

SOME CONSEQUENCES OF GENDER STRATIFICATION

Authority and Gender

The term **authority** refers to the legitimate exercise of power. As Max Weber observed, those with authority assert a right to make decisions affecting others, who believe they have a duty to obey.[19] This shared definition of right and obligation usually means that force does not have to be used. Thus, from the point of view of traditional gender norms, men have the right to exercise authority in the United States. Women's acceptance of male authority is reflected in traditional marriage vows: They pledge to love, honor, and obey. Although this prerogative has been challenged in recent years (marriage vows are changing), men dominate public life.

In economic matters, men, not women, set policy. Internationally, U.S. companies apparently have the highest proportion of women in management jobs in the world.[20]

That is, however, not saying much. Among Fortune 500 companies (the largest publicly traded corporations), eight have women chief executive officers and only 5 percent of the top five most well paid corporate officers are women.[21] Moreover, in these large companies, only 16 percent of all corporate officers at any level are women. In general, the higher in an organization's hierarchy one looks, the fewer the women are to be seen. Thus, men decide the height of assembly lines and the size of airplane cockpits, which affect women's ability to work in better paying blue-collar jobs (recall the distribution in Table 3.1). Men decide how occupations are to be evaluated, which may be part of the reason engineering is seen as more important than teaching. Pay levels follow.

This same pattern occurs in government. Men, not women, make laws and dictate how they will be enforced.[22] Only 14 percent of all Senators and 14 percent of all members of the House of Representatives are women. It is not accidental that until just a few years ago women were denied many basic civil rights. These included the ability to own property, obtain credit, and sue in court. Men made these laws, which codified traditional gender norms. They still do. When bills about day care, or Head Start, or domestic violence (wife or child abuse) come before Congress, women have little impact.

Religion is no different. Men, not women, talk to God. Only 15 percent of all members of the clergy are women.[23] Those religious groups excluding women from leadership roles do so for varying reasons. Most, however, appear to assert that although men and women are equal in the eyes of God, however known, scripture says men ought to be in positions of formal leadership. It should be no surprise, then, that God is defined as masculine and those interpreting His intentions have always justified men striking and chastising women and children.[24] It should be no surprise that, in His name, they chose to defend developing embryos over the needs of women. It should be no surprise that some Protestant faiths still assert that every woman should "submit herself graciously" to her husband's leadership.[25] Father knows best.

The situation is similar in court. Men dominate; they decide how laws are interpreted and enforced. It is not accidental that child support payments in the United States are set very low and poorly enforced.[26]

When people seek medical treatment, men dominate. They decide who should enter the field of medicine and its priorities. So men define who is sick and how they will be treated. In fact, organized medicine drove women from the field during the nineteenth century.[27] It is not accidental that this process began just when abortion became a safe medical procedure and increasing numbers of women sought to regulate their fertility.[28]

Finally, men dominate higher education. Walk down the hallway where administrators and faculty are housed; nearly all are men. The secretaries, of course, are women. This pattern includes sociology.[29] It is not accidental that just thirty years ago, women's studies courses and departments were almost unheard of. It was assumed that analyses of women's experiences would yield little new insight. This assumption was, of course, buttressed by sociological theory.[30]

Although much change has occurred, women in authority remain rare. Imagine women in jobs of real authority: as the Chief Executive Officer of General Motors, as the Majority Leader of the United States Senate, as the parish priest. Think about how women in positions of dominance are described: "lady policemen" and "lady doctors." The diminutive term, "lady," relegates those performing such roles to unequal status. It implies they should not be there. This situation also occurs on campus, where the expression "lady" designates many women's athletic programs—as in "Lady Gators" and "Lady Bruins." Women's sports are, of course, always unequal compared to men's. Thus, the term "lady" still implies, as it always has, that women belong in the home, where men can protect them. Unfortunately, the paradoxical result of traditional gender norms is that women are not protected, either at home or at work.

Victimization and Gender

Although often unrecognized, traditional gender norms and the inequality that follows lead to female victimization. Sexual harassment, rape, wife abuse, and child sexual abuse all involve the assertion of power by men over women. **Power** refers to people's ability to achieve their goals, whether legitimate or not, even if opposition occurs. Power often requires force or coercion. It was mentioned earlier that authority relies on a shared acceptance of the right to dominate. In this case, traditional gender norms imply agreement that men belong on the job and women at home, dependent. Nonetheless, anyone approached by an armed police officer knows that the threat of force always underlies authority. Relations between men and women are similar. The combination of differences in physical size and men's dominance of public life means that the threat of force always exists and sometimes occurs. Women become victims. They are the only exploited people who have been idealized into powerlessness.

Sexual harassment is a form of discrimination that occurs under one of two conditions.[31] First, a person pressures another for sexual cooperation in exchange for something, such as a job, promotion, grade, letter of recommendation, or class notes. Second, an intimidating or hostile environment is created on the job or at school such that people find it hard to work or study—and thereby find it harder to succeed. A hostile environment is created by such behaviors as offensive jokes or remarks, invading one's personal space, being touched or grabbed, the display of sexually offensive material, being cornered or followed or forced into sexual contact (such as kissing). Of course, some contexts exist where sexual banter is expected and women sometimes take such jobs knowing that fact, as when eating establishments require servers to wear skimpy outfits and flirt with customers.[32] By contrast, the key to understanding sexual harassment is that it is unwanted, upsetting, and prevents people from doing well, either at work or at school.

It is also widespread.[33] For example, about 60 percent of women aged 25 to 26 report they have been harassed on the job. Among women college students, about 62 percent say they have been harassed. Some men are harassed as well, usually by homophobic comments, gestures, or touches. These data mean that on a campus with, say, 5,000 female students, about 3,000 will have someone (nearly always a male) make sexually explicit comments about them, brush up against them, grab them, block their way or follow them, and the like. Yet many, if not most, women find that sexual harassment is a crime without a remedy. In *Measure for Measure*, written around 1603, William Shakespeare shows why.[34] In Act II, scene iv, Isabella tells Angelo:

> *With an outstretched throat I'll tell the world aloud*
> *What man thou art.*

Angelo responds:

> *Who will believe thee, Isabel?*
> *My unsoil'd name, th'austereness of my life*
> *My vouch against you, and my place i'th'state*
> *Will so your accusation overweigh*
> *That you shall stifle in your own report,*
> *And smell of calumny.*

Like Angelo, harassers often try to make the victim into the victimizer by accusing her of making untrue assertions harming his reputation (calumny). Like Angelo, they then move on with their careers, becoming chairs of academic departments (including sociology), administrators in Fortune 500 corporations, and judges and politicians.[35]

The consequences of sexual harassment can be adverse.[36] Many women blow it off, viewing it as just another barrier to get over in order to get a job or learn. In some cases, however, victims lose their jobs, either by being fired or quitting, or drop out of school. Sometimes their lives are transformed: They lose self-confidence, become anxious, and suffer from headaches, ulcers, and other physical ailments. Some become clinically depressed. This term does not mean they merely feel bad; everyone feels bad sometimes. Rather, **depression** occurs when people become psychologically incapacitated; they lose interest in daily activities for an extended period; they have little energy, feel worthless, and find it difficult to concentrate; they sometimes contemplate suicide; they often use and abuse drugs. As should be clear, harassers use sex as a means to express power.[37] As women enter traditional male occupations or majors, men often become insecure; they believe women are invading their territory. Hence, they try to put women "in their place" by telling them they are not welcome and not respected. The resulting trauma inhibits educational, occupational and, ultimately, economic success for many women.

So does rape. Studies consistently show that about 17 percent of women and 3 percent of men are raped at some point in their lives, most while young, often as children.[38] Some variation occurs by race and ethnicity, with Native American women more likely to be victimized than either white or African-American women. Asian American women are least victimized. Rape keeps women unequal in two ways. First, fear of rape leads many women to alter their behavior. At an early age, women learn to avoid placing themselves in situations where they may be vulnerable, such as working at night. Yet many high prestige and well-paying jobs require such extra hours. Thus, women who have not been raped are victims to the extent that they change their behavior, act cautiously, do not take a job, or avoid an opportunity out of fear. But most rape victims know the assailant, who is their father, husband, boyfriend, or friend.[39] Second, actual victims display many problems.[40] About 30 percent become clinically depressed at some point in their lives, while another 31 percent develop **post-traumatic stress disorder.** The term refers to reactions to trauma: intense anxiety, inability to concentrate, becoming easily startled, nightmares, flashbacks, and insomnia. Physical symptoms are common: stomach aches, ulcers, and bulimia, among others. In addition, rape victims are more likely to use and abuse drugs of all sorts. Finally, about 33 percent of rape victims contemplate suicide and 13 percent eventually try it. So the impact of rape is long-lasting and inhibits occupational success. Like sexual harassment, rape is an assertion of power by men, a means of controlling women and keeping them in their place: at home and out of the labor force.[41]

So is **wife abuse:** threatening or harming one's wife or companion. Men initiate most violence in families, which is why this term is used here rather than the more common "spouse abuse."[42] About 25 percent of women say they have been physically assaulted or raped by a spouse or companion.[43] Native American and African-American women have higher rates of victimization than do Whites, with Asian American women lower. Most injuries are scratches and welts (as when someone is hit), but broken bones occur about 11 percent of the time and even more serious results less often. In addition to physical injuries, abused women suffer in other ways as well. Although numbers are hard to obtain, battered women are at greater risk for post-traumatic stress disorder, depression, and suicide. Emotionally abusive and controlling behavior often accompanies violence against women. Once again, the issue is power: keeping women dependent. Abused women have less occupational or economic success over time.

Child sexual abuse has the same impact. It refers to molestation or sexual penetration of children by adults. Official data indicate that about 87,000 cases occur per year, a rate of about two per 1,000 girls and less than one per 1,000 boys.[44] But these are events reported to state authorities and, hence, significantly underestimate the true incidence. Self-report studies show rates ranging between 6 to 38 percent of girls, depending on the nature of the sample and question wording. As a reasonable guess, about 20 percent of girls and 10 percent of boys are sexually abused as children, nearly always by adult males. As with the other behaviors described here, child sexual abuse is about power rather than sex.[45] Thus, male adults engage in sexual behavior with young persons in order to feel powerful and in control. And the victims frequently react by feeling powerless. Men who are victimized tend to have inconsistent responses, some become depressed and others aggressive (often toward women). Women who are victimized also tend to become depressed and to see themselves as dependent on men. Such women often become sexually active at younger ages and endure early pregnancy (and abortion or birth), early marriage, and early divorce. Victims of both sexes frequently use and abuse drugs, and think about suicide.[46] These results limit their employment and income as adults.

This discussion suggests that women need to be protected from men rather than by men. If a few men assert power via sex, all men benefit to the extent that women stay home, stay dependent, and provide domestic service. This pattern reinforces gender as a system of domination. Thus, while it may never occur to men who resemble the fictional Jim Anderson to threaten women like the fictional Margaret, traditional family life is buttressed by the victimization of women. In *Trauma and Recovery*, Judith Lewis Herman emphasizes that the most common locations of trauma for women are the home and workplace.[47] Such locations continue to be regulated by traditional gender norms. Because these norms dictate that men ought to dominate women, they lead to silence when trauma occurs. In fact, Herman argues that it is the silence that haunts women even more than the crimes themselves: bystanders' denial that crimes have been committed. She says that the study of trauma endured by women depends on a political movement for equality: **feminism.** The term refers to an ideology and a social movement emphasizing that women and men should be equal. It seeks the generation of egalitarian norms for women and men. It argues that the roles women play as adults cannot be like those of men until women are no longer victimized, until sex is no longer a means of power by men over women.

THE INDIVIDUAL AND GENDER
STRATIFICATION

Think about certain events in the life of Carol Hanson. She enrolls at State College with excellent test scores and good grades. Nearly any major is available to her. She initially considers engineering and takes a couple of courses. But ultimately she selects education.

Carol graduates at age 23 and begins teaching in an elementary school. She marries Bertram ("Bertie") Robinson, who is still working on his engineering degree, so Carol supports them for two years. After Bertie graduates, he gets a job and they settle in Dawson Creek (well, why not?). She teaches fourth grade for five years and also does nearly all the housework. Then Bertie is offered a job in Chicago. Carol opposes the move; they argue and at one point Bertie throws the phone at Carol, giving her a black eye. They move. After relocating in a big new house, they decide to start a family (a common pattern). After the birth, which took place at Chicago Hope (of course), Carol, now 30, quits her job and focuses on child rearing, housework, and taking care of Bertie. After three years, she begins teaching again but starts near the bottom of the salary scale because her previous tenure only partially transfers. Thus, Carol's income is less than both Bertie's and others who obtained their teaching certificates at the same time but remained in the labor force. Carol continues, of course, to be responsible for child care and housekeeping. After two years, Bertie gets another job offer. Carol again opposes the move, but to no avail. They move to a new zip code: 90210. A second child is born and Carol quits working (that is, she quits working for pay; child care is hard work). She returns to teaching after two years. But once again she starts near the bottom of the salary scale. Five years pass, and Bertie is now making serious money but hating the rat race. He begins seeing his (much younger) secretary, Ms. Bimbo. After the divorce, he takes his engineering degree (remember, Carol supported him), his pension (Carol provided support services while this was building), Ms. Bimbo, and the dog, Toto, back to Kansas. Because Carol has a good job, she receives no income support. What she gets is child custody and child support. After a short time, however, the latter stops. Carol now takes care of her children on her teacher's salary of $35,000 per year.

Though stereotypical, the vignette reflects the experiences of many women. Carol decided on a teaching career instead of, for example, designing highways. As shown in Table 3.1, women often select occupations that require helping others.[48] One reason for this choice lies in her socialization at home (more on this in the next section). Another reason is that she became serious about Bertie and married him right out of college. Such women may lower their aspirations or choose a major (and a job) that appears congruent with traditional gender norms. In either case, like many other women, Carol quit her job each time the family relocated and she gave birth.[49] She paid the wage penalty for motherhood, as shown in Table 3.5. It shows that when children are present in the home, women often drop out of the labor force and, when they do work for pay, earn far less. Recall, here, the high proportion of women employed part-time (displayed in Table 3.4). Finally, she went through a divorce and found child support to be unreliable. Again, this is common.[50] Note that, except for the break-up of her marriage and its consequences, each of these choices was Carol's. Women often make such decisions. Why?

TABLE 3.5 Presence of Children and Income for Men and Women

CHILDREN PRESENT AT HOME 10 OF 15 YEARS, 1983–1998		
	Women	*Men*
Average Number of Years out of Labor Force	3.3	.05
Average Annual Earnings When Employed	$19,000	$48,400
Women's Income Gap	33%	

Notes: Annual earnings are only for years in which income is reported. Income data are in 1999 dollars.

Source: Rose and Hartmann (2004:28).

Women's Choices

When people enter the labor force, they make decisions about what skills to acquire and the relative priority their job will have compared to leisure time, child care, housework, and the like. Economists postulate an "efficient" job market in which these choices affect income variations independent of gender, race/ethnicity, or any other ascribed characteristic. From this point of view, Carol earns less than Bertie because she is less productive. Productivity is assessed by people's **human capital:** their skills (education, work experience, and tenure on current job) and employment priorities (labor force continuity, choosing part-time employment, absenteeism due to a child's illness, leaving a job due to a spouse's mobility, etc.). This argument can be phrased as the *Human Capital Hypothesis: The less valuable the skills people acquire and the lower the priority employment has versus other activities, the lower their income.* Education and work experience reveal the job skills individuals like Carol and Bertie have chosen to develop, their employment priorities, and, hence, income. So Carol's selection of education over engineering produced skills (presumably) worth less than Bertie's. In addition, she chose to stop working for pay on two occasions, which also made her "less productive." This argument is generalizable beyond the vignette. Many women make similar decisions, which make them less productive—albeit in the narrow sense of producing goods and services. This angle of vision suggests, then, that such women deserve lower incomes because they are less skilled and less devoted to paid work. They value (economists would say they have a "taste for") housework, child care, and following their husbands. Earnings inequality follows.

Three observations, however, suggest there is more going on here than gender-related difference in "taste."[51] First, the logic of the *Human Capital Hypothesis* implies that women emphasizing family obligations would pick jobs that fit with these activities. But many of the occupations in which women cluster (shown in Table 3.1) do not fit with caring for children and husbands because, for example, the required hours are usually less flexible. Secretaries and private household help must typically keep rather rigid schedules. Nurses must often work nights and weekends. In fact, men's jobs often have more flexible hours, more unsupervised leave time, and more sick leave and vacation, which means that their jobs are more compatible with family responsibilities. Second, the hypothesis implies that single women (whose family responsibilities are less) would cluster in higher-prestige, higher-paying occupations. But this does not occur; the occupational distribution of single women does not differ from married women.[52] These observations imply that "productivity" is not the only source of gender-related differences in income, that the job market is not "efficient." Third, tests of the hypothesis suggest just how inefficient.[53] Only about one-third of the variation in men and women's income results from so-called human capital factors, with another one-third reflecting the industry, union status, and other job-related factors. This finding means that the human capital hypothesis only partly explains why women like Carol make less than men. More is going on here.

Discrimination Against Women

The "more" that is going on is **discrimination.** The term, you may recall from Chapter 1, refers to the unequal treatment of people or groups because of their personal characteristics. Today, such behavior is often illegal. But not at home, where the unequal treatment of women and men begins and a gender-based system of domination is established anew in each generation.

First, the victimization of women constitutes discrimination. When Carol objected to moving to Chicago, Bertie threw the telephone at her. From that moment on, Carol was aware that force might be directed either at her or their future children. More generally, the threat of wife abuse, rape, and child sexual abuse makes all women careful and impedes occupational success.

Second, discrimination occurs during divorce when the tangible assets (a house) and the intangible assets (a pension) are divided.[54] Although Carol's relationship with Bertie was intimate, in callous economic terms they were business partners for many years: She provided support services while he obtained a degree and made a career. She followed him from place to place, always providing services in the expectation that she would gain economic security in return. Then he walked away with Ms. Bimbo. It is a common tale, but true: and wives are treated unequally in the aftermath of divorce, especially when they have their own (less remunerative) careers and pensions.

Third, discrimination at home goes beyond these acts of power to the more subtle issue of socializing women and men to accept traditional gender norms. Economists in the human capital tradition will argue that when women like Carol choose elementary school teaching, they are selecting a job with flexible hours and slow skill deterioration precisely so they can easily relocate with their husbands and leave the labor force to bear and raise children. But this choice reflects socialization.[55] Even when children are infants, parents project their gender expectations onto children. As children grow up, data show that girls and boys perform different chores: Girls cook and clean, boys remove garbage and mow the grass. In play, children learn "appropriate" adult roles. Playing with dolls and dollhouses constitutes practice for adult responsibilities; girls learn to enjoy and to want to do what they will have to do as adults. Why do you suppose Carol, who was career oriented, so readily accepted her responsibilities at home? Boys' play, by contrast, turns into men's play. Boys play cops and robbers, build forts, and race Hot Wheels. As men, they practice target shooting, play softball, and watch sports on television. These behaviors do not teach them to enjoy caring for others. As they grow up, children actively try to make sense of their environment. They see their parents' division of household labor and learn expectations for their own behavior. Now there are many who would disagree with this third point, possibly because they do not want to face the implications of their values.

Discrimination starts at home, but continues at work. The Equal Pay Act of 1963 and the Civil Rights Act of 1964 prohibit discrimination against women in earnings and occupation. Other federal legislation forbids discrimination in education, housing, and credit. Despite these laws, a great deal of covert discrimination occurs in the work place. The methods used to prevent individual women from obtaining a job and earning a living are straightforward: recruitment and screening practices.

When employers decide to hire people, they must recruit candidates. One relatively efficient way of doing this is to place advertisements in the media. Hiring audits show the extent of discrimination. For example, when "job seekers" with similar résumés were sent to high-priced restaurants, the female "applicant" was interviewed for the job 40 percent less often, and was only half as likely to get a job offer.[56] Another efficient way is by word-of-mouth, since this is how most people find jobs. This process means that one's network of family, friends, and acquaintances is fundamental in finding a job. It also disadvantages women due to occupational segregation.[57] Since most women work in jobs that are dominated by women, they obtain information about other women-dominated jobs.

One recent study of the hiring processes at a large firm shows that income inequality between men and women has its origin in the initial sorting of applicants into job queues in which a set of candidates is competing for particular job openings.[58] Sorting by gender occurs as applicants are assigned to queues: "Women are prevalent in queues for low pay, low status jobs." In addition, applicants' "networks play an important role," as those referred by current employees are more likely to be assigned to a queue (that is, to be able to compete for a specific job) and to be hired. In this firm, the major source of income inequality is that men and women are sorted such that they perform different jobs, not that they are paid unequally when performing the same jobs. Other studies, however, continue to report within-job wage inequality.[59]

Once people enter a hiring queue, they must be evaluated—a very subjective process. An interviewer's judgment about a candidate's "appearance," "self-confidence," "emotional make-up," and many other characteristics can affect the outcome. Symphony orchestras provide a good example of both the ascriptive basis of such evaluations and the possibility of change.[60] Historically, symphonic orchestras were a male preserve; it was common for entire orchestras to have no women players at all. But in the 1990s some orchestras began using a screen to conceal the identities of candidates for positions. This change meant that only the music mattered, not the gender of the person performing it. In the top twenty-four American orchestras (in terms of size of budget), the proportion of women rose to 29 percent in 1994 and to 35 percent in 2003. In some sections, such as the violin, women now outnumber men. In at least four orchestras, the concertmaster is now a woman. The concertmaster is, perhaps, the orchestra's most important member. He or she serves as the administrative link between the conductor and the orchestra, leads rehearsals, and often plays solos. When one orchestra auditioned for a concertmaster a few years ago and a woman stepped from behind the screen, members of the orchestra became visibly upset. The music director, however, declared that "the screen has spoken." Or, as sociologists might say, achievement trumped ascription.

In sum, when the choices women make and the possibility of discrimination are combined, then the reason so many women achieve less than their abilities or motivation suggest they should, becomes clear. Yet this form of analysis remains incomplete. It cannot reveal why the overall rate of women's accomplishment is so low. In order to answer this question, it is necessary to look at the way the social structure influences people's options.

SOCIAL STRUCTURE AND GENDER STRATIFICATION

In George Bernard Shaw's play, *Pygmalion*, originally produced in 1914, the main character, Henry Higgins, wonders why women cannot be more like men.[61] Well, they can. The data presented earlier show that much change is occurring in precisely that direction: Women have entered the labor force and now increasingly obtain resources: prestige, education, income, and power. Women are more equal to (or like) men today than in the past. Even the data on female victimization reflect this fact because such events are now controversial. Yet much remains the same: The data continue to show that—in every area—women remain unequal to men. It is useful to pause and think about this problem more abstractly.

In Chapter 1, it was noted that the forces shaping the stratification structure, with its three systems of domination (class, gender, and race/ethnicity), can be conceptualized by the degree of emphasis on achievement versus ascription. A society emphasizes achievement to the extent that performance-related criteria equally applied to all are used to evaluate people and to the extent these evaluations affect the distribution of resources. The data suggest that the United States is moving in this direction and, in this sense, women and men are becoming more alike. Conversely, a society emphasizes ascription to the extent that nonperformance-related criteria based on birth are used to evaluate people and to the extent such evaluations affect the distribution of resources. The importance of gender as a system of domination indicates a continuing emphasis on ascription, as suggested by the *Gender Hypothesis: Women at every class level have fewer and less effective choices than do men.* Although this is not the place to test this hypothesis, the data presented earlier are consonant with it: At every class level, women's life chances, their ability to share in the available goods and services, still reflects their dependence on men rather than their own achievement.

As this duality reveals, societies are not monolithic entities. Historical change usually means that contradictory tendencies coexist. The decline of gender stratification coupled with its continuation illustrates this phenomenon.

The Decline of Gender Stratification

The ideal of equality of opportunity for both men and women has become more widespread over the past half-century or so. As indicated, this is another way of talking about the increasing applicability of achievement-oriented values to both genders.

A hypothesis that accounts for this change is as follows: *The decline of gender inequality reflects: (1) economic development, (2) increasing female labor force participation, (3) advances in medical technology, (4) legal changes, and (5) the rise of feminism.*

Economic Development.   In the past, most people lived on farms, scratching a living from the soil. Husbands and wives did this together, using a simple division of labor to produce what they needed to survive. There was little surplus and, as Gerhard Lenski suggested, in such contexts people tend to share what is produced. Women were indeed like men: They worked at backbreaking productive tasks. Since modern labor-saving devices did not exist, the work required of women—baking, making soap, brewing beer, harvesting garden crops, managing barn animals, and much more—was very difficult. It is absurd to think that women were incapable of heavy work.[62] In addition, bearing children was a constant burden. The average woman became pregnant ten to twelve times and bore six to eight children.[63] But in this context, childbirth was a productive act because in just a few years children produced more than they cost.

The situation remained similar in the cities when capitalism emerged. In his *Autobiography*, published in 1795, Benjamin Franklin described how his wife, Deborah, assisted "cheerfully in my [printing] business, folding and stitching pamphlets, tending shop, purchasing old linen rags for the papermakers, etc."[64] Note that Franklin specifies that it is "my business." In the nascent market economy in which men were formally in charge, women's work constituted unpaid labor. Typically, the goods produced at home by unpaid female workers were partly consumed and partly sold or traded.[65] But no matter how such products were used, the point is the same as above: Productive activity occurred at home, where both women and men worked.

Industrialization changed this situation. As noted previously, the term refers to the transformation of the economy when new forms of energy are substituted for muscle power, leading to advances in productivity. The application of technology based on fossil, steam, and other forms of energy requires a more complex division of labor than that found at home. It also requires workers to gather at one site in order to minimize the cost of energy, raw materials, transportation, and distribution. As industrialization combined with capitalism and economic development took off, production shifted away from home. In a context where controlling pregnancy and birth remained difficult, most women remained at home. Men left; they worked to earn an income and support their families.

But economic development did more than separate home and work: It led to a decline in gender inequality by creating opportunities for women as well as men, mainly because the organization and type of work changed. As productivity increased, jobs requiring professional and technical expertise, administrative skills, sales ability, and record keeping became more plentiful. Put simply: More white-collar workers were required. As will be shown in Chapter 5, the percentage of white-collar workers rose from 18 percent in 1900 to 61 percent in 2000 (see Table 5.4). Brainpower supplanted muscle power, which meant that women could compete on equal terms with men. So they have entered the paid labor force in increasing proportions over time.

Increasing Female Labor Force Participation.   In her autobiography, written around 1905, Dorothy Richardson described her life as a working girl in the late nineteenth century.[66] She left home at age 18 and moved to New York City. There she worked for a variety of companies in entry-level positions. She titled her book *The Long Day* to emphasize the length of the working day, the hard labor, and the low wages. During the latter part of the nineteenth century, the average employed person worked ten hours per day, six days per week. Despite such requirements, Richardson eventually enrolled in night school, acquiring education and some commercial skills. She then became a stenographer and, to use her word, "prosperous" and economically independent. In those days, women like her were rare. They have become more common over time.

Women's increased labor force participation lead to a decline in gender inequality because an income, even a low one, means they need not be economically dependent on men. It changes women's options and changes family life. Some, like Dorothy Richardson, could be like men: They could support themselves. Such women sometimes never married, especially those with college degrees.[67] They simply remained employed.[68] Most women, of course, married. (Celibacy is hard on people.) During the early years of the twentieth century, marriage usually meant that women quit their jobs. As time passed, however, this pattern changed as married women increasingly entered the labor force. They did so mainly in response to expanding economic opportunities, such as those produced by economic development, rather than to declining opportunities for their husbands.[69] This fact, however, has important implications: on the divorce rate, for example. People with jobs do not have to endure a marriage filled with sorrow. Thus, female employment has an insidious implication: A rejection of traditional gender norms. The demand for equality follows, as day the night, from economic independence. This is why all employed women are feminists, in fact if not ideology, since their jobs give them both a source of prestige and the potential to live on their own.

Although industrialization provides opportunity and labor force participation an income, these two factors will not lead to gender equality unless women can control fertility. This ability required advances in medical technology.

Advances in Medical Technology.   Advanced technology creates new choices. It allows behaviors that were impossible or considered immoral a few years ago and thereby creates social problems.[70] The invention of the rubber condom, the intrauterine device, and the birth control pill contributed to rising rates of premarital sexual intercourse.[71] Similarly, the development of tools and techniques for performing safe abortions raised moral issues that continue to divide the nation.[72] The nonobvious issue underlying both these problems, however, is women's roles. Specifically, should women's reproductive roles take precedence over their productive roles?

The answer to this question is now clear. Advances in medical technology lead to a decline in gender inequality by providing women the opportunity to regulate whether and when to give birth. Although significant limits on the ability to control fertility still exist, women can increasingly balance their various roles. Without this opportunity, they cannot take advantage of the transformation of the economy. Without this opportunity, employed women would be shunted into dead-end jobs they can easily enter and leave. When pregnancy and birth can occur without warning, without planning, women must be dependent on men for economic security. This fact can be suggested by a simple mental experiment. Imagine that industrialization has occurred but neither birth control nor abortions are possible. In such a context, a bright woman wants to go into civil engineering. But is it wise for an engineering school to admit her? One can argue that, like most women, she will marry and become pregnant many times. In such a situation, one can argue that most women will not be able to use their training. Moreover, even if she obtains a degree, who would (or should) hire her? After companies invested time and money in her, she would have to quit due to pregnancy or childbirth. Now there were exceptional women who succeeded under these circumstances. But they were few. For most of history, sexual differences between men and women meant that the latter had to bear children whenever pregnancy occurred.

Yet the opportunity created by advances in medical technology was not immediately available because the law restricted women's ability to take advantage of applied medical knowledge. They enjoyed neither civil nor reproductive rights. This fact had to change in order to increase women's (and men's) choices.

Legal Changes.   In democratic societies, laws not only regulate behavior, they serve as codified norms. They represent people's collective judgment about right and wrong. They identify, preserve, and protect ways of thinking and acting that citizens believe are important. As such, people with different characteristics are often treated differently under the law. Children, for example, have both special rights and special restrictions. Their unique treatment is justified because children are viewed as relatively powerless against adults. Until recently, women have been treated differently as well, along two dimensions: civil rights and fertility rights.

The denial of civil rights to women was justified as "protective legislation." One category of laws imposed maximum working hours for women. Interestingly, no state had enforceable laws limiting women's hours of work prior to the 1880s. By 1919, however, 40 states had enacted such statutes.[73] Another category allowed discrimination against women in hiring and job retention. Thus, married women could not be hired as teachers in 61 percent of all school districts in 1928; they could not be retained after marriage in 52 percent of all school districts.[74] These laws constitute one reason women quit their jobs at marriage: they were forced to. Still another category of laws made occupational segregation legal. As a result, women were typically tracked into jobs without promotion ladders while men were tracked into jobs with promotion ladders. Thus, in 1940, a sample of 260 companies with more than 19 employees revealed that 74 percent explicitly restricted some jobs to women and 70 percent restricted some jobs to men.[75] Gender was so important that employers and newspapers published separate listings for men and women. Here are some examples from the "Help Wanted—Women" section of a Washington, DC, newspaper in 1956.[76]

- Airline Hostesses for TransWorld Airlines: High school graduate, age 20–27, height 5′2″–5′8″, weight 100–135, attractive, unmarried. Apply in person.
- Cashier-Food Checker: White, middle-aged woman, honest, alert, intelligent. Experience in cashiering or food checking.
- Fountain Girl: White, for downtown drugstore; references.
- G.H.W. [general house work]: Colored girl to live in; good with children. Age 18–30. Off Sun. and half day Thurs. $20 wk.

It was not only perfectly legal to specify the gender and race of potential employees, companies were proud of such policies. In addition to restrictions on hours of work, hiring and retention, and job type, many other limits on women's rights existed—again, by law. These constraints meant that women were unable to act as fully endowed citizens, unable to act as adults. They were denied the right to choose the kind of work they did, to strive for economic success, and to obtain power and prestige apart from men. They were denied the right to achieve—simply because they were women.

Two contradictory interpretations of protective legislation exist.[77] One is that young, single, employed women were prone to exploitation, so they had to be protected, like children. Moreover, it is argued, such laws ultimately benefited all workers, male and female. Hours of work per week, for example, dropped from about 60 in the nineteenth century to about 40 by 1930. Another interpretation, however, is that these laws were designed to restrict opportunities available to women. Note that many protective statutes were passed during the period 1880 to 1930, as economic development accelerated and women began entering the labor force. It can be argued that these laws were not designed to protect women at all. They were, rather, reactions by men and their representatives (male legislators) to increased competition and an attempt at retaining their power and privilege—within both the family and society. Conveniently, such statutes were justified in terms of traditional gender norms, thus codifying gender as a system of domination.

But the drive to protect women did not occur without conflict. Some feminists proposed equality. For example, shortly after women obtained the right to vote in 1919 the National Woman's Party was organized and, under the leadership of Alice Paul, introduced the Equal Rights Amendment. But while equality is a morally powerful stance, such efforts were relatively ineffective for many years. From about 1890 until 1960, the law emphasized women's "protection." This constituted a collective normative judgment about right and wrong behavior. It expressed a traditional gender-based value: Women should not be equal to men; they should remain dependent, like children; their access to valued resources should be determined by ascription.

This collective judgment changed, like so much else, during the 1960s, when women gained full civil rights. The legislative history of the Civil Rights Act of 1964 is interesting, however, because the inclusion of women occurred by accident. The Act did not mention equal rights for women until the day before its passage when a southern congressman introduced an amendment to include sex along with race. Reportedly, some male members of Congress laughed out loud. The *New York Times* described the bizarre effects that would follow from granting women civil rights: "Executive training programs will have to be opened to women, who are almost universally excluded from them," "barbershop owners [will have] to take job applications from women who want to wield razor and scissors," a "dizzy blonde" might drive a tug boat or work as a dog warden. The *New Republic* advised its readers not to take this "mischievous joke" seriously.[78] The southern strategy was to load the bill with "absurd" amendments in order to defeat it. They miscalculated. As a result, women are now supposed to be treated equally in seeking and keeping jobs. Coupled with the Equal Pay Act of 1963, which requires that men and women be paid equally for equal work, Title IX of the Educational Amendments Act of 1972, and other statutes, the legal basis for gender discrimination ended. Thus, the trend in law has been transformed. Norms, codified into law, dictate that women and men should now be evaluated by performance-related criteria applied equally to all.

This is a clear instance of the change from ascription to achievement in orientation. As emphasized in Chapter 2, when Thomas Jefferson wrote that "all men are created equal" the concept of equality was initially applied very narrowly: to white men who owned property. Historically, however, the trend toward greater inclusiveness has proven to be inexorable: Immigrants, religious minorities, racial and ethnic groups, and women have sought to be treated as full citizens. The logic is that human beings should not be treated unequally based on their personal characteristics. (It is not much of an extension to include sexual orientation. By what logic should homosexual men and women be denied civil rights, including the right to marry?) Women, however, find themselves in a peculiar situation because only they can bear children. It is hard to imagine gender equality without the ability to regulate pregnancy and birth.

The second dimension of unequal treatment under the law was the denial of fertility rights, including both preventing and terminating pregnancy. Such rights have been restricted by law until recently. Thus, beginning about 1870 and continuing in various states until the 1960s, the distribution of contraceptive information and devices was illegal under obscenity statutes.[79] Similarly, every state made abortion illegal between 1860 and 1890.[80] Now there are two ways of interpreting restrictions on birth control and abortions. One is that they were statements of moral principles: Sex outside of marriage is wrong and abortion is murder. But the underlying issue is the roles women can play, both in the family and the larger society. These laws made women's reproductive ability the center of their lives. Barring celibacy, women's ability to obtain an education, have a career, enter politics, and participate equally in all spheres of life could be undermined at any time by pregnancy and birth. Hence, these laws kept women at home, like children, unequal to men. It is not accidental that they were passed during the same period as so-called "protective" legislation. As opportunities increased with industrialization, men (and some women) sought to keep women at home. It did not work.

As with civil rights, the denial of reproductive rights began to end during the 1960s. In a series of decisions, the Supreme Court declared that women and men had a right to obtain birth control regardless of their age or marital status. Legislative enactments facilitated this right. Various states, led by California in 1967, began changing their abortion laws. Ultimately, however, the Court's 1973 decision in *Roe vs. Wade* invalidated all state laws proscribing abortions. Hence, the collective judgment of society is now different. The law guarantees women's ability to work for pay and, indeed, to participate fully in every area of society precisely because fertility can be controlled. Underlying these legal changes was the rise of feminism.

The Rise of Feminism.   The drive for equality by oppressed people usually requires both an ideology and a social movement. Feminism provides them. Ideologically, it emphasizes that men and women should be equal. Most feminists support the development of egalitarian gender norms. Without this orientation, the traumas experienced by women—the arbitrary denial of a job, rape, abuse—remain personal tragedies and the process of bearing witness becomes meaningless.[81] Traumatic acts are not acknowledged; they are forgotten. But placed in the context of a movement for equality, these same acts are understood as examples of gender-based oppression. They allow victims to find a transcendent meaning in their experiences. They galvanize others and translate a personal tragedy into a social problem.

Feminism leads women to see themselves as individuals capable of doing more than bearing children. The Protestant Reformation, the Enlightenment, the abolitionist movement, the development of capitalism, and the French Revolution, among other factors, all contributed to a recognition by some women that they could fill productive roles in the society. A feminist movement followed.[82]

The history of the feminist movement is usually described in two waves.[83] The first wave took place between the years 1848 and 1920 or so. Beginning with the Seneca Falls Convention of 1848, women began pressing for the removal of barriers to education and political participation. The mobilizing issue was the right to vote. This goal served as a symbol of women's status as full-fledged citizens: Women voters are adults, like men, who can and should participate in societal decision making. Apart from this issue, not all feminists of the period shared the same goals. Some argued for equality while others emphasized the uniqueness of women. Many of the latter supported "protective" legislation of the sort described earlier. After passage of the Nineteenth Amendment to the Constitution, which secured the right to vote, the movement became quiescent. Protection seemed like enough, with the result that the many traumas women experienced went unnoticed, at least publicly. The second wave emerged during the 1960s and continues to the present. Responding to a new-found ability to prevent pregnancy, to ideological manifestos, to the Civil Rights movement, and other factors, women began organizing again.[84] The National Organization for Women was founded in 1967 to press for full equality. As before, however, the feminist movement has various branches, each of which pushes a somewhat different agenda.[85] In all of them, however, the mobilizing issues have been birth control, the right to an abortion, and ending violence against women. These goals serve as symbols of women's ability to control their lives. Without this ability, equality remains an illusion.

Notice how a variety of historical events coalesced. Feminism arose just as capitalism combined with industrialization to transform the economy. The ideology of equality buttressed expanded opportunity. In this context, women joined the labor force in steadily increasing numbers. Advances in medical technology, the fruits of scientific progress that originated several centuries ago, made it possible for women to regulate and control pregnancy and birth. Even though legal changes were delayed and continue to be contentious, they finally allowed women to regulate fertility. These changes, of course, were stimulated not only by the existence of technology but by the overarching value of equality. One of the dominant trends in Western history has been the freeing of individuals from dependence on others, another way of talking about an emphasis on achievement. Increasingly, when men and women join together, they do so out of desire, not need; and they remain together as a (truly) free choice rather than out of dependence. The historical trend is clear: increasing equality between men and women.

The Continuation of Gender Stratification

Despite the changes described above, gender inequality continues. Why is this so? The answer must be structural. The hypothesis offered here is that *the continuation of gender inequality reflects: (1) the salience of traditional gender norms and (2) institutionalized discrimination.*

The Salience of Traditional Gender Norms.   As noted earlier, traditional gender norms direct women and men into different spheres. Accordingly, the choices men and women make ought to differ. Even though they may be smart or creative, or both, and even though they may desire to become artists or scientists, women should focus their energy on family obligations. Most followed this dictum until recently. They became housewives, dependent on their husbands. Those who were employed worked at menial jobs, for low pay, or both, enduring discrimination. In a historical context where their choices were highly restricted, these ordinary women found whatever satisfaction they could. In certain respects, this situation has not changed, as suggested by four indicators of the continuing salience of traditional gender norms:

   1.   A significant minority of women does not work for pay. Thus, Figure 3.1 reveals that 68 percent of all married women are in the labor force. This datum means, of course, that the remaining 32 percent of all married women do not have an income. Excluding the aged and disabled, they are housewives, dependent on their husbands for economic support. Whether they like it (or admit it), they adhere to traditional gender norms.

   2.   Voluntary part-time employment is common among women: Table 3.4 shows that 26 percent of employed women in the United States have part-time jobs, most by choice. In comparison, only 11 percent of men work part-time. Women choose part-time employment to reduce the role conflict arising from job and family obligations. This priority is another way of adhering to traditional gender norms, of remaining dependent on their husbands.

   3.   Most employed wives have lower incomes than their husbands. Even though spouses usually have similar levels of education, Table 3.3 reveals that women earn only 77 percent as much as husbands. The table also shows that such differences occur regardless of education and age, and occurs among all racial and ethnic groups. Moreover, as displayed in Table 3.5, women are more likely to drop out of the labor force when children are present in the home, sacrificing income and long-term security. So wives are more dependent on husbands than husbands on wives. This economic relationship usually occurs by choice, as indicated by family decisions to relocate for husbands' jobs—even when wives are opposed, even when wives' income suffers as a result. Income differences are important because they translate into power within a marriage: When a man earns the most, he can impose his desires on his wife. Moreover, wife abuse is more common and harder to stop when women are economically dependent on men.[86] Men rarely drop out of the labor force to do child work. The fact that many women remain dependent reflects and reinforces traditional gender norms.

   4.   Finally, the relative unwillingness of men to do housework suggests that home remains contested terrain.[87] Imagine it is 30,000 years ago: Men hunted mastodon while women swept the cave and suckled the young. Now fast forward in your imagination to the 1950s and 1960s: Men hunted a paycheck while women vacuumed the house, cleaned the toilet, suckled the young, and drove them to gymnastics. Fast forward again to 2004: Men and women both hunt paychecks. Women still vacuum, clean the toilet, suckle the young, and drive them to gymnastics. Men hunt for the remote.

This description is, of course, a caricature. Or is it? According to recent data on time use, when both spouses are employed full-time, men usually work on the job about 8.3 hours per day and women 7.7 hours.[88] Men also average about 39 minutes per day participating in sports or exercise, compared to 20 minutes for women. In families with both spouses employed, however, women spent an hour a day more caring for children. In addition, women spent six hours a day in "secondary care," like taking the children with them while shopping; men spent about four hours a day. About 20 percent of men report doing some housework, compared to 55 percent of women. About 66 percent of women cook or wash dishes, compared to 35 percent of men. Thus, most men today "help" women do "their" work and thereby contribute more than their fathers did around the house, but men are relatively choosy. They are much more willing to change diapers than clean the toilet. That, as one observer, points out, remains a bottom-line barrier.[89] These data suggest that while the comic's assertion that "a man around the house is an inanimate object" is too extreme, the division of labor in many marriages still reflects and reinforces traditional gender norms. In terms of time allotted, employed husbands and wives rarely divide the household and family tasks in half.

These four indicators reveal the degree to which many people believe that women ought to focus on breadserving and men on breadwinning, and that everyone will be happier as a result. Although such beliefs are changing, their continued salience perpetuates gender inequality.

Institutionalized Discrimination. The inequality of women and men is also buttressed by **institutionalized discrimination:** the unequal treatment of individuals or groups based on their personal characteristics that is embedded in the social structure. Here are two indicators of institutionalized discrimination against women.

1. A skewed gender ratio in competitive contexts can lead to discrimination and affect women's ability to succeed.[90] Please look back at Table 3.1, which shows that women remain rare in many competitive jobs, like engineering and medicine, and many skilled blue-collar jobs, such as carpenter and electrician. Such work settings often display a skewed gender ratio: a large proportion of men and a small proportion of women. Most of the latter occupy entry-level positions. In such a context, women constitute tokens, representatives of their kind, subject to performance pressures and social isolation.

Because there are so few of them, women are highly visible to peers and supervisors, which creates performance pressures: One's mistakes cannot be hidden. Furthermore, women are often expected to avoid making men look bad on the job, even though it is a competitive situation. As might be expected, women in high-visibility jobs sometimes respond inconsistently, which makes their behavior unpredictable and social relations difficult. A self-fulfilling prophecy can occur in that women are expected to fail and do, often with a little help from male colleagues and supervisors. Women in such contexts have few choices. They can try to over achieve, a difficult tactic. Alternatively, they can seek success more covertly, thereby limiting their visibility but also reducing the chance for success via promotion.

Women in skewed gender ratio settings also suffer discrimination due to their isolation. Boundaries are established that isolate the "female intruder." Such contexts allow more opportunity for sexual harassment and other forms of unequal treatment. As a trite example, one innocuous strategy is to deliberately interrupt the flow of group events in some fashion in order to emphasize the presence of a woman. One might ask if it is okay to swear or apologize for doing so. The question emphasizes to a woman that she is different, that she disrupts normal behavior merely by being there: She is trespassing on a male domain. Other forms of harassment are much more serious, of course, and they inhibit success. In addition, such a context also makes it more difficult for women to secure mentoring, whether formally via on-the-job training or (just as importantly) informally. When male supervisors and colleagues meet informally—whether at exclusive clubs or just for drinks after work—they share sources of information, knowledge of short cuts, and other factors vital to advancement. Sometimes these processes occur without (much) malice; rather, the female intruder is simply different, threatening, and left out as a result. Success, via promotion, becomes more difficult. Such processes may be one reason why women, even professional women, sometimes leave the labor force.

2. Occupational segregation also builds unequal treatment into the social structure. A variety of interconnected factors lead to occupational segregation: traditional gender norms, the structure of the labor market, and discrimination, among others.[91] The focus here will be on the impact of traditional gender norms, as depicted in Table 3.6. It identifies some common stereotypes attributed to women that reflect traditional views: that women are caring, have skill at household tasks, do not like to supervise others, and the like. These imputed characteristics have practical consequences in terms of the kinds of jobs women want and get, which are often lower prestige and lower paying. It might seem that it is not so bad, even natural, that women want to work in occupations that require them to teach children and assist or care for men. And this may be true, but the value-laden question is whether it is desirable for women and men to remain prisoners of their reproductive abilities, to continue to be assigned to jobs based on ascriptive requirements.

Taken together, traditional gender norms and institutionalized discrimination constitute inertial forces, preserving gender-based domination of women by men. Much remains the same.

But think back: In October 1781, George Washington defeated Lord Cornwallis at the Battle of Yorktown. This win over the British forces, it can be argued, did not end the American Revolution. Nor did the signing of the Treaty of Paris two years later. Nor did the Constitution's adoption in 1789. Despite their importance, these events only marked the end of Part I of the struggle for freedom. They secured for

TABLE 3.6   Traditional Gender Roles, Stereotypes of Women, and Occupational Segregation

SOME STEREOTYPES OF WOMEN REFLECTING TRADITIONAL GENDER NORMS	EFFECT ON OCCUPATIONAL SEGREGATION	ILLUSTRATIONS OF AFFECTED OCCUPATIONS
Women have a caring nature.	Qualifies women for lower paying jobs in which others are cared for: children & men	nurse, secretary, teacher, social worker
Women have skill & experience at household work.	Qualifies women for lower paying jobs often done at home or resembling those done at home	maid, housekeeper, restaurant server, bartender
Women have superior manual dexterity (smaller, nimbler fingers).	Qualifies women for lower paying jobs where this trait is useful	typist, sewing machine operator, massage therapist, hairstylist
Women are more willing to take orders and do monotonous work.	Qualifies women for lower paying jobs & industries with poor working conditions	retail sales, agriculture, & textile industries
Women do not like to supervise others.	Disqualifies women for higher paying supervisory & managerial positions	sales supervisor, production supervisor, many professional jobs
Women have less physical strength (see note).	Disqualifies women for higher paying jobs appearing to require heavy lifting or physical effort	carpenters, electricians, machinists, plumbers

Note: Although women have less physical strength than men on average, there is much overlap. The illustrative occupations are taken from Table 3.1 and from United States Bureau of the Census (2006:401).

Source: Adapted from Anker et al. (2003).

white men certain fundamental rights: to vote, to be represented, and to obtain an education and a job based on hard work and ability. They reflected a long-term process by which white men are increasingly evaluated based on their achievements.

Women had none of these rights. They were still evaluated based on ascriptive criteria. Part II of the American Revolution began in a chapel in Seneca Falls, NY, in July 1848, where 240 people gathered and issued a declaration of the rights of women against men's oppression. It asserted that "we hold these truths to be self-evident: that all men and women are created equal; that they are endowed by their Creator with certain inalienable rights; that among these are life, liberty, and the pursuit of happiness." It went on to outline most of the elements necessary for the freedom and equality of women: the right to vote, to obtain an education, and to secure a job and income, among others. The Seneca Falls Declaration had little impact at the time. And, as the existence of this chapter indicates, gender still constitutes a system of ranking separate from class. But the moral force of ideas is strong. The Declaration began a fundamental transformation not only in the way men and women relate to one another but in stratification processes generally. Much has changed. Perhaps in the future class, with its greater emphasis on achievement, will supercede gender as a basis for stratification.

SUMMARY

Married women's labor force participation rate rose steadily in the twentieth century. In addition, married women with children also increased their rate of employment (Figure 3.1). One implication of these changes is a higher divorce rate, which does not necessarily benefit women. Although some changes have occurred in recent years, men and women are still occupationally segregated (Table 3.1) and this is true regardless of race or ethnicity (Table 3.2). Occupational segregation means women are unequal in both prestige and income. Among full-time employed workers, women earn about 77 percent as much as men (Table 3.3) and this is true regardless of education, age, or race/ethnicity. Economic inequality by gender remains typical in all Western societies (Table 3.4).

Men still exercise authority in the United States and women are still victimized, as indicated by sexual harassment, rape, wife abuse, and child sexual abuse. Underlying all these differences are traditional gender norms. Quantitative research shows that women's own choices, skills, and labor force attachment, only account for about one-third of the income difference between the genders. Thus, discrimination must cause the inequality experienced by individual women.

The history of this century reveals a duality: the decline and perpetuation of gender stratification. It is hypothesized that five variables have lead to a decline in gender stratification: economic development, gender differences in labor force participation, advances in medical technology, legal changes, and the rise of feminism. In contrast, two variables are hypothesized to continue gender stratification: the salience of traditional gender norms and institutionalized discrimination. The former is indicated by the high proportion of women not working for pay, voluntary part-time employment by women, economic dependence of women on men, and men's opposition to housework. The latter is indicated by the gender ratio common in competitive groups and occupational segregation (Table 3.6).

NOTES

1. Beeghley (1996).
2. Niemi (1989:225).
3. Zelizer (1994).
4. General Social Survey (2004).
5. United States Bureau of the Census (1975; 2006:881).
6. See Warner (2005).
7. Beeghley (1996), Sayer and Bianchi (2000), Schoen et al. (2002).
8. Amato and Irving (2006), Teachman et al. (2006).
9. Stevenson and Wolfers (2006).
10. Sayer (2006).
11. For a more complete picture of changes in occupational segregation, see Goldin (1990), Weeden (2004).
12. Korupp et al. (2002).
13. Padavic and Reskin (2002), Rose and Hartmann (2004).
14. Jacobs (1990), Baunach (2002), Weeden (2004).
15. King (1992), DiNatale and Boraas (2002).
16. Gallup Poll (1994:187). Since agreement is so high, this question is no longer asked in sample surveys.
17. Bowler (1999).

18. Greenstein and Davis (2006).
19. Weber (1968 [1920]).
20. International Labour Office (2004).
21. Catalyst (2003).
22. United States Bureau of the Census (2006:257).
23. United States Bureau of the Census (2006:401). On the difficulty ordained clergy women face in gaining positions, see Bannerjee (2006).
24. Greven (1991).
25. Niebuhr (1998).
26. United States Bureau of the Census (2003).
27. Starr (1982).
28. Luker (1984), Reagan (1997).
29. Beeghley and Van Ausdale (1990).
30. Acker (1973).
31. See Uggen and Blackstone (2004). The classic work is by MacKinnon (1979).
32. Dellinger and Williams (2005).
33. Uggen and Blackstone (2004), Hill and Silva (2005).
34. Shakespeare (1991).
35. Engelberg and Sontag (1994), Welsh (1999).
36. Wolfe et al. (1998), Welsh (1999), Hill and Silva (2005).
37. Wilson and Thompson (2001).
38. Wordes and Nunez (2002), National Institute of Justice (2006).
39. National Institute of Justice (2006).
40. National Center for Victims of Crime (1992), Dansky (1997), National Institute of Justice (2006).
41. Scully and Marolla (2005). The classic study is by Brownmiller (1975).
42. Dobash et al. (2005).
43. National Institute of Justice (2000). All the data in this paragraph are from this same source. On the psychological and economic consequences, see Herman (1989; 1992), Lloyd (1998).
44. United States Dept. of Health and Human Services (2002). The self-report studies are summarized in Russell and Bolen (2000), who consider the "reasonable guess" in the text as far too low.
45. Herman (1981).
46. Boyer and Fine (1992), Jacobs (1994), Stock (1997), Rodriguez et al. (1997), Molnar et al. (2001), Strathlee et al. (2001), Pillay and Schouben-Hesk (2001).
47. Herman (1992).
48. Bridges (1989), Valian (1998).
49. Kaufman and Uhlenberg (2000), Boyle et al. (2001), Budig and England (2001).
50. United States Bureau of the Census (2003).
51. England (1982). This remains the best critique of human capital theory.
52. Padavic and Reskin (2002), Rose and Hartmann (2004).
53. Blau and Kahn (2000), Rose and Hartmann (2004).
54. Peterson (1996), Smock et al. (1999), Sayer (2006).
55. Valian (1998).
56. Neumark et al. (1996).
57. Mencken and Winfield (2000).
58. Fernandez and Mors (2005:24). See also Fernandez and Sosa (2005).
59. Petersen and Saporta (2004).
60. Goldin and Rouse (2000), Wakin (2005). The percentages reported in the text are from Wakin, as is the concertmaster story.
61. Shaw (1957). *Pygmalion* later became a Broadway musical and then a movie under the title *My Fair Lady*.
62. Easton (1976).
63. Cherlin (1992).
64. Franklin (1961:92).
65. Goldin (1990).
66. O'Neill (1972:267).
67. Rothman (1984).
68. Goldin (1990).
69. Chinhui and Murphy (1997), Goldin (2004).
70. Beeghley (1999).
71. Beeghley (1996).
72. Luker (1984), Reagan (1997).
73. Goldin (1990:190).
74. Goldin (1990:161).
75. Goldin (1990:112).
76. Taken from Padavic and Reskin (2002:ix).
77. Goldin (1990:192).
78. Members of Congress laughing is from Bird (1968). The other examples are cited in Branch (2006:47, 247–48), and Lewis (2006:1).
79. Reed (1978).
80. Luker (1984), Reagan (1997).
81. Herman (1992).
82. Degler (1980).
83. Cott (1987).
84. For example, Friedan (1963).
85. Ferree and Hess (2000).
86. Herman (1992).
87. The following vignette is adapted from McNeil (2004).
88. United States Bureau of Labor Statistics (2004).
89. McNeil (2004).
90. Kanter (1978).
91. Anker et al. (2003).

CHAPTER FOUR

SOCIAL CLASS AND STRATIFICATION: OCCUPATIONAL PRESTIGE AND CLASS IDENTIFICATION

"What do you do for a living?" A simple question usually asked shortly after strangers are introduced, it implies class as a system of domination. As mentioned in Chapter 1, class-based societies feature an inherent tension between the impact of family background and achievement.

But the ideological emphasis tends to be on the latter. An **ideology** is a set of beliefs that support the organization of a society. Ideologies, as Karl Marx emphasized, often buttress the interests of the most powerful classes. Class-based societies are dominated by an ideology that states, loosely, that you are not responsible for where you start out in life (family background) but you are responsible for where you end up (achievement).[1] In the United States, this ideology is called the **American Dream.** Everyone learns to work hard, that their place in society is determined by the outcome of a competitive struggle to succeed—as in a baseball game. And many do succeed.

Such ideologies are relatively new in history. In the past, when most people obtained positions by ascription (recall Figure 1.1), status in the community or society was based on tradition, usually religiously sanctified.[2] Kings claimed to rule by divine right. In such a context, one's job was not important; one's name, however, meant everything.[3] Thus, when William Shakespeare wrote *Romeo and Juliet* in about 1595, it mattered if one answered: "I am a Capulet" or "I am a Montague." The name conveyed all the important information one needed about the respondent's status in Europe at that time. Today, one's name conveys such information only about the very rich and famous. "Hello, my name is Donald Trump. You're fired!"

By contrast, for most people in class-based societies, their occupations have dual functions: They not only provide the focus of people's lives, both psychologically and materially, they also reflect people's level of achievement (regardless of where they started from). The answer to the question, "What do you do?," then, is like a calling card—a short-hand summary of people's share in the distribution of resources, their ability to solve problems, their claim to be someone with standing in the community. "I'm a lawyer." This answer tells you that the respondent has high prestige, possibly high income, and perhaps some degree of power and influence. "I'm an auto mechanic." This answer tells you that the person has a skilled blue-collar job and may (or may not) earn a decent income. This person probably lives in a different neighborhood and goes to a different church than the lawyer. "I work at the hospital." An interesting response. This answer tells you that the respondent is not a physician or nurse, but has some (probably much) lower prestige job. "I am unemployed at the moment." This answer tells you that the respondent not only does not earn an income but, at least for now, has little social standing. As will be described in Chapter 9, losing one's job is a major assault on a person's self-identity and increases the odds of a family ending up poor.

Students ask similar questions and for the same reason: "Where do you go to school?" "What is your major?" It makes a difference when the respondent says, "I go to Harvard" versus "I go to the University of Florida." It makes a difference when the respondent says, "I major in chemical engineering" versus "I major in sociology." The answers locate the respondent in the collegiate class structure, indicating both one's level of achievement (regardless of family origin) and perhaps some personal characteristics. The need to obtain such information early in a relationship reveals an underlying characteristic of modern class-based societies: People's self-identity, income, and power stem from their most important and time consuming activity, their jobs.[4] This fact means that what people do each day and how it is evaluated constitute central issues in the study of stratification. One need not be a great or even a good lawyer or auto mechanic. The issue is how people who perform these tasks are evaluated.

The question, "what do you do for a living?" carries another implication as well, since people often identify with a class based on their jobs. That is, they see themselves as, say, middle class, and this subjective sense of their location in the class structure guides interaction with others. Lawyers, for example, usually want to live in neighborhoods with others like themselves, who are also middle class. They share interests, ranging from who gets elected to whom their children marry. And, as both Weber and Marx observed, they act on these interests. This chapter focuses on people's sense of occupational prestige and class identification as indicators of class location.

OCCUPATIONAL PRESTIGE

Occupational Prestige in the United States

The study of **occupational prestige** assesses the social standing of the jobs people have. It is measured by giving a set of cards to a random sample of people and asking them to rate the occupations listed therein according to their standing in the society. For example, among the jobs listed would be electrician. Respondents are asked to place this card on a ladder with nine boxes on it, signifying a range from the highest to lowest standing, making 90 the highest possible score. The ratings for each job by each member of the sample are averaged to obtain a prestige score and all the occupations in the study are then placed in rank order. In the case of electricians, the score is 51, which is about in the middle of the hierarchy. Listed below are a few of the hundreds of occupations that are ranked, along with their scores.[5]

Physician	86
Lawyer	75
Registered Nurse	66
Public Grade School Teacher	64
Police Officer	61
Business Person	59
Electrician	51
Secretary	46
Automobile Mechanic	39
Real Estate Manager	38
Cosmetologist	36
Assembly Line Worker	35
Garbage Collector	28
Sales Clerk	28
Bartender	25
Janitor	22

As this short list shows, physicians and lawyers are among the highest-rated people in the United States; that is, their jobs carry the most social standing. Most (but not all) of the high prestige occupations are white collar; that is, the jobs do not involve manual labor. On the other hand, garbage collectors and janitors are among the lowest-rated jobs in the United States that is, they carry the least social standing. Most (but not all) of the low prestige occupations are blue collar; that is, the jobs usually require manual labor. Note, however, that the dividing line between white- and blue-collar workers is not precise: Some blue-collar jobs, such as electrician, rank above some white-collar jobs, such as real estate manager.

The Meaning of Occupational Prestige

The meaning of occupational prestige is significant because, along with ownership or control of capital, jobs are the major roles through which people obtain access to resources in class-based societies. In *Occupational Prestige in Comparative Perspective*, Donald Treiman proposes an interpretation of what prestige scores mean.[6] As it turns out, his argument can be challenged; but this fact is useful because it provides a way of showing how sociologists question and evaluate one another's work.

Treiman says that occupational prestige hierarchies result from the functional necessities faced by each society. Thus, he begins by outlining a set of functional necessities that must be met if societies are to survive. Like all such lists, however, Treiman's is arbitrary and slightly different from that of previous scholars, such as Davis and Moore or Parsons.[7] His argument is that the functional necessity to obtain food and other commodities, exchange goods, develop shared values, and coordinate activities produces a division of labor. The task specialization inherent to any division of labor leads, in turn, to differences in power and privilege. These differences cause, finally, variations in prestige as people use the resources available to them. Unfortunately, however, this analysis reveals the flaws characteristic of all functionalist analyses. That is, it poses an illegitimate teleology (that every society has needs) and its presupposition (that the needs of society produce a division of labor) cannot be tested.

In contrast to Treiman, an alternative interpretation explains the meaning of occupational prestige in terms of a simple hypothesis that can be tested: *The greater the skills required, the higher the prestige of an occupation.* Education provides a good (although not the only) indicator of the amount of skill required for a job.[8] As the list above implies, nearly all the jobs with higher prestige also require either a high level of formal education or considerable training.

This latter hypothesis suggests a different way of interpreting prestige rankings: That in modern societies people symbolically reward those whose jobs indicate their skill, ability, and hard work by recognizing their authority. As a result, the hierarchy of occupational prestige carries important practical implications. People defer to their superiors, as indicated by their different occupations, and accept as equals those with roughly similar jobs. This process affects people's lifestyle and life chances, since those considered equals comprise the population with whom one typically entertains, marries, shares meals, and engages in other forms of intimate social interaction. As will be described in Chapter 5, who one knows constitutes a form of social capital that can be used to facilitate occupational status attainment. Finally, people derogate their inferiors by making them acknowledge in some way their own inferiority and by avoiding intimate social relationships with them. For example, the use of titles such as "Sir" and "Doctor" during interaction is often a tacit way for one person to recognize the prestige (and income) of another. Thus, prestige rankings embody society-wide patterns of domination and subordination, of power, in class-based societies.

In everyday life, of course, people do not think about prestige scores. They represent quantitative summaries of people's subjective judgments of others' standing in the society. Consider for a moment some of the differences between white- and blue-collar work. The image, white collar, suggests people who wear suits and ties on the job, and it is a fairly accurate symbol. As mentioned above, white-collar jobs involve nonmanual labor. A college degree or professional training is often required of those types of jobs. People employed in such occupations usually sit behind desks, stay physically clean while working, and often have high income. They are usually paid at a fixed yearly salary rather than by the hour. In addition, a relatively high proportion of white-collar jobs entail supervisory responsibility and many involve the risks of entrepreneurial (or business) activity. White-collar people usually direct blue-collar people and often run or manage businesses. This combination of characteristics, not all of which occurs in every job, means that white-collar workers typically have higher occupational prestige and more political power (the two go together) than do blue-collar employees. In addition, these characteristics, along with income differences, indicate why white-collar people usually have more and better options available when confronted with personal crises, such as a divorce or a drug problem.

In contrast, the image, blue collar, suggests people who wear work clothes on the job and, as before, it is a fairly accurate symbol. As mentioned, blue-collar jobs often involve manual labor of some sort. People employed in these occupations frequently work with their hands, often become physically dirty while doing their jobs, and usually have less income and education than do white-collar workers. Most of the time, their occupations do not involve either supervising others or the risks of entrepreneurship. They are usually paid by the hour rather than at a fixed salary. This combination of characteristics means blue-collar workers generally have lower occupational prestige and less political power than do white-collar employees. They also have fewer choices when faced with personal crises.

Although the characteristics above mean that blue-collar jobs often have lower prestige, they involve a wide range of skill. Service occupations—such as police officer (prestige score 61), cosmetologist (36), and bartender (25)—provide a good example. In a way, people in these jobs are special cases because they often stay clean. Moreover, some blue collar jobs require college education and carry great responsibility. Superior police officers, for example, must be both street-psychologists and crime fighters, a tough combination. The amount and difficulty of physical effort varies a lot in blue-collar occupations: In some automated industries, such as oil and chemical, the jobs are interesting but not physically arduous; in other industries, such as auto and steel, automation means boring and strenuous work. These variations mean that social scientific systems of classification are often imprecise.

Nonetheless, people make discriminatory judgments in everyday life (without hesitation) based on the answer to the question, "What do you do?" Sometimes these appraisals are straightforward: "She and her husband are teachers and, hence, like us." Often, however, they involve subtle distinctions. Consider an auto mechanic by the name of William Meadows (prestige score 39). Although he becomes rather dirty on the job, he charges $50 per hour for repairs. Moreover, he owns the business, so he is also a business person (score 59) with all the risks that entails. Mr. Meadows usually has two or three employees who also work on cars. He pays them (much) less than $40 per hour (with no benefits) and pockets the rest for himself. The business does well and Mr. Meadows makes a good living; his home is on a lake in an exclusive development. He happens to be African American and so are most of his employees.

Racial/Ethnic and Gender Differences in Occupational Prestige

As implied above, prestige rankings affect interaction between members of different racial and ethnic groups, and between men and women as well. "What do you do?" On average, African Americans and a Hispanic Americans will state a lower prestige job than people from other groups. For example, average prestige scores in one study were 51 for Asian Americans (the scale is 1 to 90), 49 for white Americans, 41 for Hispanic Americans, and 41 for African Americans.[9] These scores have practical implications. When customers drop off or pick up their cars at Mr. Meadows's business, his employees sometimes greet them with "Sir" or "Ma'am" but he never does. This tacit recognition of differences (and similarity) in prestige and power also occurs between men and women. This is so even though average prestige scores by gender are rather similar: Men's average is about 49 and women's 47.[10] But this similarity is misleading. First, significant differences exist among women in various racial and ethnic groups. Second, many women are not in the labor force and, hence, do not obtain the social standing (and potential for economic independence) that follows from earning a living. "I am just a housewife." Third, as shown in Chapter 3, the occupational distribution of employed women and men differs; women work at lower-ranking jobs (for example, men as physicians and women as nurses). Thus, people's judgment of others' standing also reflects nonclass patterns of domination and subordination.

The Stability of Occupational Prestige Over Time

The literature on occupational prestige is very long and has resulted in an empirical generalization: *Hierarchies of occupational prestige are similar over time within the same society.* Thus, the correlation in prestige rankings from one study to another are well above .90 in the United States.[11] This finding means that the rankings of, for example, physicians and nurses, have been essentially identical over the last half century or so. This same result occurs in other nations as well. For example, in the Netherlands the correlation between 1953 and 1982 was .97.[12] In Japan the correlation between 1952 and 1964 was .96.[13] When correlations approach 1.0, as these do, it means almost perfect agreement exists.

This same finding also occurs in less economically developed nations, such as Brazil, India, Nigeria, and the Philippines.[14] For example, in Poland the ratings correlated .93 from 1957 to 1975, and .94 from 1975 to 1987.[15] But there are problems with the samples for many of these studies. The data tend to come from urban areas and respondents are often college students. Hence, they do not represent the entire population but, rather, its most Westernized segments. This problem becomes more significant with the next finding.

The Stability of Occupational Prestige Across Societies?

Another empirical generalization is that *hierarchies of occupational prestige are similar across societies.* A question mark was placed after the heading above to indicate that even though this finding is stable, it may not be correct.

Donald Treiman assessed the hypothesis with data for 52 countries from all regions of the world.[16] He reports that "all the available evidence points to the same conclusion: There is high agreement throughout the world regarding the relative prestige of occupations." He finds a correlation of about .80 among all these studies. Although lower than the temporal correlation reported above, this figure still means that substantial agreement exists from one society to another about which jobs carry the most and least standing. According to Treiman, whose book *Occupational Prestige in Comparative Perspective* remains the best, this finding holds even when problems of terminology, weaknesses in the samples used, and disparities in type of society are resolved. But his conclusion is probably too strong. Findings are labeled empirical generalizations because, as in this case, a large number of studies have been done and the results are uniform. Nonetheless, it turns out that criticisms of this finding are serious enough to call it into question.

The first problem is with the samples. Treiman argues that it makes no difference whether the samples are composed of rural or urban people, college students or nonstudents, that the judgments of occupational prestige in Ghana, Mexico, Turkey, and other societies are essentially the same as in the Netherlands or United States. Other researchers, however, recalculated (that is, tried to repeat) Treiman's findings and showed that rural and urban people in various societies disagree regarding the evaluation of occupations.[17] This issue is important because many studies in less industrialized nations use samples of the population that are most influenced by

Western values—college students and urban people, for example. Treiman says that use of such samples does not matter. He may be wrong.

The second problem is the comparability of job titles across societies. Treiman goes to extraordinary lengths to resolve this issue, but probably does not succeed. Many studies, especially of less developed societies, use very few occupational titles (only ten in some cases) that are comparable to those in the United States and other industrialized nations. This situation means the occupational structure itself is not comparable, since the vast majority of the jobs people do are so different.

Surprisingly, then, despite the number of studies that have been done, the only way to resolve the issues mentioned here is with more data. Subsequent attempts at replication should be designed so as to address these two problems. Until that time, a less sweeping empirical generalization is more appropriate: *Hierarchies of occupational prestige are similar across all Western industrialized nations.* This finding reflects the long-term process of **rationalization,** described by Max Weber (recall Chapter 1). The basis for standing in the community in class-based societies is authority based on knowledge, especially scientific knowledge.[18] Thus, it is possible that what Treiman found reflects a worldwide process of convergence: As nations become more economically developed they may come to resemble the West in certain respects, such as their occupational structure, even though their own cultural values remain unique. If true, then similar occupational prestige hierarchies may emerge in these societies over time.

One last note before considering class identification. It is important for you to recognize that Treiman's book constitutes brilliant and enormously difficult work, one representing years of thought. It remains an excellent example of high quality social science. As Max Weber once suggested, over the long run, all good scientific research is superseded as subsequent scholars address the same issues and bring more knowledge to bear on them.[19]

CLASS IDENTIFICATION

Occupational prestige scores are assessments respondents make of others' social standing, based on their jobs. **Class identification** is an assessment respondents make of their own social class. Sociological concern with this topic stems from Karl Marx's work. He was interested in understanding the conditions under which exploited groups would become class conscious and rebel against their oppressors. This concern, however, has proven to be less relevant in Western industrial nations because classes (at all levels) may act cohesively without revolutionary intent. For this reason, studies of class identification simply analyze people's ability to locate themselves in the class structure and assess the impact this fact has on their lifestyles and life chances.

Patterns of Class Identification

Class identification was first measured by Richard Centers in his seminal book, *The Psychology of Social Class.*[20] He asked this question: "If you were to use one of these four names for your social class, which would you say you belonged in: the middle class, lower class, working class, or upper class?" Subsequent research still uses essentially the same question, with results as shown in Table 4.1. The data show that most people have little difficulty placing themselves into a class and that most see themselves as either working or middle class. In 1945, just as World War II ended, Centers found that 51 percent of

TABLE 4.1   Class Identification Among Men and Women, 1945, 1972, 2004

CLASS IDENTIFICATION	1945	1972	2004
	Men		
Lower Class	1%	4%	6%
Working Class	51	45	46
Middle Class	43	47	43
Upper Class	3	3	5
	98%	100%	100%
	Women		
Lower Class	5%		8%
Working Class	45		48
Middle Class	48		42
Upper Class	2		3
	100%		101%

Notes: 2% of the sample did not answer the question in 1945. 101% represents rounding error.

Sources: Centers (1949), General Social Survey (2004).

men identified as working class and 43 percent as middle class. Since then, the percentages have become more even, with about 42 to 48 percent of both genders identifying with each class. Only about 6–8 percent identify with the lower class, probably because people perceive the term as invidious and do not wish to see themselves in this way. Even fewer people identify with the upper class, in part because research samples typically do not include rich persons (who are most likely to view themselves at the top) and, in part, because many of those who are relatively well-off do not see themselves as such.[21]

Patterns of class identification are highly correlated with occupation, such that blue- and white-collar men usually identify with different classes.[22] The result says a great deal about their lifestyle. White male workers in blue-collar occupations with the lowest prestige scores nearly all see themselves as working class. White male workers in white-collar occupations with the highest prestige scores nearly all see themselves as middle class. White male workers in the middle section of the prestige hierarchy divide themselves based on their occupations; thus, given similar prestige scores, those in blue-collar jobs usually see themselves as working class and those in white-collar jobs usually see themselves as middle class. These findings remain after controlling for education and income. The issue of employed women's class identification will be discussed later.

Patterns of class identification vary by race and ethnicity, as shown in Table 4.2. Almost half of Whites see themselves as middle class. The order is reversed, however, among other minority groups. A majority of African Americans see themselves as working class as do nearly half of Hispanic Americans. This pattern correlates with the occupational distribution of these groups shown in Chapter 2.

TABLE 4.2   Class Identification by Racial and Ethnic Group, 2004

	WHITE AMERICAN	AFRICAN AMERICAN	HISPANIC AMERICAN
Lower Class	5%	13%	7%
Working Class	42	58	47
Middle Class	48	26	43
Upper Class	5	3	3
	100%	101%	100%

Note: 101% represents rounding error.

Source: General Social Survey (2004).

These data imply the existence of discrete and identifiable classes in the United States, not just as statistical constructs but as subjectively relevant categories in people's minds. It appears that working-class and middle-class labels reflect a division between those who do manual and nonmanual labor; they are not merely prestige judgments.[23] Thus, people see their jobs as an indicator of their location in the class structure: Those with similar occupational characteristics generally see themselves as belonging to the same class. This argument is consonant with studies of social mobility to be presented in Chapter 5, where it will be shown that the division between blue- and white-collar work constitutes a semipermeable barrier to upward and downward mobility.

The Meaning of Class Identification

In his analysis of the stratification structure in modern societies, Max Weber argued that people who share common lifestyles and values tend to discriminate against others who are different. He said that this process occurs naturally, without classes being formally organized, as people enjoy each others' hospitality and friendship, marry, select houses and neighborhoods in which to live, and practice social conventions with others who are like themselves. Such differences, correlated with class, express people's lifestyles and values. And they affect life chances.

Weber, in short, was right. When people identify with a class, they are saying something, in a symbolic way, about their experiences and their lifestyle preferences: They are identifying those with whom they prefer to interact in intimate ways, and they are commenting upon their taste in entertainment and other leisure-time activities. This fact is clearly shown in the best analysis since that by Centers, Jackman and Jackman's, *Class Awareness in the United States.*[24] In this study, nearly 80 percent of the respondents report they feel strongly about their class identification, which suggests it is important to them.

Just how important can be seen when the notion of class identification is linked to other arenas of life. Thus, the Jackmans found that people expressed "a marked tendency toward preference for [social] contact with one's own class," especially with regard to friendship choice, neighborhood preference, and marriage partners. For example, more than half of those people who identify themselves as working class say they prefer living in working-class neighborhoods and a similar proportion of those who identify as middle class assert a desire to live in middle-class neighborhoods.

These preferences are realized in practice, since class, racial, and ethnic segregation characterizes most U.S. cities.[25] Such segregation means that informal interaction, friendship ties, and other forms of relatively intimate social relationships are usually class based. As described in Chapters 2 and 3, this fact has important implications for life chances, because most people find jobs via word-of-mouth.

With regard to marriage, Jackman and Jackman reported that people who identify themselves as poor or working class usually prefer that their children "marry up." That is, they want their children to marry someone from a higher class. This preference reflects the fact that marriage can be a vehicle for upward mobility in terms of standing in the community. In contrast, people who see themselves as middle and upper class generally want their children to marry someone from the same class. As it turns out, most spouses come from similar class backgrounds. Hence, this most intimate form of interaction is typically class based. In sum, the evidence suggests that patterns of class identification reflect a fundamental division in U.S. society. People from different classes have different lifestyles and these variations affect life chances.

A Note on Employed Married Women

It was observed earlier that all good scientific research is superseded as subsequent scholars address an issue. The problem of class identification among employed married women illustrates this process. Historically, women who were housewives assumed the class of their husbands. This process is called "status borrowing." It made sense in a context where most women had no other source of standing in the community. But the situation is not as clear-cut today when so many married women have entered the labor force. Employed married women have a source of prestige and income independently of their husbands. Hence, researchers have become interested in this issue and found support for two different hypotheses.

The first is the *Status-Borrowing Hypothesis: Employed married women ignore their own jobs and education, and consider only their husbands' characteristics in deciding with which class to identify.* This argument implies, for example, that a secretary or an elementary school teacher married to an electrician would see herself as working class, since her husband's job involves manual labor. The logic behind the hypothesis lies in traditional gender norms. From this point of view, women's primary adult roles should revolve around the household: bearing children, rearing them, and caring for their husbands. Hence, their major interest should be in the home—even if they are employed. By extrapolation, then, such women should see their position in the community as resulting from their husband's job. Solid, technically sound research supports this hypothesis.[26]

The second argument is called the *Status-Sharing Hypothesis: Employed married women take both their own and their husbands' characteristics into account in deciding with which class to identify.* This argument implies rather different patterns of class identification among employed married women. For example, on the one hand, a secretary married to an electrician might see herself as working class because, even though she has a white-collar job and has many of the fringe benefits connected to such occupations, it is nonetheless the lowest prestige white-collar work. On the other hand, the same person might emphasize the fact that her job is white collar regardless of its relatively low income, assess her husband's job as a highly skilled and relatively prestigious occupation, and identify herself as middle class. (Recall that the occupational prestige score for electricians is higher than that of many white-collar jobs.) In each case, respondents evaluate both spouses' position in the community when determining their overall social standing. Hence, status sharing occurs. The logic behind the *status-sharing hypothesis* lies in egalitarian gender norms. From this point of view, women and men should be equal; that is, equally obligated to support the family, rear children, and care for one another. By extrapolation, then, employed married women should see their position in the community as resulting from a combination of their own and their husband's characteristics. Again, technically sound evidence supports this hypothesis.[27]

Obviously, both the hypotheses and the empirical findings cited above flatly contradict each other. Both cannot be right. Or can they?

Beeghley and Cochran examined this issue and show that the research results cited above may be correct, even though the findings are contradictory.[28] Rather, the inability to confirm one or the other hypothesis may reflect the historical process of changing gender norms. Thus, over the past few years, U.S. society has been moving, in fits and starts, from an emphasis on traditional gender norms to an acceptance of egalitarian gender norms. Such changes do not come easily or fast because they involve drastic alterations in the way people view themselves, the world they live in, and the way they organize their lives. Previous research may simply reveal this confusion: At one time respondents display a status-borrowing pattern and at another a status-sharing orientation.

Yet there must be some method of sorting these differences out, and Beeghley and Cochran suggested that married women's orientation to gender norms might provide a way. They argue that such normative orientations set the context in which married women adopt either a status-borrowing or a status-sharing stance. Hence, they tested the following hypotheses: (1) *Employed married women who believe in traditional gender norms will consider only their husbands' characteristics in deciding with which class to identify.* And: (2) *Employed married women who believe in egalitarian gender norms will take both their own and their husbands' characteristics into account in deciding with which class to identify.*

In testing these hypotheses, Beeghley and Cochran used married women's support for the Equal Rights Amendment (ERA) and attitudes toward married women working outside the home as indicators of gender norms. They found that those supporting the ERA and favoring women's employment use a status-sharing approach in identifying with a class. In contrast, those opposing the ERA and opposing married women's employment, even though they have a job themselves, use a status-borrowing approach in identifying with a class. Beeghley and Cochran conclude by predicting that as an increasing proportion of women work outside the home and more people of both genders accept egalitarian gender norms, then the status-sharing hypothesis will be supported by an increasing proportion of employed married women.

One last observation. It is important for you to recognize that neither the findings reported by Beeghley and Cochran nor their prediction ends the matter. Recent data, for example, show that the class identification of employed wives continues to be in flux.[29] Gender norms remain in flux and further research on this and related topics will show the direction in which they move. It is in this sense that Max Weber described the social sciences as blessed with eternal youth.

"What do you do for a living?" It is a question that has become meaningful only in the last 200 years or so. With industrialization, the rise of capitalism, and other historical changes, however, the criterion by which people evaluate each other has changed. One's name remains important, of course, but what people do and the class with which they identify provide an initial guide to their place in the community and the respect they should be given.

SUMMARY

This chapter describes the implications people's jobs have for their class location and suggests the meaning such views have for their lifestyle. Studies of occupational prestige assess the social standing of occupations. The basis for prestige assignments appears to be the level of authority required in various jobs. Prestige hierarchies indicate patterns of domination and subordination characteristic of the class structure. These hierarchies vary by race/ethnicity and by gender. There are two main empirical generalizations: The hierarchy of occupational prestige is stable over time within and across societies. The second, however, probably needs to be modified. It is more likely that hierarchies of occupational prestige are similar in all Western industrial nations.

Class identification assesses the extent to which people see themselves as belonging to different classes and the implications this fact has for their lifestyles. In the United States, people find it easy to identify with a class, mainly the working and middle classes (see Table 4.1). Class identification is highly correlated with occupation and says a great deal about people's lifestyle: for example, who they live near, their friends, and potential marriage partners. Patterns of class identification among employed married women are unclear, mainly because of changing gender norms. When this factor is controlled for, however, the finding becomes intelligible. It appears that employed married women who accept egalitarian gender norms use a status-sharing orientation, while those who accept traditional gender norms use a status-borrowing orientation in selecting a class with which to identify.

NOTES

1. I am paraphrasing a line from McNamee & Miller (2004:3).
2. Weber (1968 [1920]:9297–36).
3. Shakespeare (1989).
4. Glick (1995).
5. Nakao and Treas (1994), General Social Survey (2004).
6. Treiman (1977:1–25).
7. Davis and Moore (1945), Parsons (1951).
8. MacKinnon and Langford (1994), Zhou (2005).
9. Xu and Leffler (1992).
10. Xu and Leffler (1992).
11. Nakao and Treas (1994).
12. Sixma and Ultee (1984).
13. Treiman (1977).
14. Treiman (1977).
15. Sawinski and Domanski (1991).
16. Treiman (1977:96).
17. Treiman (1977).
18. Zhou (2005).
19. Weber (1949 [1904]).
20. Centers (1949:233).
21. Jackman and Jackman (1983).
22. Vanneman and Pampel (1977).
23. Vanneman and Pampel (1977:435).
24. Centers (1949), Jackman and Jackman (1983:21 and 195).
25. Massey (2001).
26. Felson and Knoke (1974), Jackman and Jackman (1983).
27. Ritter and Hargens (1975), Van Velsor and Beeghley (1979).
28. Beeghley and Cochran (1988). See also Zipp and Plutzer (2000).
29. Yamaguchi and Wang (2002), Edlund (2003).

CHAPTER FIVE

SOCIAL CLASS AND STRATIFICATION: MOBILITY AND STATUS ATTAINMENT

William H. Gates II was a prominent lawyer in Seattle in the 1950s. As such he would probably have seen himself as middle class. His son, William H. Gates III, was born on October 28, 1955. As he grew up in this class of origin, young Bill developed an abiding, indeed compulsive interest in computer programming. Although his father helped him get into Harvard, Bill dropped out to pursue his business interests. He had the insight to realize that computer technology (like oil a century earlier) was about to become a valuable commodity. Eventually, he founded the Microsoft Corporation, bought DOS, and in 1981 persuaded IBM to use a revised version of it as the operating system for its line of personal computers. When Microsoft became a publicly traded stock corporation in 1986, its Chief Executive Officer, Bill Gates, became an instant multimillionaire and eventually a multibillionaire.[1] The third Mr. Gates' experience implies an interesting question: Can you become a billionaire?

More prosaically, how much opportunity is there—really? What factors determine people's occupational location and, hence, their income, prestige, and ultimately their life chances? This is, of course, another way of presenting the basic question posed in Chapter 1: Who gets what and why? In the past, most societies were relatively rigid and nearly everyone was assigned positions at birth—by ascription. In contrast, modern class-based societies display a built-in tension between ascription

113

and achievement. Most people earn a livelihood from their jobs, which they obtain based on a combination of family background, hard work, and ability—with some luck thrown in. Compared to the past, then, modern societies are relatively fluid, with more opportunity to succeed.

Sociologists assess the degree of opportunity in a society in two ways: by examining mobility rates and the status attainment of individuals. **Mobility** refers to changes in the occupational distribution of people, either intra- or intergenerationally. **Intragenerational mobility** occurs during people's own careers, beginning from their first main job after the end of formal education. Thus, for students "first main job" is not at the fast food place when you were sixteen or at the restaurant while in college. For the high school dropout, however, that job at the fast food place may be the starting point. **Intergenerational mobility** compares parents' occupations to children's eventual main job. In both cases, the question being asked is this: How many people move and how far? The answer, of course, must be in terms of rates of movement and the explanation must be structural. **Status attainment** refers to the study of how individuals enter specific occupations. The question here is this: What combination of ascribed and achieved factors leads individuals into one occupation rather than another and why? The answer, of course, must be social psychological—either directly or indirectly.

As a brief methodological note, there are several possible indicators of mobility and status attainment. Sociologists generally use occupation as the indicator because of its centrality to most people's lives.[2] "What do you do for a living?" As the data on occupational prestige and class identification suggest (recall Chapter 4), most people see themselves and others in light of the answer to this question. Economists usually focus on income mobility, both intra- and intergenerationally. Each indicator has advantages and disadvantages. Occupations reveal status differences. A bartender and a public school teacher, for example, who each earn $40,000 per year, have different status in the community. The use of occupation as an indicator also has some practical advantages: Compared to income, it is more easily measured and assessed across generations. There are two drawbacks to looking at people's occupation. First, it omits the very rich, whose status in the community is often not dependent on their jobs. Thus, most analyses of mobility and status attainment say nothing about how ownership of capital (such as stock in the Microsoft Corporation) leads to incredible wealth and power. Second, income provides an important resource affecting both life chances and lifestyles. So, as will be shown later, it is sometimes useful to look at both occupational and income mobility.

SOCIAL MOBILITY

Social Mobility in the United States

It is probable that Emily Perrin produced the first quantitative study of mobility in 1904. She compared the occupations of fathers and sons in order "to determine how far ancestral bent and how far environmental conditions influence a man in his choice of occupation in life."[3] Put differently, she wanted to understand how family background and achievement affect a person's occupation. As mentioned earlier, subsequent scholars have divided Perrin's questions in two: the study of mobility rates and status attainment by individuals.

The best early analysis of mobility was Pitirim Sorokin's, *Social Mobility*, originally published in 1927.[4] Sorokin, like all subsequent observers, recognized that a job is most people's main source of income and prestige in modern societies. Thus, he focused on how fathers' occupations were linked with their sons' occupations and thereby charted the rate of mobility across generations. The emphasis on the nexus between fathers and sons made sense at the time because few women were employed and most people believed they should remain at home (recall Chapter 3). Sorokin analyzed the data then available, including Perrin's, and concluded as follows: First, much intergenerational occupational inheritance occurs. For example, he noted that "the hereditary transmission of occupation still exists. . . . The fathers' occupation is still entered by the children in a greater proportion than any other." Second, a lot of intergenerational mobility takes place such that a significant proportion of children moves into different (usually higher prestige) occupations than their fathers. This fact, he noted, makes modern societies unique compared to the past because they display more opportunity. Third, intergenerational mobility is usually short distance. In his words, "The closer the affinity between occupations, the more intensive among them is mutual interchange of their members." Although Sorokin's data were not very good, his findings anticipate later research.

Such research has developed reasonably accurate data for the late nineteenth and twentieth centuries. The result is three major findings about mobility rates among men, with women considered later.

First, there is a great deal of occupational inheritance in the United States. The dominant intergenerational pattern is for fathers in white-collar occupations to have sons who also work in white-collar occupations, while fathers in blue-collar jobs generally have sons who also work in blue-collar jobs. The extent of occupational inheritance means that the class structure is reproduced from one generation to another as people with a certain level of access to resources pass them on to their children. Unlike Sorokin, the term "inheritance" does not mean that sons take the same job as their fathers or even enter the same occupational category. Rather, they end up in the same social class: as white-collar or blue-collar workers, respectively. Panel A of Table 5.1 illustrates this finding. It shows, for example, that even during the nineteenth century, most sons of professional workers ended up in the white-collar workforce. Similarly, most sons of blue-collar workers and farmers followed in their fathers' footsteps. Thus, most sons (and daughters, see below) inherit the class of their parents. This finding shows that ascription was important in the nineteenth century and remains important today. In terms of the baseball metaphor used in Chapter 1, if a man occupied first base, his son is likely to as well.

The sons of farmers, however, constitute an anomaly. Although they displayed high levels of occupational inheritance during the nineteenth century, the historical pattern (explained in more detail in a few moments) has been for sons to move into blue-collar occupations (usually in cities) where some farm-related skills could be used. This trend means that there are now two occupational classes in the United States: the middle class composed of white-collar workers and the working class composed of blue-collar workers, with farm workers constituting a recessive class. The boundary between these two classes forms a semipermeable barrier to social mobility.

The usual interpretation of this barrier is that the need for the prestige of being "white collar" together with the lack of saleable manual skills prevents a great deal of downward mobility among the children of white-collar workers. Similarly, much

TABLE 5.1   Illustrations of Occupational Mobility Among Men, United States

PANEL A: INTERGENERATIONAL OCCUPATIONAL INHERITANCE

Year	Percent	Result
1880–1900	56%	of the Sons of Professionals became White-Collar Workers
"	78%	of the Sons of Service/Laborers became Blue-Collar Workers
"	60%	of the Sons of Farmers became Farmers
1963	68%	of the Sons of Salaried Professionals became White-Collar Workers
"	72%	of the Sons of Laborers became Blue-Collar Workers
1973	68%	of the Sons of Salaried Professionals became White-Collar Workers
"	71%	of the Sons of Laborers became Blue-Collar Workers
1982–1985	72%	of the Sons of Salaried Professionals became White-Collar Workers
"	60%	of the Sons of Laborers became Blue-Collar Workers

PANEL B: INTERGENERATIONAL OCCUPATIONAL MOBILITY

Year	Percent	Result
1880–1900	26%	of the Sons of Crafts Workers became White-Collar Workers
1963	41%	of the Sons of Crafts Workers became White-Collar Workers
1973	45%	of the Sons of Crafts Workers became White-Collar Workers
1982–1985	45%	of the Sons of Crafts Workers became White-Collar Workers

PANEL C: LONG-DISTANCE INTERGENERATIONAL OCCUPATIONAL MOBILITY

Year	Percent	Result
1880–1900	3%	of the Sons of Farmers became Professional Workers
1963	<1%	of the Sons of Farmers became Professional Workers
1973	<1%	of the Sons of Farmers became Professional Workers
1982–1985	0%	of the Sons of Farmers became Professional Workers

Note: Occupational categories vary from one study to another.

Sources: Guest, Landale, & McCann (1989:359); Blau & Duncan (1967:28); Featherman and Hauser (1978:535); Hout (1988:1396).

upward mobility into white-collar jobs is prevented by lack of necessary skills and, often, lack of respect for those sorts of jobs. Many blue-collar people do not believe that "pencil pushers" really work. After all, they do not sweat or get dirty or become physically tired from their jobs. The result is the reproduction of the class structure.

Second, social mobility is widespread in the United States. This empirical generalization means that, despite the first finding reported above, the occupational structure in modern societies is relatively fluid. A great deal of opportunity exists compared to the past. Panel B of Table 5.1 provides illustrations. Craft occupations are used in the table because they comprise the highest prestige blue-collar jobs (recall Chapter 4) and constitute a sort of jumping off place for upward mobility. Thus, about 26 percent of the sons of craft workers became white-collar workers during the years 1880 to 1900. This rate increased significantly during this century. By 1963, it had risen to about

41 percent and by 1973 to about 45 percent. Beginning in the 1890s (and probably earlier), each generation of men has been upwardly mobile compared to their fathers.[5] All this movement suggests is that there has been lots of opportunity in the United States over the last two centuries and that the importance of achievement has increased.

Although historical data are unsystematic, intergenerational inheritance coupled with relatively high rates of upward mobility describe the occupational structure in the United States since colonial times. The ability of white immigrants to improve their economic and social positions by acquiring land, entering a trade, or starting a business was one of the most important attractions of the colonies. After winning independence, it has been argued that America became the "first new nation," meaning one organized by different principles compared to the past.[6] In terms of the baseball metaphor, some people can now advance around the bases regardless of where they started from. As described in Chapter 1, widespread mobility is one of the markers of modernity.

Third, short distance movements exceed long distance ones. In their now classic work, *The American Occupational Structure*, Peter Blau and O.D. Duncan mimic Sorokin's words: "The closer two occupations are to one another in the status hierarchy, the greater is the flow of manpower between them."[7] Panel C of Table 5.1 illustrates the pattern by showing how few people move long distance. Thus, from 1880 to 1900 only 3 percent of the sons of farmers moved to the top of the prestige ladder by becoming professional workers. More recently, such mobility has occurred less than 1 percent of the time. Do not be mislead by the 0 percent for 1982 to 1985; it reflects the small sample size. A little (very little) long-distance mobility takes place.

Although these three findings are stable and evidence suggests that the pattern remains the same today, some recent data indicate that downward mobility is increasing.[8] More data are needed. It is now time for a new large-scale analysis of the American occupational structure—one that includes women and minority groups in addition to African Americans.

Throughout most of the twentieth century, studies of mobility focused on men. Data from small-scale studies of women did not become available until the 1980s and they show a similar pattern.[9] First, a great deal of occupational inheritance takes place. For example, 95 percent of the daughters of salaried professional fathers become white-collar workers, usually above the level of clerks. Second, much mobility occurs. For example, 74 percent of the daughters of craft worker fathers became white-collar workers. This figure falls to 37 percent, however, if administrative support workers are excluded. As described in Chapter 3, when women work for pay they are often guided into "support jobs," such as clerks; that is, they take jobs that involve assisting men. Finally, most movement is short distance. For example, less than 1 percent of daughters of farmers become professional workers. As shown in Chapter 3, however, these similarities understate the differences in mobility rates of men and women over time.[10] "Gender-based occupational discrimination" (another way of talking about the importance of ascription) has always inhibited daughters' occupational mobility and continues to do so.

Mobility data on minority groups are limited to African Americans and the historical pattern is much different than for Whites. As recently as 1962, only 5 percent of African American men had professional or managerial jobs.[11] Unlike Whites, however, little occupational inheritance occurred for men in these categories. Rather, the sons of African-American professionals usually displayed downward mobility: 63 percent of them had service, operative, and laborer jobs. In fact, the vast majority of

African-American men, 68 percent, were employed in these three occupational categories as recently as 1962. And nearly all of them displayed great occupational inheritance from one generation to another. Thus, unlike Whites, who often advanced intergenerationally over the centuries, the debilitating effects of discrimination kept most African-American men confined to menial jobs regardless of their parents' status. The year in which these data were collected is significant, as it was just prior to passage of the Civil Rights Act of 1964 and other measures designed to guarantee civil rights. This fact suggests that between the end of the Civil War and the mid-1960s, little opportunity existed for African Americans, regardless of their ability or hard work. As argued in Chapter 2, the Civil War freed African Americans in name only.

Since the 1960s, however, the situation has changed considerably. The class structure among African Americans elongated, as it also has, it is reasonable to suspect, among Hispanics and other minorities. Table 5.2 suggests how much increased mobility has occurred. Today, more than half of all African Americans are white collar and 27 percent are in either professional or managerial jobs (18 percent plus 9 percent in the table). Moreover, although this conclusion is tentative, it appears that the pattern of mobility is beginning to resemble that of Whites: occupational inheritance (in particular, a greater rate of inheritance at the upper occupational levels) and an increasingly high rate of upward mobility compared to the past.[12] As mentioned, these changes reflect the impact of civil rights and affirmative action. When people became free and found some opportunity, they began displaying upward mobility. The word "tentative" in the conclusion above is important, however, because recent data suggest that African Americans have displayed disproportionate intragenerational downward mobility over the last few years.[13]

TABLE 5.2   Occupational Distribution by Racial and Ethnic Group, 2005

	WHITE AMERICAN	AFRICAN AMERICAN	HISPANIC AMERICAN	ASIAN AMERICAN
Professionals	21%	18%	11%	31%
Management	15	9	7	17
Sales	12	10	10	10
Office & Admin. Support	13	17	12	12
Total White-Collar	61%	54%	39%	71%
Production & Transportation	12	16	18	10
Construction & Extraction	7	4	14	2
Installation & Maintenance	4	2	3	2
Service	15	24	23	16
Total Blue-Collar	38%	46%	58%	30%
Farmers, Foresters, Fishers	1%	0%	2%	0%
Total	100%	100%	100%	100%

Note: 0% means less than 1/2 of 1%.

Source: United States Bureau of Labor Statistics (2006:191).

Table 5.2 also shows the occupational distribution of Hispanic and Asian Americans. Although these data are relatively crude, since mobility rates probably vary by ethnicity (for example, Cuban Americans may display higher rates of mobility than Mexican Americans), they are the best to be had at the moment. With that caveat, the table reveals that a smaller proportion of Hispanic Americans, 39 percent, are white collar compared to both African Americans and Whites (non-Hispanics). It is probable, however, that the figures in the top half of the distribution represent all-time highs for Hispanics. This is also probably true for Asian Americans, who exhibit the highest rate of white-collar workers among all groups, 71 percent. This high proportion mainly reflects the 31 percent of Asian Americans in professional jobs, which is in turn a reflection of high levels of educational attainment. As described in Chapter 2, racial and ethnic equality has increased in recent years. These data suggest one dimension of this process.

Social Mobility in Cross-National Perspective

Cross-national studies show that while considerable variation occurs among nations, patterns of occupational mobility are rather similar: (1) a high level of occupational inheritance, (2) a significant amount of mobility, and (3) short distance mobility.

Table 5.3 uses data from the United Kingdom to illustrate these findings. Although the occupational categories used in this table differ somewhat from those used in Table 5.1 as do the specific occupations subsumed in these categories, the findings are essentially the same. For example, with regard to inheritance of social class (shown in Panel A), cumulative data over the twentieth century in the United Kingdom show that 74 percent of the sons of professionals became white-collar workers, while 61 percent of the sons of skilled blue-collar workers became blue-collar workers. Panel B uses the sons of skilled blue-collar workers to illustrate the extent of mobility: 31 percent became white-collar workers during the twentieth century. Finally, long distance intergenerational mobility is rare, as illustrated in Panel C. In the United Kingdom, "increasing room at the top has meant that there could simultaneously be improved chances of people from privileged backgrounds remaining in the salariat [professional and managerial jobs] and also improved chances of people from less privileged backgrounds gaining access to the salariat."[14] As will be seen later this same conclusion applies to mobility in all economically developed nations.

But considerable variation occurs, as can be illustrated by intragenerational mobility.[15] You should recall that the issue here is how many people are occupationally mobile over the course of their careers. Presented below are the chances of men who begin their careers as skilled blue-collar workers ending up as professionals and managers:

Sweden	22%
United States	20%
England	16%
France	15%
Ireland	8%

These data lead to two conclusions. First, with regard to the United States, the intragenerational finding presented here parallels the intergenerational finding presented earlier: Most people are occupationally stable while a significant (although smaller)

TABLE 5.3   Illustrations of Occupational Mobility Among Men, United Kingdom, Cumulative Data for the Twentieth Century

PANEL A: INTERGENERATIONAL OCCUPATIONAL INHERITANCE

Percent	Result
74%	of the Sons of Professionals and Managers became White-Collar Workers
61%	of the Sons of Skilled Blue-Collar Workers became Blue-Collar Workers

PANEL B: INTERGENERATIONAL OCCUPATIONAL MOBILITY

Percent	Result
31%	of the Sons of Skilled Blue-Collar Workers became White-Collar Workers

PANEL C: LONG-DISTANCE INTERGENERATIONAL MOBILITY

Percent	Result
9%	of the Sons of Unskilled Blue-Collar Workers became Professional Workers

Note: Occupational categories differ from those in the U.S. Data are from British Election Surveys, 1964–97, which include those who entered the labor market over the course of the twentieth century.

Source: Heath and Payne (2000:262).

proportion is mobile. Second, although U.S. mobility rates are not unique, there is considerable cross-national variation. Thus, in the United States and Sweden the odds of a man who begins his career as an electrician ending up as an engineer are about one in five. In England and France, however, they are about one in six, and in Ireland one in ten. So these three nations display less intragenerational mobility than does the United States.

Social structures in modern societies display three tendencies, all of which are illustrated by the study of mobility. First, they are stable over time. This is why so much occupational inheritance occurs and movement is short distance. Comprising networks of relationships and values that tie people together, social structures set the range of opportunities and limitations that are available. So people grow up within a context that provides specific skills and experiences: schools, role models, and the like. Hence, the class structure is reproduced as the children of farmers learn to appreciate the land, children of blue-collar families learn how to work with their hands, and children of white-collar families learn how to succeed in school. The phrasing here is stereotypical, of course, simply to point out that there is a great deal of intergenerational occupational inheritance. Second, social structures in modern societies change over time, and deliberately so in light of political decisions and technological change. This is why so much mobility occurs. For example, productivity increased when people invented machines to take advantage of fossil fuels. Not only was more food produced, but problems of expertise and coordination arose that lead to the creation of more white-collar jobs. The plausible range of opportunities expanded. Hence, mobility became widespread as people took advantage of new choices. Third, social structures vary internationally. This is why differences in mobility occur from one nation to another. The next section offers an explanation for these tendencies.

SOCIAL STRUCTURE AND MOBILITY

Mobility refers to changes in the occupational (or income) distribution of people. The issue is how many people move and how far. As Gerhard Lenski showed, mobility rates were minimal for nearly all of human history because low productivity limited opportunity.[16] Most people's positions in society were determined by ascription (recall Figure 1.1). The importance of birth began declining, however, in the eighteenth and nineteenth centuries as the emphasis on achievement increased. The key finding in studies of mobility reported above is the second one: Social mobility is now widespread, not only in the United States but in all economically developed nations. A relatively high rate of mobility (compared to the past) characterizes all modern, class-based societies. In trying to explain this phenomenon, sociologists distinguish between two types: **Structural mobility** refers to people's upward rate of movement from their class of origin due to historical changes in the occupational structure. The idea, here, is that economic development and other elements of modernization stimulated upward mobility and, hence, improvements in people's life chances and lifestyles. These changes in the social structure provide one indicator of how much opportunity exists. **Circulation mobility** refers to the rate of upward and downward movement between class of origin and class of destination that occurs independently of historical changes in the occupational structure. The idea, here, is that while most people end up more or less where they started, some move up and some move down (forming a "circle"). All this movement provides another indicator of how much opportunity exists.

Structural Mobility

Common sense, American style, suggests that individuals are upwardly mobile because they work hard and have ability; in so doing, they live by dominant cultural values. And data reviewed earlier (see Figure 5.1) show that this sequence occurs relatively often. But a focus on individual behavior does not explain why the rate of mobility increased over the last two centuries and remains relatively high today. In reality, the social structure changed such that a great deal of opportunity became available for certain kinds of people, as described by the following hypothesis. *The rate of mobility in the United States reflects the impact of: (1) economic development, (2) class differences in fertility rates, (3) immigration rates, and (4) affirmative action for white males.*

Economic Development.   In the past, the occupational structure did not display much variation. Virtually the entire population farmed, generation after generation. It was not the charming life of pastoral legend. Hamlin Garland's memoir of growing up on a farm in the Midwest, *A Son of the Middle Border*, published in 1917, provides an unsentimental portrait that dispels the myth of yeomen (and women) living idyllically. Farming was a monotonous and brutal life in which "the poor and the weary predominate."[17] Working the land meant being at the mercy of the seasons and the elements, which could destroy crops, and of commodities markets in far away places (like Chicago or New Orleans), that set the prices crops could bring. For most people, not only at the beginning of the twentieth century but throughout the great span of human history, farm life consisted of backbreaking labor, worry, and—above all—poverty.

But a great transformation occurred. Industrialization meant that new forms of energy—such as steam, fossil fuels, and (later) nuclear energy—allowed the substitution of machines for human and animal muscle power. This fundamental change was based, of course, on scientific advances. They combined with capitalism, democracy, notions of individual dignity, and the other dynamic factors described in Chapter 1, and productivity increased radically. Such changes mean that machines increasingly performed many tasks that animals and people used to do, a process that continues today.

As economic development took off in the nineteenth century, generating opportunities for a better life, people left the farm, moved to cities, and took newly available jobs. As recently as 1800, for example, 74 percent of the employed labor force was engaged in farming occupations, an all-time low at that time.[18] And this figure did not include slaves, women, children, and others who worked the land without pay. In any case, it fell steadily. As shown in Table 5.4 (look across the bottom row): By 1900, farmers constituted only 38 percent of the workforce; by 1950, 12 percent; and in 2005, less than 1 percent. As readers of this book, how many of you have or know anyone who has ever milked a cow, plowed a field, looked for rain to nourish a parched field, or cursed the hail for beating down crops or grasshoppers for eating them.[19]

TABLE 5.4   Occupational Distribution 1900, 1950, and 2005

	1900	1950		2005
White-Collar			*White-Collar*	
Professionals	4%	9%	Professionals	15%
Managers	6	9	Management	20
Sales	5	7	Sales	12
Clerical	3	12	Office & Admin. Support	14
	18%	37%		61%
Blue-Collar			*Blue-Collar*	
Crafts	11%	14%	Production & Transportation	13%
Operators	13	20	Construction & Extraction	6
Laborers	12	7	Installation & Maintenance	4
Service	9	10	Service	16
	45%	51%		39%
Farmers	38%	12%	Farmers, Foresters, Fishers	1%
Total	101%	100%	Total	101%

Note: Percentages do not add to 100 because of rounding. As implied by the name changes, the occupational categories are not exactly comparable between 1950 and 2005.

Sources: United States Bureau of the Census (1975:139), United Status Bureau of Labor Statistics (2006:191).

Today, farming is rather remote to most people. If one had to select the single best indicator of the impact of economic development on social life, it might be the declining proportion of people in farming occupations.

This movement off the farm created the modern class structure—first the working class and then the middle class—signifying increased opportunities for everyone. Almost everyone's life chances and lifestyles improve in class-based societies.

Table 5.4 provides a simple summary of the rise and fall of the working class over the last two centuries (see Chapter 9). It shows that jobs requiring people to work with their hands constituted the largest class by 1900, 45 percent, and became the majority in 1950, 51 percent. That figure, however, has dropped off since then to 39 percent in 2005. Even though the names of the categories have changed as have many of the specific occupations (fewer barrel makers and more cable installers) the proportion of skilled blue-collar occupations displays a curving pattern in the form of an upside-down bowl over the twentieth century. The table shows, however, that service workers constitute an exception. Over the last 30 to 40 years, the proportion of service workers has risen dramatically. Importantly, these jobs often pay less than other working-class trades, such as construction work, especially in nonunion settings. As a result, the life chances and lifestyles of working-class people have suffered in comparison to the middle class in recent years. Part of the reason for this change lies in economic development, especially globalization, and part lies in old-fashioned class conflict: As will be suggested in a few moments, middle-class people are often better able to protect their occupational sinecures than working-class people.

Table 5.4 also provides a simple summary of the rise of occupations "in the middle" between the working class and the rich (see Chapter 8). Looking again across the rows, by 1900 a small middle class had formed, indicated by 18 percent of the workforce in white-collar jobs. This figure rose steadily, however, to about 61 percent in 2005. Again, although the category names in the white-collar workforce have changed over time and the occupations subsumed under them have changed as well (there are fewer corset makers today and many more engineers), the pattern is evident: Economic development has meant more professionals, more managers, more sales persons, and more office workers.[20] In the past, who needed accountants, computer programmers, corporate financial officers, and so many more? For most of you reading this book, the jobs your parents have simply did not exist two centuries ago.

The existence of these classes means that as economic development occurred vacant job slots were created in the top categories, which served as a "pull" factor stimulating upward mobility. Thus, while no individual was forced to be upwardly mobile, these jobs came into existence; they were attractive in terms of pay, perquisites (or privileges), and other characteristics (such as the ability to remain physically clean and avoid manual labor); and many individuals strove to attain them. It is important to understand, however, that the motives or abilities or any personal characteristic of those who filled them cannot explain the existence of these jobs. They reflect changes "in the nature of the society itself" that produced a high rate of mobility over time.[21] People's opportunities expanded. If that had not happened, most people would still be farmers today and the rate of social mobility over the last two centuries would have been nil. Hard work would not have produced improvement in life chances, no matter how much ability people possessed. In sum, "changes in the occupational structure are the [primary] source of systematic variation in rates of intergenerational occupational mobility."[22]

Class Differences in Fertility Rates.   The term **fertility rate** refers to the average number of children each woman has. With the exception of the post-World War II "baby boom," the long-term trend in fertility rates has been downward. The average woman born in the early 1800s had about eight children, while the average woman born since 1935 has had about two.[23] But the fertility rate of women from different classes has probably always varied such that lower-class women had more and upper-class women had less than average. Scattered data from throughout the nineteenth century show this tendency clearly.[24] Data from 1910, when the process of economic development was in full swing, also display this pattern: rural and farm women had around five children on average, urban women married to blue-collar workers had around four children, and urban women married to white-collar workers had about three.[25] These differences are significant, since large families in farming and lower-level blue-collar occupations provided most of the people to fill the jobs opening up above them in the stratification hierarchy. In effect, class differences in fertility constituted a historical "push" factor, stimulating upward mobility in the United States.

Immigration Rates.   The United States is a nation of immigrants, and the years from 1870 to 1920 saw the highest level of immigration in American history. In the decade from 1900 to 1910, for example, the immigration rate was ten persons per 1,000 U.S. citizens, an all-time high.[26] These new residents typically entered society at the lowest rungs. Nonetheless, immigration laws during this period required that new arrivals come equipped with skills.[27] The sheer force of numbers combined with education, literacy, and other vocational abilities constituted another "push" factor, stimulating upward mobility.[28]

Despite current controversies over immigration, the significance of class differences in fertility and immigration for mobility rates has declined in recent years. Since about 1920, for example, the level of immigration into the United States has been kept at one or two persons per 1,000 citizens. Similarly, although class differences in fertility continue to exist, they have declined over the years.

Affirmative Action for White Males.   As you should recall from Chapter 2, the term **affirmative action** refers to public policies giving advantages to members of one group over others. Historically, white males have ensured that they receive most of the benefits, which meant they were free to achieve occupational and economic success. Women and members of minority groups have been held back by ascribed barriers.

Unequal treatment has been built into the social structure in the form of **traditional gender norms.** These rules emphasize that men and women ought to have separate spheres: Women should bear and raise children, and take care of their husbands. Men should provide for the family economically and dominate public life. In the past, such norms were implemented by denying women the right to vote, despite the fact that they were productive citizens. Such norms were also used to justify driving women out or keeping them out of high prestige and high-paying jobs in medicine, education, business, and the like. Although these norms are changing, as indicated by the fact that many forms of unequal treatment have become illegal in recent years, they continue to influence behavior (see Chapter 3). They inhibit women's occupational success.

Affirmative action has also benefited white males at the expense of African Americans and other racial and ethnic groups. In Chapter 2, it was shown that three factors inhibited mobility by non-Whites. First, variations in the conditions of settlement—free versus slave and citizen versus debt peonage—placed people of color at a disadvantage. Second, patterns of prejudice and discrimination (especially institutionalized discrimination) inhibited occupational success. And third, affirmative action aimed at Whites, mainly males, promoted their occupational success. The impact of such policies can be seen in the nineteenth century land acts and the development of land grant colleges, which provided conduits of mobility that were unavailable to African Americans. Although discrimination has become illegal today, some of the mechanisms by which it continues were described in Chapter 2.

The result of these limitations has been greater upward mobility by white males, at least until recently. For both minority groups and women, mobility has increased over the last half century as discrimination has declined.

These elements of social structure—economic development, class differences in fertility rates, immigration, and affirmative action for white males—existed independently of individuals and influenced them, affecting their range of choices. The best single summary of the source of structural mobility in modern, class-based societies remains that by Peter Blau and Otis Dudley Duncan: "The pressure of displaced manpower at the bottom and the vacuum created by new opportunities at the top [started] a chain reaction of short distance movements throughout the occupational structure. This push of supply at the bottom and pull of demand at the top [created] opportunities for upward mobility from most origins, as the vacancies left by sons moving up [were] filled by sons from lower strata."[29] In short, the social structure changed, providing more opportunity.

Circulation Mobility

In class-based systems of domination, some mobility occurs independently of changes in the social structure. The overall pattern resembles a circle as some move up and others down. This process can be illustrated by shifting the focus from occupational mobility to intergenerational income mobility, as shown in Figure 5.1.

Figure 5.1 divides the income distribution into deciles (tenths) and displays the income of those born into the lowest and highest deciles, respectively. The data refer to individuals born between 1942 and 1972 and followed over 32 years.[30] Parents' income was averaged during the subjects' childhood (typically about nine years) and then averaged again in the years after age 26 when the subjects established themselves in their own households as adults (typically for about ten years). As a rough guide, the upper limit of the lowest income decile was $10,900 in 2004, which means people with incomes below that level found themselves in the lowest 10 percent of earners. By contrast, the lower limit of the top decile was $121,000, which means people with incomes above that level found themselves in the highest 10 percent of earners.[31] This guide really is "rough" for two reasons: First, because of inflation, both of these numbers would have been lower in previous years. Thus, in thinking about the results you have to mentally adjust for that variation. Second, and more seriously, the fact that people entered the top decile in 2004 with incomes of only $121,000 indicates that the mobility being described ranges from being poor to being middle class (and vice versa). The very rich are omitted.

The data in the figure can be interpreted in three ways that replicate the findings reported earlier. First, most of those who start near the bottom or the top of the income distribution end up there. About 62 percent of those born into the lowest income group

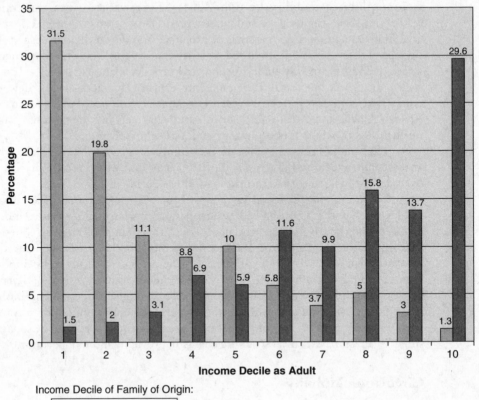

FIGURE 5.1   Income Distribution of Adults Born in the Top and Bottom Deciles

Note: Data refer to 6,273 individuals born 1942–1972. Parents' income averaged during subjects' childhood. Subjects' adult income measured after age 26 & typically averaged over 10 years.

Source: Hertz (2005:186).

ended up, as adults, in the lowest three deciles (31.5 + 19.8 + 11.1 in the figure). Conversely, about 59 percent of those born into the highest income group ended up in the highest three deciles (29.6 + 13.7 + 15.8). This finding suggests that just as most people are occupationally stable intergenerationally, they are also stable in terms of income. This is so after controlling for inflation. Second, both upward and downward mobility occur. About 38 percent of those born poor displayed significant upward mobility, while about 41 percent of those born "middle class" displayed significant downward mobility. Finally, long distance moves are rare. Only 1.3 percent of those born at the bottom of the income distribution ended up in the top decile, while 1.5 percent of those born at the top (middle class) ended up in the bottom decile. Thus, the pattern displayed in the figure suggests circulation mobility in that upward and downward movements roughly balance.

The first task is to explain all the movement shown in the data. The structural sources of circulation mobility can be found in the way modern societies, as described in Chapter 1, create opportunities. In **industrialized** societies, **capitalism** and **democracy** combine to produce a competitive environment regulated by the rule of **law.** The logic of **science,** with its emphasis on using reason and conclusions based on systematic observations, permeates these societies. All these structural factors are buttressed by the **culture of capitalism,** which stresses achievement, individualism, and merit as bases for evaluating people. Formal education becomes increasingly important in this context because the skills required in many jobs are relatively complex. Thus, modern societies are often called meritocracies and the schools constitute the vehicle by which merit is recognized. The schools function like elevators, vehicles for **upwar**d mobility for some people as talent and hard work are recognized. The result is **circula**tion mobility; some people make it and others do not.

The second task is to explain the intergenerational stability shown in the figure. Given that the class structure is reproduced across generations, the notion of modern societies as meritocracies overstates the case.[32] Paradoxically, the same variables that produce mobility also generate both income and occupational stability across generations. This stability makes complete sense sociologically, since it is a truism that the social structure sets the range of options available to people. Ascription still operates, even though individuals do not inherit class position in modern societies and even though they must get and keep jobs based on achievement. For most people, then, the schools function more like those livestock sorting devices that channel animals down different chutes depending on their weight. In effect, schools channel most young people into the classes from which they came. For children of poor families, this process often involves staying in school or dropping out. If they stay in school, perhaps they can attend the community college and learn a trade. But they often live on the margin. For children of middle-class families, it involves getting good grades, taking advanced placement courses, getting into the state university, and perhaps going on to professional school. For children of rich families, it involves attending a private prep school (that the rest of us have often never heard of), being admitted to a college like Yale, joining exclusive clubs (Skull and Bones), and gaining access to entry-level positions that can lead to elite jobs. Note that while many people (like readers of this book) work extremely hard in school to achieve success later, most end up in the class bequeathed them by their parents.

An Example of Upward Mobility

Although sociologists study mobility in structural terms, an example can be useful as a way of describing the interplay between ascription and achievement. It also provides a transition to the study of status attainment.

Angela Whitaker is an African American who was raised in poverty by a single mother.[33] Her father was not part of her life. She began life poor and made poor decisions. As a young adolescent, she used men as a substitute for her father, becoming pregnant by age 15. For awhile she was addicted to crack cocaine. By age 23, she had five children and lived in the Englewood section of Chicago, one of the most violent neighborhoods in the city.[34] Gangs ran the projects; elevators were sticky with urine; gunfire provided the background noise. In this context, "each day meant trying to piece together enough to take care of herself and her kids—one day petitioning the fathers for child support, the next counting what was left of her food stamps; one minute rushing to an administrator's office to get bus vouchers for school, the next bargaining with the electric company to get her lights turned back on."[35] This is where she began.

Wanting something better, Ms. Whitaker got off drugs. She worked two jobs for several years. She made a long commute to a fast food place, becoming an assistant manager, but still earned little more than the minimum wage. She also worked nights as a security guard in one of the projects, living with the danger in order to earn a bit more. At the latter, she met Vincent Allen, a police detective, and they eventually married. He encouraged her to go to nursing school, which she did.

> [She slowly began to see] a new way of managing one's life. The professional people she met in college and [her husband] had different ways of thinking about spending money and carrying oneself. They tended to plan and save for things. She had never had enough money or reason to save. They paid attention to things like late fees and interest rates; she [had] mostly ignored them because she couldn't pay the bills anyway. They set long-term goals for themselves; she just tried to get through the day. It all rubbed off on her, and it changed her.[36]

While working more than full-time and trying to care for her children, it took Ms. Whitaker six years, from 1996 to 2002, to get a two-year nursing degree. In order to do it, she had to shut out the outside world. "I blocked everything and everybody out."[37] Her success is remarkable because she had to overcome so many social deficits: Without family connections or a mentor (in the jargon, she lacked social capital), "she didn't know anyone who could give her the ins and outs of the field or tell her what to expect." She had to figure it all out for herself. And she did. Armed with a degree she took and passed the nursing boards, her "pass–fail entrance exam into the American middle class."

Ms. Whitaker's position, however, remains tenuous and involves many personal difficulties. Even though she won academic awards, the reality of her life is that the two-year degree is as far as she will go. Also, she does not have the contacts (another social deficit) to get a job at one of the teaching hospitals in Chicago, where she would earn more and get additional training. She makes good money now, working nights to earn even more, and has some of the accoutrements of middle-class life: a credit card and car payments. For the latter, she pays 17 percent interest, far higher than most people would have to pay.* Her success invites obligations stemming from her past, as friends and family ask for loans (which are really gifts) and other forms of support. It is very hard to refuse these requests because kin and non-kin exchange networks imply the obligation to help one another.[38] Such exchange networks are useful survival techniques in impoverished environments but hinder mobility. Finally, two of her children have dropped out of school and had extensive drug and legal problems. It is hard to know what will happen to them in the future.

Ms. Whitaker has had more time, however, to raise her younger children. One just graduated from high school. Another is in the gifted program at a middle-class school. So there is a chance that at least these two children will be able to maintain themselves in their new status. Apart from her children, Ms. Whitaker's goal is simple

---

*This high interest rate may simply reflect her credit history. Recall from Chapter 2, however, that African Americans pay higher interest rates for housing and auto loans than do Whites, even with the same income and credit history.

now: She wants to buy a house, the final symbol of being in the middle class. In this regard, she is like many individuals striving for success.

STATUS ATTAINMENT

Individuals make decisions in a specific historical context. There are about 139 million employed persons in the United States, which means that about the same number of jobs exist.[39] **Status Attainment** refers to how each individual enters one of those occupations. The issue is how ascribed and achieved factors combine, because each person enters an occupation based on the way their parents' status produces advantages and disadvantages, their own efforts and abilities, and a degree of luck. Peter Blau and O.D. Duncan showed that this process can be studied as a causal sequence that identifies the factors in individuals' lives that influence attainment and how much each factor affects later ones.[40] In their words:

> We think of the individual's life-cycle as a sequence in time that can be described, how-ever partially and crudely, by a set of classificatory or quantitative measurements taken at successive stages. . . . Given this scheme, the questions we are continually raising in one form or another are: How and to what degree do the circumstances of birth condi-tion subsequent status? And how does status attained (whether by ascription or achievement) at one stage of the life-cycle affect the prospects for a subsequent stage?

Status Attainment in the United States

The major variables in the status attainment process are shown in Figure 5.2, which depicts a sequence of ascribed and achieved factors.[41] A person's family background influences one's occupational status attainment, both indirectly because of its strong relationship to one's educational accomplishments, but also directly. Thus, while the importance of ascribed factors is greatest when a child is young, one's family influences a child's accomplishments throughout life. At the same time, however, achievement at each stage of life decisively affects prospects at subsequent stages. This fact means that issues over which individuals have more control assume greater importance with age. The boxes in the figure are numbered to correspond with the order of findings reported below. As with mobility, the initial studies of status attainment dealt with men.

  1. *The social class of a person's family of origin, as indicated by such variables as father's education, father's occupation, mother's education, and family income are all highly correlated and influence status attainment at all subsequent stages of a child's life.* Put simply, birth matters. It directly affects each stage of status attainment: the development of ability, academic performance, the encouragement one gets from significant others (such as teachers and friends), educational and occupational aspirations, educational attain-ment, and eventual occupational attainment. For example, some combination of genetic inheritance and nurturance in the family predicts tested ability even before children enter school. These differences affect educational performance. Finally, they also affect eventual occupational status attainment.[42] In practice, then, preschool children from poor backgrounds who score low on ability tests usually do poorly in school and they end up achieving less over the long term. And, without some sort of intervention,

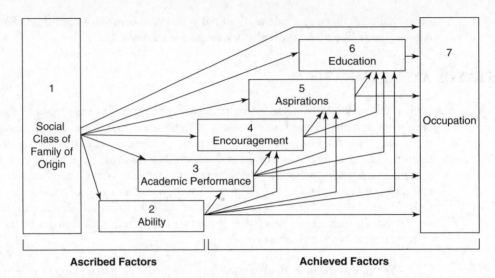

Ascribed Factors　　　　**Achieved Factors**

FIGURE 5.2　The Status-Attainment Process

preschool children from poor backgrounds who score high on ability tests also usually do poorly in school and achieve less over the long term. The reason is that poor children with high ability are often not taught the skills necessary to succeed in school. The findings are exactly opposite for children from the middle class: Whether of low or high ability, they achieve at a relatively high level in school. The reason low-ability middle-class children do better in school is that their families are often able to better prepare them. Thus, the overall impact of a person's family on eventual occupational and economic success fits with most people's intuitive observation. This is a case where research shows that "common sense" is correct.

2. *Ability influences every subsequent stage of the status-attainment process.* People of high ability usually do better than those with less. "Ability" is usually measured by either an achievement or intelligence test and, hence, refers to academic aptitude rather than other kinds of skills. Thus, ability most strongly affects academic performance (for example, grade point average) and educational attainment. But ability also influences the other intervening variables as well: educational and occupational aspirations and the encouragement a child receives from significant others. Finally, in addition to education, ability also affects the job a person ultimately gets. As an aside, you should remember that while ability has a biological basis, its development is socially determined.[43] Thus, middle-class children often possess advantages over others who have the same ability but come from working-class and poor backgrounds. This is because, for example, middle-class children often enter school better prepared and, hence, display better performance. The long-term impact increases the odds of occupational success for middle-class children.

3. *Academic performance directly influences subsequent status attainment: the level and kind of encouragement received from others, aspirations, and eventual educational and occupational* *attainment.* The dual impact of the schools becomes apparent early in people's lives. On the one hand, the schools facilitate achievement (they are like elevators). Ambitious parents encourage and prepare their children, who enter the schools ready to use their abilities. As a result, they receive encouragement from teachers, develop aspirations, and get tracked into a college preparatory curriculum. They become less likely to drop out of schools and more likely to attend college.[44] And a college degree is often what separates those in the middle class from those in the working class. On the other hand, schools often channel people (they are like livestock sorting devices). This process occurs because school personnel often use ascriptive (nonperformance) criteria in evaluating and placing children. Teachers assess (even if imperfectly) each child's class of origin; they expect, and get, better performance from middle-class students.[45] Just as important, however, track placement typically reflects class background. Tracking is how the public schools prepare some students for college and others with vocational skills.[46] One guess is that this practice constitutes a reaction to large class size: Heterogeneous groups of 25 (or more) are much harder to teach than 15 or so. Tracking makes teaching large groups easier. Class size is a function of funding, of course, much of which is dictated by middle-class voters (see Chapter 6). In this context, then, the schools provide some children with a vehicle for upward mobility. For many, however, they lock people in place.

4. *Encouragement by significant others affects aspirations and educational and occupational attainment.* The term **significant other** was coined by the psychiatrist Harry Stack Sullivan, who used it to refer to people who are emotionally important to individuals and, hence, especially influential on them.[47] Sullivan emphasized that the impact is strongest when individuals are young. Thus, parents, teachers, and peers constitute significant others who affect children's aspirations and their ultimate educational and occupational attainment. This influence occurs in combination with the effect of academic performance and other previously mentioned variables. Thus, children develop aspirations according to the evaluations they receive from others and their own self-assessment based on their academic performance, familial obligations, and the like. Further, children's peers are also significant others who influence the development of aspirations and educational and occupational attainment.

5. *Educational and occupational aspirations influence educational and occupational attainment.* **Educational aspirations** refer to children's plans and expectations about their ultimate level of schooling, such as going to college. **Occupational aspirations** refer to the kind of jobs children expect or would like when they become adults. Aspirations are the filter through which significant others influence children. Thus, parents who have college degrees provide role models and encouragement for their children to attend college. In addition, when people's friends comprise children of parents with college degrees, a collective expectation about college attendance develops. The result is higher educational attainment. In contrast, children raised in different contexts often develop lower aspirations, which results in lower educational attainment.

6. *Educational attainment strongly influences occupational attainment.* College attendance is crucial to getting many white-collar jobs. The best predictor of college attendance remains family background, with all the other variables shown in Figure 5.2 serving as filters for this factor. It has been known for a long time that middle-class children are

much more likely to attend college than working-class or poor children, even if the latter have high ability.[48] What happens, of course, is that middle-class parents are more likely to encourage higher education and more capable of making it happen. This is so even if their children do not have as much ability as others, at least when measured by standardized tests. At the same time, however, a smaller proportion of working-class and (a few) poor parents whose children display high ability also get their children into college. As the experience of Angela Whitaker suggests, *educational attainment is probably the most important factor weakening the impact of family background (ascription) on eventual status attainment.* Interestingly, class of family of origin does not predict either performance once a person enters college or graduating from college. And graduating is important. Those with a college degree have a significant occupational advantage over those without one. This means that in the race for prestige (and income), it is not attendance but the credential that counts. In this regard, the dual impact of education becomes clear once again. On the one hand, an educational credential constitutes a vehicle for preserving class boundaries. Middle-class parents ensure that their children reap the rewards of prestige and income associated with white-collar jobs. On the other hand, a significant minority of working-class children gets into and completes college, and their achievement translates into white-collar prestige and income. To repeat: The status-attainment process constitutes an interrelated chain of ascribed and achieved factors. And this is also true for African Americans (and probably other minority groups) and women.

The status-attainment process shown in Figure 5.2 describes African Americans' experiences as well as Whites.'[49] Yet this fact masks significant change that has occurred. During the 1960s, African Americans were less able than Whites to pass on whatever status advantages they achieved. Over time, however, more intergenerational continuity is occurring among African Americans and racial differences in educational and occupational attainment have declined.[50] Nonetheless, it remains true that, on average, African Americans and Whites begin at different status levels and end up at different status levels. This is, of course, also true for other minority groups. Put bluntly, while everyone benefits from increased schooling, white males still benefit more. This variation reflects discrimination. Alas, models of the status-attainment process, such as Figure 5.2, do not include this factor as a variable. So they do not get at a key issue.

The situation is similar with regard to gender differences.[51] The status-attainment process is similar for women as well as men. But significant variations exist: Mothers' characteristics affect daughters' status attainment more than fathers' do. Women's first job tends to be higher in prestige then men's, but men's main job increases their prestige more. This difference occurs because women get locked into jobs (as clerks, for example) without a promotion ladder. Ultimately, however, while the status-attainment model shown in Figure 5.1 describes both women's and men's experiences, it reveals little about the impact of discrimination.

Status Attainment in Cross-National Perspective

The process of status attainment appears to be similar in all economically developed Western nations, although the models include fewer variables than shown in

Figure 5.2: *(1) Family background exerts a weak but significant and direct impact on one's occupation. (2) A child's education exerts a strong and direct impact on one's occupation.*[52]

But while the pattern is similar across Western societies, significant variation exists. For example, one study compared the relationship between father's occupation and son's job in the United States, the former West Germany, Great Britain, the Netherlands, and Sweden. The association is much lower in Sweden compared to the United States and other nations, while that between son's education and his job is much higher.[53] This finding suggests that ascription is less important than achievement in Swedish society. The Netherlands, by contrast, displayed the highest relationship between father's and son's jobs, and the lowest relationship between son's education and job. This finding suggests that ascription has a greater impact in the Netherlands, compared to the United States and other nations.

Another study looked at the relationship between father's and son's income. In Sweden, the association is relatively low compared to the United States, again suggesting Sweden's greater emphasis on achievement. In Great Britain, however, the association is roughly similar to the United States, suggesting a similar relationship between ascription and achievement.[54]

The process of status attainment illustrates how ascription and achievement combine in modern societies to affect the jobs people get and thus where they end up in the class structure. As outlined in Figure 5.2, the class of a person's family of origin indicates the opportunities with which one begins seeking a place in society. At the same time, what individuals accomplish makes a difference.

THE INDIVIDUAL AND STATUS ATTAINMENT

As children grow up, they enjoy the benefits of their family's income and wealth, as when one's father is a successful lawyer in Seattle or one's mother an impoverished single parent in Chicago. Children also participate in their family's social network, developing contacts and connections, which may facilitate getting into Harvard. Finally, children learn what's going on in the larger culture, such as the development of computer technology or the crack epidemic. In so doing, children are **socialized,** as described in Chapter 1; they learn norms and values, internalize needs, develop skills and knowledge, and enact roles. The result makes a huge difference in life chances, as suggested by the status-attainment process.

Two Vignettes

Figure 5.2 shows the way these differences play out. Each of the arrows in the figure represents a quantitative measure of the interrelated factors affecting the status-attainment process. But boxes and arrows convey insight in a relatively impersonal way. This section illustrates the relationships shown in the figure with vignettes about two fictional families: the Smiths, a working-class family on the edge of poverty, and the Joneses, a middle-class family. Be warned: The differences between the two families are portrayed in ways that emphasize the disadvantages of growing up near poverty and the advantages of growing up middle class. Hence, they do not do justice to the full range of familial experiences children in different classes have. There is some danger of caricature, of assuming that the family background of poor and working-class children is always inferior to that of middle-class children. Nothing could be further from the truth. Nonetheless, the types of events depicted here are class-related: Poor and working-class families are more likely to display characteristics like the Smith's, while middle-class families are more likely to resemble the Joneses. This difference is reflected in the socialization process and, as a result, in status attainment. As a last point, problems of prejudice and discrimination are not considered here, either by race/ethnicity or gender, as they have been dealt with in previous chapters.

The Smiths.   Jane and Edward Smith are married and live in Cedar Key, Florida, a town of about 1,000 people located on the gulf coast. Jane's mother and father both have high school degrees. Although past retirement age and in poor health, her parents remain employed because they do not have pensions. Her mother works as a waitress and her father earns an uncertain living fishing in the gulf. Edward's mother graduated from high school and works as a retail clerk. Although his father did not finish high school, he works steadily as a janitor at a local fish processing plant.

They married when they were both 17 years of age. Jane was pregnant at the time with her first child, Joyce. At age 19 they had a second child, Belle, and at 20, a third, Sam. Initially, they tried to establish their own household, but moved back into Jane's parents' home on two occasions. Living conditions were crowded, which adds stress.[55] For several years they had spells of unemployment and part-time employment. They were "officially" poor at times and received public assistance twice, totaling about a year and a half (see Chapter 10 on the poverty line). They are now 30, and both work full-time. Jane operates a machine at a textile factory and earns about $18,000 yearly. Edward's father learned about an apprentice electrician program at his plant and helped Edward get into it. As a result, Edward is now a nonunion electrician at the plant, earning about $25,000 yearly. Today, their total income of $43,000 places them well above the poverty line.

But this family income level is relatively recent. The financial hardships the Smiths experienced early in their marriage mean that the children lived in an environment of economic want without satisfaction. In this context, they learned that their parents could not control what happens to the family: how much there is to eat, what kind of house they live in, and other fundamental aspects of life. Although Jane and Edward stayed together and eventually achieved a stable living standard, their lifestyle remains precarious. And children internalize this knowledge, it becomes part of their interior vision of the world and their place within it, and it affects their behavior throughout life. They may learn, for example, to live for the moment, since waiting around for future rewards is likely to bring disappointment. What such orientations mean in terms of the socialization process is that children learn to believe they are vulnerable and not in control of what happens to them. This lesson affects future behavior in school, making it more difficult to succeed occupationally later on.

In addition to the financial limitations, the Smiths married and started a family while still young and inexperienced. Hence, the children were raised by parents who were still, in years and experience, children themselves. Because Jane and Edward passed from girl and boy to wife and husband to mother and father so swiftly, they had less time to integrate and assimilate the psychological orientations and behaviors necessary for their new roles. So, at least initially, they lacked both marriage and parenting skills. As before, this fact means that their children's early years were spent in an environment in which want without satisfaction was everywhere, only in this case the thing wanted was psychological security. To be raised by people who are unsure of their own adulthood can mean that children are responded to in very inconsistent ways. In this case, Edward and Jane have always tried to be loving parents. There were, nonetheless, periods of neglect in which their own needs (they were young adults, remember, 18–22 years of age) took precedence over their children's needs. Moreover, they struggled economically and lived in a crowded environment. Inevitably, they fought sometimes. So there were some occasions when Edward and Jane took out their frustrations on the children: They hit them. The long-term effects of such lack of predictability are straightforward: Children become angry and frustrated and, as a result, display inconsistent and inappropriate behaviors. For example, they may be aggressive in the wrong way or passive at the wrong time. Such characteristics have important negative implications for success in school and for occupational attainment later on.

Even though the Smiths are now mature adults and steadily employed, their income barely allows them to meet expenses and their social circle remains rather limited—circumscribed by family and religion. They attend the True Life Evangelical Church, most of whose members are blue-collar workers like themselves; none have college degrees. With their limited circle of friends and acquaintances, who is going to help them when a problem arises?

For the children, growing up in a rural environment like this is relatively safe. Joyce, Belle, and Sam all learned to fish at young ages. They hung out on the dock, listening to stories told by the men. Most of them had spent their entire lives in Cedar Key, fishing in the gulf or working at one of the local factories.

That same environment, however, can be boring. Neither Jane nor Edward was read to when they were little and, hence, did not recognize the importance of reading to their own children. In the summers, Joyce and her siblings stayed with their grandmother and spent much of the day watching television. Rural life also makes other forms of stimuli unavailable—trips to museums, computer camps, and the like—that can help prepare children for school and expose them to the dominant culture. These activities are important when the children enter school and throughout the school years. Teachers identify which children are going to have difficulty in the first grade. Those who have not learned certain skills at home—naming colors, counting, and alphabet, among others—enter school at a disadvantage.

Joyce provides a good example of these disadvantages as well as illustrating how the Smiths' social deficits limited their ability to help their children. After enrolling in Cedar Key Elementary School at age five, Joyce was a low achiever from the beginning. Jane Smith had meetings at the school and tried to respond to the teachers' suggestions, but she was not forceful in dealing with educators. The Smiths were dimly aware that they could have Joyce tested for some sort of learning disability but could not afford to do so. By the beginning of third grade, Joyce was placed in a special education class even though she appeared to be of normal intelligence. Joyce is now in middle school, but reading at an elementary school level.

Yet children, even in the same family, have different experiences. Recall that schools have a dual impact, facilitating high achievement for some that is independent of family background. The Smiths' minister, as luck would have it, was an undergraduate music major at the University of Florida and saw that Belle (the middle child) had unusual musical ability. She encouraged the child, even buying her a violin. With the Smiths' support, she taught Belle for several years without charge. She also occasionally took her to the museum and to concerts in Gainesville, about 90 miles away. Finally, Belle was able to attend a music camp in the summer, where she met people from all over the state and became friends with a few. As a result of this attention, teachers took an interest in her, both academically and musically, and she is at the top of her class.

As shown in Figure 5.2, the status-attainment process begins with "family of origin," which provides an important baseline (ascriptive) starting point, affecting ability, school performance, encouragement, aspirations, educational attainment, and ultimately one's occupation. The variables following "family of origin" also have their own independent and cumulative effects. The future is always uncertain, but Joyce's situation suggests a certain pessimism. Belle's future, however, at least at this point, seems more positive. (You may have observed that the Smiths' third child, Sam, has not been mentioned. His travails will be described in Chapter 10.)

The Joneses.   Mary Anna and David Jones live in Gainesville, Florida, where the University of Florida is located. Mary Anna's parents both have college degrees. Her father is an engineer and her mother a computer programmer. David's parents also have college degrees. His father is an accountant and his mother is an elementary school teacher. Although none are retired because they are healthy and enjoy their jobs, both sets of parents have good pensions to look forward to when that time comes. Thus, as with the Smiths, both Mary Anna and David come from similar class backgrounds. Unlike the Smiths, however, Mary Anna and David remained in school, obtained their college educations, and started their careers before thinking about marriage. They met at age 26 and married at 28. Their child, Michael, was born two years later. Although, like her father, Mary Anna is trained as an engineer, she writes crime novels (good ones that sell). David is a college professor at the university. Their combined income is over $120,000 per year. Not only is their joint income relatively high, but Mary Anna's parents gave them the money for the down payment on their house in an exclusive area with good schools.

The Joneses enjoy a wide circle of friends and acquaintances. They belong to the Episcopal church and to professional associations. Peter is active in local politics. Harriet sits on the board for the public library. They regularly entertain people from various backgrounds in their home, where discussions range from public policy dilemmas to moral issues to the fate of the Gator football team this year.

Being raised in a relatively privileged (middle-class) environment produces many advantages for Michael. It has never occurred to him to wonder about whether there will be enough food to eat. Moreover, their home is large and, hence, it has been easier to separate when people became frustrated with one another. Hence, Michael experienced a stable and predictable lifestyle from a very young age. When he wanted a bicycle, he was told to save enough money to pay for half of it, which he did. In this and other ways, Michael learned that life is not precarious and that delaying immediate gratification will often bring greater rewards in the future. Thus, his interior vision of himself included a sense of personal efficacy (the ability to solve problems and overcome obstacles) and a belief that he has some control over what happens to him. Such experiences fundamentally affect behavior in school, making it easier to succeed subsequently as an adult.

In addition, Michael was "affluent" in a second way as well. Mary Anna and David were mature when Michael was born. Secure in their adulthood, they responded to him as consistently as possible and tried to create a family environment in which he could thrive. While he was young, for example, they read to him every night. They limited his time in front of the television. One result is that Michael developed superior verbal and interpersonal skills at a young age. Such characteristics produce more success in school and increase the level of achievement as an adult. So Michael entered school knowing his colors, able to count, and capable of using the computer to find sites his parents did not want him to see. Nonetheless, it became apparent in the first grade that Michael was a low achiever, primarily because he had trouble paying attention. Mary Anna and David attacked the situation directly: They consulted with an acquaintance at the university, a specialist in attention deficit disorder, and had the child tested. The cost, while significant, was never a problem. They volunteered to work in the classroom, worked with him daily at home, and had him tutored over the summer. Finally, they requested and got a more structured second grade teacher. Michael was working at grade level by the end of second grade.

Over the years, Mary Anna and David provided Michael with many experiences—preschool, lessons, camps, computers at home, and the like—that not only increased his cognitive skills but also taught him about the dominant culture. They vacationed in Europe. He is now in middle school, performing extremely well, and is something of an athlete. Last summer he attended a basketball camp, a music camp (the same one Belle went to), and computer camp at the local university, where he met children from around the state.

Consider once again how family background and the other variables in the status-attainment process combine. Although, as before, the future is uncertain, at this point one might be reasonably optimistic about Michael's.

A caveat: As indicated earlier, these two vignettes are designed to suggest how the status-attainment process described in Figure 5.2 occurs and the relative advantages middle-class people enjoy. You should understand, however, that some middle-class couples have children but dodge parenting; they are unable to put their children's needs before their own. Some are absent from their children due to their occupational ambitions. Some abuse their children. Some use their children as weapons during divorce. At the same time, many working-class and poor families are stable and nurturing. So you should take the Smith and Jones lives as illustrative of the impact of social class on status attainment, not as definitive examples.

Social Class and Status Attainment

The vignettes raise three questions: How do the Smiths and Joneses differ? How do these differences affect the status-attainment process? What implications does the status-attainment process have for understanding the structure of stratification?

One obvious difference is family income, an important ascribed factor. One of the characteristics of "social class of family of origin" shown in Figure 5.2, it is important because *the higher the family income (especially in early childhood), the greater the achievement of children.*[56] The reason for this relationship is that family income influences the quality of the home environment: the nature of parent–child interaction, opportunities for learning, the physical condition of the home, the ability to pay for unexpected expenses as well as amenities, among other factors.

Think about the differences in parent–child interaction portrayed in the vignettes. The Smiths are good people who struggled mightily, indeed heroically, to establish a stable family life—and they succeeded. Nonetheless, much of their interaction early in the marriage was harsher than occurred in the Jones family. The finding is this: *The lower the family income, then the greater the economic pressures and the greater the stress between parents—which leads to harsher parent–child interaction.*[57] It follows that *the harsher the parent–child interaction, the lower the children's self-confidence and the lower their achievement.* These findings are one reason why Joyce Smith's future looks bleaker than Michael Jones's. But such results are not inevitable. Recall that significant others besides parents affect status attainment. When a minister recognized Belle Smith's musical talent, her aspirations rose and improved the odds of her finishing high school and, perhaps, attending college. The future is not given; it is impossible to know what will happen to Joyce, Belle, or Michael. But there is no question that the quality of the home environment, in this case parent–child interaction (along with others who are emotionally significant), affects their future.

Social capital constitutes another, perhaps less obvious, difference between the families. The term refers to who one knows and where they are located in the class structure.[58] Such relationships provide connections to the larger society and, hence, opportunities for success. These relationships underlay the variables measured in the status-attainment process (Figure 5.2).

Educational opportunities of children vary, for example, in terms of family social capital. Consider the experiences of Mary Smith and Michael Jones when both were identified as "slow learners" in elementary school. Michael's parents called on an acquaintance who happened to be an expert on his problem and they had the money to pay for testing services. Joyce's parents did not have the contacts or the money to do this. Moreover, Michael's parents approached teachers and other school personnel much differently than Joyce's. This difference can be expressed by a hypothesis. *The less knowledge and self-confidence parents have, the less likely they are to see themselves as the status equal of teachers.*[59] Mary's parents were more diffident and less forceful in dealing with school teachers and administrators. Michael's parents volunteered in the classroom and had their son assigned to a more appropriate teacher. The result is not accidental; middle-class people dominate the public schools. They get to know members of the school board, teachers, and administrators. As a result, their children's educational needs are better served: teachers take a more personal interest, are more tolerant, and are quicker to spot and resolve potential problems.

Economic opportunities also vary in terms of family social capital, thus affecting status attainment. In the vignettes, Edward Smith's father got him into an apprentice electrician program, an example of nepotism that occurs at all class levels.[60] Historically, working-class Whites were able to dominate crafts unions, keeping African Americans and other minorities from good jobs, by getting their sons and friends into similar apprentice programs.[61] Of course, middle-class and rich parents also use their contacts to smooth their children's way.[62]

People display inconsistent responses to the existence and use of social capital.[63] On the one hand, if you go to your college career counseling center, one of the first pieces of advice you will get is to "network," another way of saying to cultivate your family's personal ties. And if these connections lead to a job, you will be grateful to "get a foot in the door." On the other hand, if you get bypassed for a job by an "inside candidate" (whom you will inevitably see as less qualified), you will be outraged. But obtaining such bypasses is precisely what family, friends, and acquaintances are for. Without these relationships, as the experience of Angela Whitaker suggests, occupational and economic success is far more difficult.

Cultural capital constitutes a third difference between the families in the vignette. The term refers to familiarity with the dominant culture. In order to fit in, one must possess an awareness of beliefs, customs, and ways of life. At every class level, Pierre Bourdieu argues, small distinctions of style constitute the basis for social judgments.[64] What is the Head of the Charles Regatta? What is open wheel auto racing? What is the Debutante Cotillion and Christmas Ball? Such knowledge is important in certain segments of American society. As Max Weber argued when he distinguished between "class" and "status," snobbery occurs in every class and it affects economic and occupational success.

Although he did not use the concept, inequality of cultural capital is the theme of George Bernard Shaw's play, *Pygmalion*, originally produced in 1914. In the play, Professor Higgins makes a cynical wager that he can turn a lower-class flower girl, Eliza Doolittle, into a member of high society by teaching her language and taste. He succeeds and falls in love with Eliza. And she succeeds as well, rebelling against him and eventually marrying a fatuous young man of the genteel class.[65] Sociologically, the play is about how social, economic, and political power inheres to and follows from class position, as signified by patterns of speech and aesthetic judgment.

In the vignettes, this same point is illustrated (more altruistically) by Belle Smith, whose minister taught her the violin and introduced her to middle-class lifestyle via trips to the museum, concerts, and the music camp at the university. The example illustrates how young people can acquire, often with considerable difficulty, cultural capital independently of their families. Admission to and graduation from a college or university provides for this transition; the diploma certifies both knowledge and cultural competence. Michael Jones also learned to be middle class, like his parents, via the advantages they provide. Children obtain cultural capital from their parents in three ways: First, they simply live at home, go on vacation (to Europe, for example), and participate in their parents' social networks. Second, they benefit from their parents' strategic investments (computer camps, for example). Third, they visit in their friends homes, since families with similar status characteristics tend to associate with one another in neighborhoods, churches, and schools.[66] This tendency is one reason why housing and school segregation by class and race are so important; they constitute mechanisms by which children are constrained to meet and socialize with others like themselves.

These differences have enormous implications for understanding the structure of stratification. Family income, social capital, and cultural capital represent fundamental elements of status in the community, in Max Weber's sense. That is, as described in Chapter 1, class and status are interrelated, and inequality in the distribution of resources is maintained as families in each class act—individually and collectively—to protect their interests. They extend hospitality to social equals, restrict their children's potential marriage partners to social equals, practice unique social conventions (a form of cultural capital), and safeguard their economic interests. Inequality follows; yet opportunity exists. This is the paradox of modernity.

ANOMIE, THE AMERICAN DREAM, AND STRATIFICATION

Although the findings in the study of mobility and status attainment occur at different levels of analysis, structural and individual, they mirror each other. Structurally, the rate of mobility in modern societies is limited (intergenerational continuity is the mode) but significant (upward mobility occurs much more often compared to the past). For individuals, status attainment in modern societies depends on a combination of ascription (in the form of family background) and achievement (especially via education). In this process, the schools and other factors function like a sorting device for most, but like an elevator for some.

Figure 5.3 illustrates these findings by depicting how ascription and achievement combine as people from each class of origin compete for economic success in modern societies. This competition can be seen as like a baseball game, the metaphor introduced in Chapter 1. In this game, people start out with some ascribed advantages or disadvantages. Given a particular starting point, everyone then competes, using whatever abilities they have, working hard, and sometimes getting lucky. Some people, of course, are born very, very rich (see Chapter 7). In effect, they begin life at home base. Everyone else, however, has to work their way around the bases. As described earlier, economic development and other factors have produced a great deal of structural mobility. And the emphasis on competing, politically and economically, under a rule of law and buttressed by the American Dream (the value everyone places on achievement and merit) produces circulation mobility. The net impact of all this competition, however, is that many people achieve a little—symbolized in the figure by the dashed lines inside the ovals. Only a few go beyond the ovals (either backward or forward). The dashes in the figure also provide a way of conceptualizing degrees of achievement. They suggest that those few who move from poor backgrounds (at bat) into the middle class (2nd base) actually display more "units" of achievement than do those who leverage their family contacts, work incredibly hard, and move from being well-off (3rd base) to being very rich (home).

The mobility and status-attainment findings make it possible to understand why modern societies are **anomic;** that is, opportunity exists but is restricted at the same time. The cynical but sociologically accurate reason for restrictions on opportunity is that the competition is rigged. But it is not rigged by a conspiracy; it is rigged by people acting in terms of their social, economic, and political interests. Although he had a grandiose and foolish dream, Karl Marx correctly identified the mechanism by which an anomic society is created and maintained: class conflict. As he recognized, classes have different and often opposing interests. And they act on these differences, both collectively and individually, even though classes are not formally organized.

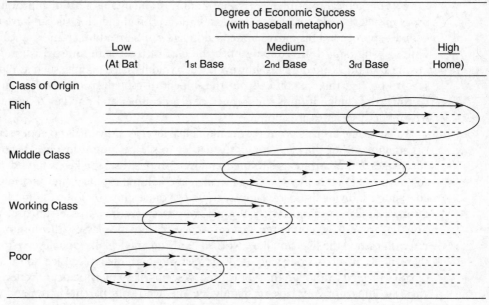

Key

Solid arrows: Impact of ascription, where people start based on class of orgin
Dashes: Potential for Achievement, each dash equaling one unit of achievement
Ovals: Area in which most people circulate

FIGURE 5.3   A Model Illustrating the Relationship Between Class of Origin and Subsequent Economic Success in Modern Societies

But occupational groups are often organized and they illustrate how collective behavior protects class interests. As Max Weber emphasized in *Economy and Society: An Outline of Interpretive Sociology*, occupational groups "become interested in curbing the competition."[67] Some succeed and some do not. Please look back at Table 5.4, noting the rising proportion of people in service jobs coupled with declining proportions in other blue-collar jobs between 1950 and 2005. Most of these changes occurred in the last 20 years and they indicate fundamental dislocations in the labor market.[68] This change does not reflect purely economic forces; it also indicates class conflict. When these workers (or their unions, which are blue-collar occupational groups) asked for trade protection, Congress refused. Over the long run, the argument went, everyone benefits from the lower prices that follow from globalization. Now consider middle-class radiologists, whose incomes average $300,000 or so per year.[69] It is actually faster to send a medical image (an MRI or CT scan) to India to be read by a radiologist there than to take it from one floor of a hospital to another. Although the training necessary to recognize and read images is long and arduous, there is no particular reason that it must be done on site—other than the ability of American physicians to regulate who can practice medicine. The credentialing requirements (an American hospital residency, passage of American radiology board exams) both guarantee qualifications and restrict lower-priced competition, thus protecting the incomes of American radiologists and raising the cost of medical treatment. Britain, by contrast, maintains a list of approved training programs worldwide and non-European Union-trained radiologists can have their credentials approved. This means a medical image can be read much more cheaply in the United Kingdom, thus reducing both the cost of treatment and British radiologists' incomes. In the United States, however, when middle-class people, such as radiologists, seek to protect their incomes from the impact of globalization, they often succeed. Curbing the competition is the essence of class conflict and one key to understanding why modern societies are anomic.

This same process occurs at the individual level as individuals go about seeking status attainment but the class conflict is harder to see because it involves parents giving advantages and disadvantages to their children. In this case, the key is to understand the significance of family income, social capital, and cultural capital as they are leveraged by competing individuals. For example, some of you reading this book come from backgrounds similar to that of Michael Jones, who was described in the vignette. You know how hard you have competed: the advanced placement classes, the summer jobs or internships, and the like. You have worked hard and you feel like you deserve the benefits that will eventually accrue: a good job, a relatively high income, a nice house. And most of you will get it. Although the whole process seems like a meritocracy, it reflects, in large part, the impact of your parents' family income, who your parents know, and what they know. These factors have functioned like a lever, giving you class-based advantages from the time you were born. The competition was rigged to your advantage. By contrast, as Figure 5.3 suggests, these differences stack the odds against competitors from the lower classes, often preventing them from achieving the same level of economic success. In order to overcome these deficits, they must display more merit than you.

Apart from your personal experience, modern societies are anomic because class conflict structures the competition—both collectively and individually—determining who wins. In the United States, more than in other nations, that fact is hidden under the guise of the American Dream. The cultural values embodied in the American Dream have a paradoxical impact. On the one hand, they do help to level the playing field; everyone can compete and the smartest and hardest workers have a chance to succeed. Both Angela Whitaker and (the fictional) Michael Jones illustrate this process. Increased opportunity is the marker of modernity. In this context, Americans are told (especially by the rich) that the high level of mobility makes this country exceptional, obviating the need for an extensive set of welfare protections such as those common in the European Union nations.[70] But the data show that U.S. rates of mobility do not differ much compared to other nations. So, on the other hand, the belief in the American dream is, Marx would say, "the opium of the masses." It is like a siren song, a deceptive and alluring appeal. Sirens occur often in popular culture, in film, video games, and music. In the song "There There" from the 2003 album *Hail to the Thief*, the British band, Radiohead, sings:

> *There's always a siren*
> *singing you to shipwreck.*
> *(don't reach out, don't reach out)*
> *Steer away from these rocks*
> *we'll be a walking disaster.*
> *(don't reach out, don't reach out)*

Culturally, the siren call is precisely to reach out: to work hard and strive for success. Failure, Americans are taught, consists in giving up. Sociologically, Robert K. Merton argues, most people conform to that directive.[71] But, inevitably, some take Radiohead's advice: They "don't reach out" because they see it as a set-up for failure (a shipwreck). Or, as Merton would say, some people end up going through the motions, withdrawing, and acting out. Can you become a billionaire? You are more likely to win one of those state-run lotteries.

SUMMARY

The study of mobility focuses on changes in people's occupation, either intra- or intergenerationally. The study of status attainment focuses on how individuals enter specific occupations. Together, they indicate the relative emphasis on ascription and achievement in a society.

The major findings in the study of mobility are (Table 5.1): (1) Inter- and intra-generational stability occurs most often. (2) Yet mobility is widespread. (3) Most movement is short distance. The combination of stability and mobility has characterized the United States since the seventeenth century. Women and men show similar patterns of mobility. Historically, mobility for African Americans, Hispanic Americans, and other minority groups differed significantly from Whites, with less occupational inheritance. But since the 1960s, racial and ethnic differences have been declining (Table 5.2). These same three findings occur in other economically developed nations (Table 5.3).

The class structure is stable across generations because people in each class pass their resources (wealth, education, interpersonal contacts) on to their children. Structural mobility refers to people's upward rate of movement from their class of origin due to historical changes in the occupational structure. The most important factors affecting structural mobility are: economic development, class differences in fertility rates, immigration, and affirmative action for white males. Circulation mobility refers to the rate of upward and downward movement that occurs independently of historical changes in the occupational structure. The structural sources of circulation mobility are industrialization, capitalism, democracy, the rule of law, science, and the culture of capitalism. Thus, the rewards of hard work go mainly to those who start out with some advantages.

The status-attainment process reflects an interrelated chain of ascribed and achieved variables, as shown in Figure 5.2: family background, ability, academic performance, encouragement, aspirations, and educational attainment lead to occupation. Subsequent work shows that the basic status-attainment model also describes the experiences of African Americans and women, with the caveat that it does not take the impact of discrimination into account. The status-attainment process in other Western industrial nations resembles that in the United States. Underlying the status-attainment process is family income, social capital, and cultural capital, which vary by social class. Because children from different classes often (not always) have different experiences at home and at school, their status attainment varies accordingly. The study of mobility and status attainment suggests why modern societies are anomic (Figure 5.3).

NOTES

1. Wallace (1993).
2. Erikson and Goldthorpe (2002), Breen and Jonsson (2005).
3. Perrin (1904:967).
4. Sorokin (1927).
5. Ferrie (2005), Long and Ferrie (2005).
6. Lipset (1963), Main (1965). The argument here is about "American exceptionalism" and it has a long history. Shafer (1999) provides a useful summary.
7. Blau and Duncan (1967:36).
8. Treiman (2000). On downward mobility, see Rytina (2000), McBrier and Wilson (2004).
9. Hout (1988:1395), Biblarz et al. (1996), Korupp et al. (2002).
10. Biblarz et al. (1996).
11. Featherman and Hauser (1978:326).
12. Featherman and Hauser (1978), Davis (1997), Fosu (1997), G. Wilson et al. (1999).
13. McBrier and Wilson (2004).
14. Heath and Payne (2000:270). See also Long and Ferrie (2005).
15. Erikson and Goldthorpe (1993). The data below are from p. 333.
16. Lenski (1984).
17. Garland (1917). The quotation is from the epigraph to Garland's *Main Travelled Roads*, published in 1893(1995). The sentence beginning with "working the land . . . " paraphrases a line from Allitt (2005:26).
18. United States Bureau of the Census (1975:139).
19. I am paraphrasing a line from Allitt (2005:24).
20. Wyatt and Hecker (2006).
21. The phrase is Durkheim's (1982:28[1895]).
22. Hauser (1975:585), Sawhill (2000).
23. Cherlin (1992).
24. Whelpton (1928), Jaffe (1940).
25. Graybill et al. (1958).
26. United States Bureau of the Census (2006:9).
27. Lieberson (1980).
28. Sibley (1942).
29. Blau and Duncan (1967:66).
30. Hertz (2005).
31. United States Bureau of the Census (2006:40).
32. McNamee and Miller (2004).
33. Wilkerson (2005).
34. Beeghley (2003:81–84).
35. Wilkerson (2005:206).
36. Wilkerson (2005:211).
37. Wilkerson (2005:212–13).
38. Stack (1975).
39. United States Bureau of the Census (2006:387).
40. Blau and Duncan (1967:63).
41. The figure is intended as a summary of many empirical studies. See, for example, Blau and Duncan (1967), Sewell et al. (1970), Hout and Morgan (1975), Alexander et al. (1975), Featherman and Hauser (1978), Jencks (1979), Krymkowski (1991), England (1992), Duncan et al. (1998), Lin (1999), Treiman (2000), Mayer (2001), Warren et al. (2002).
42. Klebanov et al. (1998), Feinstein (2003).
43. Duncan et al. (1998), Feinstein (2003).
44. Haveman and Wolfe (1995).
45. Rosenthal and Jacobson (1968).
46. Jencks (1979), Oakes (1985).
47. Sullivan (1940), Sewell and Shah (1968a; 1968b).
48. Coleman (1966), McPherson and Shapiro (1998).
49. Blau and Duncan (1967), Winship (1992).
50. Jaynes and Williams (1989).
51. England (1992).
52. Treiman and Ganzeboom (1990), Krymkowski (1991).
53. Treiman and Yip (1989).
54. Solon (2002).
55. Beeghley and Donnelly (1989).
56. Mayer (1997), Duncan et al. (1998), Mayer and Peterson (1999), Lin (1999).
57. Conger et al. (1997).
58. Bourdieu (1986), Lin (2000).
59. Lareau (1989).
60. Bellow (2003).
61. Waldinger (1995), Royster (2003).
62. Granovetter (1995), Lin (2000), Bellow (2003), Keister (2005).
63. The next three sentences paraphrase lines from McNamee and Miller (2004:72).
64. Bourdieu (1986; 1987). On Bourdieu, see DiMaggio (1979).
65. Shaw (1957). The movie based on the play, *My Fair Lady*, ends rather differently.
66. Mohr and DiMaggio (1995). On status similarity, see the classic study by Lazarsfeld and Merton (1954) and the review of the literature by McPherson et al. (2001).
67. Weber (1968[1920]:341).
68. DiPrete and Nonnemaker (1997).
69. Leonhardt (2006), Levy et al. (2006). The remainder of this paragraph relies on these two sources.
70. This is the argument about "American exceptionalism." See Shafer (1999).
71. Merton (1968a).

POLITICAL PARTICIPATION AND POWER

In a democracy, citizens elect their representatives and hold them accountable for their decisions. But democratic societies have other attributes as well. For example, they are capitalist. Democracy and capitalism fit together because in both goals are achieved via competition under the rule of law. The law not only regulates conflict, channeling it in nonviolent directions, it also reflects still another characteristic: a respect for individual dignity and civil rights. In addition, democratic societies also emphasize the use of science to solve problems. Finally, democratic societies are buttressed by a set of unique cultural values, called the culture of capitalism. As described in Chapter 1, these structural attributes have what Max Weber called an "elective affinity" for one another; although lots of variation exists from one nation to another, they are typical of all modern societies.

In this context, the democratic political process should display, at least ideally, two features.[1] First, competitors should act within the law to influence public policy. The idea here is that correct procedures are followed. The constant danger, however, is that the law itself can be used to make procedures unfair, thereby protecting the political and economic interests of the most powerful classes and groups. With regard to voting, for example, the right to vote can be restricted or electoral districts can be constructed to dilute the impact of certain people's votes. Such distortions of the political process are analogous to a company seeking increased market share (even a monopoly) in order to increase profits at the expense of consumers. Second, in order to avoid this danger, access to the political arena should be open so that the contest for power is competitive and fair. The degree of **political participation** is an important indicator of openness. It refers to people's attempt at influencing who gets elected or the appointments, policies, and laws passed by government at all levels—federal, state, and local. The more people can and do participate in the political process, the more easily are decision makers held accountable. Political scientists often use the term **pluralism** to describe political systems displaying these two features.

The democratic political process, then, provides a nonviolent, competitive mechanism for dividing up shares in the available goods and services: jobs, income, wealth, and other resources that affect people's life chances. In a democracy, those ending up with inferior life chances accept the outcome. And make no mistake: There are always winners and losers. Even so, democracies are stable because the inequality that results from political decisions is perceived by the people (especially the losers) as fair.

In fact, however, no democratic society displays the two features of a pluralist system described above in pure form.[2] An inherent tension exists between them that can never be resolved. This tension often manifests itself as class conflict, which is the focus of this chapter, but also race and gender conflict. In general, those classes with the most resources inevitably try and to some extent succeed in limiting the ability of other groups to participate in the political process. Inequality results. For example, as stated in the *Political Power Hypothesis* in Chapter 1: *The higher the social class, the greater the influence over the distribution of resources in the society.* Even so, the pluralist ideal provides a standard by which to evaluate how democratic a society is.

TYPES OF POLITICAL PARTICIPATION

Voting

Elections are the mechanisms by which eligible citizens vote for their desired candidates or political parties, who then act as their representatives. Thus, ideally at least, elections function simultaneously as a method for participants to express their desires and to hold decision makers accountable. But achieving this goal is not easy. The degree to which elections are free, fair, and competitive reflects the structure of elections, which is determined in turn by such decisions as who gets to vote, how electoral districts are determined, and several other factors to be explained later on. Moreover, elections do not end the political process; they begin it. After all, people pursue their interests (they exercise power) as public issues are defined, policies considered, and laws implemented. In a democratic society, will decision makers listen to their constituents who vote or to someone else, such as wealthy contributors?

Partisanship

Partisans are people who identify with, work for, and try to influence a party, candidate, or issue. Average middle- and working-class citizens sometimes become partisans. During elections, they may wear a button, put a sign on their car, do volunteer work, or contribute small amounts of money. Between elections, the main form of partisanship consists of **lobbying,** the attempt at influencing legislators or other decision makers in favor of (or against) a specific decision. Again, average citizens sometimes lobby. They might, for example, telephone a member of the school board or write a note to their congressional representative. These contacts are taken very seriously by decision makers; for they know that people who contact them in this way are especially likely to have voted and to vote again. Also, those who contact officeholders can then be solicited for campaign contributions at the next election.

The most influential partisans, however, are those constituents with large amounts of cash to spend. This is a key point: Contributions of money provide the lubricant for successful lobbying, which is mostly done by very wealthy people and hired professionals. They are effective precisely to the extent they can funnel cash to candidates, either directly to their campaign funds or indirectly via a political party. Candidates, both liberal and conservative, Republican and Democrat, rely on cash constituents to get elected. Thus, understanding the twin issues of accountability and power in a democracy requires recognizing the role of money in elections.

Unruliness

Ideally, when citizens become dissatisfied, they elect a new mayor, senator, or president to represent their interests, either by voting, campaign contributions, or both. But those who do not or cannot participate do neither. When significant numbers of people lack the ability to participate effectively, democracy becomes a sham. Such persons often feel powerless (the jargon term is **alienated**) and this feeling is realistic. When those left out become angry, as periodically happens, they sometimes take to the streets, acting out in violent and destructive ways. Such unruliness is sometimes the only power the weak have.

During the 1960s, poor people and racial and ethnic minorities took to the streets repeatedly. Similar events have occurred in the last decade or so in Los Angeles, Miami, and other cities.[3] The obvious interpretation is to see such episodes as riots. From this point of view, the perpetrators are criminals, who should be prosecuted for vandalism, mugging, even murder. Although this interpretation is correct, a nonobvious explanation also exists: In an anomic context, one can see anger in the streets as rebellions on the part of oppressed and disenfranchised people. They are political acts by individuals for whom few options exist. They seek the right to vote, the ability to hold decision makers accountable for decisions affecting them. From this rather different angle of vision, violence and other forms of unruliness constitute political claims to be considered.[4] But collective violence only occurs under conditions of extreme frustration; it is a signal to those with power from those left out of the system. Unruliness, then, constitutes the political underbelly of a democratic system. It is ignored with peril.

THE RATE OF VOTING

Voting is the primal democratic act; it is the first and most important indicator of a democratic society. All other modes of participation are adjuncts to this act. After all, while wealthy constituents may contribute money to candidates, gain access to the winners, and lobby for the creation of laws beneficial to themselves (and against laws that would harm them), even if they are successful, elected representatives must ultimately appeal to ordinary citizens. Voters, then, can hold decision makers accountable—at least in principle—against the interests of those with money. Alas, many Americans either do not vote or their vote is not effective. By way of anticipation, the finding is that *the lower the social class, the lower the rate of voting.* This finding means that elected officials are held accountable by those at the top and that the interests of those at the bottom are not represented.

Voting in the United States

Historically, the number and characteristics of citizens eligible to vote has steadily expanded in all democratic nations.[5] As explained in Chapters 2 and 3, voting in this country was generally restricted to white male property owners over age 21 when the Constitution was adopted.[6] Today, however, nearly all persons over the age of 18 have gained the ability to participate (at least in principle), regardless of property owner-ship, immigrant status, race, or gender. In the United States, as in other nations, this process occurred mainly because those left out of the democratic process fought to be included.[7] There is a lesson here: The extension of the franchise resulted from unruly (and often illegal) activities—riots, demonstrations, and other forms of rebellion—by those excluded from a presumably democratic system. Such persons and groups had no other option. Historically, then, the American political system has responded to the unruliness of those left out by including them. The outcome has been (again, at least in principle) a more democratic society.

But that ideal is not fully realized today. This fact is revealed by Figure 6.1, which displays the rate of voting in presidential elections from 1876 to 2004. In the 2004 presi-dential election, only 58 percent of the adult population voted—and this was above aver-age for the United States. There was a time, however, when most people voted. Almost 80 percent of all eligible citizens took part in presidential elections during the last quarter of the nineteenth century. Moreover, in the non-Southern and most densely populated states, turnouts during the years 1876 to 1896 were much higher than displayed in the figure. For example, average turnouts in presidential elections were 93 percent in Indiana, 92 percent in New Jersey and Ohio, 89 percent in New York, and 83 percent in Pennsylvania.[8] In nonpresidential election years during this period, these same states had average turnouts of 84 percent in Indiana, 77 percent in New Jersey and Ohio, 68 percent in New York, and 71 percent in Pennsylvania. It thus appears that nearly all eligible citizens, rich and poor alike, voted in those states where most of the population lived.

This, then, is the first important example: Even given structural constraints (to be discussed), the current low rate of voting is not inevitable; people in every class have voted in the past. Even so, you might remember that during the late nineteenth century, women and young adults could not vote by law. Moreover, although African Americans gained the franchise for a brief time after the Civil War, it was taken from them after 1876 by Whites' imposition of Jim Crow laws.[9] So the assertion that low rates of voting can be avoided should be interpreted with caution for now.

In addition, some have argued that turnout data during the later nineteenth century may be artificially high because of vote fraud.[10] Most scholars conclude, however, that the data shown in Figure 6.1 are reasonably accurate, at least with regard to the total rate of participation.[11] The problem of fraud during elections of this period is separate from the issue of electoral turnout. All observers agree that most elections were controversial and competitive—usually decided by small margins. So high rates of participation make sense. Moreover, as will be shown in a few moments, the levels of voter turnout reported in Figure 6.1 for the late nineteenth century United States resemble the proportion of

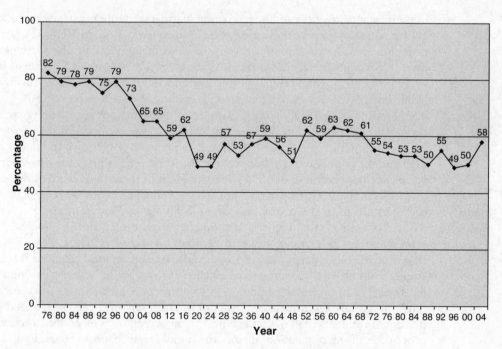

FIGURE 6.1   Rate of Voting in U.S. Presidential Elections, 1876–2004

Source: United States Bureau of the Census (1975:1071; 2006:264)

middle-class and rich people who vote today, the proportion of registered citizens who now vote, and European turnout rates. These similarities suggest that reported levels of participation in the last quarter of the nineteenth century are plausible.

Most fraud during this period involved vote buying, voter intimidation, miscounting of votes, and the manipulation of small numbers of ballots in highly competitive elections.[12] Thus, the nature of the ballot is extremely important. Before 1890, each party printed and distributed its own ballots, called "party strips" or "tickets," which listed all its candidates. These ballots were of varying size and color, which made it difficult to conceal one's preference as the ballot was dropped into the box. Voting during this period was raucous and public. Citizens selected one ticket, sometimes for a price, and turned it in—in full view of everyone gathered around the polling place. Adoption of the Australian ballot at the turn of the century changed this situation.[13] This type of ballot identifies all the nominees for office on one piece of paper and asks voters to mark their choices. It not only reduces the possibility of fraud but also makes it easier for people to vote a "split ticket." That is, they can select candidates for various offices from either party.

Figure 6.1 shows that electoral turnout began dropping with the presidential election of 1900. As will be explained, laws requiring registration were introduced in every state during this period. Participation rates fell steadily through the election of 1924. Part of this decline occurred because women obtained the franchise for the first time in 1920, which depressed rates for two elections. But as women developed a sense of political effectiveness and began voting in greater numbers, turnout rose somewhat, averaging about 56 percent during the elections from 1932 to 1948. With this exception, however, the decline in turnout was concentrated among the working class and poor.[14] Turnout rose again for the next five elections, averaging 61 percent from 1952 to 1968. In 1971, the voting age was lowered to 18 from 21. Voter turnout has not been above 60 percent since that time, averaging about 53 percent in the presidential elections of 1972 to 2000. Even allowing for lower turnout rates among young adults, those who do not vote are still mainly working class and poor. Since just over half of all adults now vote in the United States, the necessary majority to choose the president and other public officials elected at the same time is just over one-quarter of the voting age population (half of 53 percent). Most of these people are middle class.

Electoral turnout during off-year congressional elections is even less; for example, only 35 percent of the population voted in House of Representative races in 2002.[15] These low voting rates in off-year elections mean that many decision makers—senators, representatives, governors, and state legislators—are selected by only 18 percent (or less) of all eligible citizens (half of 35 percent). Turnout in local elections that occur separately from off-year Congressional elections is lower still. In many communities, voting rates of 15 percent are common in local elections, which mean that local officials (city and county commissioners, school board members) can be selected by only 8 percent of residents (half of 15 percent).[16] Low voting rates mean that a relatively small proportion of the population, mainly the middle class, chooses elected public officials. They, in turn, orient their decisions to the interests of those who voted. Such low turnouts, as will be suggested later (see Figure 6.2), have become self-perpetuating: Nonvoters—meaning the poor and working class—are not contacted or mobilized and do not develop a sense of political effectiveness; so they do not vote. This pattern suggests that the United States departs rather far from the democratic ideal.

Low turnouts do not, however, occur everywhere in the United States.[17] On the mainland, Puerto Rican Americans display low rates of voting similar to those of other ethnic groups whose members are disproportionately poor. For example, in the 1996 presidential election, only about 47 percent cast ballots. On the island, however, turnout is much higher. In the three presidential elections of 1992, 1996, and 2000, Puerto Rican citizens' turnouts averaged 84 percent. Here, then, is a second example of very high rates of voting. On the island, people from all social classes vote.

An important restriction on voting is the registration requirement and its impact reveals one of the most important causes of low electoral turnout. Table 6.1 displays by income, the proportion of eligible voters (not the voting age population) who reported they registered and voted. (The difference between voting age population and eligible voters will be discussed in a few moments.) Please look down columns (2) and (3). Note that as family income decreases, the percent reporting that they registered and voted decreases as well. The poor vote at the lowest rate. But this result is not inevitable, as can by seen by looking down column (4). Although the percentage of those registered who reported voting falls with income, the rate of decline is much less. In fact, column (4) shows that most of those who are registered actually vote, and this is so at all income levels. This fact has been true for many years: In the last nine presidential elections, the proportion of those registered who voted has ranged from 83 to 91 percent, with little variation by social class.[18]

TABLE 6.1   Participation by Citizen Population in the 2004 U.S. Presidential Election by Family Income

(1) FAMILY INCOME	(2) PERCENT ELIGIBLE VOTERS REGISTERED	(3) PERCENT ELIGIBLE VOTERS WHO VOTED	(4) PERCENT REGISTERED ELIGIBLE VOTERS WHO VOTED
All Incomes	72%	64%	89%
> $100,000	86%	81%	95%
$75,000–99,999	83%	78%	93%
$50,000–74,999	80%	72%	90%
$40,000–49,999	77%	68%	89%
$30,000–39,999	72%	62%	86%
$20,000–29,999	69%	58%	85%
< $20,000	61%	48%	79%
Percent Difference Lowest to Highest	25%	33%	16%

Note: "Eligible voters" excludes legal residents who are not citizens and ex-felons who cannot vote. See below for an explanation of the significance of this issue.

Source: United States Bureau of the Census (2006b:4).

These data lead to a third example of high rates of voting: The turnout rate among those registered resembles that which existed toward the end of the nineteenth century and occurs today in Puerto Rico: More than four of five of those registered vote, which means people from all social classes cast ballots. The low turnout among working-class and poor persons cannot be explained away as due to lack of motivation. Some observers try; they argue that those who do not vote must be satisfied with public policy.[19] This argument, a sort of "don't worry, be happy" orientation, implies that poor and working-class people are the most satisfied of all citizens, since they vote at the lowest rates. This interpretation is not only absurd, it masks a hidden reality: The middle class and rich dominate the political process in the United States and receive most of the benefits.

Voting in Cross-National Perspective

The pattern of electoral participation is greater in other Western nations, which come closer to the democratic ideal than does the United States. Economically developed democracies around the world display an average electoral turnout rate of about 73 percent.[20] The range of variation is illustrated by turnout among the voting age population in recent elections for the five nations shown below:[21]

Sweden, 2002	80%
Germany, 2005	78%
Canada, 2004	61%
United Kingdom, 2005	61%
United States, 2004	58%

The key point to remember, as suggested by the hypothesis presented earlier, is that *differences in the rate of voting among the lower classes account for almost all the cross-national variation in electoral turnout.*[22] Thus, in nations displaying low turnout the poor vote at a relatively low rate, which means that elected officials do not have to take their interests into account. The United States provides an example, as shown in Table 6.1. Conversely, in nations displaying high turnout, the poor vote at a relatively high rate, which means that elected officials must take into account the interests of all social classes when making policy decisions. Electoral turnout in the most recent Swedish parliamentary elections by family income (in Swedish Crowns) illustrates how little variation can exist in turnout by social class:[23]

≤ 99,999	72%
100,000–149,999	78%
150,000–199,999	83%
200,000–299,999	87%
≥ 300,000	92%

There is only a 20 percent difference in turnout between the poor and rich. This difference is far less than occurs in the United States (and, indeed, in other nations), which displays a 33 percent variation (see column (3) of Table 6.1). In fact, class differences in Swedish voting resemble those found in the United States among people who are registered, as shown in column (4) of Table 6.1.

The cross-national data provide a fourth example of high rates of voting: Many nations (not just those reported above) show electoral turnouts resembling the level of voting seen in this country in the late nineteenth century, in Puerto Rico today, and the percent of registrants who vote. These examples suggest that neither low rates of electoral participation nor vast differences by social class are inevitable.

SOCIAL STRUCTURE AND VOTING

The conventional view of voting is simple: citizens cast ballots and elect their representatives. But the structure of voting is actually relatively elaborate. There is no "correct" way for, say, technical experts, to create electoral structures. The rules of the game by which democracy is practiced are constructed and maintained by people in light of their values and political interests. This is as it should be: Politics in a democracy is a competitive (pluralist) process and the outcome—in the form of regulations, programs funded (or not funded), and tax policy—affects the level of inequality, another way of describing differences in life chances and lifestyles. The data presented above show not only low rates of electoral participation but also that participation is negatively related to social class. Why might this be so? The hypothesis offered here is: *The rate of voting in the United States reflects the impact of (1) type of electoral system, (2) who gets to vote, (3) gerrymandering, (4) election day, (5) registration requirements, and (6) degree of inequality.*

Type of Electoral System

Americans have a peculiar electoral myopia. They think there is only one way to vote. But all sorts of electoral systems are practiced around the world, each of which has advantages and disadvantages.[24] In the United States and Europe, the most common electoral systems are (1) plurality/majority systems and (2) proportional representation systems.

Plurality/majority systems are winner-take-all arrangements. There are several types, the most common is **first past the post (FPTP),** used in the United Kingdom, the United States, and several other nations. In this system, an election is like a horse race, with the first candidate past the post being the victor and losers getting nothing. This system has several advantages: It is simple, produces clear results, and promotes a link between constituents and their representatives. Its disadvantages are that significant political views may go unrepresented as well as the interests of minority groups, which leads to "wasted votes." As a winner-take-all system, FPTP nearly always produces two broad-based parties.[25] In this context, citizens who anticipate being on the losing side may feel they have no realistic chance of electing a candidate of their choice. Also, FPTP systems depend on the drawing of electoral boundaries (gerrymandering, see below), which can reduce competitiveness.

Table 6.2 displays the cross-national rates of voting mentioned earlier and illustrates how turnout is related to structural factors. For example, as shown in column (2) electoral turnout tends to be lower in first past the post systems.[26]

In proportional representation systems a party's share of the vote gets translated into a corresponding proportion of seats in the legislature. The party with the most votes (the winners) gets the most seats; the party with the second most votes gets the second most seats, and so on. Such an arrangement means that many parties—and, hence, many points of view—may obtain representation. Although there are many types, the most common (at least in the European Union) is **list proportional representation (list-PR),** in which each party presents a list of candidates for citizens' consideration. The main advantage of list-PR is that electoral results represent the range of voter preferences, so minority views and groups gain representation. This means there are fewer wasted votes. Also, gerrymandering (the drawing of electoral boundaries) has less impact because each district has several representatives. The disadvantage of list-PR is that as more parties can win seats in the legislature, coalition governments may be formed. One result can be that parties must compromise their policy goals in order to govern. As illustrated by column (2) Table 6.2, turnout is often higher in list-PR systems.

Who Gets to Vote

Although the right to vote is fundamental to democracy, it has always been contested terrain.[27] After all, who gets to vote can swing an election, altering the priorities of government, affecting the distribution of resources. Inevitably, then, some participants want to increase electoral turnout while others want to decrease it—both for partisan purposes.

The right to vote was not mentioned in the Constitution until ratification of the Fifteenth Amendment in 1870. It states: "The right of citizens of the United States to vote shall not be denied or abridged by the United States or by any State on account of race, color, or previous condition of servitude." Over the next 10 to 15 years, African Americans voted in large numbers.[28] One result was that more African Americans were elected to political office than at any other time in American history. Another result was that state legislatures set aside laws denying minority groups civil rights, among them laws prohibiting intermarriage, and began enacting programs for the public good, such as integrated public education. But this period was short-lived, despite the Fifteenth

TABLE 6.2 Social Structure and Electoral Turnout in Five Countries

COUNTRY, ELECTION YEAR	(1) ELECTORAL TURNOUT	(2) TYPE OF ELECTORAL SYSTEM	(3) RESTRICTIONS ON VOTING	(4) IMPORTANCE OF GERRYMANDERING	(5) ELECTION ON WORK DAY	(6) REGISTRATION REQUIRED	(7) INDEX OF INCOME INEQUALITY
Sweden, 2002	80%	List-PR	Few	Low	No	No	.21
Germany, 2005	78%	List-PR	Few	Low	No	No	.27
Canada, 2004	61%	FPTP	Few	Low	Yes	No	.28
United Kingdom, 2005	61%	FPTP	Few	Low	Yes	No	.34
United States, 2004	58%	FPTP	Some	High	Yes	Yes	.45

Notes: Electoral turnout: voting age population. Electoral system: List-PR refers to proportional representation with a party list of candidates; FPTP refers to first past the post. The index of income inequality is the Gini coefficient. It varies from zero to 1.00, with a higher number indicating greater inequality. The Gini is for 2000 in Sweden, Germany, and the United States for 1999 in the United Kingdom and 1998 in Canada.

Sources: United States Bureau of the Census (2006b:3), International Institute for Democracy and Electoral Assistance (2005), United Nations (2005:270).

Amendment's mandate. The law (buttressed by murderous violence) was used to disenfranchise African Americans and other minorities and deny them civil rights. As described in Chapter 2, lack of civil rights meant that minority groups could not compete for economic success. Instead, they were trapped, first as sharecroppers and then in urban ghettos. How would the next century of American history have differed if African Americans, Hispanic Americans, and Asian Americans had been allowed to vote?

The vote was contested terrain for women as well. During the same period the nation (not just the South) began depriving minority groups their civil rights, women began agitating for theirs—especially the right to vote. For example, Susan B. Anthony and fourteen other women persuaded a sympathetic registrar to allow them to register and vote, which they did in the presidential election of 1872.[29] They did this as both an act of political unruliness and a test of whether the equal protection clause of the Fourteenth Amendment could be a vehicle for expanding women's rights. It was not, at least at that time. All were arrested, including the registrar. In a speech given before her trial, Anthony argued:

> One half of the people of this Nation today are utterly powerless to blot from the statute books an unjust law, or to write a new and just one. . . . This form of government, that enforces taxation without representation—that compels [women] to obey laws to which they have never given their consent—that imprisons and hangs them without a trial by a jury of their peers—that robs them, in marriage, of the custody of their own persons, wages, and children—[leaves] half of the people wholly at the mercy of the other half.

When called to the stand during her trial, the prosecutor objected, stating that, as a woman, "she is not competent as a witness on her own behalf." Her lawyer took the stand and testified for her. All were found guilty and fined, although Anthony never paid hers. Women did not obtain the right to vote until ratification of the Nineteenth Amendment in 1920 and did not gain full civil rights until the 1960s.

Underlying the argument about who gets to vote are two competing points of view.[30] The first justifies limiting the vote as prudent to insure good government. The fear is that ill-informed citizens (i.e., the poor or others who have been marginalized) might be goaded by a demagogue into abrogating essential freedoms. For example, a movement arose during the 1930s to deny the vote to the poor and welfare recipients because they might be unduly influenced by President Franklin Delano Roosevelt.[31] This idea lingers. Should today's welfare recipients vote? After all, they are often not as well-educated as other citizens. The other point of view is that universal suffrage (the right to vote) gives everyone a stake in the political system, making government and its decisions legitimate and stable. The argument is that all individuals can understand their interests well enough to cast a ballot, including the poor and downtrodden. Although this approach is embodied in the pluralist ideal, described earlier, which point of view one adopts usually depends on a calculation of political and economic interests. Who gets to vote dictates, in part, who gets to divide up the pie and for whose benefit.

In the United States, today, every adult over age eighteen is formally eligible to vote, with two exceptions. First, legal residents who are not citizens cannot vote. This may seem like an obvious restriction, but in the past, white men who were not citizens voted even as minority groups were denied the suffrage.[32] Second, convicted felons cannot vote in 48 states, an issue that has become controversial in recent years.[33]

About 4.7 million Americans, more than 2 percent of the adult population, are barred from voting because of a felony conviction. Many are African-American men, of whom 13 percent cannot cast ballots.[34] Consider: An eighteen-year-old first-time offender who pleads guilty in exchange for probation may unintentionally give up the right to vote forever. The question is whether this result constitutes wise public policy.

The United States is unique in disenfranchising convicted felons. Nearly all the nations comprising the European Union allow persons who have completed their prison sentences to vote. At least five—Ireland, Spain, Sweden, Denmark, and Greece—allow prison inmates to vote.[35] The rationale for restoring voting rights to former offenders is that it provides a clear marker of their reintegration into society and recognition that, as citizens, they have a stake in the distribution of resources. It thereby reduces political alienation and the possibility of unruliness. This rationale fits with the pluralist ideal.

In American elections, however, the impact of voting by ex-felons is potentially significant. Because they are drawn disproportionately from the ranks of racial and ethnic minorities and the poor, it is probable that their disenfranchisement takes more votes from Democratic than Republican candidates. Computer simulations suggest that the outcome of the 2000 presidential election, as well as several senatorial elections over the past several decades, would probably be reversed if they had voted.[36] Which party controlled the Senate could have been effected. Not surprisingly, then, allowing ex-felons to vote is a partisan issue, a form of class and race conflict. Also not surprisingly, arguments over this issue mirror the competing points of view described above. Those in opposition argue that "there are certain levels of loyalty, responsibility, and trustworthiness . . . required in order to vote. People who have committed crimes against their fellow citizens do not have these qualifications. Allowing felons to vote will dilute the quality of self-government." Those in favor argue "once people start voting, they're less likely to commit new crimes. . . . There's no threat to public safety by permitting prisoners and felons to vote." And, most importantly, "the right to vote is fundamental in a democratic system."[37] As illustrated in column (3) of Table 6.2, restrictions on the right to vote reduce turnout in the United States.

Gerrymandering

Gerrymandering refers to the deliberate rearrangement of the boundaries of electoral districts in order to influence the outcome of elections. In 1812, Governor Eldridge Gerry, a signer of the Declaration of Independence, tried to disadvantage his political opponents by packing their supporters into a few strongholds. Because the outline of one of the resulting districts looked somewhat reptilian, a creative newspaper editor said that it resembled a "salamander. Call it a Gerrymander." The term has been used ever since.[38]

The goal of gerrymandering is to minimize the impact of opponents' votes and maximize the impact of supporters' votes in order for incumbents to insure their reelection and parties to protect their majority in a legislative body, such as the House of Representatives. The impact of gerrymandering is illustrated in Figure 6.2. Panel A depicts a hypothetical state's congressional districts arranged to insure competitiveness.

PANEL A: This state has four Congressional districts with boundaries designed to encourage competition.

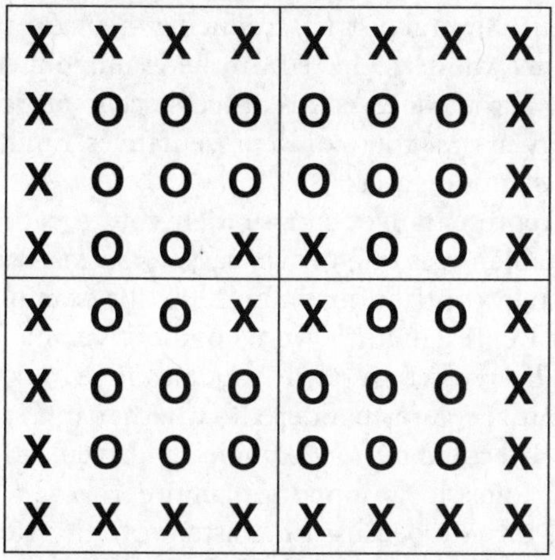

These four districts each have sixteen voters, eight affiliated with party X and eight affiliated with party O. Elections are competitive and turnout is likely to be high. In order to win, candidates for office must appeal to a broad spectrum of interests.

PANEL B: This state has four Congressional districts that have been gerrymandered.

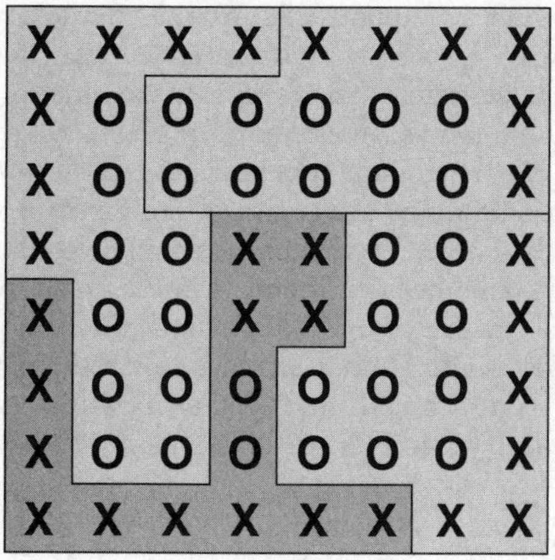

These four districts also have sixteen voters. Fourteen X voters, however, have been "packed" into the dark gray district and the rest "cracked" into the three light gray districts. In this scenario, O office-holders are guaranteed three districts and X officeholders one. Elections will not be competitive in any of these districts and candidates can be more ideologically driven because they must only appeal to their own supporters. Electoral turnout will fall as citizens see their votes are wasted. For example, why should the X voters in the light gray districts bother to cast ballots when their candidate has little chance of winning?

FIGURE 6.2   An Illustration of Competitive and Gerrymandered Electoral Districts

Source: Adapted from "Gerrymandering," an article in Wikipedia. Author unknown.

In this example, each district contains eight citizens identifying with party O and X, respectively. In order to win, candidates will have to appeal to a broad spectrum of citizen interest. In a competitive context, interest is likely to be high, as will turnout. This is one of the most stable findings in the literature on elections: "More people vote when the election is close."[39] For example, turnout in the 2004 U.S. presidential election was higher than normal because everyone knew the outcome was going to be close. Panel B depicts the same hypothetical state's congressional districts after they have been gerrymandered. Two tactics are used in combination: "Packing" places many voters of an opposing party into a single district, usually one it would win anyway. "Cracking" spreads opponents' voters into several districts, reducing their impact. The result almost guarantees that incumbents will be reelected. In the example used here, party O will win three seats while party X wins one. As this process occurs nationwide, it translates into a congressional majority in the House of Representatives. Similar outcomes occur in many state and city legislative districts.

Gerrymandering works because representatives choose their voters (rather than voters holding representatives accountable). It is one of two reasons so many incumbents are reelected (the other is campaign contributions). In 2004, for example, only about 40 of 435 seats in the House of Representatives were competitive and 98 percent of incumbents were reelected.[40] This reelection rate is about average over the last quarter century. Legislative bodies that are gerrymandered—whether in Congress, state legislatures, or city commissions—become more ideologically driven, since candidates must only appeal to their party's most loyal supporters in order to win.

Gerrymandering lowers electoral turnout because of "wasted votes."[41] Recall for example, that only 35 percent of the population voted in House of Representatives races in the 2002 off-year elections. Panel B of Figure 6.2 suggests why. Supporters of party X in the light gray districts have little chance of casting meaningful ballots and so some of them choose not to vote. Similarly, supporters of party O in the dark gray district know their candidate will not win—if there is a candidate.

Nations with first past the post electoral systems (FPTP) are most prone to gerrymandering.[42] The United Kingdom and Canada, both of which have FPTP systems, minimize its impact by using nonpartisan commissions to set electoral district boundaries, with the goal of ensuring that elections are competitive. In the United States, by contrast, which also has an FPTP electoral system, elected officials nearly always arrange district boundaries and they do so in their interests—which is to say, they want to be reelected. As illustrated in column (4) of Table 6.2, this process constitutes another reason why turnout in the United States is lower than in other nations.

Election Day

The day on which elections are held influences participation rates.[43] In many Western European nations, as in Sweden and Germany, elections occur on Sunday or a national holiday, which means there is leisure time available to vote. This fact helps to explain why turnout rates are very high in these nations, often 70 to 80 percent or more, and class differences minimal. In contrast, Election Day is a working day in some nations, such as England, Canada, and the United States.

In the United States, federal elections are held on the Tuesday after November 2nd.[44] This date was first established for the presidential election of 1848 and subsequently mandated for use in elections to the House of Representatives and the Senate. In a predominantly rural nation, November constituted the most convenient time for farmers to travel over unimproved roads. Tuesday allowed for travel on Monday without disrupting attendance at worship services on Sunday. Delaying election day until after November 2nd allowed farmers to balance their books from the preceding month on the first. This logic, of course, is a vestige of the past and no longer relevant. For nearly everyone, Election Day is a work day. On the island of Puerto Rico, however, it is a national holiday.[45] Political parties spend the day mobilizing their supporters and people spend the day celebrating the election. This is one reason why electoral turnout is higher on the island than on the mainland.

Voting on a working day is a structural barrier to participation. Those who overcome this obstacle in the greatest numbers have longer lunch hours, leave time built into their jobs, more physical energy at the end of the day, child care available, and a belief in their own political effectiveness. These traits, however, are class related, which is one reason why voting is also class related and turnout is lower. The impact is illustrated in column (5) of Table 6.2.

Registration Requirements

In all Western European nations, the state automatically registers citizens to vote, another fact that partly accounts for their high voting rates. Only in the United States are citizens responsible for their own registration. As illustrated in column (5) of Table 6.2, the registration requirement reduces turnout.

Voting and registration differ in fundamental ways. Voting is a political decision in which citizens decide whose positions best reflect and protect their own interests. Registration is an administrative act in which citizens must deal with regulators who assess their credentials and process forms, a situation that makes some people uncomfortable—especially those who are unfamiliar with professional settings.

In the past, registering to vote was difficult because citizens had to appear during working hours at a registration office (usually City Hall or the county seat) well before Election Day. Passage of the National Voter Registration Act (NVRA, or "motor voter" law) in 1993 was supposed to make this process easier by increasing the number of locations where registration could take place.[46] Seven states are not subject to the Act; they are North Dakota, which does not have registration, and Idaho, Maine, Minnesota, New Hampshire, Wisconsin, and Wyoming, which use Election Day registration (more on this later). As of January, 1995, when the Act went into effect, the other 43 states are supposed to offer citizens the opportunity to register when they appear at Department of Motor Vehicle offices, public assistance offices, and other state agencies. In addition, the NVRA also stipulates that citizens be allowed to register by mail (but not online).

The impact of the NVRA on electoral turnout has been minimal; registration has not kept up with the growth in the number of eligible voters.[47] This is so for three reasons.

First, in most states the process is antiquated.[48] Although Americans can now do their banking, pay taxes, register their cars, and perform other tasks requiring security and identification online, they cannot register to vote online in any state except Arizona. In all other states, they must rely on a stamp and patience (in many states the forms are available online but then must be mailed). You should ask yourself why such procedures remain in place. One possibility is concern about fraud. Another, however, is concern about who might vote and how many they might be.

Second, states have actively opposed implementation of NVRA.[49] In many states, citizens who registered at motor vehicle or other state offices were not, in fact, added to the voting lists. In the presidential election of 2000, for example, it is estimated that between 1.5 and 3 million citizens were denied the vote for this reason.[50] In addition, one study shows that the number of persons registering to vote at public assistance agencies declined by 60 percent between 1995 and 2004.[51]

Third, in many states, registration deadlines are 60 to 90 days before the election. Nationwide, the average closing date for registration is three weeks before Election Day. A century and a half ago, the French observer Alexis de Tocqueville noted the significance of this time difference: "As the election draws near, intrigues grow more active and agitation is more lively and wider spread."[52] He thought a presidential election is like a national crisis, which motivates people to get involved—by voting—as it draws near. And he was right. As an election approaches, debates occur, candidates increase their advertising in order to get their message across, and many races tighten, especially for the presidency. As a result, citizens become increasingly interested and develop a sense of political effectiveness; they think their vote matters. In the 2000 campaign, for example, 59 percent of the public reported they were giving "quite a lot" of thought to the campaign in September, nine weeks before the election. This figure rose steadily to 75 percent by the week before the election.[53] As another indicator of increasing interest, registration rates also increase during the run-up to elections, at least in those states where the deadline has not passed.

Table 6.3 illustrates how the registration deadline affects turnout by focusing on the six states that use Election Day Registration (EDR), along with North Dakota, which does not have a registration requirement, and Oregon, which allows citizens to vote by mail ahead of time. Taken together, average turnout in the eight

TABLE 6.3 Turnout in States with Election Day Registration (EDR), No Registration, or Mail Voting, 2004 U.S. Presidential Election

STATE	REGISTRATION OR VOTING PROCEDURE	VOTING AGE POPULATION TURNOUT
Minnesota	EDR	77%
Wisconsin	EDR	73%
Maine	EDR	72%
Oregon	Mail Voting	71%
North Dakota	No Registration	71%
New Hampshire	EDR	69%
Wyoming	EDR	66%
Idaho	EDR	59%
Average in 2004 for the 8 states		70%
U.S. turnout in 2004		58%

Notes: EDR established in 1976 in Minnesota, Wisconsin, and Maine, in 1996 in New Hampshire, Wyoming, and Idaho.

Source: United States Bureau of the Census (2006:264).

states shown in the table was 70 percent, compared to only 58 percent for the nation as a whole. Puerto Rico also uses Election Day Registration, contributing to the high electoral turnout mentioned earlier. This, then, is still another example about electoral participation: If voting is made easier, turnout goes up. Indeed, this finding is consistent over several elections. Despite this fact, EDR is nearly always rejected by state legislatures. Such bills have been introduced in 34 states since 2001, including some of the most populous (such as New York, California, Florida, and Ohio), but passed only in Montana. It began EDR in the 2006 off-year elections.

The original and continuing rationale for imposing registration was to prevent electoral corruption. Yet fraud rarely occurs.[54] There has been no fraud in North Dakota, which does not require registration. Nor has it occurred in states using Election Day Registration. Nor does it happen in other Western nations. Finally, as noted earlier, it is likely that introducing the Australian ballot reduced fraud more than registration. If registration is unnecessary to prevent corruption, then such requirements must have a less obvious purpose. One guess is that it helps to insure middle-class dominance of the electoral process.

Degree of Inequality

All societies display stratification. The unequal distribution of resources is important because it affects people's life chances: their ability to share in the available goods and services. Measuring inequality can be done in a variety of ways. You have seen in previous chapters that occupational prestige scores are sometimes used. So are differences in educational attainment. Because income is fundamental to people's life chances, it provides a straightforward measure. But comparing income inequality across societies is tricky, so researchers often employ an index, called the Gini Coefficient. It translates the income distribution of each country into a standard score that varies between zero and one, with a higher number indicating greater inequality. Thus, a score of zero would mean that all incomes are completely equal, while 1.00 would mean that one person receives all the income. Of course, neither of these extreme results occur in any nation. In practice, the standard interpretation of the Gini is that values between .20 and .24 indicate a "small" level of income inequality; .25 to .29, a "moderate" level; and .30 to .34, a "high" level. Any nation with a Gini above .35 displays a "very high" level of inequality.[55]

Please look back to column (7) of Table 6.2, which displays Gini Coefficients of income inequality for five nations. As the data reveal, the United States displays much greater income inequality than do these other nations, and (although not shown in the table) the gap has become greater over the past quarter-century. In fact, as will be discussed in subsequent chapters, the level of income inequality has increased in this country to a point not seen since the 1920s, just before the Depression. It is so high that this nation ranks 92nd in the world, with a level of income inequality higher than that of Bolivia, China, Cameroon, Uganda, and many others.[56]

Income inequality affects electoral turnout in all Western nations.[57] The finding is straightforward: *The higher the degree of income inequality, the lower the turnout.* In addition, the finding also occurs in subnational units within these societies. For example, in this country, states displaying higher levels of inequality also display lower turnout.

The reason for this relationship is straightforward: Modern societies, as you should recall, are **anomic,** which refers to a disconnection between cultural values and the legitimate means to achieve them. The impact of anomie is greatest when the level of inequality is high. One response to an anomic situation is rebellion, described earlier in terms of political unruliness. Another response is withdrawal (called "retreatism"), a simple unwillingness to participate.[58] When inequality is especially high, large segments of the population feel powerless and do not participate in political decision making; they do not vote, for example.

In sum, Table 6.2 displays factors affecting electoral turnout cross-nationally. As the table illustrates, nations with the highest rates of voting maximize the opportunity to vote. For example, by holding elections on a Sunday or holiday, they make it easier to vote. Conversely, nations holding elections on working days have imposed a barrier to voting that some people cannot cross and, hence, they display lower levels of participation. The United States places the most restrictions on the opportunity to vote.

A Note on Voting Technology

Assuming citizens are registered, nearly all of them vote (recall Table 6.1). In this country, five quite different technologies are used for voting. Each has strengths and weaknesses. Each affects the accuracy of the count and thus electoral outcomes in close races.[59]

First, hand-counted paper ballots are still used occasionally, mainly in rural areas. This is the simplest, least technologically sophisticated way of voting. Recall that in the nineteenth and early twentieth centuries, Americans simply dropped a preprinted ticket into the ballot box or marked their ballots with a simple X. Even the Australian ballot used today makes voting easy, especially if there is only one choice to make. Paper ballots make auditing the election relatively straightforward: They are simply recounted. But there are drawbacks: Counting is slow, labor intensive, and can be error prone when more than one choice is marked on the same ballot. This is important because choices on many offices and initiatives may appear on each ballot in some elections and jurisdictions today. The advantage, then, of using more advanced technology is that it provides a speedier and, presumably, more reliable way of counting the votes.

Second, mechanical lever machines require that citizens record their votes and then pull one or more handles. These machines eliminate paper but make auditing the election difficult because there is no separate record of each voter's intent, only the results captured by each machine. Also, this equipment can be intimidating and confusing to voters. Although some jurisdictions still use these machines, they are being phased out.

Third, punch card ballots require citizens to depress a lever that creates a hole in a card, which is then counted by a sorting machine. This technology is not as daunting as mechanical machines, nor is it difficult to use. Moreover, the count goes quickly and auditing voter intent during a recount is possible. But punch cards are, alas, one of the most error prone of all voting technologies. The experience in Florida in the 2000 presidential election, where the phrase "hanging chad" entered the national consciousness, was not unique. Several other states had similar problems, which occur whenever an election is close and this technology is used.

Fourth, touch screens, called direct-recording electronic (DRE) voting machines require that citizens record their votes on an "interface" by touching various sections of the screen. The result allows for a swift counting of the votes. When they are not equipped with a paper backup, however, auditing each voter's intent becomes impossible. Some states require that these machines be equipped with "voter-verifiable paper audit trails" (VVPATs), a paper record of each vote that is retained by election officials (not voters). In effect, two versions of the vote are produced—one digital and one paper. This would allow auditing the vote and a recount if necessary. The advantage of these machines is that they are easy to use. But there are several disadvantages.[60] (1) They generate a relatively high number of unrecorded votes because they are confusing to many persons, especially the poor and others who are not used to computers. (Yes, they exist.) (2) Critics argue that, like any computer, they can be hacked into, which would affect both the digital and paper record. The outcome of elections could thus be influenced. (3) These machines are very expensive to purchase and complex to maintain.

Fifth, optically scanned paper ballots require citizens to mark their selections and then insert the ballot into a scanner, which reads and counts the votes. Like all paper ballots, they are less intimidating to voters, the count goes swiftly, and it can be audited relatively easily. Optically scanned paper ballots also display fewer errors than any other form of voting technology. Moreover, these machines are much less expensive to purchase than other equipment, such as touch screens.

Voting technology clearly affects the accuracy of the count and of a recount, if necessary.[61] In this regard, optically scanned paper ballots seem to provide the best choice. Citizens mark their ballots on paper. The count occurs quickly. If a recount becomes necessary, each voter's intention can be accurately assessed. And these machines are much cheaper to purchase and maintain.

Implications

Other Western nations display much higher levels of voting than the United States. If the pluralist ideal is used as a standard, then low rates of electoral turnout mean that this country is much less democratic than other nations. Moreover, while low electoral turnout is concentrated among the working class and poor in all nations, it is especially pronounced in the United States (recall Table 6.1). The result affects both who gets elected and the public policies they espouse. The great political scientist, V.O. Key, explained why, more than half a century ago: "The blunt truth is that politicians and officials are under no compulsion to pay heed to classes and groups of citizens who do not vote."[62] Regardless of the issue—job benefits (such as health insurance), housing policies (such as segregation), educational spending, or income protection—those who do not vote have little influence on decision makers. This is also true of issues unrelated (at least directly) to the distribution of resources, such as abortion policy, gun policy, or environmental policies. Unless threatened with unruliness from below or (more likely) co-opted by money from above, decision makers represent the interests of voters.

Low electoral turnouts have existed for so long that they have become part of a self-perpetuating electoral system. Figure 6.3 presents a model of the impact of structural inhibitions on the ability to vote.[63] As described in the model, structural inhibitions on voting lead to lower electoral turnouts, which in turn lead candidates and parties to stress policies of interest to likely voters, who are mainly middle class. This emphasis, of course, reinforces the low voting rate. Over the years, the candidates and parties have stopped contacting nonvoters and trying to mobilize them. As a result, nonvoters do not develop

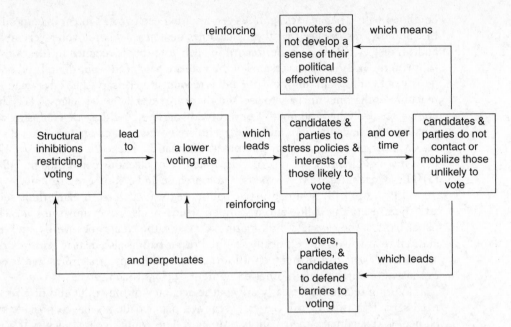

FIGURE 6.3   **The Impact of Structural Inhibitions on the Rate of Voting in the United States**

a sense of their potential political effectiveness, which again reinforces low turnouts. In addition, since they do not contact (or care about) nonvoters, those who vote, candidates, parties, and some academic researchers find themselves defending barriers to voting, which perpetuates structural inhibitions (such as registration).

Low electoral turnouts are not inevitable. Although a first past the post electoral system is embedded in the Constitution, all of the other factors restricting turnout can be changed. From the point of view of the pluralist ideal, democracy would be better served if ex-felons were allowed to vote, if electoral districts were drawn by nonpartisan commissions, if Election Day occurred on a Sunday, if election day registration were instituted around the country, and if the level of inequality was reduced. Commentators propose changes like these in the name of greater democracy all the time.[64] Such changes involve more than conforming to an ideal value, they are partisan political issues. If turnouts approached, say, 80 percent, the political power of the middle class and rich would be diminished. If elections become more competitive, incumbent lawmakers would be at greater risk. Some people benefit from low turnouts. They also enjoy access to decision makers as a result of their campaign contributions.

PARTISANSHIP AND THE ROLE OF MONEY IN ELECTIONS

To most people, elections seem straightforward. Candidates present themselves to the public via television commercials, sound bites on the nightly news, public forums, and other venues. Based on this presentation, ordinary citizens select the winners on Election Day. Although this view is accurate, it is incomplete. Behind the veil, the real business of election campaigns (at any level) is money. This business is conducted over the telephone, at cocktail parties, and at private meetings with partisans, especially wealthy contributors. Those with money are attracted to political campaigns like a moth to light. Their money provides a source of power not available to ordinary voters. Their goal is to obtain a bigger piece of the pie, a bigger share of the available resources. Money trumps voting as the rich hold decision makers accountable. In order to see why money provides power, consider the cost of winning.

The Cost of Winning

In the straightforward version of elections, winning requires a candidate with a timely and articulate message, appropriate experience, an effective campaign organization, and an attractive presentation of self and issues. In addition to these necessary attributes, however, a candidate requires money. In the 2004 presidential campaign, the two main national parties raised more than $1.6 billion, divided as follows: Democrats, $730,900,000, and Republicans, $892,800,000.[65] Spending will be even higher in the 2008 campaign. These enormous sums imply a fundamental truth: It costs so much money to be elected to public office, especially at the federal level, that one must be wealthy or well connected or both to conduct an effective campaign. In fact, millionaires and multimillionaires now comprise more than 40 percent of the United States Senate.[66] Listed below are the average amounts spent by the winner and loser, respectively, in Congressional campaigns during the 2004 election:

	WINNER	LOSER
Senate	$8,614,000	$1,720,000
House of Representatives	$1,127,000	$ 277,000

These averages hide sharp variations in expenditures.[67] Representative Pete Sessions of Texas, who spent $4,504,000 to retain his seat, ran the most expensive House campaign in 2004. Campaign costs are usually much higher in Senate races because they are statewide. Senator Tom Daschle of South Dakota, who spent $21,105,000, ran the most expensive Senate campaign, although he lost to John Thune. The principle that running for office costs a lot of money applies to campaigns at all levels: governor, state legislator, or city commissioner. Money is necessary to pay for television and radio spots, staff salaries, transportation, and the myriad tasks that must be performed in a modern campaign in order to win.

Money, Winning, and Reelection

Here is an empirical generalization: *The more money spent on a political campaign, the greater the odds of winning.* There are exceptions, of course, candidates who become targets of opportunity (such as Daschle) or who lack a credible message or other necessary attributes noted above (does anyone remember Steve Forbes?). Even so, money is essential to winning. Look, for example, at the gap between the amount spent by winners and losers in

House of Representatives elections displayed in the informal table above. In 2004, winners outspent losers by an average $850,000, or 75 percent. Most House races, in fact, are financial mismatches: The winner vastly outspends the loser. This principle applies, of course, to elections at any level. And most winners are incumbents being reelected.[68] In 2004, as mentioned earlier, 98 percent of members of the House of Representatives who ran for reelection won. Similarly, 96 percent of Senators running for reelection won. Again, this principle—that incumbents usually win reelection is true at every level: city, county, and state. This result occurs partly because incumbents have many natural advantages. Their name recognition is high; they provide services to their district or state; they receive regular news coverage; and they enjoy the congressional franking privilege, which allows them to mail "newsletters" and other items to constituents without paying postage. Moreover, in many instances they also benefit from gerrymandering. Finally, incumbents have an established network of contributors, both wealthy individuals and Political Action Committees (PACs). Those who win hold the levers of power.

Incumbent members of Congress get most of their campaign contributions from two sources: (1) individuals and industries in their district or state and (2) interest groups that are aligned with the member's committee assignment. For example, members of the Financial Services Committee in the House will receive disproportionate contributions from people associated with credit companies and the securities industry, regardless of the location of their district. In fact, the financial sector (banks, accountants, real estate, etc.) is usually the single largest contributor of campaign funds in American elections.[69] Members of Congress, then, have loyalties to two groups: wealthy contributors and voters—in that order. Both must be (and usually are) kept satisfied. Thus, except when challengers are already wealthy or have personal ties with people who can generate huge funds, they face a difficult race. Most lose.

Where Does the Money Come From?

Challengers lose because incumbents are supported with money—lots of it. For example, Table 6.4 depicts the sources of campaign contributions during the 2004 congressional elections. The business contributions of more than $1.2 billion come from every industry imaginable: finance, agriculture, communications, utilities, defense, medical treatment, law, lobbyists, transportation, and many others. Labor contributions of $61 million come from some of the same industries, at least where unions exist. Ideological contributions come from special interest groups, both liberal and conservative, such as abortion groups (both sides), human rights groups, organizations interested in reducing or enhancing gun availability, and the like. The data reveal that business contributors overwhelm all other categories. The table shows that at least 71 percent of all contributions to Congressional campaigns come from business interests ($1.2 out of $1.7 billion).

"At least" is used above because candidates have other sources of money as well. **Political Action Committees** (PACs) are special interest groups organized to elect or defeat candidates for public office as well as to support or oppose legislation. They are nearly always funded by wealthy contributors. Under Federal Election Commission rules they can contribute up to $5,000 per candidate per election (e.g., a primary and general election). This may not seem like much, but the money adds up rather quickly.

TABLE 6.4 Campaign Contributions, Congressional Elections, 2004

SECTOR	AMOUNT OF CONTRIBUTION	PERCENT TO DEMOCRATS	PERCENT TO REPUBLICANS
Business	$1,223,400,000	36%	64%
Ideological/Single Issue	180,700,000	62%	38%
Labor	61,500,000	87%	13%
Other/Unknown	264,100,000	53%	46%
Total:	$1,729,000,000		

Source: Open Secrets (2006).

For example, seventy PACs dealt with "agricultural services and products" in the 2004 election cycle. Among them are such organizations as the Alabama Veterinary Medical Association, the Archer Daniels Midland Company, and the Fertilizer Institute. Taken together, these seventy PACs raised $3.2 million dollars, giving 70 percent of it to Republicans and 30 percent to Democrats.[70] A similar pattern occurred in every industry imaginable. In addition, PACs can spend unlimited amounts of money supporting legislation or issues of interest to them. The line between issue support and candidate support often becomes blurred. An additional source of funding comes from **527 Groups,** which are tax-exempt groups (named after a provision of the tax code) created to engage in issue advocacy. Again, they are nearly always funded by wealthy contributors. These groups are not regulated by the Federal Election Commission and, hence, can spend unlimited amounts of money. And they spend big money. The top twenty 527 groups spent about $441 million in 2004 on presidential and congressional campaigns.[71] Two of the most well-known at that time were MoveOn.org (which supported mostly Democrats) and Swift Boat Veterans for Truth (which supported mostly Republicans). And, again, the line between issue support and candidate support often becomes blurred.

The metaphor that is sometimes flippantly used to describe these varied sources of campaign contribution is that PACs run in packs. They are like wolves on the hunt. Such animals want to be fed. Phrased less glibly, people do not give away such large sums of money on a whim. Campaign contributions are investments and those making them expect results. They expect their interests to be protected. In this context, who will lawmakers listen to? Where does that leave ordinary voters? What about the public's interest?

An Example

Representative Dennis Hastert is a Republican from Illinois. His 2004 campaign for reelection provides a convenient example of the role of money in elections.

Representative Hastert spent $5 million for his reelection.[72] His Democratic opponent raised only $18,000. This vast difference meant that the election in this district was basically uncontested. Hastert won 69 percent of the vote. Nearly all the money Hastert raised came from business interests. The top five sectors contributing to his campaign are shown below.

The data refer to both individual and PAC contributions.

Finance/Insurance	$511,000
Health	450,000
Misc. Business	440,000
Construction	180,000
Lawyers/lobbyists	267,000

Although the amounts received and their sources will vary, every member of the House and Senate who gets elected and reelected must raise funds in this manner—liberal and conservative, Democrat and Republican.

In addition, Representative Hastert has had his own political action committee, called "Keep Our Majority," for many years. This PAC raised an additional $2.6 million, again nearly all from business interests. Hastert distributed this money to the campaigns of 59 other members of the House and Senate, some of whom were in contested elections in which a little more money helped a great deal. This tactic is not unique. Every House and Senate leader along with other prominent members of Congress have formed personal political action committees designed to aid other members. Money thus distributed becomes a favor that can be called in when a vote is close.

This example illustrates a fundamental point: Elected officials at every level maintain themselves in office based on large contributions from wealthy constituents. These constituents have access to the levers of power unavailable to ordinary voters.

SOCIAL CLASS AND PARTISANSHIP

Although anyone can be a partisan, few citizens actually try to influence decision makers. They vote (or do not vote) and let it go at that. Ordinary people have jobs, spouses, and children, plus assorted other obligations—which keep them busy. In addition, most decisions made "inside the beltway" (the freeway that surrounds Washington, DC), or at the "state capital," or "downtown," seem remote to their daily lives. But the policies that result mean tens of millions of dollars to companies and large fortunes for individuals. It is a rarefied world, one where business and politics converge. The rich predominate in this world. In order to protect their interests, they are active partisans, trying to influence legislation at every stage.

Protecting their interests constitutes the rationale for making campaign contributions. Although data on the characteristics of those giving money to political campaigns are hard to obtain, two recent studies are suggestive.[73] Nearly all donors, especially large donors, have very high incomes. Nearly all are White men, most of whom are in high prestige occupations. And they are well connected: 61 percent personally know their congressional representative, 39 percent know one of their senators, and 32 percent know both. Not surprisingly, they want to preserve their income and wealth: More than half support tax cuts, even if government services must be reduced. Donors give in two ways, either directly to candidates themselves or to professional lobbyists employed by PACs who work for or against specific issues.

There are about 33,000 registered lobbyists in Washington, DC, and many more who are not registered.[74] A similar army of lobbyists exists, of course, in every state capital and large city. These are the professionals whose job it is to affect legislation and policy implementation. Many former members of congress comprise a special category of lobbyists, since they retain access to the floor of the House and Senate chambers, to members' dining rooms, the House gym, and parking. Like most lobbyists, former members of Congress have policy expertise, an understanding of the legislative process, and personal contacts with key representatives and senators.

The term lobbyist originated in the 1870s during the administration of President Ulysses S. Grant. Favor seekers would gather in the lobby of the Willard Hotel to importune the President as he went to lunch. He called them lobbyists and the term stuck. Even today, the Willard remains a favorite gathering place for lawmakers and those who seek access to them. The most important task of the lobbyist and individuals who contact decision makers is to explain their views about the nature and impact of pending legislation or regulations. This is important because those who get to make an argument have a chance to win it.

The mechanism for succeeding in this task is the campaign contribution and other gifts. Thus, because of the need for money, it has become common for members of Congress to solicit a campaign contribution soon (sometimes immediately) after concluding a meeting with a lobbyist.[75] One lobbyist described the procedure this way: After meeting with a member of Congress, a lobbyist will be invited to the member's next fundraiser. If the lobbyist gives, he or she will get another meeting. If the lobbyist does not give, then access dries up. Thus, the millions of dollars raised by candidates in order to get elected and reelected sets up a simple exchange relationship in which each side has something the other wants.

Now, campaign contributions are not necessarily bribes. Nor are the vacations, payments for "speeches," skybox tickets to the Super Bowl and Kentucky Derby, and other gifts that members of Congress casually accept.[76] One would have to be cynical to see them in this way. Rather, as noted above, what contributors and gift givers say they are "purchasing" with their monetary support is access, the ability to make their case, to be heard in the policy-making and rule-development process. This is how power works. The empirical generalization is: *The higher the social class and the greater the campaign contribution, then the greater access to public officials.* Thus, since rich people contribute disproportionately, they have more access to decision makers (either directly or indirectly), more ability to have their interests get a hearing.

A simple thought-experiment can illustrate why: Imagine yourself as a member of Congress considering legislation to "reform" the tax code. This issue is important because it affects how much money people get to keep for themselves rather than contributing to the common good. Now suppose your secretary tells you that two telephone calls have come in at once; one is from an ordinary voter constituent and the other from a wealthy contributor. Which call would you take? And whose position would be most persuasive to you? This logic is why public policy often favors the interests of those contributing to campaigns. It is why elections are like auctions, with the winner being the highest bidder.

It should be noted that campaign contributions constitute only one way lobbyists (whether wealthy individuals or professionals) influence legislators. Decision makers often rely on lobbyists for information, since in many cases they are experts in the field, capable of explaining complex and difficult subjects clearly. Moreover, on specific issues, lobbyists can often generate "grass roots" support for their positions by having ordinary citizens write, telephone, and visit legislators.[77] These contacts work because members of Congress (and decision makers at every level) want to please their constituents, especially those who are likely to vote. For these reasons, then, the rich often have access to policy makers.

And access means influence. Envision a common scenario on Capital Hill in Washington (or in your state capital or city hall).[78] The nation needs to maintain its infrastructure, such as highways, bridges, and the like. (1) A bill is introduced to fund highway construction. (2) A rich constituent wants to build a go-kart track, visits a member of Congress to talk about how the track will generate more (minimum wage) jobs in the district. (3) The constituent subsequently makes a contribution to the representative's forthcoming campaign. (4) The representative convinces the chair of the House Appropriations Committee to add a $350 million "earmark" to the bill allowing for an "alternative sustainable research facility" in her district. (5) The committee chair, of course, adds similar earmarks for other members of the House of Representatives. (6) The bill is subsequently passed by a huge majority. Who cannot support better roads? (7) A similar bill, also containing earmarks proposed by various senators, passes the Senate. (8) The President complains that the bill contains too much "wasteful spending" but signs it anyway. (9) When the go-kart track opens, the representative attends an elaborate ceremony in which the number of new jobs is mentioned prominently. (10) That evening, the rich constituent hosts a fund-raiser for the representative.

As an aside, **earmarks** refer to legislative provisions that appropriate funds for a specific purpose. They are usually added as sidebars to bills (especially large and complex legislation) and rarely voted on individually. They are often favors given by party leaders or committee chairs in exchange for votes on this or some other unrelated item. Members of Congress often support a bill others have earmarked in exchange for similar treatment. The use of earmarks has accelerated since the mid-1990s.[79]

Note the process that is occurring. A serious problem is identified. Various ways of dealing with the issue are debated on the floor of the House of Representatives and the Senate. Behind the scenes, however, the bill passed actually protects the interests of those contributing to lawmakers' campaigns—reflecting the outcome of the auction. Lawmakers, of course, describe the act as in the public interest. This is a veil. Politics in a democratic society is never about finding the "best" solution to a problem. Politics is about finding the answer that can be passed by a legislative body. In figuring out what can pass the House and Senate (or your state legislature or city commission) one of the oldest sayings in politics should be kept in mind: "You gotta dance with them who brung ya." In most cases, "them who brung ya" are those who supplied the cash for political campaigns. Thus, you will not understand politics in America until you see it as a series of exchanges between candidates who need votes and those who have the money to pay for campaigns. Their "purchase" is effective. As one veteran observer comments, "there is no . . . investment with a greater return on capital than political contributions."[80] Figure 6.4 presents a cynical but accurate model of the relationship among campaign contributions, access to members of Congress, and their votes.

So how is the distribution of resources affected by the relationships depicted in Figure 6.3? In part, it depends on the industry: Banking, insurance, resource extracting, telecommunications, agriculture, food processing, pharmaceuticals, accounting, and many more, all reap benefits from their campaign contributions in the form of bills passed, bills passed in weakened form, bills defeated, or loopholes added to bills. As discussed in Chapter 7, the very rich own most of the stock in these industries.

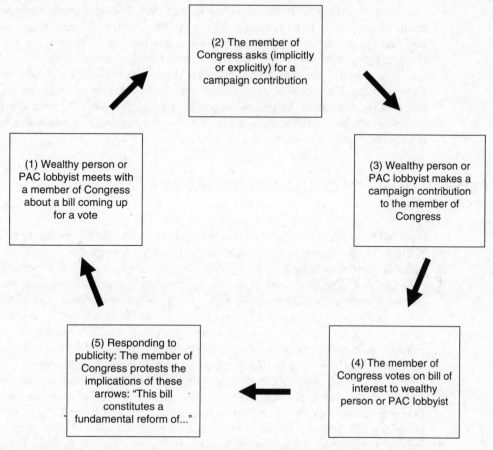

FIGURE 6.4   Campaign Contributions, Access, and Congressional Voting

But the rich benefit personally and directly as well, affecting their life chances. Inequality has increased in recent years. For example, top tax brackets were reduced from 70 percent to 50 percent in 1981, and then to 28 percent in 1986, before rising to 39 percent in 1993. As a result, the rich can now retain an enormous amount of income and become even wealthier than in the past. In addition, as will be shown in subsequent chapters, a "hollowing out" of the income and job structure occurred during these same years such that lower-middle-class, working-class, and poor people are increasingly left behind; they get a smaller share of the available goods and services. More recently, high-income people contributed over $1.8 billion to political campaigns during the years 1999 to 2002.[81] It is probably not accidental that the most recent round of tax cuts amounts to $1.35 trillion over ten years, $769 billion of which will go to high-income Americans (the richest 1% of the population). Moreover, internal revenue audits of the wealthy, who have much greater ability to hide income, have declined. One result will be huge governmental deficits over the next few years, necessitating cuts in services. There will be less money for disaster relief, staffing the Internal Revenue Service offices and Head Start, research into the causes of disease at the Centers for Disease Control, and myriad other tasks. There will be less money for Medicare, Medicaid, and Social Security. It will be said that the nation cannot afford to protect the public. Actually, however, the Congress chose to enact these tax cuts. It chose to provide benefits to the wealthy.

Once again, this is how power works. Whenever tax bills are passed, members of Congress develop sound bites for the nightly news, making statements like "this is a major effort to reform the tax law and make it more equitable."[82] Such sonorous platitudes have little relationship to reality. Rather, they are exercises in lowering the veil, in deceiving ordinary citizens.

CONCLUSION: POLITICAL PARTICIPATION AND ANOMIE

The veil hides the reality of class conflict over the possession of resources in an anomic context. In this country, those with the most money finance the campaigns of elected officials, thus restricting the ability of the vast majority to affect decision making. The only way to inhibit the power of the rich is by voting, the primal democratic act. But the electoral structure inhibits voting, especially among the working class and poor. As a result, candidates for office find themselves in a peculiar situation. To be successful they must campaign as though they care about improving the lives of ordinary citizens. In governing, however, politicians as decision makers must satisfy the interests of those who provided the money to be elected and voters—usually in that order.

The game is rigged. As indicated by the hypothesis presented earlier: *the higher the social class, the greater the influence over access to resources in the society.* In *The Culture of Contentment*, the economist and iconoclast, John Kenneth Galbraith suggests why.[83] He speculates that those at the top of the class hierarchy develop a sense of entitlement, a feeling that their wealth and other benefits reflect merit: their virtue, intelligence, and hard work. This is a myth, of course, but a powerful one. Economic doctrine, Galbraith proposes, accommodates that view. In his pithy description, supply-side economics argues that "if the horse is fed amply with oats, some will pass through to the road for the sparrows." Phrased in this mildly scatological way, the crackpot nature of the argument becomes clear. Nonetheless, it provides an intellectual veil for what is really class conflict over possession of resources. Moreover, Galbraith suggests, middle-class people accept the enormous benefits going to the rich as "the price the contented electoral majority pays for being able to retain what is less but what is still very good."[84] In effect, it appears that the middle class allows the rich to be favored in return for some limited economic protection for itself. The result can be seen in the distribution of wealth and income, and the lifestyle of each class, as described in the following chapters.

SUMMARY

In a democratic society, people are supposed to act within the rules to influence public policy and access to the political arena is supposed to be open so that everyone can compete fairly. The term for this state of affairs is pluralism. A dilemma results, however, because classes with resources want to limit the ability of other classes to increase their share. Three types of participation were reviewed: voting, partisanship, and unruliness.

Although the proportion of adults eligible to vote expanded steadily over time, the actual rate of voting has declined, especially over the last 40 years (Figure 6.1). Today, only about half of those eligible participate in presidential elections and the middle class dominates voting. But this fact is not inevitable. (1) About 70 to 80 percent of those eligible voted during the last quarter of the nineteenth century. (2) Today, about 80 percent of those registered actually vote (Table 6.1). (3) About 60 to 80 percent of adults vote in other Western industrial societies. Differences in the rate of voting among the lower classes account for almost all of the cross-national variation in electoral turnout. This tendency is especially true in the United States.

Voting rates are influenced mainly by the type of electoral system, who gets to vote, gerrymandering (Figure 6.2), day on which elections are held, the registration requirement, and the level of inequality (Tables 6.2 and 6.3). A model of the structure of elections shows the impact of a situation in which middle-class people dominate: candidates lose interest in the working class and poor because they do not vote, the working class and poor fail to see their interests, and everyone defends barriers to participation (Figure 6.3).

In order to understand elections, it is important to understand the role of money. The cost of winning has risen steadily over time. Most officeholders are reelected, mainly because they spend the most money. Incumbents raise money from large contributors, both individuals and political action committees, or PACs (Table 6.4). Contributions from people and organizations tied to business overwhelm those with labor and ideological affiliations. Decision makers are accountable, then, to those who supply the money necessary to win elections.

Although anyone can be a partisan, the rich possess the resources to pursue their interests most effectively. They take advantage of access in order to receive benefits (Figure 6.3).

NOTES

1. The classic analysis of pluralism is by Robert Dahl (1967).
2. This portrayal of a democratic society is an "ideal type," to use a phrase of Max Weber's (1968 [1920]:6). The strategy consists of setting up an example that is logically perfect and then assessing empirically (by observation) how actual occurrences differ from the "pure" construct. See Turner, Beeghley, and Powers (2006).
3. Gamson (1975), Piven and Cloward (1977), Special Advisor to the Board of Police Commissioners on the Civil Disorders in Los Angeles (1994).
4. Coser (1967:84), Merton (1968a).
5. Acemoglu and Robinson (2000).
6. Keyssar (2000).
7. Keyssar (2000), Acemoglu and Robinson (2000).
8. Burnham (1980).
9. Woodward (1966).
10. Converse (1972).
11. Burnham (1980).
12. Argersinger (1986), Allen and Allen (1981).
13. Rusk (1970; 2001).
14. Arneson (1925), Gosnell (1927), as cited in Lijphart (1997).
15. United States Bureau of the Census (2006:264).
16. Teixeira (1992:7), Ansolabehere and Iyengar (1995:145–46).
17. Freeman (2003).

18. Calculated from United States Bureau of the Census (2002b:4; 2006:263).
19. Conway reviews this argument (2000).
20. Freeman (2003).
21. International Institute for Democracy and Electoral Assistance (2006).
22. Freeman (2003).
23. Statistics Sweden (2005).
24. International Institute for Democracy and Electoral Assistance (2005).
25. Duverger (1954).
26. See the classic studies by Powell (1982; 1987). Blais observes that this finding probably only applies to economically developed nations (2006).
27. The definitive analysis of the history of voting in the United States is by Alexander Keyssar (2000).
28. Foner (1988; 2005), Keyssar (2000).
29. Frost-Knappman and Cullen-Dupont (1997). The quotations below are from p. 312. See also Keyssar (2000:180).
30. Keyssar (2000:10–14).
31. Keyssar (2000:240–41).
32. Keyssar (2000:32).
33. Mauer and Kansal (2005), Uggen and Manza (2002).
34. Mauer and Kansal (2005).
35. Uggen and Manza (2002).
36. Uggen and Manza (2002).
37. Quoted in McRae (2006).
38. On Gerry, see Bradsher (2006). On the history of gerrymandering, see Monmonier (2001).
39. Blais (2006:119).
40. Open Secrets (2006).
41. Blais (2006), Toobin (2003), Monmonier (2001).
42. Toobin (2003), Monmonier (2001).
43. The material in the next three sections expands on my earlier analyses (Beeghley, 1986; 1992).
44. Federal Election Commission (2006).
45. Freeman (2003).
46. Kavanagh (2005).
47. Election Assistance Commission (2005).
48. Electionline.org (2006).
49. Martinez and Hill (1999), Tobias and Callahan (2002), Kavanagh (2005).
50. Caltech/MIT (2001:8).
51. Kavanagh (2005).
52. Tocqueville (1954 [1835]:135).
53. Gallup Poll (2001). See also Tobias and Callahan (2002).
54. Minnite and Callahan (2003).
55. Gottschalk et al. (1997).
56. United Nations (2005:270).
57. Lijphart (1997), Mahler (2002), American Political Science Association (2004).
58. Merton (1968a).
59. Caltech/MIT (2001:18–23), Norden et al. (2006).
60. Norden et al. (2006).
61. Caltech/MIT (2001), Norden et al. (2006).
62. Key (1949:527).
63. The model is adapted loosely from some comments made by Piven and Cloward (1988:16–23).
64. For example, Ornstein (2006).
65. Open Secrets (2006). This is a Web site run by the Center for Responsive Politics that provides the most accurate data on campaign financing available.
66. Loughlin and Yoon (2003).
67. Open Secrets (2006).
68. Open Secrets (2006).
69. Open Secrets (2006).
70. Open Secrets (2006).
71. Open Secrets (2006).
72. All the data in the next two paragraphs come from Open Secrets (2006).
73. Green, Hermson, Powell et al. (1998), Lake and Borosage (2000).
74. Purdum (2006).
75. Public Campaign (2002).
76. Barlett and Steele (1994:213).
77. Mitchell (1998).
78. Adapted from Tierney (2006).
79. Center for Media and Democracy (2006).
80. Quoted in Morgenson (2002).
81. Public Campaign (2003).
82. Quoted in Barlett and Steele (1994:252).
83. Galbraith (1992:27).
84. Galbraith (1992:26).

THE RICH

They are the most talked about social class. Its members are both resented and envied, and for the same reason: because they have so much. In the jargon, their life chances far surpass those of other social classes. Their notoriety is, perhaps, the reason why few people admit to being a member (recall the results of the class identification question in Chapter 4). They are the rich. Americans like to believe that ours is a society of opportunity and the existence of this class of people appears to epitomize the American Dream: Anyone can become rich, or so it seems.

But, as F. Scott Fitzgerald once commented, the rich "are different from you and me."[1] The poor are characterized by relatively low wages and periodic dependence on public aid as a source of income. Working- and middle-class people rely on their occupations for income and prestige. Indeed, because these three classes comprise nearly the entire population, the usual tendency is to focus on people's occupations and the incomes they produce as the key to understanding their life chances and lifestyles. And this is a reasonable strategy. It is the logic, for example, underlying the literature on social mobility and status attainment reviewed in Chapter 5. But the rich are different. In his story, "The Rich Boy," written in 1925, Fitzgerald describes the sense of privilege, arrogance, and cynicism of the very rich. As you will come to see, the rich are different in another way as well: They own capital—a great deal of capital.

THE CHARACTERISTICS OF THE RICH

Counting the Rich: Income and Wealth

Surprisingly, however, little agreement exists about the criteria for inclusion in this small class of people. One argument is that the rich are simply those with the highest incomes. And, in fact, most discussions of economic inequality begin with the distribution of **income,** which refers to the flow of dollars received during a period of time, usually a year—whether from one's job, the sale of goods, or profit from investments. This emphasis occurs because the vast majority of people derive nearly all their income from their jobs. But the distribution of income is rather limiting if the goal is to either count the rich, especially the super-rich, or to understand their true economic circumstances.

In order to see why, consider physicians and lawyers. It is common for people in these and other occupations to have incomes of $160,000 per year or more, which places their households in the top 5 percent of the income distribution.[2] Although they live well, most people would see them and they would see themselves as middle class. They live in nice neighborhoods; in fact, most of their incomes go to purchasing their house; it is often their biggest asset. And they can pay for new cars, college for their children, country club memberships, and the like. But their income-producing assets are minimal. It is hard to call them rich, even though their incomes are so far above average.

Consider, however, people whose occupations lead to truly high incomes because demand for their services is high and talent is limited.[3] Some college football coaches make several million dollars per year or more, placing them in the top 1 percent of the income distribution. They are clearly rich. So, too, are the small number of professional athletes and entertainers who make the big bucks, say $10 million per year or even more. They live in rarefied economic circumstances. But coaches get fired. Athletes get injured. Entertainers stop selling records. More important, people who earn a high income and spend it are living well and accumulating nothing. Income, even extraordinary income, is unstable—unless it is converted into wealth.[4]

Wealth provides a much better measure for counting the rich. It refers to the value of everything a person or family owns minus its debts. The things owned can be consumer durables, like housing or automobiles, which satisfy people's needs. More importantly, they can also be various forms of capital, such as stocks, bonds, commercial real estate, or other income-producing assets. Debt includes mortgage and auto loans, credit card balances, and the like. Although wealth can vary over time, it provides more stable long-term security for a family. Wealth is also more unequally distributed than income. For example, while the top 5 percent of all households obtain about 22 percent of all the income in this country each year, the top 1 percent of all households possesses 33 percent of all the wealth.[5]

If the rich are defined as those households possessing wealth of more than $1 million, then the size of this class has increased a great deal over the past few decades. For example, the percent of households possessing wealth of more than $1 million increased from about 3.3 percent in 1983 to about 7.0 percent in 2001. This figure translates into about 17.5 million persons, or roughly 5 percent of the population that can be considered rich. Although this estimate is a little high, it provides a rough guide.

The reason it is a little high can be seen when this small aggregate of people is divided into two types. First, most of those with wealth above $1 million (but sometimes much higher) are job-rich. They have acquired their wealth based on their jobs and frugality.[6] It is increasingly plausible, for example, for a professional couple (say, a college professor and a lawyer) to acquire over time, by means of the value of their pensions and small investments, wealth of greater than a million dollars. Although they live well, often in large homes in exclusive neighborhoods, it remains true that their most valuable assets are their house and pensions. Again, many of these people, especially at the lower end of the wealth continuum, would define themselves as upper-middle class. So the dividing line between the middle class and rich is not precise. Second, the owner-rich comprise a much smaller group; they live off their ownership of capital: mainly stocks in large corporations, government and corporate bonds, business ventures, and commercial real estate. Only about 0.9 percent of households possess wealth greater than $5 million, which translates (roughly) into about 2.3 million people—less than 1 percent of the population. These wealthy people are super-rich. They comprise a tiny apex that owns most of the wealth in America.[7]

The Basis of Great Wealth

The basis for great wealth is ownership of capital, especially corporate stocks and bonds, but other income-producing assets as well. Information from income tax returns not only provides an initial way of visualizing this fact but also shows once again that the truly rich comprise a very small aggregate of the population. Table 7.1 presents the distribution of tax returns and the percent of "adjusted gross income" from wages and salaries. Tax returns, of course, can be filed individually or jointly (by couples). "Adjusted gross income" is placed in quotes to remind you that it is income for tax purposes, not total income received during a year. It represents taxable income after a series of transfer payments and exclusions are subtracted from couples' and individuals' gross (or total) income. These deductions (called tax expenditures) occur for business expenses, depreciation of income-producing assets, individual retirement accounts, capital gains exclusions, and the like. They make it possible for people, mainly the upper-middle class and rich, to show an income for tax purposes that is lower (often much lower) than their total income. Observe again that, as shown in column (2), the rich constitute a very small segment of the population.

The importance of capital as the basis for wealth is shown in column (3) of Table 7.1. Those tax returns displaying "adjusted gross incomes" of less than $200,000 receive nearly all their income from wages and salaries. Thus, for the vast majority of the population, about 98 percent, their jobs constitute the center of their lives, determining their life chances. But those returns showing "adjusted gross incomes" above $200,000 reveal a steadily decreasing proportion of income resulting from wages and salaries. At the top, among individuals and couples showing an "adjusted gross income" above $10 million, only about a fifth of their incomes are obtained from salaries; the remainder comes from capital. Finally, at the very extreme, data for the 400 wealthiest taxpayers in 2000, whose adjusted gross income averaged $174 million, show that their salaries accounted for less than 1 percent of the total.[8] These numbers reflect an empirical generalization: *The higher the income, then the greater the reliance on capital as the source of income.* And, it should be added, the greater their share of the available goods and services in the society.

TABLE 7.1   The Distribution of Tax Returns and Adjusted Gross Income from Wages and Salaries, 2003

(1) ADJUSTED GROSS INCOME (AGI)	(2) PERCENT OF TAX RETURNS	(3) PERCENT OF AGI FROM WAGES AND SALARIES
$0 – <15,000	29.1%	75%
$15,000 – <30,000	22.7	80
$30,000 – <50,000	18.4	82
$50,000 – <75,000	13.3	81
$75,000 – <100,000	7.3	82
$100,000 – <200,000	6.8	78
$200,000 – <500,000	1.5	64
$500,000 – <1,000,000	0.27	52
$1,000,000 – <2,000,000	0.89	42
$2,000,000 – <5,000,000	0.037	36
$5,000,000 – <10,000,000	0.008	32
$10,000,000 and higher	<u>0.005</u> 100%	20

Source: Parisi and Hollenbeck (2005:25).

This fact has important implications, for those who obtain income based on capital have several advantages over those who live on wages and salaries. One advantage is economic security. People without capital who work for a living can be injured, laid off, or see their occupational skills erode if they pause to start a family. Their life chances are always precarious as a result. Another advantage is lifestyle. People who derive high income from assets can choose to be employed or not and, since nearly all do work, they can select an occupation which suits their interests and develops their human potential most fully. Persons without capital do not enjoy this luxury. A final advantage, one discussed in Chapter 6, is political influence. Although they constitute a very small segment of the population, those with great wealth gain access to lawmakers via their campaign contributions and protect their assets. The result affects the structure of stratification.

The Concentration of Wealth

At the extreme end of the stratification structure, wealth is very concentrated, as shown in Table 7.2. The top 1 percent of the population possesses a stunning 33 percent of all the wealth in America, $13.85 trillion. The top 10 percent holds 69 percent of all the wealth, which does not leave much for the remainder of the population. Thus, percentile 50 to 90 percent possesses 27 percent of the wealth while the bottom half of the population possesses a meager 3 percent. In considering the table, the most astonishing indicator of the degree of inequality is the fact that the top 1 percent of the population is wealthier than the bottom 90 percent. And this estimate of wealth concentration is probably low.[9]

TABLE 7.2   The Concentration of Wealth, 2001

POPULATION PERCENTILE	VALUE OF WEALTH	SHARE OF WEALTH (PERCENT)	CUMULATIVE SHARE OF WEALTH (PERCENT)
Top 1%	$13.85 trillion	33%	33%
Next 90–99%	15.75 trillion	37	70
Next 50–90%	11.60 trillion	27	97
Bottom 0–50%	2.80 trillion	3	100%
	44.00	100%	

Source: Kennickell (2003:21).

Table 7.3 elaborates on this issue by displaying the assets owned by the rich and the rest of the population. The richest 1 percent own most of the capital that provides significant income. They own 64 percent of bonds, 58 percent of business assets, and 46 percent of trust funds. As financial advisors constantly remind investors, the single asset that goes up in value the most over time is stocks; the richest 1 percent of the population own 53 percent of all privately held stocks. Although many ordinary people invest in the stock market, the poorest 90 percent of the population own only 12 percent of all stocks. In fact, the table shows that the poorest half of the population owns almost no capital, nothing that produces an income. The ownership pattern is reversed for other kinds of assets. The poorest 90 percent of the population owns 63 percent of residential housing, most of which is mortgaged (often heavily). This debt means that an average family that purchases a home for, say, $200,000, will pay three or four times that amount in interest to a lending agency—owned by the rich. As will be shown in Chapter 8, this interest is deductible from income tax, which placates middle-class people. Similarly, 86 percent of all installment debt is owed by the poorest 90 percent of the population. Although this statement simplifies the situation, it can be said that a few people live rather well off the interest payments of middle-class families. The combination of assets and liabilities shows again that wealth is concentrated in this country.

The data above focus on individual wealth. Using individuals as the unit of analysis makes sense as long as they serve as a proxy for a nuclear family. Most people today think of the family as comprising adults living together, often with their immediate children. Family members typically have much less contact with relatives in their extended family, such as aunts, uncles, and cousins. But such ties are vitally important to the owner-rich. This is so for two reasons.[10] First, kinship indicates who can share in the family fortune. Thus the founders pass on wealth to children; they, in turn, marry and bear children, passing on wealth again. This continuing process involves an ever-widening range of people and, it would seem, diminishes the fortune. Yet great wealth usually remains intact. This fact leads to the second reason family ties are important to the rich: Family members combine their assets via trusts and holding companies so as to control many large corporations. It turns out, then, that families, not individuals, own most fortunes.

TABLE 7.3 Assets and Debts by Level of Wealth, 2001

| | SHARE OF WEALTH | | | | |
| | Population Percentile | | | | |
	Top 1%	90–99%	50–90%	0–50%	Total
Assets					
Owned Mainly by the Richest 10% of the Population					
Bonds	64%	32	4	0*	100%
Business Assets	58%	32	10	0*	100%
Trust Funds	46%	40	13	0*	100%
Stocks	53%	35	11	1	100%
Other Assets**	40%	38	17	4	100%
Owned Mainly by the Poorest 90% of the Population					
Checking & Money Market Accts.	26%	35	33	6	100%
Pension Accounts	14%	47	36	3	100%
Life Insurance (cash value)	13%	34	47	7	101%
Home	9%	28	51	12	100%
Automobiles	5%	19	48	28	100%
Debts					
Installment & Credit Card	4%	11	38	48	101%
Home Mortgage & Home Equity	5%	20	52	24	100%

* Less than ½ of 1%

** Antiques, paintings, jewelry, oil leases, and all other economically valuable assets.

Note: Some totals do not add to 100% because of rounding.

Source: Kennickell (2003:21).

Here is a simple example. In one tabulation, J. Paul Getty was included in a list of the fifty wealthiest people of the last 1,000 years.[11] Prior to his death in 1976, Getty controlled a majority of stock in Getty Oil, receiving dividend income of about $29 million per year (look back to Table 7.1 to see where this amount would place him). This stock was worth at least $1 billion at the time. But Getty was not really a billionaire. The reason is that while he controlled the stock, he did not own it. He served as the trustee of a trust established by his mother, voting the stock and receiving dividends from it. Both he and his sons were lifetime beneficiaries: entitled to the income but unable to touch the principal. The trust will not be dissolved until the death of the last surviving grandchild. At that time, a holding company will probably be formed in order to preserve the principal for subsequent generations. In effect, the assets of this fortune constituted the collective property of the entire family. According to Michael Patrick Allen in *The Founding Fortunes: A New Anatomy of the Super-Rich Families in America*, this pattern is typical among the rich and it carries important implications.[12]

In the data displayed above, the many individual members of the Getty family are included in the top 1 percent even though in reality they function as a unit. Allen presents data and a host of interesting stories about 160 families, each of which was worth at least $200 million in 1986 and much more today. This is a rather small community of people who have tremendous economic and political resources.

THE HISTORICAL TREND IN THE DISTRIBUTION OF WEALTH

The historical trend in the distribution of wealth, especially the share possessed by the very rich, is a matter of considerable controversy. Many people, even today, agree with the French observer, Alexis de Tocqueville, that the United States is and always has been a relatively egalitarian society.[13] In *Democracy in America*, originally published in 1835, Tocqueville argued that in the United States an equality of "condition gives some resources to all members of the community [and] prevents any of them from having resources to any great extent." Furthermore, Tocqueville asserted, "most rich men were formerly poor" and when wealth is amassed it is not passed on to relatives but circulates with "inconceivable rapidity." In contrast to this argument, other observers claim that wealth always has been highly concentrated in the United States. Gabriel Kolko, for example, argues that "a radically unequal distribution of income [and wealth] has been characteristic of the American social structure since at least 1910 and despite minor year-to-year fluctuations . . . no significant trend toward income equality has appeared."[14] The way to resolve these different interpretations, of course, is with a hypothesis and data.

The Kuznets Hypothesis

Like Gerhard Lenski, the economist Simon Kuznets hypothesized that when less economically developed societies, such as Brazil and Nigeria, are compared to more economically developed societies, such as the United States and Sweden, the relationship between economic growth and inequality is curvilinear in the form of a bowl turned upside down.[15] Phrased formally, the *Kuznets Hypothesis* goes like this: *Inequality of wealth and income increases during the early phases of economic development when the transition from preindustrial to industrial society is most rapid, stabilizes for a while, then decreases in the later phases of economic development.*

This pattern is not accidental, Kuznets said. Economic development, especially in the early stages, cannot occur without large-scale capital formation. Those who are not rich spend all or nearly all their income. Only rich persons can invest their incomes in sufficient quantity to transform a society from preindustrial to industrial. The result, however, is greater inequality, as wealthy people reap a considerable return on their investments. But Kuznets argued that a variety of factors produce a stable and then a declining level of inequality as economic development continues. One of them is what Kuznets called "legislative interference" with the "free market," by means of taxes, government-induced inflation (which erodes the value of wealth), and other policies designed to redistribute wealth. Such "interventions," Kuznets suggested, "reflect the view of society on the long-term utility of wide-income inequalities."[16] As described in Chapter 6, voters hold decision makers in a democracy accountable—at least in principal—which can (at least in some nations) lead to more egalitarian public policies. Another factor reducing inequality over time is continued economic development combined with political freedom. The occupational structure changes, stimulating upward mobility as workers shift from agricultural and low-skill jobs to higher paying blue- and white-collar occupations (recall Chapter 5). In addition, the more or less constant growth of new technology based on scientific advances (remember that capitalism, democracy, and science are all interrelated in modern societies) leads to the rise of new industries, which means old wealth declines in value and is superseded by new wealth. Thus, the Kuznets Hypothesis says that the impact of these changes first raises, then stabilizes, and, over time, reduces inequality as economic development continues.

This hypothesis implies that a historical process occurs. Yet, as noted above, the data used to test it are nearly always cross-sectional: comparisons of less and more developed societies existing today. One reason for this strategy is that such information is readily available. In any case, the hypothesis implies a historical pattern that needs to be traced empirically. The following paragraphs sketch the trend of wealth inequality in the United States from colonial times to the present. The result will show that the Kuznets Hypothesis must be modified.

The Colonial Era

The colonial era constituted a preindustrial period and the overall level of wealth inequality remained relatively low. It was greater, however, in colonial cities than in rural areas. For example, as early as 1693, the richest 10 percent of the population owned about 24 percent of the wealth in Chester County (Philadelphia), Pennsylvania. This figure rose steadily. A century later, in 1793, the richest 10 percent owned approximately 38 percent of the wealth in Chester County.[17] Wealth appears to have been similarly concentrated in Salem, Boston, and New York.[18] But cities comprised a very small proportion of the total population, less than 10 percent. The vast majority of people lived in rural areas and on the frontier, where conditions were much more equal. Thus, the most reasonable estimate is by Williamson and Lindert in *American Inequality: A Macroeconomic History*.[19] They surmise that in 1774, on the eve of the Revolution, the richest 1 percent of free households owned about 13 percent of the wealth (see Figure 7.1).

The Nineteenth Century

The first half of the nineteenth century is often called the "age of equality" in America. Yet this is the period in which industrialization began in the United States and it is also a period of sharply increasing inequality. Millionaires appeared. The first was probably Elias Derby, of Salem, Massachusetts, whose wealth reportedly rose above $1 million in the 1790s. If so, the estimated ratio of his assets to the median income at the time is about 4000/1. In 1804, William Bingham of Philadelphia died, leaving an estate of $3 million.[20] More generally, data for various

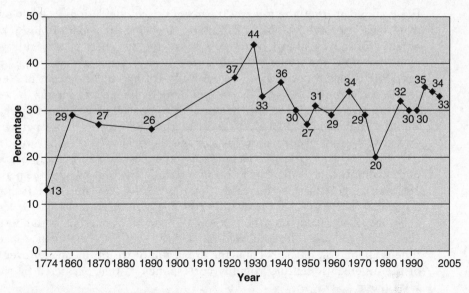

FIGURE 7.1 Share of Personal Wealth Held by Richest 1% of Population, 1774–2001

Sources: Williamson (1980:38–39), Wolff (2000:81), Kennickell (2003).

cities show increasing inequality.[21] In New York City, for example, the richest 4 percent of the city's population owned about 49 percent of the wealth in 1829, rising to 66 percent by 1845. In Brooklyn, a separate city then, the richest 1 percent owned 42 percent of the wealth in 1841. In Boston, the richest 1 percent owned 37 percent of the wealth in 1848. A similar trend occurred in the south, where the richest 10 percent of families held about 72 percent of the wealth in 1830 and 82 percent in 1860. By 1848, the richest man in America was John J. Astor, worth about $20 million. The estimated ratio of his wealth to the median income at the time is about 50,000/1.[22] Note how much greater this ratio is compared to Elias Derby's. It illustrates the size of the first really great fortunes that were amassed in the early nineteenth century. This pattern contrasts with Tocqueville's assertion but fits the *Kuznets Hypothesis.*

Not only did wealth inequality increase during these years, most was inherited and very stable over time. For example, on the one hand, economic development provided opportunity, just as Kuznets suggests. John J. Astor, for example, entered this country as a poor immigrant.[23] But, on the other hand, between 1828 and 1848, 92 to 95 percent of rich persons also had rich parents in the cities of New York, Philadelphia, and Boston. Only 2 percent had poor parents. Thus, even allowing for increased opportunity that accompanies economic development, the dominant pattern was for inherited wealth to be built up to higher levels with each generation. As one historian concludes, "the extent of an individual's early wealth was the major factor determining whether he would be rich later." This conclusion remains true today.[24]

During the second half of the nineteenth century, the economy continued its transformation and the distribution of wealth stabilized at very high levels of inequality.

For example, in 1860 the richest 20 percent of the population probably owned more than 90 percent of the wealth in Baltimore, New Orleans, and St. Louis.[25] Data for ten other cities show a similar pattern. As today, the distribution of wealth was skewed. Consider now the richest 1 percent in those same three cities: This small aggregate owned 39 percent of the wealth in Baltimore, 43 percent in New Orleans, and 38 percent in St. Louis.[26] As was typical in the nineteenth century, however, urban areas displayed more inequality than rural or frontier regions. Thus, for the nation as a whole, Williamson and Lindert report that in 1870 the richest 1 percent probably owned 27 percent of the nation's wealth and the richest 10 percent owned 70 percent (see Figure 7.1).[27] They conclude that the best interpretation of the pattern to this point in time is that "wealth concentration rose over most of the period 1774 to 1860, with especially steep increases from the 1820s to the late 1840s. It should also be noted that these two or three decades coincide with early industrial acceleration." By 1890, the richest person in America was William H. Vanderbilt, with a fortune worth about $200 million. The estimated ratio of this wealth to the median income at the time is about 370,000/1.[28] Thus, the expansion of wealth inequality over the course of the nineteenth century roughly corresponds to that predicted by the Kuznets Hypothesis.

The Twentieth Century

The extraordinary concentration of wealth reached in the nineteenth century continued to increase in the early years of the twentieth century. The richest 1 percent of all adults owned about 37 percent of the wealth in 1922 and 44 percent in 1929, an all-time high to that point in history. During these years, the richest person in America was John D. Rockefeller, whose wealth totaled more than $1 billion. The estimated ratio to the median income at that time is 800,000/1.[29] Beginning with the Depression, however, wealth inequality declined. The extent of its decline is shown in Figure 7.1, which depicts estimates of the share of the wealth held by the richest 1 percent of the population for selected years over the past two centuries.

In addition to scattered data for the period 1774 through the 1920s, which have been mentioned previously, the figure shows that the years between about 1945 and 1980 displayed the lowest levels of wealth inequality during the twentieth century. Thus, the share of the wealth held by the richest 1 percent of all adults fell to about 27 percent in 1949, rose slightly during the 1950s, and dropped again in the 1960s and 1970s. By 1976, the richest 1 percent of American adults held approximately 20 percent of the total wealth, its lowest point in the century. One indicator of declining inequality during this period lies in the assets of the richest person during this period: In 1962, this distinction fell to J. Paul Getty, whose wealth totaled about $1 billion, more or less the same as John D. Rockefeller's thirty-three years earlier. More telling, perhaps, the ratio of his wealth to the median income was "only" 138,000/1, a much lower ratio than Rockefeller's.[30] Thus, these years marked a relatively low degree of wealth inequality.

As Figure 7.1 reveals, the long-term historical pattern through the 1970s suggests—tentatively—that the Kuznets Hypothesis may be correct. Wealth inequality apparently increased with the onset of accelerated economic growth in the early part of the nineteenth century, remained very high between the Civil War and the Depression, then declined and stabilized at a relatively low level. On this basis, Williamson and Lindert, writing in the late 1970s, concluded that "the American record thus documents a 'Kuznets inverted U' for wealth inequality."[31] Alas, sometimes conclusions, even tentative ones, do not last long in the social sciences. Figure 7.1 shows that the story does not end in the 1970s.

The Trend Since 1980

The figure presents data for the 1980s through 2001, revealing sharply increasing wealth inequality. The richest 1 percent now own about 35 percent of the wealth, an amount not seen since the 1920s. As one indicator of this huge increase, the richest person in America is now Bill Gates, whose wealth totals about $85 billion. The ratio of his wealth to the median income today is far greater than ever before: 1,416,000/1.[32] Recall that in 1790, the ratio for the first millionaire, Elias Derby was 4,000/1 and that as recently as 1962 the ratio of J. Paul Getty's wealth to the median income was 138,000/1. And Bill Gates is not alone. As shown in Tables 7.1 and 7.3, a relatively small aggregate of about 229,000 households (comprising a few thousand families) now possess 34 percent of the nation's wealth—approximately $10 trillion ($10,000,000,000,000).

These data show that Kuznets is wrong, or at least partially wrong: Inequality does not necessarily decline with advanced economic development.[33] Rather, modernity—based on industrialization, capitalism, science, democracy, the rule of law, and the culture of capitalism—leads to greater control over all aspects of the environment, physical and social. The level of inequality, whether by wealth, income, or any other measure, is now chosen. This new fact means that the Kuznets Hypothesis must be modified in the following way: *Inequality of wealth and income increases during the early phases of economic development, when the transition from preindustrial to industrial society is most rapid, stabilizes for a while, and then becomes subject to political negotiation.* It is known, of course, from Lenski's work, that power determines the distribution of surplus in most societies.[34] So the issue will be which classes can influence public policy so as to garner as much wealth and income as possible, ideally without prompting the losers to revolt. This is tricky business. As argued in Chapter 6, the rich and the middle class dominate the political process, the rich because they have the most money to spend and the middle class because they have the most votes. The data presented in Figure 7.1 suggest that the rich had enormous influence over public policy in recent decades. They won the auction.

Beginning in the 1980s, so-called "supply-side" economic theory was used to justify reducing taxes on the rich on the grounds that the benefits of their investments would "trickle down" to the rest of the population via increased jobs and increased tax revenue. The logic behind the assertion that reducing taxes would increase tax revenues was never clear.[35] Even so, the crackpot nature of the argument was ignored, with the results shown in Figure 7.1. But, as the modified Kuznets Hypothesis suggests, the present level of wealth inequality in the United States is not inevitable; it reflects the outcome of class conflict.

CROSS-NATIONAL VARIATIONS IN WEALTH INEQUALITY

Other Western nations display far less wealth inequality than does this country. For example, the richest 1 percent in France possesses 26 percent of the wealth and in Canada 17 percent. The Gini Coefficients for wealth inequality in these nations are correspondingly lower as well.[36] Historical data are available for Sweden and the United Kingdom. In Sweden, the share of the wealth possessed by the top 1 percent steadily declined between 1920 and 1970, from about 40 percent to 17 percent. Since that time, it has risen to about 19 percent, still far lower than in the United States. A similar pattern has occurred in the United Kingdom: The richest 1 percent of the population held 61 percent of the wealth in 1923, far higher than in the United States—37 percent in 1922 (look back to Figure 7.1). Over the next half century, however, the proportion fell more or less continuously in the United Kingdom—to 23 percent. Table 7.4 takes up the story from that time, comparing the United Kingdom to the United States. As shown in the table, the two nations resembled each other during the 1970s, with the richest 1 percent possessing about one-fifth of the wealth. Since then, however, the two nations have diverged. In the United States, as is now familiar, wealth inequality increased greatly. In the United Kingdom, by contrast, the richest 1 percent held only 18 percent of the wealth during the 1980s and early 1990s, and then increased it to 22 percent in 2000. In other Western nations the rich are, indeed, very rich. But the distance between them and the rest of the population is not nearly so great as in the United States.[37]

These differences between the United States and other Western nations have not developed accidentally. Public policies in Sweden, the United Kingdom, and other nations, have lead to greater equality in wealth. Class conflict occurs in every nation. Its outcome varies.

TABLE 7.4   Share of Wealth Possessed by Richest 1%, United Kingdom and United States

YEAR	UNITED KINGDOM	UNITED STATES
1974	23%	—
1975	—	20%
1986	18%	32%
1992	18%	30%
1998	23%	34%
2000	22%	—
2001	—	33%

Sources: Wolff (2002:33), Inland Revenue (2003), Kennickell (2003:21).

THE ORIGIN AND EXPANSION OF WEALTH

In the United States, most people believe that hard work and ability will produce occupational and, by extrapolation, economic success. From this point of view, the way to wealth is through a process of long-term, self-limiting behavior in which savings and investments accumulate over time. This strategy works, especially for middle-class people who manage their pensions and other investments wisely. Truly great wealth, however, is another matter. There are at least five strategies for wealth creation and expansion. They are described below in order to illustrate the interplay between the great opportunity that exists in modern societies and the continuing role of inheritance.[38]

The first is windfall profit, which is to say that an asset generates a sudden, extraordinary return on an investment of time or money. In the jargon economists use, the financial markets capitalize an asset at an extraordinary rate of return. In plainer language, a person possesses something whose value increases exponentially, leading to what economists call capitalization: a high rate of investment. This development can lead to the creation of large fortunes in a very short time. Patient saving and investment have little to do with this process. The great fortunes mentioned earlier—of John J. Astor, John D. Rockefeller, and Bill Gates—all illustrate how, in a modern society, a few persons armed with insight, hard work, and luck can either generate or select an asset in which an extraordinary rate of return is about to be capitalized. The early years of the Apple Computer Company provide another good example. Steven Jobs and Stephan Wozniak produced the first personal computer in a garage in 1976. A year later, they found a wealthy investor to underwrite their fledgling corporation. When Apple offered stock to the public in 1980, the value of the company suddenly ballooned. Their 37 percent share of its stock became worth $630 million, and much more today. Thus, like Astor, Rockefeller, and Gates, these two men parleyed a certain genius, hard work, and a peculiar asset into great wealth in just a few years.

But windfall profit is a limiting case. The great fortunes of the owner-rich are rarely created in such a short time. Rather, they often take one or more generations to reach their zenith as the family builds its assets. This argument fits with the nineteenth-century pattern described earlier: Most of the great fortunes today constitute inherited wealth that has expanded over time.

A second strategy for wealth creation and expansion is to own a small company in a new field that becomes a growth industry and to pass it on to one's family heirs. The Motorola Corporation provides an example. The Galvin brothers founded the predecessor of Motorola in 1928 with an investment of about $1,300. The company became the sole supplier of radios to the fledgling automobile industry, which expanded steadily for over a half-century. By 1952, the Galvin family (including children and grandchildren) owned only 31 percent of Motorola stock, but it was worth $21 million dollars. The company has continued to prosper, expanding into new areas of electronics, such as cellular phones, and the family's stake is now worth well over $550 million. The Johnson & Johnson Company provides another example. It sells medical equipment, supplies, and drugs to both hospitals and individuals. When Robert Johnson died in 1910 his estate, including shares in Johnson & Johnson was worth "only" about $3 million, still a lot of money in those days. By the time the company went public in 1944, however, that same stock was worth $30 million. By 1971, the 34 percent of Johnson & Johnson stock held by the descendants of Robert Johnson was worth $2.2 billion. It is worth considerably more today. Note that both companies started small but were part of growth industries. Note also that in both cases the family fortunes continued increasing long after the founding entrepreneurs left the scene. Like J. Paul Getty, family members receive incomes of millions of dollars each year based on their assets.

A third strategy for creating and expanding wealth is to own a corporation that radically increases its share of an important market, with the benefit going to family heirs. The Anheuser-Busch Company provides an example. Incorporated in 1875 by Adolphus Busch, it was for many years simply one of several hundred breweries supplying local markets around the country. As recently as 1952, Anheuser-Busch produced only 7 percent of the beer sold in the United States. At that time, the company had a market value of about $100 million, which meant the 50 percent share held by the children and grandchildren of Adolphus Busch was worth "only" about $50 million. Since that time, however, the company has become the dominant brewery in the nation, producing about 37 percent of all beer sold. The Busch family, which now owns only 20 percent of the stock, is worth at least $1.1 billion. Again, wealth expansion continued long after the founder left the scene and family members receive huge yearly incomes based on this asset.

A fourth strategy for wealth creation and expansion is for inventors of new products to establish their own companies, which then grow in value over time—to the benefit, again, of the family heirs. Thus, unlike the inventors of the personal computer (who found a wealthy investor to underwrite their company), Cyrus McCormick developed the mechanical reaper and, along with his brothers, founded McCormick Harvester Machine Company in order to sell this product. The company eventually became International Harvester. Similarly, Charles Kettering invented a number of automotive devices, such as the self-starter, and founded Dayton Engineering Company to sell them to auto manufacturers. The company later merged with General Motors. A more recent example is Edwin Land. He founded the Polaroid Corporation in 1937 to sell polarizing filters he had invented. Other inventions followed, such as instant photography. By 1978, the 12 percent of Polaroid stock held by Land and his family was worth over $330 million. In all these cases, the inventors are also entrepreneurs, creating fortunes through their own efforts and passing them on to their descendants.

In most cases, as the examples suggest, the members of rich families watched their wealth grow over many years, benefiting from hard work by others. Recall the baseball metaphor from Chapter 1: These are (mostly) people who are born at third base and think they hit a triple. Saying this does not denigrate the importance of hard work and ability in producing success. It does mean, however, that these characteristics do not distinguish those who become very rich from those who do not. What separates most of those who are extremely wealthy from people in other social classes is, quite simply, luck. Many rich persons work hard, but then so do most people in all social classes. For the rich, however, the result is the possession of political resources (money) that can be used to protect their interests even though their numbers are relatively small.

POWER AND WEALTH INEQUALITY

Power is difficult to observe, especially with the methods normally used in the social sciences. Its effect can be seen indirectly in terms of who decides what issues are important and the outcome of key decisions. Many issues that roil the public are of little interest to the rich, who are mainly concerned with the preservation of wealth. As a general principle, those classes possessing the most resources want to preserve them and limit the ability of other classes to increase their share. Recall that this argument can be stated formally as the *Political Power Hypothesis: The higher the social class, the greater the influence over the distribution of resources in the society.*

Tax law provides an important indicator of the ability of the rich to preserve their wealth. Taxes have two purposes. One is to collect funds in an equitable way in order to finance government activities that provide for the common good.[39] These tasks include national defense, highway construction, immunization programs, public aid for the poor, disaster relief, harbor dredging, medical insurance, old age support (social security), regulation of industries to protect the public (food, water, air), and much more. The other, less recognized, purpose of taxes is to redistribute income. Many people believe that taxes are too high; in fact, the very rich always believe this, no matter at what level they are set. In any case, the real problem is not the size of the tax burden but its distribution.[40] Consider: Taxes can be set so that the rich have enough money left to buy several houses and everyone in the middle and working classes can buy one house. Or taxes can be set so that the rich are left with enough money to buy many houses and large estates while middle- and working-class people cannot buy even one. This relative ability to buy one or many houses is, of course, a metaphorical way of describing people's life chances, their ability to share in the available goods and services. The house metaphor suggests that taxes affect this ability by channeling income up or down the class structure.

This fact results in two dilemmas. First, the political dilemma is who benefits; that is, which class can keep most of its income and wealth. Do not be naïve; fairness is never a choice. For example, cutting back in the Medicare program hurts elderly people; similarly, a tax increase for the top 1 percent makes the rich worse off. The issue is always whose ox will be gored. Even though politicians often use the phrase "tax reform" when describing changes in tax law, this is really a euphemism for making someone else pay. Second, the value dilemma is the common good; that is, should taxes be set so that everyone has plenty or that some have plenty and others not enough? Over the past 30 years or so, these dilemmas have been resolved to the advantage of the rich, as federal income tax rates declined, especially at the top, and this decline is one (but not the only) reason inequality increased.[41]

Figure 7.2 suggests this result by displaying the top bracket for each year since the income tax was imposed in 1913. Observe that the two periods with low top tax brackets were the 1920s and since about 1980. By contrast, between the years 1945 and 1980 the top bracket was set very high, 70 percent and above. Now look back to Figure 7.1 and compare it to Figure 7.2. The two periods when wealth inequality has

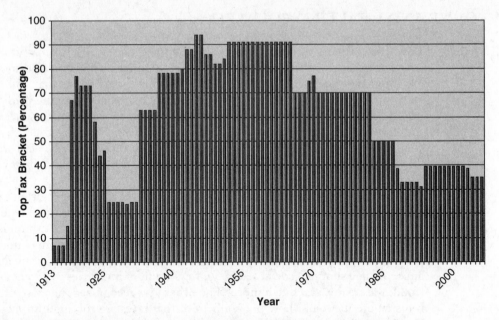

FIGURE 7.2   Federal Income Tax: Top Bracket Rates, 1913–2005

Sources: United States Bureau of the Census (1975:1095), Tax Policy Center (2003), International Revenue Service (2006).

been greatest were during the 1920s and since 1980 or so, and the period with the lowest degree of wealth inequality was between 1945 and 1980. Moreover, recall as well, the cross-national data on wealth mentioned earlier: The United States displays much more wealth inequality than do other Western nations, and these other nations also have significantly higher top brackets than does the United States.[42] These correlations are not accidental.

They are achieved, in part, by establishing only a few brackets and setting the highest at a relatively low income. For example, from 1945 to 64 there were 24 brackets.[43] The impact of having so many brackets is that people at similar income levels were treated similarly. In contrast, as of 2006 there were only six brackets, as listed below for married couples filing jointly:[44]

INCOME BRACKET	TAX RATE
$0–15,100	10%
$15,101–61,300	15%
$61,301–123,700	25%
$123,701–188,450	28%
$188,451–336,550	33%
Over $336,550	35%

The impact of having only a few brackets is that people with different economic problems and possibilities are treated as if they are the same.[45] Families with incomes of $61,300 and $123,700 face different economic obstacles. Families with incomes of $188,450 and $336,550 have different abilities to purchase a home and send their children to college. And families with incomes of $336,550, $1 million, $5 million, or $10 million have vastly different lifestyles—and ability to acquire wealth. The existence of so few tax brackets channels income upward, improving the life chances of the rich and creating more inequality.

You should remember, however, that the analysis above deals with the top tax brackets rather than effective tax rates—which are lower because of expenditures for deductions and exemptions. Even so, the point remains. Although most people benefit from deductions and exclusions that reduce their tax obligations (explained in Chapter 8), the rich benefit the most.

One indicator of how the rich benefit is the number of persons with "adjusted gross incomes" greater than $200,000 who paid no taxes whatsoever in various years:[46]

YEAR	NUMBER
1966	155
1974	244
1980	198
1990	1,183
1995	2,676
2000	2,766
2003	5,839

Although this threshold seems low ($200,000 is what the Internal Revenue Service uses to define high-income taxpayers), only the very rich have sufficient deductions to allow them to avoid paying taxes altogether and retain their income.

Another indicator of how the rich benefit is revealed by the 400 wealthiest taxpayers.[47] Their average income rose from $47 million in 1992 to $174 million in 2000, a nearly fourfold increase in just eight years. The main reason for this huge windfall is that their average effective tax rate fell from about 29 percent to about 22 percent during this period. As one observer suggested, tax cuts targeted to the very affluent "give people with plenty of cash to spare even more cash to spare."[48] Yet, as will be shown in a few moments, these tax cuts do not increase employment rates or overall prosperity very much.

Still another indicator of how the rich benefit can be seen by looking at the impact of tax cuts enacted between 2000 and 2005, as shown in Table 7.5. When fully implemented, those with adjusted gross incomes in the top 1 percent will reap more than half of the benefit, a cumulative average of $483,000 (although the benefit will be much higher for the super-rich).[49] Everyone else gets much less.

Between 1966 and 2005, Congress amended the tax code nearly every year. Many of these "reforms" reflect the success of various groups that lobby members of the tax-writing committees of Congress to obtain special treatment—against the interests of the majority of the population. The overall effect, once again, has been to increase the ability of the rich to retain their income, which is one factor leading to an increase in wealth inequality.

TABLE 7.5   Cumulative Impact of Tax Cuts Enacted 2000–2005

POPULATION PERCENTAGE	CUMULATIVE SHARE OF TAX CUTS
Poorest Fifth	1%
Second Fifth	6
Middle Fifth	9
Fourth Fifth	13
Next 19%	20
Top 1%	51
	100%

Source: Citizens for Tax Justice (2006).

The arguments justifying low taxes on the rich have a time-honored quality. Thus, during the 1920s, Secretary of the Treasury (and one of the wealthiest men in the United States at that time) Andrew Mellon asserted that low taxes on the rich would produce greater tax revenue and reduce tax evasion and avoidance.[50] He added that high rates reduce investment, retard economic prosperity, and, besides, constitute a communist plot against the United States. These are precisely the same arguments used during the 1980s, recycled as "supply-side" economics. The only difference is that instead of a "communist plot," it was argued that high rates constitute a form of "class warfare" that is somehow unfair. As a United States Senator argued a few years ago, there is something "very dangerous taking place in this nation. . . . It is class warfare under the theory of 'let's get the rich guy, the richest 1 percent.' So we set them up, target them; those are the people we are going to get."[51] Of course, members of every class want a bigger piece of the economic pie and describe dieting as unfair; that is the essence of class conflict in a modern society.

But the federal income tax only constitutes part of the story about taxes. In general, as the federal income tax has been reduced over the years, especially to benefit the rich, other taxes have been increased to make up at least part of the revenue shortfall. In addition to income taxes, the federal tax system also comprises payroll taxes (for Social Security and Medicare), excise taxes (on gasoline, alcohol, tobacco, and more), the estate tax (on very high income estates), and corporate income taxes. Under current law, taxes on estates will be eliminated and taxes on corporations are now very low. The focus here is on the payroll tax, which is higher than the income tax for most households. But the payroll tax is regressive, meaning that lower income people pay at a much higher rate than do those with higher incomes. Thus, the maximum payroll tax rate for each individual taxpayer who is employed amounts to 7.65 percent on the first $90,000 of income (employers pay a matching amount).[52] So the payroll tax for a middle-class person who earns precisely that amount will be $6,885. In comparison, the person with an income of $1 million will also pay $6,885, a rate of only 0.01 percent. And the few individuals with incomes of $10 million will also pay $6,885, a rate of 0.001 percent. In addition, taxes levied by states, counties, and cities are also very regressive and have been raised over the last few years. This fact is illustrated in Table 7.6, which shows the percentage of state and local taxes paid by the poorest 20 percent of the population, the middle 20 percent, and the richest 1 percent. As revealed by the table, state and local taxes take a greater share of income from middle- and low-income families—which lowers the tax burden on the rich. The disparity is even greater in the nine states without an income tax and those states whose income tax is either nominal or regressive.

Taken together, the overall tax structure now bears far more heavily on working-and middle-class people than it did only thirty years ago. Remember, this change reflects deliberate decisions. As the modified Kuznets Hypothesis states, the level of inequality is now subject to political negotiation. The nature of this negotiation was described in Chapter 6: Those who donate money to political campaigns have access to decision makers, and access means influence. Moreover, donors and legislators come from similar class backgrounds; many personally know their senators and representatives. Finally, decision makers themselves are often wealthy. This is how the rich, as a social class, affect the distribution of resources in the United States.

But for many years, people like Andrew Mellon and "supply-side" economists have argued that reducing taxes on the rich and shifting more of the burden to the middle and working classes would lead to greater economic prosperity for all, such as higher employment rates and an overall increase in prosperity. Alas, it probably does not, as suggested by Table 7.7, which juxtaposes the average top bracket over three periods during the last half century and average annual productivity growth. In economics, one measure of prosperity is change in the level of **productivity.** The term refers to the percent of the total output of goods and services in private business. The table shows that when tax brackets (and by extrapolation, effective tax rates) are higher, productivity is higher; when brackets are lower, productivity is lower. In considering this relationship, however, you should understand that the table hides a lot of "statistical noise." Prosperity reflects the impact of a great number of factors and varies significantly from year to year, even when taxes remain the same.[53] Even so, the data suggest that the "supply siders" have it exactly backwards; there is an association between high taxes on the rich and the level of economic prosperity—which benefits the entire population. Instead, we have chosen

TABLE 7.6   The Distribution of State and Local Taxes, Two Quintiles and Richest 1%, 2002 (Non-elderly Taxpayers)

	POOREST 20%	MIDDLE 20%	RICHEST 1%
Average Income in Group	$9,300	$31,900	$1,081,000
Sales & Excise Taxes	7.8%	5.1%	1.1%
Property Taxes	3.1	2.5	1.4
Income Taxes	.6	2.3	4.8
Deduction from Federal Income Taxes	−0.0	−0.3	−2.0
Total	11.4%	9.6%	5.2%

Source: Institute on Taxation and Economic Policy (2003:118).

TABLE 7.7   Top Tax Brackets and Economic Productivity, 1950–2002

YEARS	AVERAGE TOP TAX BRACKET	AVERAGE ANNUAL PRODUCTIVITY GROWTH
1950–1964	91%	3.6%
1965–1981	71%	2.1%
1987–2002	37%	1.9%

Note: Productivity refers to percent of gross domestic product (the total output of goods and services) produced in private business sector.

Sources: Tax Policy Center (2003), Bureau of Labor Statistics (2003).

to allow the rich to retain their income, to have plenty of cash to spare. Their lifestyle is more opulent as a result. It is worth thinking about whether this fact adds to the common good.

SOCIAL CLASS, LIFE CHANCES, AND LIFESTYLE

In 1899, Thorstein Veblen published *The Theory of the Leisure Class*, a satirical look at the attempts by wealthy people in the late nineteenth century to appear sophisticated.[54] They did this by purchasing items that were both expensive and superfluous. In effect, the rich at this time were trying to express (and gain) social status by displaying the extent of their wealth. Veblen, a mordant critic, had a gift for descriptive phrases. Thus he portrayed a wealthy class engaged in "conspicuous consumption," "vicarious consumption," "conspicuous leisure," and "conspicuous waste." One of his many examples was the walking stick, a popular affectation in those days. Excluding the infirm, this item is entirely without purpose—for walking. Its function was to demonstrate idleness based on wealth. Hence, walking sticks (as opposed to ordinary canes) were often very ornate. Such forlorn efforts still occur today, especially among the job-rich and people who are new to wealth. They seek out publicity so that the public (middle- and working-class people) will know about their glitzy lifestyle: the collection of expensive automobiles, the $10,000 watches, the appearance at swank clubs—all designed to draw attention to themselves.[55]

In contrast, many of the very rich, especially those whose wealth has been passed down across generations, lead "intensely private lives" organized so as to make themselves as invisible as possible.[56] This orientation reflects a desire to elude those searching for money, to enhance their personal security, and to avoid becoming a focus of political attention. The emphasis on privacy means that consumption tends to be inconspicuous.

Privacy combined with wealth brings much more personal autonomy than the rest of the population has. Although they are concerned with many political issues, especially those (such as tax law) that are related to the preservation of their wealth, many of the disputes that vex the public appear less important to the rich. Thus, they tend to be uninvolved in issues like the abortion controversy. A wealthy woman wishing to terminate her pregnancy has always been able to do so, precisely because she possessed economic resources. Since Medicaid money cannot be used to pay for abortions, many poor women do not have a choice: They must bear children. Without medical insurance, many working-class women lack a choice as well (see Chapter 8). More generally, it seems to me, the fight over cultural values (for example, sex, abortion, and drugs) in the United States over the last several decades provided useful political cover for the rich, who have increased their wealth without much reaction from ordinary people.

In addition, the combination of privacy and wealth brings luxury that adds to the quality of life, such as palatial homes, longer vacations, and amenities that are more pleasant. But these purchases tend to be designed to ensure their status within the upper class itself rather than to demonstrate it to ordinary (nonrich) people.[57] Hence, rather than purchasing useless items, "the ideal expenditure [today] is one that represents a sound financial investment and that simultaneously enhances the social status and political influence of the family."[58]

Here are several examples. First, a ranch in Montana not only provides a second home for vacations in a pristine location, it serves as an income-producing asset. Second, an art collection not only demonstrates taste and brings pleasure, it constitutes an investment. This is because the prices paid for original works can multiply in a very short period.[59] Third, owning racehorses provides a certain cachet while also producing a profit or a tax-deductible loss. In all these cases, the search for status combines with a financial investment. According to the tax code, breeding racehorses constitutes a farming business. So owners can deduct from their taxes the cost of food, housing, employees, insurance, transportation, state and local taxes, interest charges, depreciation (as horses age), stud fees, attending horse shows, and visiting (friends at other) horse farms.[60] Thus, second homes, the pleasure of great art, and horses provide perfect expenditures in that a rich person's lifestyle is underwritten by the majority of taxpayers.

A similar process occurs with elite education, which is important because it affects life chances—the share of goods and services people possess. In order to place this issue in perspective, it is useful to recall the literature on mobility and status attainment reviewed in Chapter 5. This research shows that occupational status attainment reflects the impact of ascription and achievement, with the latter having greater impact over time. The dominant image in this literature is of an increasingly meritocratic society in which ability provides the key to occupational success.

This image is consonant with the American Dream shared by most middle- and upper-middle-class parents, who see education as an investment in their children's occupational future and, hence, white-collar status. So it appears that much anguish occurs over getting their children into "gifted" programs, into select public high schools, and into good universities. For some, the latter translates into the state-supported Flagship University; for others, the goal is one of the elite private schools, especially in the Ivy League. Because the vehicles for admission are typically test scores and grades, middle-class parents see this process as based on merit. In comparing themselves to the poor and working class, they do not wish to recognize the impact of family background, with its advantages and disadvantages.

The rich are not so myopic. They know the meritocratic image is misleading, that family background is fundamental. In Chapter 1 a baseball metaphor illustrated both the reproduction of the class structure as a whole and the existence of the rich, a group whose position in society does not depend on occupation but source of income. Since their children's economic future is assured, education is designed to facilitate their children's entrance into the exclusive social circles of the upper class.[61] This process begins with attendance at one of the elite private prep schools.

The prep school has always served as a means for inculcating upper-class values, preparing students for socially desirable universities (the Ivy League plus a few others), and building networks of friends and acquaintances who will become important in the future for both business and marriage.[62] About 16 of these schools form the elite core; among them are Phillips Exeter Academy, Groton School, Kent School, Deerfield Academy, and Woodberry Forest School. All are located in the Northeast. Most are unknown to middle-class people, which constitutes another example of the ability of the rich to keep their lifestyles relatively private.

It should not surprise you that those attending such schools enjoy a decisive advantage over public school applicants in gaining admission to Ivy League Universities.[63] This is, of course, a form of affirmative action for the rich, most of whom are white (recall Chapter 3). Unlike public school advisors, college advisors at these prep schools typically have long-standing personal relationships with college admissions officers. During the spring, when decisions are made, prep school college advisors often sit-in on admissions committee meetings. In addition, universities apparently make an effort to recognize applicants from elite prep schools; for example, by color-coding their files. This process means that the public high school student from the Midwest with outstanding credentials who applies to Harvard is sometimes denied admission in favor of an undistinguished prep school applicant. When merit and pedigree clash, the latter often wins.

The result is the reproduction of the class structure over time. For example, graduates of elite prep schools are much more likely than nongraduates to rise in the hierarchy of Fortune 500 corporations.[64] Of course, as seen earlier, such graduates are also more likely to own or control stock in these corporations. Over the long-run, then, the rich comprise a relatively well-integrated network of people who know one another, marry one another, share similar experiences and values, and—most importantly—have access to resources that allow them to exercise political power.

SUMMARY

Wealth refers to the value of everything a person or family owns, minus its debts. The source of great wealth in the United States is ownership of capital, income-producing assets. This chapter explored some of the implications of this fact. The rich comprise a relatively small proportion of the population, about 5 percent of households—roughly 17.5 million persons. This is a liberal estimate. The reliance of the wealthy on assets is shown by the fact that only 42 percent of the income from tax returns with an adjusted gross income above $1 million comes from wages and salaries; the remainder comes from capital (Table 7.1). The higher the income, the greater the reliance on capital as the source of income.

The concentration of wealth is shown by the fact that the richest 1 percent of families own 33 percent of the nation's wealth. In fact, the richest 1 percent of families in the United States is worth more than the poorest 90 percent (Table 7.2). The rich own most of the bonds, business assets, trust funds, and stock (Table 7.3). The table understates the concentration of wealth because it focuses on individuals rather than families.

The historical trend in the distribution of wealth in the United States shows that the Kuznets Hypothesis of an upside-down U must be modified to take into account the huge increase in inequality since 1980 (Figure 7.1). Thus, it appears that wealth and income inequality increase with economic growth, stabilize, and then become subject to political negotiation. Cross-national data show that other Western nations display far less wealth inequality than does the United States (Table 7.4).

Although wealth can result from hard work and thrift, this characteristic does not distinguish the truly rich from those not so fortunate. Rather, most rich people inherited their wealth. It is created or expanded by means of windfall profit, owning a small company in a growing industry, owning a company that increases its market share, or developing a new product and founding a company to market it. Other strategies probably exist.

Increasing inequality reflects the power of the rich, especially their ability to obtain reduced taxes while shifting the burden to middle- and working-class people (Figure 7.2). This change was justified by asserting that low taxes on the rich would produce greater tax revenue, retard economic prosperity, and constitute a form of "class warfare" against the rich. Over the last few decades, the tax burden has been shifted from the rich to the remainder of the population (Tables 7.5 and 7.6). Whether the common good is served by low taxes on the rich can be questioned, especially since economic prosperity seems to be related to high taxes on the rich (Table 7.7).

Finally, with some exceptions, the lifestyle of the rich reflects an attempt at preserving privacy. In this context, wealth allows for personal autonomy and considerable luxury. But in expressing their lifestyle most people with a lot of money try to combine social status with sound financial investments. These can range from second homes that are working ranches to art that appreciates in value. Education in elite prep schools provides a vehicle for both preserving the lifestyle of the rich and access to power.

NOTES

1. Fitzgerald (1954:318).
2. United States Bureau of the Census (2005:40).
3. The classic analysis is by Rosen (1981). See also Crook (2006).
4. O'Brien (2006).
5. Income data are from United States Bureau of the Census (2005:40). Wealth data are from Kennickell (2003:9).
6. Stanley and Danko (1998).
7. Wolff (2002:15). See also Johnson and Raub (2006).
8. Parisi and Strudler (2003).
9. Keister and Moller (2000), Parisi and Strudler (2003), Keister (2005), Johnson and Raub (2006).
10. Allen (1990).
11. Phillips (2002:206). The data on Getty come from Allen (1990).
12. Allen (1990).
13. Pessen (1971), Tocqueville (1954:250–58).
14. Kolko (1962:13).
15. Lenski (1984), Kuznets (1955).
16. Kuznets (1955:9).

17. Pessen (1971:1019).
18. Williamson and Lindert (1980).
19. Williamson and Lindert (1980:38).
20. Phillips (2002:9, 19, 39).
21. Pessen (1971:1022, 1973:36, 133).
22. Phillips (2002:39).
23. The data are from Pessen (1973:85). The quote is from Pessen (1971:1006). The point about Astor comes from Phillips (2002).
24. Allen (1990), Solon (1992).
25. Gallman (1969). The other ten cities are in Soltow (1975).
26. Pessen (1973:41).
27. Williamson and Lindert (1980:46).
28. Phillips (2002:39). The richest 1% is from Williamson and Lindert (1980:38–39).
29. The richest 1% is from Williamson and Lindert (1980:387–39). Richest person is from Phillips (2002:39).
30. Phillips (2002:39).
31. Williamson and Lindert (1980:63).
32. Phillips (2002:39).
33. Nielsen and Alderson (1997).
34. Lenski (1984).
35. Galbraith (1992).
36. Wolff (2002:35). The Swedish historical data are from Wolff (2002:32–34).
37. Saez (2006).
38. All the examples that follow come from Allen (1990).
39. Century Foundation (1999), Institute on Taxation and Economic Policy (2006).
40. Barlett and Steele (1994), Johnston (2003), Graetz and Shapiro (2005).
41. For a review of the issues surrounding the relationship between tax structure and inequality, see Slemrod and Bakija (2004). For a historical overview of tax policy toward the rich, see Brownlee (2000).
42. Century Foundation (1999:20).
43. Barlett and Steele (1994).
44. Internal Revenue Service (2006). For single persons, the cut points below $336,550 differ.
45. Barlett and Steele (1994).
46. Barlett and Steele (1994:40), Balkovic (2006:11).
47. Parisi and Strudler (2003).
48. Krugman (2003).
49. Citizens for Tax Justice (2006).
50. Mellon (1924).
51. Quoted in Barlett and Steele (1994:93).
52. Social Security Administration (2006).
53. Slemrod and Bakija (2004).
54. Veblen (1979 [1899]).
55. Frank (2004), Heffetz (2005).
56. Allen (1990:2), Stanley and Danko (1998).
57. Higley (1995).
58. Allen (1990:248).
59. See Gross (2006), Mei/Moses Fine Art Index (2006).
60. Barlett & Steele (1994).
61. Allen (1990:249).
62. Baltzell (1958; 1964), Kendall (2006).
63. Persell and Cookson (1985), Golden (2006).
64. Persell and Cookson (1985), Kendall (2006).

THE MIDDLE CLASS

The middle class has not always existed. The essence of middle-class life is to do nonmanual labor in what are called white-collar jobs. Persons in white-collar jobs usually sit at desks, nearly always stay physically clean while they work, often supervise others, sometimes engage in entrepreneurial activity, and frequently have high incomes. More polemically, they do not "bend, lift, scrub, shovel, haul, or engage in other potentially damaging exertions for a living."[1] They join fitness clubs instead. But the rise of a class of people who need physical activity as a respite from work is new in history.

In colonial times, the structure of stratification did not include a large segment of the population who could survive and prosper doing nonmanual labor. Nearly everyone worked with their hands; most plowed the land using their own muscles as the energy source. A few people, however, were anomalies—pointing to the future. For example, in *Paul Revere's Ride*, the historian David Hackett Fischer observes that Revere saw himself as both an artisan (a silversmith) and a gentleman—without any sense of contradiction.[2] As a gentleman, he was part of the political elite of Massachusetts. He was not the loner described in the myth of *Paul Revere's Ride*. Rather, he organized and directed resistance to the British in the Boston area during the 1770s. The ability of such a man to rise to the top suggests that the stratification structure was simple. Indeed, all societies before industrialization can be divided into two main classes: a small ruling class and the great mass of people.[3] Colonial America was no different; the vast majority of people farmed small plots of land while an elite group of large landowners and entrepreneurs dominated the new society. The colonial stratification structure was unique in history, however, because it was relatively open, which meant that exceptional (white) individuals like Revere could rise to the top and plausibly claim to be "gentlemen." But he worked with his hands. Indeed, Fischer shows that Revere was one of the finest silversmiths in the colonies. He was an artist.

Today, the combination of artisanship and elite membership is unlikely; few silversmiths get elected to Congress or belong to the clubs of the rich. Revere's position was significant historically and sociologically because he was part of a very small group of "middling sorts," people who were highly skilled, relatively autonomous, earned a cash income, and on that basis had sufficient leisure time to be able to participate in the political life of the community.[4]

Over the years, as Max Weber recognized, the stratification structure became more complex and these "middling sorts" eventually turned into what we now call the middle class. What happened, of course (as you should recall from Chapter 5), is that economic development during the nineteenth century lead to the creation of more and more white-collar jobs, which resulted in a great deal of upward mobility. People in these new occupations began being paid by salaries instead of hourly wages, and the spatial separation of blue- and white-collar jobs occurred because the latter worked at desks in offices.[5] In this context, a unique **lifestyle** gradually developed that set the nascent middle class off from the working class. You should recall that the term refers to people's way of living as indicated by their consumption habits, use of leisure time, and fundamental choices and values. Thus, the greater income of the middle class allowed for larger homes equipped with amenities and filled with more elaborate furnishings. Patterns of housing segregation by class developed and those doing white-collar work tended to live in one place for many years, indicating that their jobs were stable. For example, in Boston from 1840 to 1850, only 36 percent of unskilled manual workers remained residentially stable for the entire decade, compared to 69 percent of white-collar workers.[6] Although the emerging middle class was very small, its stability meant that people with similar characteristics began associating with one another: in neighborhoods, churches, clubs, and the like. They began keeping their children in school and even sending them to college. Young people with similar backgrounds and experiences began marrying one another. This pattern continued with economic expansion over the decades and the middle class developed a historically unique lifestyle, one that still exists today. As these similarities became clear, the middle class crystallized as a more-or-less self-aware aggregate around the turn of the twentieth century.

As Marina Moskovitz points out in *Standard of Living: The Measure of the Middle Class in Modern America*, middle-class notions of a decent, socially proper, and economically conservative lifestyle was established at that time and continues today.[7] For example, the purchase and use of silver flatware not only epitomized proper dining etiquette, they symbolize certain family values, such as eating together at the end of the day. The purchase and use of kitchen and bathroom fixtures symbolizes the importance of cleanliness, both at home and at work. And the purchase of a house symbolizes not only an economic but an emotional investment: A house is a home, the advertisers emphasized, perhaps the most important symbol of a family's hopes and aspirations, character and tastes, and place in the community. Zoning, Moskovitz shows, became the vehicle for providing and protecting domestic order—at least for Whites. By the 1920s and 1930s, when the Lynds investigated a small town in Indiana, they chose an apt name for it: *Middletown*. It epitomized the characteristics of a nationally standardized middle-class lifestyle that continues to exist today.[8]

Middle-class people define themselves as representing what is best about the United States: hard work, frugality, economic and occupational success, and individual autonomy—all the elements of the American Dream. These attitudes seem—to them—to be characteristic of this country, to be uniquely middle class. Thus, as shown in Chapter 2, the class identification question reveals that most people with white-collar jobs say they are middle class. And, along with the rich, they dominate the political process in the United States. In the case of the middle class, they do so as voters. And they are perfectly aware of their interests. They want "perks" to go along with their jobs—medical insurance, pensions, and the like—and they want a decent income to follow from their labor. Class conflict occurs as a result, as the middle class acts to protect its life chances.

SOCIAL CLASS AND JOB PERQUISITES

Job perquisites (the jargon term for the more common "perks") consist of any protections, privileges, or benefits tied to one's employment status. Their history coincides with the emergence of the middle class. For example, a 1913 Bureau of Labor Statistics study described 50 companies that provided their white-collar employees with such perquisites as on-site eating facilities, pension plans, paid vacations, and the like.[9] Although such benefits were the exception then, they are common now. Today, the list of potential perquisites includes such benefits as holidays, disability insurance, on-site child care, parental leave, free parking (very important in large cities), college tuition for children, and much more. In addition to these sorts of "perks," many companies provide upper echelon employees with rather special benefits, such as expense accounts, use of company-owned cars, membership in private clubs, entertainment, and stock options. Often called "fringe benefits," job perquisites are not fringe at all; rather, they are important aspects of remuneration and constitute a fundamental element in the structure of stratification in the United States, significantly affecting people's life chances. Indeed, they are so central to the middle class that people cannot envision being without these benefits and privileges. For this reason, they act politically to obtain a greater share of the distribution of resources than do the working class and the poor.

Yet the importance of perquisites is not salient to many observers, partly because they are difficult to measure and partly because they are so taken for granted. In general, people with higher prestige jobs and higher incomes generally have the best protections, privileges, and benefits, as expressed by the *Job Perquisite Hypothesis: The higher the social class, the greater the job perquisites.* Although the hypothesis is probably accurate, it is not described as an empirical generalization here because measurement problems exist and the research literature omits certain topics. For example, while considerable work has been done on the job perquisites available to ordinary workers, there is very little social scientific research on the additional perquisites enjoyed by top-level executives. Hence, the most conservative strategy is to pose a hypothesis and present what data do exist. The job perquisites reviewed in the following paragraphs are typical of those available in private industry.

Paid Time-Off Benefits

Many employees, not all, are paid for certain amounts of time even though they are not required to be at work, such as holidays, vacations, and sick leave. **Holidays,** for example, are days of special significance—for religious, patriotic, or cultural reasons—for which many employees receive time-off with pay. Typical paid holidays are New Year's Day, Memorial Day, Independence Day, Thanksgiving Day, Christmas Day, and some others. Moreover, when a holiday falls on the weekend, a compensatory day off is sometimes scheduled on Friday or Monday. Table 8.1 shows that a higher proportion of white-collar workers have paid holidays compared to blue-collar workers. Service workers are broken out in the table because their benefits tend to be lower, not only here but across the entire range of job perquisites. Many employees in this group are low-paid hourly workers and do not get paid holidays. When the business shuts down for Christmas or New Year's Day, they are out of luck.

Similarly, white-collar workers in private industry receive more paid **vacation time** compared to blue-collar workers. Again, service workers are much less likely to enjoy this benefit, especially among the lowest paid. For those eligible, a paid vacation usually begins after a certain length of service. For example, white-collar workers average about 15 days of vacation after five years of service, while blue-collar employees get 12 days or less.[10]

Finally, **sick leave** constitutes a very important form of paid time-off.[11] It allows workers the chance to return to full productivity after becoming ill and avoids spreading disease to coworkers (who would then have to stay home). As shown in Table 8.1, most middle-class people, at least 72 percent, assume they can stay home when they become ill (or have to care for an ill child) and still draw their salary. Only 45 percent of blue-collar workers and 38 percent of service workers enjoy this benefit. Those who do not have sick leave face a stark choice: work and get paid or stay home and do not get paid. Moreover, even though their working conditions are both more dangerous and more likely to expose them to disease-causing toxins, blue-collar and service workers typically have fewer days of paid sick leave.

It should be emphasized that the data on paid time-off understates class differences because very few white-collar workers punch time clocks, which means their working hours are less regulated. Even among the lowest prestige white-collar workers, informal norms often develop that allow for daily and situation-specific variations in established schedules, especially when family or personal problems arise. White-collar workers, in short, are much more capable of coming and going—as long as their work gets done. In any case, the benefit of more paid time-off goes disproportionately to middle-class people, who see it as an occupational right.

The data in the first section of Table 8.1 conform to the *Job Perquisite Hypothesis*. You should note that this pattern is nearly invariant across the rows of the table: Those at the top of the prestige hierarchy receive more "fringe benefits" and their life chances improve as a result.

Medical Benefits

Medical insurance pays for treatment when people become sick or injured. The earliest known coverage for medical treatment in this country occurred in 1798, with the establishment of the U.S. Marine Hospital Services.[12] Under this plan, seamen had deductions taken from their salaries in order to pay for hospital services. Several mining, lumber, and railroad companies in the far west developed insurance plans in the 1870s and 1880s. They set up clinics and prepaid doctors to provide their

TABLE 8.1 Percent of Workers with Employee Benefits, by Occupational Category, Private Industry, 2005

	EMPLOYEE BENEFIT											
	PAID TIME-OFF			MEDICAL			FAMILY		PENSION			
Occupational Category	Holidays	Vacation	Sick Leave	Medical Ins.	Long-term Disability	Long-term Care Ins.	Child Care	Defined Benefit	Defined Contrib.	Combined		
White collar	84	83	72	67	40	17	20	53	52	60		
Blue collar (except service)	80	79	45	60	22	7	8	40	40	52		
Service	50	59	38	27	11	4	10	20	26	24		

Note: Data for defined benefit and defined contribution pension participation do not add to combined total because some persons participate in both types of plans.

Source: United States Department of Labor (2006:7, 10, 24, 28).

employees with medical services. Although few people had medical insurance coverage in this country at the turn of the twentieth century, they were nearly all middle class. A movement advocating some form of nationwide medical insurance developed during those years, partly because most European nations had already enacted such plans. It was opposed in this country, however, by unions (which thought they would be weakened), physicians (who assumed their salaries would be lower), and private insurance companies (which wanted to retain a lucrative business for themselves).[13] This movement failed. Legislation mandating nationwide health insurance also failed in 1994.

This failure means that for most people today, only about 84 percent of the population has medical insurance. For most, about two-thirds, it is tied to employment. The remainder obtains insurance via a government program unconnected to employment, most often Medicaid (which serves the poor) or Medicare (which serves the aged). About 16 percent of all Americans, 41 million people, have no insurance coverage.[14] This means they cannot get medical treatment when the need arises. By contrast, in other Western nations everyone is covered by medical insurance; it is viewed as a right of citizenship. As a result, everyone has better life chances in these nations.

Among those with employer-based medical insurance, their plans typically cover hospitalization, surgery, and treatment in a physician's office—although the way this process occurs varies considerably. Some plans, especially those held by middle-class persons, provide more complete coverage than others. People become eligible to participate in these plans when they are hired and for as long as they continue employment with the sponsoring company. Companies frequently pay half or sometimes more of the cost of medical insurance for employees, thereby helping them to pay lower income taxes. The remainder paid by employees will often come out of pretax income, which means they do not pay taxes on that portion of their wages or salaries. (These savings are called tax expenditures, explained later). People who are laid off, fired, or quit for any reason lose insurance benefits—just when they are most needed.

Medical insurance coverage varies by social class. For example, as shown in Table 8.1, 67 percent of white-collar and 57 percent of blue-collar employees in private industry have coverage, but only 47 percent of service workers. That these are predominantly low-income, hour-wage employees is suggested by the fact that 24 percent of those persons earning less than $25,000 have no insurance coverage.[15]

These data illustrate that individuals not participating in employer-based group medical insurance plans are disproportionately working class and poor, and nearly all of them do not participate because they cannot. Their employers do not give them a choice. Although Medicaid presumably aids poor persons without other means of obtaining medical treatment, Chapter 10 will show that coverage is inconsistent and a significant proportion of the poor are not eligible. Most middle-class people, however, do not suffer from these problems and, hence, are relatively unconcerned.

Long-term disability insurance constitutes protection against income loss from long periods of physical incapacity. Thus, given coverage, long-term disability payments can be combined with social security disability, workman's compensation, and other government benefits such that total compensation provides a relatively high proportion of people's full pay for an extended period of time.

The first long-term disability insurance policy was probably written in Massachusetts in 1850. For a premium of fifteen cents, a policy holder would be paid $200 in case of injury due to a railway or steamboat accident—a lot of money in those days.[16] The nation's first group health policy was long-term disability insurance purchased by Montgomery Ward and Co. for its employees in 1910. It provided benefits up to half of an employee's weekly salary. Benefits today are somewhat greater but participation in employer-paid long-term disability plans varies by occupation, as revealed in Table 8.1. About 40 percent of white-collar workers in private industry have employer-paid long-term disability plans, compared to 22 percent of blue-collar and only 11 percent of service workers. Those employed at companies not offering disability insurance must pay for it themselves, something middle-class people find easier to do, since they earn more than their working class counterparts to begin with. Many of the latter simply go without, even though their jobs are more dangerous and more likely to lead to serious injury (and even death, see Chapter 9).

Long-term care insurance covers some or all of the cost associated with nursing home care, home care, or adult day care for aged persons.[17] These benefits are usually initiated when an insured person or an insured spouse can no longer perform several activities of daily living, such as dressing oneself, eating, bathing oneself, going to the toilet, or taking medicines. The cost of living in a nursing home or some other facility can range from $36,000 to well over $100,000 per year, not amounts most families can finance by themselves. Neither Medicare nor its supplemental insurance covers long-term custodial care. The odds of needing such care rise with age. For example, only about 1 percent of those aged 65 reside in nursing homes, a figure that increases to 18 percent by age 85.[18] The necessity for other forms of care rises in a similar way. The implications can be bleak: In the *Star Trek* movies, Mr. Spock often closed conversations by saying "live long and prosper." In today's world, however, in which many people live into advanced old age, a more accurate comment might be "live too long and face financial ruin."

In order to avoid this fate, people increasingly purchase long-term care insurance, at rates ranging from $500 to $2,000 per year or (much) more, depending on the age of the insured, whether a spouse is covered, and the extent of coverage desired. Given their income (described later in this chapter), white-collar people are better able to afford these rates. A lucky few, however, obtain long-term care insurance for themselves and sometimes their spouses as a perquisite of their employment. As shown in Table 8.1, about 17 percent of white-collar employees in private industry enjoy this benefit, compared to only 7 percent of blue-collar and 4 percent of service workers. People's life chances in old age are decisively affected by their possession of long-term care insurance.

Family Benefits

Some perquisites come in the form of cash payments. In addition to saving employees money, these perquisites often reduce their tax bill as well. One example is **child care,** which fully or partially subsidizes the cost of caring for employees' children in a nursery, day care center, or by a sitter. Such care is important not only for preschool children, but after school as well. As shown in Table 8.1, about 20 percent of white-collar workers in private industry receive this benefit, compared to 8 percent of blue-collar and 10 percent of service workers. Those who do not receive this benefit must either pay for child care out of pocket (in after tax dollars), leave their children at home alone after school, or one parent must remain at home. Any of these choices affects the life chances of employees and their families.

Pension Benefits

Pensions constitute earnings deferred until retirement. Pensions were unnecessary until recently because so few people lived into old age. In 1890, for example, only 4 percent of the population was over age 65. But that figure was an all-time high and apparently triggered the discovery of "old age" as a social problem and the need for pensions.[19] Thus, in 1903, Edward Everett Hale (himself more than 80 years old at the time) published an article titled "Old Age Pensions" in *Cosmopolitan* magazine. He proposed that workers contribute $2.00 per year to a pension fund until they were 69, after which they would receive an annuity of $100 for the remainder of their lives.[20] This principle—contributions during people's working years (either by the employer, employee, or both) and yearly payments after retirement—remains the basis of all pension plans.

Although the principle remains the same, pension plans today can be divided into two types: defined benefit and defined contribution. Defined benefit plans provide participants with annuities equal to a percentage of employees' preretirement earnings, usually calculated based on years of service to a company. An annuity is a monthly income. Under defined contribution plans, usually both the employer and employees contribute a percentage of employees' wages to a pension fund each month, with the eventual benefits after retirement dependent on the employees' ability to manage their money. Participation in such plans is important, as people live longer now and the proportion of the population over age 65 has increased to 13 percent today. And this figure will rise to 20 percent or (probably) more during the next century.[21] Today, about 42 percent of all workers participate in employer- or union-sponsored retirement plans in addition to social security.[22] This relatively low level of participation means that less than a third of all persons over age 65 actually receives a pension (from any source: private or public) in addition to social security.[23] Aged persons living only on social security benefits endure a very restricted lifestyle.

Participation in an employer-funded private pension plan varies by occupation, as shown in Table 8.1. If participation in both types of pension plans is combined (some contribute to both), 60 percent of white-collar workers are enrolled in a plan, compared to 52 percent of blue-collar and 24 percent of service workers. Thus, regardless of the size or type of plan, blue-collar workers are least likely to participate in pension plans. This is so even though the law requires that if a pension plan is offered to some employees it must be offered to all. Companies find all sorts of ways around this requirement. These data are important because they mean that pension benefits and, hence, lifestyle after retirement reflect the preretirement class structure.

In sum, it appears that the *Job Perquisite Hypothesis* accurately summarizes the relationship between social class and employee fringe benefits. And these benefits not only make life easier and more pleasant, they also improve people's life chances.

Paid time-off in the form of holidays and vacations allows those who have them to maintain their lifestyle while they refresh themselves through leisure. Medical insurance means that sickness or injury does not represent a financial catastrophe. Long-term disability insurance allows people the time they need to recover from poor health without loss of income. Long-term care insurance means that aged people do not have to spend down their assets in order to qualify for nursing home care paid for by Medicaid. Child care benefits reduce the daily expenses that families face. And pensions mean that people who have worked for many years can have a pleasant retirement. All these benefits accrue mainly to the middle class, and especially for those in higher prestige and higher income white-collar jobs. They are not "fringe benefits"; those who have them possess a greater share of the resources available in the United States. This fact suggests that middle-class people have a greater ability to protect their economic situation and lifestyle than do working-class or poor people. They possess a greater share of the resources in American society.

The advantages enjoyed by middle-class people and the way job perquisites increase inequality can be illustrated by the experience of Mary Mendez, a 40-year-old single mother.[24] She sorts apples in a packinghouse in Wenatchee, Washington, for $8.00 per hour. After a minor injury at work forced her to stay home for a few days to recover, her employer simply did not pay her for the time-off. It is hard to imagine such harshness toward white-collar employees. Moreover, although the firm she works for offers medical insurance to employees, it does not cover other family members. Ms. Mendez, therefore, must spend $21 per month out of pocket to cover her child. She does this on a budget that is only slightly above the poverty line. By cross-national contrast, the state takes care of all pension, medical, and disability needs in most Western European nations, which means that class differences are minimal. Hence, the millions of European citizens in jobs like that held by Mary Mendez have much more economic security than she does. As a result, these nations display less inequality. But this fact is irrelevant to most middle-class people in the United States because they have all the job perquisites they need. So they do not demand the development of government programs that might provide such benefits for everyone. Hence, those working-class and poor people who remain without adequate income protection are politically isolated and ineffective. Compared to the middle class, they lack power, especially (as shown in Chapter 6) voting power.

In the past, some argued that white-collar people are politically impotent and alienated.[25] Yet those who are powerless should not be able to garner for themselves more paid time-off, better medical insurance, more family benefits, and better pensions. Moreover, these differences indicate that middle-class employees have greater control over their lives, both on and off the job, than do working-class employees. The ability to obtain and protect a greater share in the available resources—in the form of job perquisites—indicates the power of the middle class in American society.

Top-Level Perquisites

The job perquisites available to middle-class people, however, are far less than those enjoyed by those at the top of the class structure. Although top-level people in private industry are paid a great deal of money, sometimes millions of dollars, companies believe that high salaries alone are not enough to recruit and retain them. "Perks" are the thing. After all, many of them are tax free to the recipients.

People in upper management receive essentially the same holidays and vacations as others, although the length of the latter may be longer. But they also get additional leisure time amenities.[26] Examples of a few of them are country club memberships (such as at Augusta National Golf Club, for example, site of the Master's Tournament), memberships in private clubs (such as the Union League in Philadelphia and similar organizations in other cities), and access to sky boxes and season tickets to sporting events. As an example of the latter, someone gets to sit courtside at National Basketball Association games, such as those played by the Los Angeles Lakers or the New York Knicks (okay, maybe the Knicks are not such a great deal these days, but you get the idea). Ordinary people, in contrast, watch the games on television, the leisure time amenity of the middle and working classes.

The medical benefits available to top-level executives are juiced-up versions of those offered to ordinary employees.[27] Their medical insurance, for example, may have no deductibles, no copayments, no yearly dollar limits. Their yearly physicals may be paid for by the company. Even when they are insured, middle- and working-class people pay for these things out of pocket. The disability insurance offered to top-level executives may contain higher benefit levels and be written more restrictively so that policy holders would not have to take a lower paying job, even if qualified. Their long-term care insurance premiums may be paid for life, with more expensive benefits guaranteed.

Family and other cash benefits, however, are what really distinguish top-level people from the middle class.[28] To begin with, many companies provide amenities that save top executives significant amounts of money, regardless of how well the company performs. Housing subsidies, expense accounts, and personal use of company cars and airplanes are some common examples. Private dining rooms, and laundry and dry cleaning services, and financial planning services are some others. These "perks" go tax free to top-level people; everyone else pays for them out of pocket.

Companies also protect top executives' jobs and salaries. Although few middle-class or working-class employees receive severance pay, top-level people are often given the "golden parachute" (in the jargon, a "change of control agreement"). If the company changes hands and an executive is forced out, she or he may receive a severance package worth many millions of dollars, along with what is called "gross-ups," additional money to cover the cost of excess taxes stemming from such large lump-sum payments.

Finally, companies add to top executives' compensation with stock options, guaranteed bonuses, and no-interest loans (often forgiven). Stock options can bring a huge financial windfall.[29] Although many white-collar employees also receive stock options, most companies reserve nearly all of them for top executives. A stock option gives the holder the right, but not the obligation, to purchase a certain number of shares of a company at a fixed price (called the exercise price) over a specified time. The exercise price usually equals the stock price at the time the option is granted. The profit can run to millions of dollars, as illustrated with the following example. Let us say the Widget Corporation grants its CEO 50,000 stock options, which can be exercised any time after one year but before ten years from the date of granting. Let us also say the stock price on the day of granting is $50, so the cost of 50,000 shares would be $2.5 million at that time. Finally, assume that the stock goes up in value by exactly 10 percent a year (this keeps the arithmetic simple). In the tenth year, the stock price will be $100 and the cost of 50,000 shares would be $5 million. The executive then takes (or borrows) $2.5 million and exercises his options and buys 50,000 shares of the Widget Corporation at the exercise price of $50. This is so even though it is currently selling at $100. The result is a windfall of $2.5 million. Although simple, the amounts in this example are not extreme. In order to offer these options, many firms simply issue new shares of stock—thereby diluting the value of all the other outstanding shares, such as the 200 owned by a middle-class person in a retirement account. But stocks do not always go up in value or do not go up very much. In such cases, companies have been known to lower the exercise price retroactively. Ordinary middle-class people do not get many stock options and, when they do, the exercise price remains unchanged regardless of the direction of the stock price.

In addition to ordinary pensions, companies offer top-level executives Supplemental Executive Retirement Plans (SERPS) designed to insure that their huge incomes continue after they withdraw from the workforce.[30] In fact, use of SERPS is increasing, even though an estimated 40 percent of large companies either have or are considering reducing pension benefits for rank-and-file employees. The advantage of SERPS is that, unlike the pension plans available to middle- and working-class people, there are no upper limits on contributions. Moreover, executives are eligible for these pension plans, often amounting to millions of dollars per year, immediately on employment. Companies simply credit a newly hired chief executive officer with 20 or 25 years service. They then place the money in trust funds so that top executives get them even if the company goes bankrupt in the meantime. Such protection is not available to ordinary middle- and working-class employees.

As mentioned in Chapter 6, the political game is rigged in the United States and the structure of stratification reflects this fact. The structure of elections means that the middle class dominates the electoral process. They appear to accept the huge share of the distribution of resources going to the rich as the price of their own contentment: The middle class obtains a lesser share, but what they do obtain remains very good—much more than goes to the working class.[31]

SOCIAL CLASS, INCOME INEQUALITY, AND INCOME TRANSFERS

But the job "perks" discussed above, while fundamental, are not the same as a paycheck. For middle-class people, the income they receive from their jobs combines with the perquisites they enjoy to make their lifestyle possible and it is lifestyle (as will become clear) that separates them from the working class.

Social Class and Income

The top row of Table 8.2 reveals that the median income for people working full-time all year long was $42,400 for males and $31,900 for females in 2005. As it turns out, the median highlights the economic difference between the middle and working class: Most white-collar workers earn more than the median while most blue-collar workers earn less. Thus, the average male white-collar worker, an administrator of some sort or a professional worker, earns well over the median (for men), more than $60,000 or so per year. Similarly, women in management and professional occupations also earn well over the median (for women), more than $40,000. Among men, the only white-collar job category in which they do not earn more than the median are those in office and administrative support occupations. Among women, those in sales and administrative support usually do not earn above-average wages. Even so, most people in white-collar jobs find that their work pays off, not only in pleasure and prestige, but monetarily as well.

In contrast, individuals in blue-collar jobs nearly always earn less than the median. The typical male in production and transportation jobs earns about $34,600 each year, not much to live on, even with a spouse who is, say, a secretary. As one looks down Table 8.2 each occupational category includes a higher proportion of jobs with lower prestige and income (recall Chapter 4). So work pays off for these people, but barely.

The income distribution shown in Table 8.2 reveals the importance of both spouses in maintaining family lifestyle—even though the table reveals that women earn less than men in every occupational category (recall Chapter 3). It is an empirical generalization that husbands and wives tend to be from the same social class; that is, white-collar men usually marry white-collar women, and blue-collar men marry blue-collar women.[32] The most prevalent cross-class marriage pattern is for blue-collar men to marry women in administrative support jobs.

This finding of class homogeneity can be used to suggest the implications family income has for class differences in lifestyle. For example, assume that a male physician is married to a female lawyer. Although not shown in the table, their incomes would usually be above the average for professional workers. Let us assume for a moment that the physician earns $200,000 and the lawyer $150,000. These plausible figures mean that their total income of $350,000 makes them rich—statistically, at least. In identification, however, they would undoubtedly see themselves as upper-middle class.

**TABLE 8.2 Median Income by Occupation and Gender, 2005
Year-Round, Full-Time Workers**

OCCUPATION	MALE	FEMALE
All Workers	42,400	31,900
White-Collar		
Management	66,700	46,800
Professional	61,000	42,000
Sales	42,200	26,700
Office & Administrative Support	34,900	30,000
Blue-Collar		
Production & Transportation	34,600	22,900
Construction & Extraction	32,100	30,700
Service	26,700	20,700
Farming, Forestry, & Fishing	22,300	18,700

Source: United States Bureau of the Census (2006c)

A few years ago they were called "Yuppies," young urban professionals, with unflattering connotations. In comparison, assume that a female nurse marries a male high school teacher. Again, both are professional workers. She earns, let us say, $50,000 per year, and he $45,000. Their combined income of $95,000 makes them solidly middle class and they would undoubtedly identify as such. But their lifestyle is much restricted compared to the physician–lawyer couple. Finally, consider a male police officer married to a female secretary. Police officers are service workers, and they usually earn above the average for that category. Let's assume he earns $35,000 per year and she earns $30,000. Their combined income of $65,000 requires a more restricted lifestyle. That is to say: These three couples live in different neighborhoods, shop in different stores, take different vacations, and usually send their children to different colleges (although working-class youth are less likely to attend college). Such variations suggest what it means to be upper-middle, middle, and working class in the United States. All these people have been buffeted, although in different ways, by changes in the distribution of income over the past half-century.

Trends in Income Inequality

Whether the United States has become more unequal over time is a controversial topic, and not just among academics. During the quarter century after World War II, real incomes (adjusted for inflation) rose among all social classes.[33] Hence, most people were better off and could afford an improved lifestyle. For example, rates of home ownership among Whites expanded significantly during this period. But the degree of income inequality remained more or less unchanged during these years. Since about 1970, however, income inequality (like wealth inequality) has increased significantly.

Income Inequality, 1950–1970.   Two alternative hypotheses describe income inequality during the years after World War II until about 1970: the *Inequality Reduction Hypothesis* and the *Inequality Stability Hypothesis*. The *Inequality Reduction Hypothesis* states that *the lower the social class, the greater the benefit from income transfers and the lower the level of inequality from 1950 to 1970.* The term **income transfers** in the hypothesis refers to government spending that provides money or benefits to individuals without obtaining goods or services in exchange, which means there is no increase in the gross domestic product (GDP). Thus, an income transfer occurs whenever money or an in-kind benefit, such as medical treatment, is simply given to recipients by the government with no expectation of receiving goods or services in return. Beginning in the mid-1930s, the federal government developed a variety of programs providing economic benefits to various segments of the population. Some of the most well-known assist the poor and the aged. Welfare programs are especially salient to the public and appear (the word is important) to reduce income inequality. After all, cash programs like Temporary Assistance to Needy Families (or its precursor, Aid for Families with Dependent Children) provide income, while noncash programs like Medicaid and Food Stamps provide economically valuable resources (see Chapter 10). Other programs target the aged: such as Social Security and Medicare. Social Security does reduce income inequality among the aged. So the *Inequality Reduction Hypothesis* sounds like common sense.

It turns out, however, that the hypothesis suffers from three problems. First, the literature supporting it fails to include all cash income transfers to various population groups.[34] One example would be the impact of farm price supports, which go mainly to the largest and richest farmers, is omitted.[35] Farm price supports are income transfers from the government to farmers that make up the differences between the selling price of a crop and an arbitrary target price. Second, this argument assumes that public assistance reduces poverty, ignoring the fact that recipients must remain poor in order to continue receiving benefits and that the cash they spend ends up going into the pockets of middle-class people (see Figure 10.3). The different impact of such programs as Temporary Assistance to Needy Families and Social Security reflects the means test that characterizes the former but not the latter. Thus, precisely because it has no means test (that is, it does not require that recipients remain poor), the Social Security program reduces inequality among the aged. Third, the *Inequality Reduction Hypothesis* flies in the face of theoretical understanding. Gerhard Lenski, remember, found that power has determined the distribution of resources over most of human history.[36] Now theory can be refuted by evidence, of course, but those proposing the *Inequality Reduction Hypothesis* fail to address the issue. In sum, despite the redistributive effect of Social Security, the *Inequality Reduction Hypothesis* does not explain the facts.

Rather, the best explanation of the pattern of income inequality between World War II and about 1970 is the *Inequality Stability Hypothesis: The higher the social class, then the greater the benefit from income transfers such that the overall distribution of income remained unchanged from 1950 to 1970.* Table 8.3 illustrates the *Inequality Stability Hypothesis* in two ways. Please look first at Panel A for the years 1950 to 1970. These data show that the income distribution among households was relatively stable during this period. The poorest 20 percent of households received about 5 percent of the total income, the second 20 percent about 12 percent, the third about 18 percent, the fourth about 24 percent, and the richest fifth about 41 percent. The top 5 percent of households (included in the "richest fifth") received about 15 percent of the total income. Now look at the Gini Coefficients displayed in Panel B for the years 1950 to 1970. You should recall that the Gini Coefficient is an index that measures the degree of income inequality. It varies between zero and 1.00, with a score of zero meaning that all incomes are equal and a score of 1.00 meaning that one household receives all the income in a society. Again, the data show that income inequality was rather stable during this period.

The reason for this stability lies in the impact of income transfers. The pattern shown in the left portion of Panels A and B is plausible because "income" includes cash received from virtually any source: not just earnings, but also unemployment and workers compensation, Social Security and veterans benefits, public aid, survivor and disability benefits, educational assistance, alimony and child support payments, and all other periodic cash income. Thus the impact of income transfers is included in the data. Moreover, the *Inequality Stability Hypothesis* makes sense theoretically, of course, because in most societies the more powerful classes make sure they obtain their "fair" share of the benefits from such programs. "Fair," of course, is defined as "more." Recall the pie metaphor used earlier: Classes always want a bigger piece of the pie; some are more successful than others.

Several studies have shown that the pattern displayed in Table 8.3 for the years 1950 to 1970 is accurate. One investigation looked at the impact of governmental tax

TABLE 8.3   Income Inequality Among Households, 1950–2005

	1950	1960	1970	1980	1990	2000	2005
Panel A: Percentage of Income Received by each Quintile and Top 5%							
Poorest Fifth	5%	5%	5%	5%	4%	4%	3
Second Fifth	12	12	12	12	10	9	9
Third Fifth	17	18	18	18	16	15	15
Fourth Fifth	23	24	24	24	24	23	23
Richest Fifth	43	41	41	42	47	50	50
	100%	100%	100%	101%	101%	101%	100%
Richest 5%	16%	16%	16%	15%	18%	22%	na
Panel B: Gini Coefficient of Income Inequality							
	.38	.36	.39	.40	.43	.46	.47

Notes: Totals of 101% represent rounding error. na = not available.

Source: United States Bureau of the Census (2006d:7)

and spending policies in 1950, 1961, and 1970 and included a wide array of income transfers plus some that clearly go to middle-class persons, such as "farm income" (apparently price supports) and "housing expenditures" (apparently housing subsidies). In addition, the authors also took into account governmental outlays for such public goods as "auto expenditures" (apparently roads), "estimated expenditure on higher education," and "children under age 18" (apparently public school outlays). The term **public goods** refers to government expenditures for goods and services that, presumably, anyone can take advantage of or use, such as lighthouses or airports. Their finding is that the distribution of income after governmental taxing and spending decisions was unchanged between 1950 and 1970.[37]

Another analyst came to a similar conclusion after looking at the impact of government spending on a wide range of public goods, such as expenditures for national defense, science and technology, the administration of justice, government operations, energy, the environment, community and regional development, revenue sharing, and interest on the national debt. "Over time, greatly increased government activity has not led to more income equality. There is little indication that the United States government has done much net redistributing of income."[38]

Finally, in *American Inequality: A Macroeconomic History*, Williamson and Lindert examined income inequality in decades after World War II and came to an unequivocal conclusion.[39]

> By almost any yardstick inequality has changed little since the 1940s. . . . The data that yield this conclusion differ greatly from one another. Several series are available: the Statistics of Income reported by the Internal Revenue Service, the Survey of Consumer Finances, the Census Bureau's Current Population Survey, the income distributions of the Social Security Administration, and the benchmark consumer surveys of the Bureau of Labor Statistics. . . . One would expect such diversity to produce a variety in the estimates, but in fact none of the inequality measures exhibits any dramatic trend.

So for the period between World War II and 1970, income inequality remained rather stable. Although income transfers to impoverished people became politically salient during these years as more programs benefiting the poor came into existence, the overall impact of transfers was to preserve the status quo. Two final points: First, this discussion is somewhat longer than it had to be in order to emphasize, once again, the importance of hypothesis testing in the social sciences. Researchers proceed, very imperfectly, by conjecture and refutation, to get at truth. Second, recall Max Weber's aphorism cited in Chapter 1: The social sciences are granted eternal youth. The reason is that findings vary over time (and across societies). Thus, beginning around 1970 the level of income inequality began increasing.

Income Inequality since 1970.   This increase was not fate. It did not "just happen." It reflects, rather, the impact of human decisions on the structure of stratification; it reflects, in short, the outcome of class conflict. Please look at Panel A of Table 8.3 for the years 1980 to 2005. Data for this more recent period show that the income distribution became more unequal as the bottom quintiles began receiving less income and the richest fifth (and top 5 percent) began receiving more.[40] Although the differences in percentage may not seem like much, the samples are so large that even small changes are significant. Just how significant can be seen by looking at the Gini Coefficients in Panel B. Note that the Gini rose steadily from 1970 to 2005. Moreover, these data provide a practical measure of how much better the lifestyle at the top is today compared to a few years ago: The increase in household income inequality between 1960 and 2005, as measured by the Gini, was 31 percent. The United States has become a much more unequal society in recent years.

The reasons for this increase are the following:[41] First, the Baby Boomer generation graduated from college in precisely these years and, hence, the supply of people looking for white-collar jobs increased. Salaries fell somewhat as a result, especially for the middle class. Second, the demand for people in blue-collar jobs fell with the decline of high-paying jobs in manufacturing industries and the rise of low-paying jobs in service industries. Third, and perhaps most important, so-called supply-side economic policies adopted during this period redistributed income to the rich and, to a much lesser degree, to the middle class. As described in Chapter 7, tax reductions constituted one mechanism for this redistribution. Tax expenditures represent another mechanism.

Tax Expenditures and Income Inequality

Taxes are the source of income for government. But all governments use tax policy to influence behavior; that is, they enact spending programs via tax policies that stimulate some activities rather than others and profit some citizens rather than others. So it follows that class conflict occurs as individuals and groups compete to see who can benefit from such programs. The result affects the level of income inequality.

The name for spending programs enacted through the tax code is **tax expenditures.** They constitute the least well-known type of income transfer. The term refers to provisions of the tax code that provide special or selective reductions in taxes for certain groups of citizens and corporations, thus increasing their income. Tax expenditures are "analogous to direct outlay programs." As such, the two are "considered as alternative means of accomplishing similar budget policy objectives."[42] Thus, both direct budget outlays and tax expenditures cost money and often serve similar goals. For such reasons, the cost of tax expenditures is routinely included in calculations of the federal budget.

The sense in which tax expenditures constitute tax code-based government spending programs can be illustrated with a simple (albeit fanciful) example.[43] Suppose, as part of a drive for energy independence, the government wished to encourage the construction of windmills. One way to achieve this goal would be to create a direct spending program via the appropriate process. Those willing to construct windmills would receive a check to cover their costs plus profit. Another way would be to offer a tax expenditure that allows companies (or even individuals) who build windmills to reduce their taxes by the amount of their costs. The result is functionally the same: Government spending causes the windmills to be built.

On a more cynical level, tax expenditures create pockets of privilege within the tax code that are taken for granted unless a movement arises to rescind them.[44] Such programs receive far less scrutiny during enactment than direct budget outlays and their effectiveness at achieving policy goals usually remains unclear. In practice, they often turn out to be expensive subsidy programs without much oversight.[45] Perhaps this is why a corporation that pays for season tickets to professional baseball games for its top-level employees can deduct their cost as a business expense, while parents who take their children to the same games cannot.

Some idea of the extent of government spending through the use of tax expenditures is illustrated in Table 8.4. Individuals received about $884 billion in benefits during 2005, almost all of which went to middle-class and rich people. The table has a (rough) orderliness to it. The items at the top (#1–7) refer to the value of some of the job perquisites discussed earlier, such as pensions ($126 billion), medical insurance ($91 billion), transportation ($4 billion), life and long-term care insurance ($4 billion), and employer-provided child care ($3 billion). Of course, most of the remaining tax expenditures also benefit the middle class and rich. The exceptions are items #24 to 25 at the bottom of the table, which go mainly to the poor. The amount in these two categories combined ($45 billion) constitutes only 5 percent of government spending in the form of tax expenditures.

Two examples from the table can be used to suggest how these programs work. In considering them, remember that the issue is not whether these and other governmental spending programs are good or bad, wise or unwise. The issue is how such programs benefit the middle class compared to the working-class and poor.

Housing.   Insuring that the population has adequate housing constitutes an important policy goal for two reasons. First, having a place to live is better than being homeless. Second, housing programs stimulate the economy and thereby provide people with jobs.

One way to insure that adequate housing exists is to provide cash assistance or vouchers to people. The federal government allocates and spends about $34 billion each year in direct outlays for housing assistance to the poor.[46] Such programs are, of course, very controversial.

TABLE 8.4   Tax Expenditures by Budget Category, 2005

INDIVIDUALS	PROGRAM COST (IN BILLIONS)	
Selected Employment Fringe Benefit Programs		
1. Exclusion of employer-provided pension contributions	125.6	
2. Exclusion of employer contributions for medical insurance	90.6	
3. Exclusion of employer-provided transportation (cars, limousines)	3.7	
4. Exclusion of employer-provided group term life & long term care insurance	4.2	
5. Exclusion of employer-provided child care	3.1	
6. Exclusion of various other employer-provided fringe benefits	47.1	
7. Exclusion of investment income on employer-provided life insurance & annuities	25.5	
Subtotal		299.8
Selected Investment Programs		
8. Reduced rates on long-term capital gains	92.2	
9. Exclusion of capital gains at death	50.9	
10. Exclusion of interest on state & local bonds	18.7	
Subtotal		161.8
Selected Other Programs		
11. Deductibility of mortgage interest on home	69.4	
12. Deductibility of state & local property tax on home	19.9	
13. Exclusion of capital gains on home sales	24.1	
14. Deductibility of state & local income & property taxes	36.8	
15. Deductibility of charitable contributions	29.1	
16. Tax credit for children less than age 17	46.0	
17. Deductibility of medical expenses	6.0	
18. Deductibility of long-term care expenses	6.0	
19. Exclusion of untaxed Medicare benefits	34.4	
20. Exclusion of long-term care expenses	7.3	
21. Exclusion of worker compensation benefits	2.5	
22. Exclusion of Social Security benefits	23.1	
23. Exclusion of veterans benefits	3.9	
24. Exclusion of public assistance benefits	3.4	
25. Earned Income Tax Credit	42.1	
26. All Other	67.9	
Subtotal		421.9
Total Individual Programs		883.5
Total Corporate Programs		76.0
Grand Total		959.5

Note: Some program categories have been combined for ease of presentation. Data are for fiscal year 2006, which begins on October 1, 2005.

Source: Joint Committee on Taxation (2006:30–42).

Another, more or less equivalent way to insure adequate housing is to allow middle-class and rich people to deduct or exclude from their taxes certain aspects of the cost. These programs are not very controversial, unless rescinding them becomes likely. The deductibility of mortgage interest on owner-occupied homes (item #11 in Table 8.4) provided individuals with $69 billion in 2003, more than twice the amount spent on housing assistance for the poor. What these benefits mean on an individual level is that a middle-class family in the 25 percent tax bracket which paid $20,000 in mortgage interest in that year received a $5,000 income transfer from the government. This amount is more than a poor family receives in cash via the Temporary Assistance to Needy Families (TANF) program as will be described in Chapter 10. Moreover, the Mortgage Interest deduction is supplemented by other benefits to homeowners. For example, items #12 to 14 in Table 8.4 provide an additional $81 billion in housing assistance to individuals, mainly in the middle class. The impact of these subsidies, however, is exactly the same as income transfers to the poor: They increase the incomes of middle-class people.

It is reasonable to ask whether these programs, taken together, are effective. Does the nation effectively prevent homelessness? Or do they provide a sop to the poor while comprising a pocket of privilege for the middle class?

Medical Insurance.   In all Western nations but the United States, medical insurance constitutes a right of citizenship. The idea is that modern nations can and should provide for the common good by protecting, as much as possible, the health of their citizens.

In the United States, as described earlier, most citizens obtain health insurance as a fringe benefit connected to their jobs. Employers could, of course, give employees the money to purchase their insurance but they would then have to pay taxes on this income. Instead, employers purchase coverage for their employees. The exclusion of employer contributions for medical insurance premiums (item #2 in Table 8.4) provided individuals with a $91 billion subsidy in 2005, not counting the benefits of various other medical exclusions shown in the table. What this program means for middle-class people can be illustrated with a simple example. Assume a yearly premium for family coverage costs $9,000, of which the employer pays $6,750 (75%) and the employee pays the remaining $2,250. Thus, because of the exclusion of employer contributions, the employee receives an income transfer of $1,687, assuming a 25 percent tax bracket (25% of $6,750). In addition, employees usually pay their share of the premium out of pre-tax income (this is one reason adjusted gross income is lower than total income). In this example, they also receive an additional $422 income transfer (25% of $1,687). To repeat: The reason for this result is that if an employer pays the total premium directly to its employees (in this case $9,000), who then use it to purchase medical insurance, they will have to pay taxes on the income. While the amounts will vary, those who have medical insurance as a job perquisite have a great deal more money to spend each year as a result. Again, this is real cash that can be used to take a vacation cruise or for anything else they desire. Medicaid benefits to the poor constitute an analogous program. As will be pointed out in Chapter 10, however, since the poor do not have extra money to begin with, those who do not receive Medicaid benefits simply go without medical treatment. Note also that the exclusion of employer contributions for medical insurance is not means tested: one member of a family must merely have a job with a group insurance plan.

As with housing programs, one might ask whether this system constitutes an effective mechanism for underwriting the cost of medical insurance for the population. This question seems especially relevant when, as mentioned earlier, 16 percent of American citizens, 41 million persons, have no health insurance coverage. Or does health insurance represent a pocket of privilege for the middle class? And perhaps an overly expensive one.

Table 8.5 illustrates the way tax expenditures distribute benefits across social class by examining six programs. The data are arrayed according to adjusted gross income. The table shows that most of the benefits of the earned income tax credit (column 2) go to those with low incomes. Although Social Security benefits (column 3) are spread throughout the class structure, most go to people in the middle-income brackets. Finally, as shown in columns 4 to 7, the ability to deduct medical payments, mortgage interest payments, state and local property taxes, and charitable contributions mainly provides benefits to middle- and high-income people. You should remember that "adjusted gross income" as used in the table is not people's total income; rather it is income for tax purposes, after various deductions. The pattern in the table is meant to be instructive: As one looks from left to right, from column (2) to (7), the benefit of tax expenditure programs go increasingly to middle-class and rich people. It was mentioned earlier that job perquisites exaggerate income inequality. Tax expenditures constitute one way this process occurs. Middle-class and rich people have more money to spend on the good things in life.

A final note. Tables 8.4 and 8.5 do not take into account the benefits individuals receive from public goods purchased by the federal government. While public goods are presumably for everyone, they actually provide benefits for specific groups. For example, everyone can take advantage of harbor dredging, drawbridge erection, lighthouse construction, and buoy maintenance financed by the federal government so long as they own a sailboat. This amenity, of course, is mainly reserved for upper-middle-class and rich people. People with lower incomes are much less likely to take advantage of it. Similarly, everyone can use the government-financed commercial and general aviation facilities at airports so long as they are rich enough to fly commercially, own a private plane, or use corporate aircraft. Again, these amenities are primarily reserved for middle-class and rich people. About half of the federal budget goes for such public goods; for example, internal affairs, science and technology, natural resources, commerce, community development, education, the administration of justice, general government, fiscal assistance, and interest on the national debt. These general categories include hundreds of programs like those mentioned above. Although one could question whether such public goods are income transfers, many economists treat them as such.[47] Thus the impact of spending on public goods amplifies that of tax expenditures specifically and income transfers generally.

Power and Income Inequality

The benefits of income transfers, whether as budget outlays or tax expenditures, are legislatively enacted. Politics, which produces legislative outcomes in a democracy, is a

TABLE 8.5 Distribution of Selected Tax Expenditures by Adjusted Gross Income, 2005

(1) ADJUSTED GROSS INCOME	(2) EXCLUSION OF EARNED INCOME TAX CREDIT	(3) EXCLUSION OF SOCIAL SECURITY	(4) DEDUCTIBILITY OF MEDICAL PAYMENTS	(5) DEDUCTIBILITY OF MORTGAGE INTEREST	(6) DEDUCTIBILITY OF STATE & LOCAL PROPERTY TAXES	(7) DEDUCTIBILITY OF CHARITABLE CONTRIBUTIONS
<$10,000	15%	0%	0%	0%	0%	0%
$10,000–20,000	39	9	1	0	0	0
$20,000–30,000	29	11	2	1	0	0
$30,000–40,000	14	17	4	2	1	1
$40,000–50,000	3	16	8	3	2	2
$50,000–75,000	1	33	24	12	8	8
$75,000–100,000	0	10	20	14	10	10
$100,000–200,000	0	4	33	40	33	29
>$200,000	0	1	8	28	46	50
	101%	101%	100%	100%	100%	100%

Note: Some totals do not add to 100% because of rounding. Data are for fiscal year 2006, which begins on October 1, 2005.

Source: Joint Committee on Taxation (2006:44–49).

219

competitive process in which the most powerful usually receive the most benefits. This is why laws rarely constitute the "best" solution to problems; rather, they reflect compromises among competing groups. So despite the public salience of transfers to the poor, the overall impact of transfers was to maintain income inequality for many years (1950–1970) and increase it since then.

This increase constitutes one of the great social experiments of our time. It was justified by "supply-side" economic theory, which argued that placing more money in the hands of the rich through reduced taxes would ultimately benefit everyone. This is because the rich invest (or supply) money, creating jobs and (presumably) increased tax revenues. Hence, the result of making the rich richer would "trickle down" to the rest of the population. Note what went on here: The majority of the population gave money to the upper-middle class and rich on the grounds that everyone would benefit. Regardless of your opinion about this experiment, these data imply a simple fact described in Chapter 1: Modern societies determine how much inequality exists, how much poverty exists, and the forms they take. Other Western societies, such as Sweden and England, display a more equal distribution of income than does the United States. In addition, poverty in these other nations is significantly less. The structure of stratification in each case reflects the outcome of this competitive process.

Income Inequality and Economic Prosperity

In the years after World War II, most people's real incomes rose, especially among Whites, even after taking inflation into account. Economic prosperity meant that they became better off, even though the level of inequality remained unchanged during that period. In the years between 1970 and the present, however, the level of inequality increased, with most of the benefit going to the rich and middle class—in that order. As mentioned earlier, part of this increase reflected the entry of the well-educated Baby Boomer generation onto the job market at a time when the economy was being transformed such that demand for blue-collar skills declined and demand for white-collar skills increased. But, in addition, an important part of this increasing inequality reflected political decisions about the nature and extent of income transfer programs—as illustrated by tax expenditures.

An important question is whether the two processes, income inequality and economic prosperity, are related to one another and, if so, how. Considered metaphorically, think of economic prosperity as like the size of a pie and the degree of income inequality as like the proportion of the pie going to each social class. If the pie gets bigger and each class is getting the same size slice, then everyone is better off. If the pie stays the same size, but one social class gets a larger slice, then a few people are better off and most others worse off. If the pie gets bigger and one class also gets a bigger slice, it gets most of the benefit of the increase in size while the portion of everyone else remains the same. The empirical issue is whether and to what degree income inequality leads to greater economic prosperity, as indicated by investment and worker productivity. The usual hypothesis is *the greater income inequality, the greater the economic prosperity in economically developed societies.* In the customary interpretation, "any insistence on carving the pie into equal slices would shrink the size of the pie.

That fact poses the trade-off between economic inequality and efficiency," another word for greater investment and worker productivity.[48] The logic underlying this interpretation is that greater inequality increases investment and work incentives, thus leading to an expanding gross domestic product—the size of the pie increases—and everyone prospers at their own level. This argument is, of course, a variation on supply-side economics. It also allows those who benefit the most to claim that their riches are good for the society as a whole, an argument that should remind you of the Davis–Moore thesis described in Chapter 1. There is a self-serving quality to this analysis that ought to arouse suspicion.

But the hypothesis can be tested and the empirical answer is mixed. For example, one study suggests, indeed, that nations in which the level of inequality increased during the 1990s (such as the United States, United Kingdom, and Japan) also experienced a greater increase in the GDP. During this same period, however, nations in which the level of inequality did not increase so much or actually decreased (such as Germany, France, Canada, and Italy), experienced slightly less increase in the GDP but—and this is important—most of the benefit went to working- and middle-class people.[49] In another study, covering the years 1974 to 1990, the results refuted the hypothesis: (1) Greater income inequality corresponded to lower levels of investment. (2) Variations in income inequality were not related to differences in worker effort and productivity. The author concludes that the hypothesized trade-off between income inequality and economic performance has little credence in advanced industrialized nations.[50] Interpreting these results requires some care. One guess is that a very high level of equality would, in fact, lower investment and worker productivity. But no Western nation displays this profile. At the opposite end, it can be argued that a very high level of inequality can be detrimental to economic performance over the long term by reducing consumer demand and reducing motivation on the part of those left behind. In any case, in modern societies, decision makers have a lot of room to maneuver such that inequality can be reasonably low and economic prosperity can be reasonably robust. And the distribution of benefits from the latter reflects the distribution of power in a society.

SOCIAL CLASS, LIFE CHANCES, AND LIFESTYLE

The majority of the American population today is middle class. Its members not only survive, they prosper doing nonmanual labor. Their **life chances** are pretty good. The term, you should recall, refers to people's share in the distribution of the resources available in the society, their share of the pie. Although the middle class possesses considerably less than the rich, what they do have is very good; it is considerably greater than that of the working class or poor. And the lifestyle that follows is, if not unique, also much better than that of the working class and the poor. **Lifestyle** is often taken to refer to the stuff people surround themselves with, such as houses, cars, and other amenities that one can purchase, and to the way in which people amuse themselves, such as their modes of entertainment or avocation. And these issues do indeed provide important indicators of social class.

But lifestyle also refers to how people organize their lives at home. For example, prior to World War II it was common for middle-class families to employ working-class women as servants, mainly nannies, cooks, and maids.[51] But over time they have been, as the saying goes, outsourced. The nanny now works for the day care center, often without job perquisites. The cook now works at McDonalds or one of the food delivery outfits—again, without benefits. And the maid now works for a janitorial or cleaning service—without perks. When middle-class families do employ a housekeeper, the impression one gets is that many (most?) cheat her out of social security benefits. Think of it as a small way of keeping a bigger piece of the economic pie. Lifestyle and stratification are inherently connected.

This connection is also revealed in terms of people's moral choices, another aspect of lifestyle. Put bluntly: Middle-class families cannot maintain their lifestyle if they cannot control their fertility.

Some background is necessary. As it developed during the nineteenth century, the middle class acquired some peculiar values regarding family life and gender roles that distinguished it from the working class. As the economy was being transformed, working-class families continued to need the income generated by children and wives. In an urban environment, children in the working class often brought in 30 to 40 percent of the total family income.[52] Hence, even though both parents may have been employed, many families' survival depended on their children's earnings. It is important to understand that the reference here is to the wages of young people, aged six to fourteen years. Historically, such individuals had always labored on the farm. (They continued doing so in the late nineteenth-century.) Urban living did not change this condition for working-class women and children. Thus, families in this situation continued the age-old practice of having many children.

The nascent middle class, however, found itself in a different situation and, hence, developed different interests. Upwardly mobile, often working in occupations that had not existed previously, by the second half of the nineteenth-century husbands were earning a "family wage"; that is, they could support their wives and children without them having to work for pay. As always, most housework remained labor intensive and it was asserted that women, often with the help of servants from the working class, ought to take primary responsibility for such tasks. In this context, middle-class people began wanting smaller families and the birthrate declined as a result. Thus, for every 1,000 white women of childbearing age, the birthrate fell from 275 in 1800 to 131 in 1900, with much of this reduction occurring among the middle class.[53] In this context, child rearing became central to the middle-class lifestyle and norms about appropriate levels of care and attention became stricter. For the first time in human history, childhood became a distinct stage of life, and women, it was said, ought to be the primary caretakers of children because men had to earn a living and lacked nurturing instincts. (This was, of course, an ideological stance.) Men's and women's roles, at least in the middle class at this time, became rather narrowly defined. It was during this period that what we now call **traditional gender norms** emerged. As described in Chapter 3, these rules specified that women and men ought to have separate spheres: Women should bear and raise children and take care of their husbands while men should provide for the family economically and dominate public life. Such norms grew widespread in the middle class during the latter part of the nineteenth-century. They extended to the working class later.

But these norms became unstable over time. The reduction in the birthrate referred to above was achieved by use of birth control (condoms and abortion).[54]

The rising incidence of abortion among middle-class women ignited the first abortion controversy during the latter years of the nineteenth-century.[55] As a result, restrictions on access to abortion were enacted in every state around the turn of the century. They served as a legal buttress to traditional gender norms, since the inability to regulate fertility kept women, especially middle-class women, from pursuing occupations requiring long training or cumulative expertise. This is because pregnancy could occur at any time, changing the direction of a woman's life. The situation remained this way for many years. Eventually, however, gender norms began changing—albeit mainly in the middle class. One (not the only) expression of these changing norms was the desire to **regulate** fertility. And that goal meant, in turn, access to birth control and, if necessary, to **an abortion**. Thus, the second abortion controversy developed in the 1960s and continues today. Although the ability to control fertility is an issue affecting all women (and all couples) regardless of social class, middle-class people—especially women—have always been predominant among activists favoring abortion rights. They have interests to protect.

But abortion is a moral issue.[56] All discussions of this topic revolve around the question of whether the developing embryo is a person or a potential person. If it is assumed to be a person, a baby, it follows that abortion can never be morally right because it is murder. In contrast, if the developing embryo is assumed to be a potential person, a fetus, then abortion can be morally justified and the issue becomes women's right to control their fertility. You should observe that each moral stance reflects an unverifiable assumption about the nature of developing life. This suggests that an underlying social division exists.

Some perspective on this division can be obtained by looking at data. Here are cross-national rates of abortion per 1,000 live births in 2000:[57]

Sweden	34
United States	33
United Kingdom	29
France	25
Germany	17
Netherlands	13
Belgium	11

Abortion is legal in each of these nations. In each it is relatively unregulated early in the pregnancy with increasing restrictions over time. These data suggest that a solution exists to the "abortion problem," that we do not have to live with such a high rate. That solution is contraception. Those nations with low rates of abortion place emphasis on preventing pregnancy. It is probable that encouraging contraceptive use in the United States would reduce the level of abortions by half or more, a result that would make our rate similar to that in Western European nations.[58]

In general, whenever relatively obvious solutions are rejected, you can be sure that hidden social divisions exist. In this case, the debate about abortion is not only about moral values; it is also—and perhaps more importantly—about the nature of the family and the centrality of motherhood in women's lives. It is, in short, about lifestyle. Those on each side of the abortion debate in the United States want to live in different worlds.

In a sense, they do live in different worlds, framed by their social class. Abortion is often seen as a cornerstone of the feminist movement, a movement dominated by middle-class white women acting in their interests. There is some truth to this assertion. Phrased simply, restrictions on the possibility of abortion are taken by many (not all) middle-class people as a threat to their economic interests and lifestyles. At the same time, as mentioned earlier, abortion is a moral dilemma. Most people try (albeit imperfectly) to live by their values. In this regard, most people find themselves in the middle—supporting women's right to an abortion with some ambivalence. Yet, as it turns out, people's moral positions often fit with their economic interests. So it is with abortion. This is because the conflict over abortion is one aspect of the larger conflict over fertility control and the nature of the family. These are, to some degree, class struggles.

SUMMARY

The middle class originated in the nineteenth-century as the number of white-collar jobs increased, people in these jobs began being paid by salaries, and blue- and white-collar jobs became spatially separated. As a result, middle-class people developed a unique lifestyle: They became residentially stable, lived near one another, and interacted with one another. By the end of the nineteenth-century, the middle class had coalesced into a more-or-less self-aware aggregate. Following from theory, the *Political Power Hypothesis* asserts that the middle class and the rich have greater influence over the distribution of resources than the other social classes.

The *Job Perquisite Hypothesis* specifies that middle-class people receive much more from such job perquisites as paid time-off benefits, medical benefits, cash and family benefits, and pension benefits (Table 8.1). Perquisites to top-level people are much greater, especially severance packages and stock options. Job perquisites add to the level of inequality in the United States, making middle-class and rich persons unwilling to demand government programs to provide such benefits to everyone. They illustrate the ability of middle-class people to influence the distribution of resources.

People in white-collar jobs nearly always earn more than those in blue-collar jobs (Table 8.2). Although the *Inequality Reduction Hypothesis* states that income transfers reduced income inequality between 1950 and 1970, this argument appears to be wrong. Rather, the *Inequality Stability Hypothesis* better explains the facts. That is, income transfers served to maintain the level of inequality for many years (Table 8.3). Since 1970, however, income inequality has risen, primarily because of (1) the increased supply of white-collar workers as the Baby Boom generation matured and (2) the reduced demand as a result of so-called "supply-side" economics. Tax expenditures are provisions of the tax code that allow reductions in taxes for selective groups of citizens and corporations. They constitute an important, if relatively unknown, form of income transfers. Tax expenditure programs are analogous to direct outlay programs, often attempting to achieve similar goals, such as providing housing or medical insurance for the population. Examining the array of tax expenditures by budget category suggests that some programs exist to benefit people at every class level (Table 8.4). Nonetheless, the benefits of tax expenditures appear to go primarily to middle-class and rich people (Table 8.5).

The last section of the chapter looked at how lifestyle reflects people's values by examining the abortion issue. People's moral stance often corresponds to their economic interests.

NOTES

1. Ehrenreich (1990:233).
2. Fischer (1994).
3. Marx and Engels (1971[1848]), Lenski (1984).
4. Blumin (1989), Bledstein and Johnston (2001).
5. Blumin (1989).
6. Archer and Blau (1993).
7. Moskovitz (2004).
8. Lynd (1929), Lynd and Lynd (1937), Caplow (1982).
9. Mitchell (1992).
10. United States Department of Labor (2006:26).
11. Lovell (2004).
12. Scofea (1994).
13. Scofea (1994).
14. United States Bureau of the Census (2006d:21).
15. United States Bureau of the Census (2006d:22).
16. Scofea (1994).
17. Katt (1997).
18. United States Bureau of the Census (2001:7).
19. United States Bureau of the Census (1975:15), Fischer (1978).
20. Hale (1903).
21. United States Bureau of the Census (2006:26).
22. United States Bureau of the Census (2006:368).
23. United States Bureau of the Census (2006:360). See also Costo (2006) and Lowenstein (2005).
24. Passell (1998).
25. Mills (1951).
26. Yaqub (1999).
27. Yaqub (1999), Bebchuk and Jackson (2005).
28. Yaqub (1999), Useem (2003), Bebchuk and Jackson (2005), Brush (2006).
29. Financial Markets Center (2000), Congressional Budget Office (2004).
30. Yaqub (1999), Fryer (1999), Revell (2003).
31. Galbraith (1992).
32. Shehan (2003).
33. Levy and Murnane (1992), Ryscavage (1999).
34. Danziger et al. (1981), Danziger and Plotnick (1977).
35. United States Department of Agriculture (2002), Morgan (2006). On the relationship between campaign contributions and farm price supports, see Stratmann (1995).
36. Lenski (1984).
37. Reynolds and Smolensky (1977).
38. Page (1983:144).
39. Williamson and Lindert (1980:92).
40. Piketty and Saez (2003, 2006), Saez (2006), Shapiro (2005).
41. Levy and Murnane (1992), Ryscavage (1999: 109–30), Saez (2006).
42. Joint Committee on Taxation (2006:2).
43. Institute on Taxation and Economic Policy (2005).
44. Brownlee (2000).
45. Institute on Taxation and Economic Policy (2005).
46. United States Bureau of the Census (2006:361).
47. Page (1983), Reynolds and Smolensky (1977).
48. Okun (1975:48).
49. Burtless (2001).
50. Kenworthy (1995).
51. Palmer (1989).
52. Zelizer (1994).
53. United States Bureau of the Census (1975:49).
54. Sanderson (1979).
55. Luker (1984), Reagan (1997).
56. Two classic arguments about the morality of abortion, for and against, are Warren (1996) and Marquis (1989).
57. World Health Organization (2006).
58. Westoff (1988), Marston and Cleland (2003).

■ ■ ■ ■ ■

THE WORKING CLASS

Does the working class differ from the middle class? The *Embourgeoisement Hypothesis* suggests that it does not. Although the word "embourgeoisement" is unwieldy, it stems from Karl Marx's work and attempts to account for the lack of working-class radicalism in the United States. To use his terminology for a moment, it asserts that the bourgeoisie have allowed proletarians to become sufficiently affluent that they are not very interested in political activity aiming at income redistribution, greater economic equality, or other forms of radical change. In plainer language, the hypothesis proposes that there has been long-term improvement in the occupational characteristics, income, and lifestyle of working-class people such that they now resemble middle-class persons, with the result that the members of the working class do not display distinctive political attributes.

If this argument is correct, then it should be observable. For example, researchers should find that the occupational settings of blue- and white-collar people are similar, that they have similar life chances (as indicated by, say, their incomes), and as a result that they have similar lifestyles. Such findings would mean that a separate analysis of the working class, like that undertaken here, is unnecessary because most people in the United States, excluding the very rich and the poor, are reasonably affluent and middle class.

The hypothesis originated with publication of John Goldthorpe's provocative *The Affluent Worker in the Class Structure* in 1969, but few social scientists today think the *Embourgeoisement Hypothesis* accurately portrays the working-class situation today because the evidence does not support it.[1] The argument is useful for pedagogical purposes, however, as a way of showing how an interesting idea can be put forth and refuted empirically. Phrased formally, the *Embourgeoisement Hypothesis* is: *The greater the similarity in the occupational characteristics, income, and lifestyle between the working class and the middle class, then the less emphasis on radical political change by the working class.* As stated, the hypothesis presupposes that middle- and working-class people are similar, and uses this "fact" to explain why working-class people are not politically radical. As it turns out, however, the presupposition is not correct, which means the hypothesis is false.

Previous chapters have shown that working-class and middle-class people differ in ways that are relevant to the hypothesis. For example, as revealed in Chapter 4, people who have blue-collar jobs usually display lower occupational prestige than do their white-collar counterparts and their class identification is with the working class rather than middle class. Moreover, as described in Chapter 5, the division between blue- and white-collar work serves as a semiper-meable barrier to mobility such that children of working-class parents usually end up in working-class jobs themselves. Finally, Chapter 8 revealed that working-class people enjoy fewer job perquisites (such as paid time-off, various medical benefits, severance pay, and pensions) and lower incomes than do middle-class people. Thus, the information already available casts doubt on the hypothesis: If working- and middle-class people differ so much, then the *Embourgeoisement Hypothesis* obviously cannot be correct.

In spite of these differences, however, other similarities are possible that have relevance for the *Embourgeoisement Hypothesis* For example, perhaps the work settings of blue- and white-collar people do not differ so much as is thought. If so, that would be evidence for the argument. Or perhaps their level of job security is about the same. Although income is obviously vital, a secure income—even a low one—determines lifestyle. Or, finally, perhaps there are similarities in consumption habits, tastes, use of leisure time, or other elements of lifestyle. If it can be shown that middle-class and working-class people resemble each other along these dimensions, then the plausibility of the *Embourgeoisement Hypothesis* would be greater.

SOCIAL CLASS AND OCCUPATION

Like the middle class, the working class has not always existed. In preindustrial soci-eties work was "a game against nature" as people used human and animal muscle power to obtain necessities for living.[2] Reliance on an inefficient source of energy meant that productivity was low. As a result, most people lived a rural life for nearly all of human history, struggling with the soil for subsistence.[3] In such contexts, a working class did not exist. Beginning in the nineteenth century, however, work increasingly became "a game against things" as people linked new, more efficient forms of energy (mainly steam and fossil fuel) with machines, and productivity rose greatly. As a result of industrialization, the class structure changed dramatically. Increasing numbers of people became urban and labored at new kinds of jobs in which the tasks were routinized, systematic, and mechanical—not to mention dan-gerous to health and safety. These are the people Marx called proletarians in the 1840s. They coalesced as a recognizable working class over the remainder of that century.

Working-Class and Middle-Class Occupations

Today, as you may recall, about 46 percent of the population answers the class identification question by saying they are working class (see Table 4.1). This answer correlates with the occupational distribution, as shown in Table 9.1. Column (2) reveals that about 40 percent of the population does blue-collar work. Taken together, these figures provide a reasonable estimate of the size of the working-class population in the United States.[4] But significant racial and ethnic differences exist, as also shown in Table 9.1. About 47 percent of African Americans, 61 percent of Hispanic Americans, and 30 percent of Asian Americans do blue-collar work. Nearly all of them identify with the working class as well. These different occupational distributions by race and ethnicity suggest that while most working-class people are white (since they are the largest group by far), a higher proportion of minority group people are working class—a fact that has important implications for differences in life chances and lifestyles.

The millions of people referred to in the lower portion of Table 9.1 wear some form of work clothes on the job. This is so they can do manual labor, the essence of working-class life. These are the people who fix, haul, lift, scrub, shovel, help, and otherwise engage in potentially damaging exertions for a living. Hence, one gets the impression that working-class people are less likely to join fitness clubs. Their jobs are exhaustive enough. And often dirty.

In the now classic examination of the working class, *Families on the Fault Line*, one of Lillian Rubin's respondents talks about the implications of getting dirty on the job: "I used to work in an upholstery factory. . . . The only thing I wanted to do when

TABLE 9.1   Occupational Distribution by Race and Ethnicity, 2005

(1) OCCUPATION	(2) ALL	(3) WHITE AMERICAN	(4) AFRICAN AMERICAN	(5) HISPANIC AMERICAN	(6) ASIAN AMERICAN
White Collar					
Management	15%	15%	9%	7%	17%
Professional	20	20	17	10	32
Sales	12	12	10	10	10
Office & Admin. Support	14	13	17	12	12
Total White Collar	61%	60%	53%	39%	71%
Blue Collar					
Production & Transportation	12	12	16	18	10
Construction & Extraction	7	7	4	14	2
Installation & Repair	4	4	12	4	2
Service	16	15	24	23	16
Farming, Forestry, Fishing	1	1	1	2	0*
Total Blue Collar	40%	39%	47%	61%	30%

Note: Some totals do not add to 100% because of rounding. * = less than ½ of 1%

Source: United States Bureau of Labor Statistics (2006:191–92).

I got home was take a bath."[5] The clean–dirty divide serves as a metaphor for the division between the middle class and working class. This same respondent eventually became a word processor, making slightly less money but glad for the difference in job characteristics:

> "You're a real person. . . . If you want to stop a minute and go talk to the other girls, nobody says anything. Or you can go to the bathroom and grab a smoke, and it's no big deal. I mean, they expect you to work, but they know you can't do it every minute. If it got slow in the factory, you got laid off. But in this job, they don't just dump you if there's a couple of slow days."

Being laid off is always a threat if you are working class. Nonetheless, as Rubin comments, working-class people provide the wheels and services that make the nation turn.[6] She means this not as a metaphor but literally. Someone—almost half the population—has to build, fix, haul, cut, and scrub. The context in which these tasks are performed can be extremely difficult.

Social Class and Job Setting

Recall that the *Embourgeoisement Hypothesis* presupposes that middle-class and working-class people are fundamentally alike. But in order to provide the wheels and services that make the nation run the environment in which working-class people must labor differs in fundamental ways that are logically incompatible with the hypothesis. Working-class job settings are often dangerous to health and life. They are also characterized by intense production pressures along with close supervision and petty work rules.

Dangerous Working Conditions.   Average middle-class Americans use electricity generated by coal that others have to mine, consume meat that others have to cut or grind, work in buildings that others have to build and maintain, and use paper made from trees that others have to log. Those "others" are working-class people. Indoors or out, even if the tasks inherent to blue-collar work involve some degree of autonomy and satisfaction, which is sometimes the case, the tasks are often difficult and dangerous.

One result is a high rate of job-related injuries. Manual laborers frequently operate machines that are very hazardous if unreliable or handled incorrectly, such as a meat grinder or hand-held power tools.[7] But most working people handle their machines and tools correctly. Even so, they still get injured. For example, those operating tools that vibrate often suffer "reduced epidermal nerve density" (which is to say they lose feeling) in their hands, a condition that lasts for many years and can become permanent. Equipment that produces high noise levels as it clatters and grinds leads to hearing loss. Machines that produce noxious dust, dirt, and other airborne particulates cause lung damage. Those working with substances that produce toxic odors suffer eye, ear, nose, and throat problems. Machines that give off sparks produce burns and eye injuries.[8]

In addition to the problems caused by the equipment, those who work outside must face the weather, the seasons of the year. Garbage collectors, mail carriers, soft-drink delivery drivers, and landfill workers must toil in the rain and the snow and the heat and the cold. Electricians and telephone line repairers must work in the middle of storms, in the middle of the night, no matter what the temperature, with equipment that is often dangerous; electrocutions are a constant threat. Bricklayers, carpenters, and others who construct homes and office buildings, usually cannot wear gloves and still do their jobs. So if it is cold they just suffer; if it is hot they just suffer. If they fall, they simply go to the hospital and sometimes die.[9] One of the most dangerous forms of work, however, is logging. For every 100 workers, about 16 are injured each year, with the odds of loggers dying much greater than the average for all occupations.[10] Yet their work is vital. Each year, the average American citizen consumes wood and paper products equal to what can be produced from one 100-foot high tree with an 18-inch diameter trunk. One could, of course, say the same thing about many of the jobs mentioned here. Someone has to build, fix, haul, cut, and scrub—tasks that are often dangerous. The people who do these jobs are working class.

Overall, between one and two million people are injured on the job every year, nearly all of them working class.[11] The people most likely to become injured at work are truck drivers, laborers, nursing aides and orderlies, janitors, machine assemblers, construction workers, carpenters, electricians, stock handlers, cashiers, and cooks. About 40 percent of all injuries are sprains and strains, most often involving the back from all the lifting involved. But many are disfiguring. Bobby Lee Cantley was only 15; he was not supposed to be there. But there he was anyway, working in a beef processing plant in Ohio in order to help support his family. He slipped and fell into a meat grinder and lost his entire arm. About 11,000 nonfatal workplace amputations of arms, hands, legs, and feet occur every year.[12] Less than 1 percent of all job injuries, they can serve as a symbol of all the burns, lacerations, cuts, respiratory problems, blurred vision, and headaches that people in working class jobs become used to.

Journals like *Monthly Labor Review, Compensation and Working Conditions,* and several others carry articles with titles such as "Work-related Injuries, Illnesses, and Fatalities in Manufacturing and Construction," "Exposure to Different Forms of Nickel and Risk of Lung Cancer," and (the award for the best title goes to) "Logging is Perilous Work."[13] There are no articles like "Workplace Injuries in the Office Suite." Apart from injuries due to repetitive motions at the keyboard (for example, Carpal Tunnel Syndrome), it is hard to imagine any way in which white-collar work compares to the dangerousness of blue-collar work. And no one dies from Carpal Tunnel. This difference in degree of dangerousness is why working-class people lose an estimated 32 percent more days from work each year than do middle-class people.[14] For example, the median is ten days a year away from work due to job-related injuries among electricians. The mode, however, is 30 days. Of course, when they become injured, working-class people are less likely to have health insurance, sick leave, or other job perquisites that protect their income (recall Chapter 8).

This relative lack of job perquisites is important because working-class people are much more likely than middle-class people to suffer long-term health problems and physical deterioration as a result of the jobs they have. As one study concludes, "the rate at which health deteriorates with age is faster in manual occupations than nonmanual occupations. For many [working-class] people, work wears out their health." For some, poverty results. Much of the strong relationship between poor health and poverty reflects the fact that work-related poor health makes people poor.[15]

In addition to injuries and their consequences, working-class jobs are also characterized by a high rate of job-related deaths.[16] Rolan Hoskin, 48 years old, lived in Tyler, Texas. He was married, with one daughter. He worked at a pipe foundry that produces cast iron sewer and water pipes, the kind found under neighborhood streets in most American cities. One day he was trying to adjust a conveyor belt and got caught in the machinery, which crushed his head. Rick Slusack, 29 years old, lived in Stevens Point, Wisconsin, near a branch of the University of Wisconsin. He was married with one child. Each working day, he was supposed to load large plastic bags filled with bark chips and wood shavings into tractor-trailer trucks. These bags end up at suburban shopping malls and garden stores, where they are sold as mulch to middle-class people. One morning the forklift he was operating skidded on gravel, overturned, and pinned him underneath. He was dead within the hour. Dereck Hubbard, 42 years old, lived in Muscle Shoals, Alabama, where he was an iron worker. One afternoon, he was locking roof panels into place on an office building when he fell to his death. A wife and two children survive him. Danny Newman, 46, married with three children, was an oil rigger in southeastern New Mexico who died when a mechanical failure caused a piece of equipment to crush him. Finally, an electrician named Lynda Gertner, a 31-year-old married woman with one child, died when a chemical explosion ripped through the plant where she was working and spread poisonous fumes throughout.

Every day, about sixteen people die in work-related accidents, roughly 6,000 each year. Most of them are working class, as shown in Panel A of Table 9.2. All the dangerous occupations are working class. Panel B of the table shows the causes of workplace fatalities. The most common source of injury leading to death is connected to operating some sort of vehicle. Some white-collar workers, such as those in sales, use cars regularly. But even more blue-collar workers must do so as they go from work-site to work-site, or operate moving equipment—such as forklifts. Ignoring homicides, a high proportion of deaths on the job reflect its inherent dangerousness: operating machinery or tools, the impact of the structures on which people work, environmental conditions, toxic liquids, and the like.

Fatalities on the job are the ultimate price some people pay to keep the nation running. Sewer pipes are manufactured and laid in the ground to carry water; mulch is ground and transported to stores so people can decorate their yards; the iron framework for the office buildings people work in is hoisted and fastened; meat for families' tables is cut, sliced, and ground at huge processing plants. Working-class people must perform these and myriad other tasks.

Middle-class jobs are different. Even in menial white-collar occupations, work stations are relatively quiet, reasonably clean, without offensive odors, and maintained at a constant temperature. In addition, it is common for office workers, even the lowest paid, to have windows and to surround themselves with flowers and pictures on the walls. Those who think, administer, sell, and push pencils or type keys for a living are, quite simply, subjected to fewer health hazards and, hence, are at less risk for injuries and death. Thus, even if the tasks that white-collar workers must do are routinized, the environment within which they are accomplished is, most of the time, reasonably pleasant and safe. Working-class jobs are much more dangerous than middle-class jobs.

TABLE 9.2   Occupational Fatality Rates among the Working Class

PANEL A: OCCUPATIONS WITH HIGH FATALITY RATES

Occupation	Number of Fatalities	Rate per 100,000
Fishers	48	118
Loggers	80	93
Aircraft Pilots & Engineers	81	66
Iron & Steel Workers	35	56
Refuse Collectors	32	44
Farmers & Ranchers	341	41
Power Line Installers	36	33
Truck & Sales Drivers	993	29
Agricultural Workers	176	23
Construction Workers	339	23

PANEL B: CAUSES OF WORKPLACE FATALITIES

Transportation Accidents	43%
Contact with Objects and Equipment	18
Assaults & Violent Acts	14
Falls	13
Exposure to Harmful Substances & Environment	9
Fires & Explosions	3
	100%

Source: United States Bureau of Labor Statistics (2006a).

Production Pressures.   The phrase "production pressures" refers to the attempt at regulating the rate and rhythm of work. This characteristic is especially true of assembly line occupations. What happens is that employers measure the amount of time it takes a competent person to perform a task and then set the pace of the line accordingly. And it does not matter if a person has a sprained hand or was up last night with a sick child.

Companies in the same industry, however, often take rather different approaches to the problem of maintaining production. In the pipe foundry industry, for example, some companies emphasize keeping the line running regardless of safety or environmental hazards. If 80 pipes are supposed to be produced each hour, then management expects 80 pipes—not 79. The reason is simple: "Time equals pipe, and pipe equals money."[17] These companies have high rates of work-related injuries and deaths, constant accusations of polluting the environment, and high employee turnover. But the dilemma may be false. Other companies in that same industry are very profitable while emphasizing job safety and environmental responsibility; they also have high employee morale and low turnover.[18] This rather different emphasis reduces (although it does not eliminate) the level of danger inherent to many jobs.

Production pressures also occur in most manufacturing and some service tasks, whether an assembly line exists or not. The installation of new sky boxes and renovation of a college football stadium must be completed on time, or the contractor faces significant financial penalties. So does the road builder if the repaving of a highway or city street is not finished on time.

The pressure to finish on time leads some companies to take shortcuts. Patrick Walters had missed work the day before, after being hit in the back by the bucket of a backhoe. On this day, however, after a night of rain, he was attaching sewer pipes in a ten-foot-deep trench. No one took the time to brace up the sides and they collapsed. "He was buried alive under a rush of collapsing muck and mud" and died a few moments later.[19]

Their inherent dangerousness constitutes part of the reason for so many injuries and deaths in working-class jobs. But production pressures and companies' orientation to them constitute another. Many middle-class jobs, of course, also carry production pressures. In the professions, for example, architects must have plans finished on time; accountants must review tax returns on time; lawyers must have arguments ready on time. The stress inherent to these jobs can be great. Perhaps that is one reason why vacations are so welcomed.

Close Supervision and Petty Work Rules.   Close supervision and petty work rules distinguish many working-class job settings. The pervasive time clock, at which people punch-in when they arrive to work and punch-out when they leave, suggests immediately how closely supervised blue-collar workers are. Along with supervision, of course, come rules to enforce. Working-class jobs are often characterized by work rules that resemble those in elementary school or, perhaps, boot camp. There are rules against talking, against going to the bathroom without authorization, against pausing for a moment to stretch tired muscles, against everything that would make a job more pleasant or enjoyable. The enforcers of these rules are the foreperson and line-level white-collar managers. Although the power of these supervisors is somewhat circumscribed in union plants, the millions of nonunion workers face a simple choice: do what they are told, toe the line, or be fired. Workers report that this kind of supervision makes them feel as though they are being treated like machines instead of human beings. This is a metaphorical way of describing what it means to feel powerless or, in the jargon, alienated.

Most middle-class jobs are rather different. For one thing, time clocks rarely exist; most people are paid annual salaries rather than hourly wages, which means punching in and out is viewed as less necessary. In addition, while nearly everyone has a supervisor or boss, the nature and quality of the supervision is often quite different. For example, it is hard to imagine college professors, engineers, computer programmers, salespersons, or even clerical workers having to justify going to the bathroom or a few moments on the telephone talking to their spouse. (Recall the quotation from the word processor a few pages ago.) To propose such rules is to propose an absurdity. Yet many blue-collar workers live by them everyday. In most middle-class jobs, getting the task done is the important issue, and this is accomplished with far less direct supervision and far fewer work rules.

This emphasis on production pressure and close supervision reflects a specific managerial approach that is peculiarly American. In *Fat and Mean: The Corporate Squeeze of Working Americans and the Myth of Managerial "Downsizing,"* David Gordon argues that American companies rarely emphasize raises, bonuses, and other "carrots" as mechanisms to motivate workers.[20] Rather, compared to other nations, U.S. companies typically develop rather large bureaucracies that emphasize a "stick strategy": arbitrary commands and threats of loss of job for failure to obey. This "fat" bureaucracy and "mean" management style is supposed to lead to greater productivity. It probably lowers productivity, however, as most people respond better to positive reinforcers ("carrots") than negative ("sticks"). Gordon argues that one—not the only—reason for rising inequality in this country is the existence of bloated bureaucracies in U.S. corporations whose personnel require income that might otherwise go to blue-collar workers. Working-class people toil harder at more dangerous jobs just to stay in place. From this angle, the presupposition underlying the *Embourgeoisement Hypothesis* is incorrect.

SOCIAL CLASS AND JOB SECURITY

It was mentioned earlier that working-class men and women provide the wheels and services that make this nation turn by fixing, hauling, lifting, shoveling, and helping. Although one might think that people employed in these sorts of jobs would be paid rather well for the extra danger and other difficulties, the income and job security of working-class people are less today than in the past. This fact was illustrated in the last chapter in Table 8.2, which shows median income by occupation for men and women. Please pause and look back at the table now. These data reveal that, despite the *Embourgeoisement Hypothesis*, reality for most working-class individuals and families is that they are not affluent; they are, rather, economically insecure. Nonetheless, popular stereotypes abound of the plumber, the teamster, and even the garbage collector as members of a new well-to-do working class. This perception reflects considerable misunderstanding because most people do not realize who gets the money when they employ skilled people. For example, when customers take their automobiles to be fixed, they are often charged $35 to $50 per hour for the job. While such figures seem like a high rate of pay for a "simple car repair" most of the money does not go to the mechanic; it goes, rather, to the owner of the dealership or repair shop to cover overhead and profit. Owners are classified as businesspersons, not blue-collar workers. The latter make $10 to $15 per hour ($21,000–$31,000, if they work full-time all year long—many do not). This same point applies when people employ plumbers, electricians, and other skilled blue-collar people. Those who actually do the job often earn far less than the price paid by the customer and, as a result, are much less affluent and more economically insecure than white-collar employees.

Although income is fundamental to families' economic circumstances, those who are assured a regular income, even if it is relatively low, can organize their lives to a greater degree than those for whom a steady income is more doubtful. Thus, if working-class people have job security similar to that of middle-class people, then this fact could be taken as evidence of embourgeoisement.

Unfortunately, job security, as indicated by the unemployment rate, is significantly less for those engaged in working-class occupations. This fact is illustrated in Table 9.3, which shows that unemployment rates are higher in all working-class occupations. For example, the unemployment rate among professional specialty workers was only 2 percent in 2005, compared to figures between 4 percent and 7 percent in most working-class occupations. These differences in likelihood of unemployment mean that of all those out of work at any time, most were previously in working-class jobs.

Moreover, most people who are unemployed do not leave their jobs voluntarily. Table 9.3 shows that the overall rate of unemployment was about 6 percent in 2005. This figure can be broken down in the following way.[21]

45%	Lost job
12	Left job
33	Reentering the job market
9	Entering job market for the first time

Thus, very few of the unemployed find themselves in that situation because they left their jobs by choice. Nearly all those without work, 78 percent (45% + 33%), either lost their jobs or, overcoming their discouragement, reentered the job market. Discouragement, by the way, is a major issue in discussing the unemployment rate. This is because people are only classified as unemployed if they are looking for work. If they have become so demoralized that they have stopped looking, then they are no longer unemployed—at least officially. This paradoxical phenomenon is why you occasionally see newspaper articles describing hundreds or even thousands of applicants appearing when a new plant opens up. When jobs, real jobs, become available then people re-enter the labor market—another way of saying they become hopeful of actually finding work. The number of unemployed persons has been placed in Table 9.3 in order to emphasize that millions of people are reflected in the percentages. You should remember, however, that the figures understate the number of unemployed and discouraged people: Among

TABLE 9.3   Number Unemployed and Unemployment Rate by Occupation, 2005

OCCUPATION	NUMBER UNEMPLOYED	UNEMPLOYMENT RATE
White Collar		
Management	440,000	2%
Professional	792,000	3%
Sales	873,000	5%
Office & Administrative Support	933,000	5%
Blue Collar		
Production & Transportation	1,180,000	6%
Construction & Extraction	528,000	6%
Installation & Maintenance	210,000	4%
Service	1,502,000	6%
Farming, Forestry, Fishing	85,000	7%
Overall	7,327,000	6%

Note: Data refer to persons 16 years of age and older.

Source: Bureau of Labor Statistics (2006b:table a10).

adults aged 18 to 64, there are more than 11 million poor persons in this country. Despite stereotypes to the contrary, most want to work (see Chapter 10).

One last point. Although it is not shown in the table, the mean duration of unemployment across all social classes was about 19 weeks in 2005.[22] This time has been fairly typical over the years and it implies that a far higher proportion of the total workforce, three to four times the overall rate, experience some unemployment in any specific year. The vast majority of these persons are working class, which is a typical situation, and many are poor for at least part of the time. Thus, the people who have the least job security, who have the most to fear from unemployment, are in working-class families. This finding is not consonant with the *Embourgeoisement Hypothesis*, since those who are economically insecure cannot be considered like the middle class.

The experience of insulation workers provides a good illustration of the problems and dangers many working-class people face.[23] Residences and offices that are insulated properly reduce energy consumption because they retain heat during the winter and ward it off during the summer. Utility bills are less as a result. In new construction, insulation workers cement, staple, wire, tape, or spray insulation on pipes, flat surfaces, or various enclosed areas (such as the attic of your house). They spend their days lifting their equipment while standing, bending, or kneeling. Small particles from the materials they handle (typically fiberglass, cellulose, or rock-wool) can irritate the eyes and skin, and inflame the respiratory system (making it hard to breathe over the long-term). This problem is acute because insulation workers often labor in confined spaces that are not well ventilated.

When older residences or offices are renovated, insulation workers remove the old materials. In the past, asbestos was widely used in walls, ceilings, attics, and to cover pipes, boilers, and other equipment. Because asbestos is a potent carcinogen, the law requires that it be removed. Specially trained persons (called hazardous materials removal workers) do this. Of course, the difficulties and dangers they face are significantly greater.

Insulation workers fall into the more general category of "construction and extraction" workers. Recall from looking back at Table 8.2 that the median income of men employed full-time, all year round in these occupations, was $31,100 in 2005. Experienced insulation workers had a median income of $15.66 per hour in 2005, which translates into a yearly wage of $31,320—assuming they work 50 weeks and take a two-week (usually unpaid) vacation. But, as shown in Table 9.3, construction and extraction workers display one of the highest rates of unemployment of any occupational category. Nearly all insulation workers are employed in the construction industry. Hence, they typically experience higher-than-average periods of unemployment due to the short duration of construction projects and the cyclical nature of the industry. Their incomes will be significantly lower as a result. Let us assume a person is unemployed for ten weeks. This person's actual income (before taxes) becomes $25,056. Not many people can take a one-fifth drop in income without significant economic and familial consequences.

As an editorial aside, economists often describe unemployment as "unpaid vacation," presuming, apparently, that people benefit from being thrown out of work because they have leisure time in which to enjoy themselves. But consider: Economists are usually employed in colleges and universities or come from an academic background, experiences that fundamentally influence their vision of reality.

For example, college professors are generally employed on nine-month contracts and paid sufficiently well that they frequently view the summer as free time, as unpaid vacation. Those who publish often use the summer to do research, which means that (no matter how much they enjoy their jobs) they see themselves as giving up leisure time in order to work. Moreover, college professors have unpaid leave built into the academic year: at Thanksgiving, Christmas, and spring break. Once again, this time is often used for research, which involves giving up leisure. Thus, from economists' point of view, those who (like themselves) are sometimes unemployed have "unpaid vacation" and those who (like themselves) work anyway are particularly virtuous. Perhaps economists' rather privileged position in the society leads them to make inappropriate generalizations about those in other locations, such as working-class people.

This mistake illustrates a fundamental difficulty that is peculiar to social science research: How are observers to be objective about society even as they participate in it? This is the problem Max Weber raised a long time ago. Alas, there remains no easy answer to the question and social scientists rely on the disciplined skepticism of colleagues to point out implicit bias.

Reality, in fact, is far different than the image conveyed by the phrase "unpaid vacation": Any period without a job, especially long-term unemployment, is devastating to working-class families, often destroying their lifestyle completely and sometimes creating poverty where none had existed before. This threat is a fundamental and pervasive source of stress. It means they are not affluent, that the *Embourgeoisement Hypothesis* is incorrect.

THE HUMAN CONSEQUENCES OF UNEMPLOYMENT

As will be explained in more detail in Chapter 10, a trade-off usually occurs between inflation and unemployment, and American policy makers typically choose to allow unemployment to be higher than inflation. While this choice can be defended as one that benefits the nation as a whole (the argument is that "everyone is hurt by inflation"), poor and working-class people are hurt more by unemployment than inflation. There is, however, surprisingly little research on the human consequences of unemployment. The phrase "human consequences" is used here to distinguish the suffering of individuals from the macroeconomic effects of unemployment: loss of productivity. Economists emphasize, correctly, that billions of dollars worth of goods and services are not produced when people, factories, and other resources stand idle.

The lack of research on the impact of losing one's job is important because unemployment has far-reaching economic and noneconomic consequences for those who go through it, sometimes lasting long after the experience is over. Furthermore, it is possible that these results, nearly all of which are negative, redound (or spill over) into other arenas of society. This situation means that macroeconomic policies are made in relative ignorance, buttressed by stereotypes of unemployed people enjoying unpaid vacations, rather than social scientific evidence.

A Note on the Meaning of Work

Max Weber emphasized that in modern societies people's jobs have both economic and noneconomic implications.[24] Jobs not only provide a way to earn a living, they also affect people's identity. When unemployment occurs, this identity is threatened.

One indicator of this fact is that the vast majority of people would, if given a choice, continue working even if they had enough money to live comfortably.[25] This is because many individuals view their jobs as relatively interesting and enjoyable, as a way of staying physically and mentally healthy, and as a means for justifying their existence and seeing themselves positively. Others, mainly those in less engaging and more physically arduous occupations, say they would keep working (although not always at the same job) because they do not want to be idle or bored, because their self-respect is tied to earning a living and providing for their families, and because they would "go crazy" if their work did not keep them occupied.

But work appears to have different meaning for middle-class and working-class people. Those in middle-class occupations tend to emphasize that their jobs are interesting and carry a sense of accomplishment as well as a concern with self-respect and a desire not to be idle. It should be recognized that people in white-collar jobs are often in competitive environments where individual initiative can pay off, a fact that carries intrinsic interest. (Office and administrative support workers constitute an obvious exception to this generalization.) In contrast, working-class people tend to say that their jobs occupy their time, provide them with companionship, and give them a sense of earning an "honest living," which they define as working with their hands. This orientation leads to some harsh judgments. It appears that many working-class people see white-collar jobs as scams for avoiding "real work."[26] Moreover, from this angle the work middle-class professionals do often takes the form of harassing those below them—working-class people. Hence, they believe that working with your hands is more honorable than "shuffling paper" or "working with your mouth." Whatever one thinks of these judgments, they indicate how central employment is to the lives of working-class people. Observers consistently find that "one of the best indicators of the importance of the job to these men is their discomfort when they cannot work."[27]

Men are referred to here because it appears that the possibility of unemployment raises different issues for women and men, at least in the working-class couples Lillian Rubin talked to.[28]

> Ask a [working class] man for a statement of his identity, and he'll almost always respond by telling you first what he does for a living. The same question asked of a woman brings forth a less predictable, more varied response, one that's embedded in the web of relationships that are central to her life.

Among these couples, women tended to have multifaceted self-identities that include their roles as mother, wife, friend, daughter, and sister. So even for those women who were divorced and single mothers, their job only represented part of their sense of self. Hence, while losing a job (or the potential for doing so) might be painful and anxiety producing, it did not call their identity into question. For men, however, even though they also assume many roles (as husband, father, friend, son, and so forth), going to work is what they are. Their job is what they are, the core of their being. As will become clear, these differences in orientation affect the impact of unemployment on families.

Economic Deprivation

For young couples of any race or ethnic group, usually saddled with high debts and little savings, unemployment of either spouse is an immediate catastrophe. For families in the prime earning years, however, getting laid off usually does not result in poverty—at least immediately. But it is a constant specter. In order to illustrate why, the plausible income and expenses for a hypothetical working-class couple, named Margarita and Alberto Martinez, are sketched. They have two teenage children and are active in their church—a more or less typical family. They are now doing pretty well economically because, after many years of struggle, Alberto, age 42, recently became a member of Local 14 of the Insulators and Hazardous Workers Union, located in Philadelphia. As a union member, he would earn about $42,000 per year, assuming that he works full-time all year long. Margarita, 38, is a bank teller. She also works full-time all year long and earns slightly less than the average for office workers, $28,000 (see Table 8.2). Although their total gross income is well above average for blue-collar workers, it is used here to illustrate the precariousness of lifestyle in the working class.

This uncertainty can be seen by looking at the breakdown of their gross income in Table 9.4. Although the figures in the table are tailored to fit this hypothetical example, they are comparable to amounts shown by consumer expenditure surveys for families at this income level.[29]

Although the Martinezes' gross income is $70,000, this amount is reduced in a variety of ways. Following from the discussion of job perquisites in Chapter 8, it is assumed that they obtain medical insurance through her employer, which pays most of the cost of medical insurance. In addition, each of their employers matches their retirement contribution. Their share of the cost of these two benefits is $2,000 and $5,000, respectively, which is paid before taxes (another small perquisite). So their total taxable income is reduced to $63,000.

Their income is reduced further by taxes. After normal deductions, the Martinezes' effective federal income tax rate is 8 percent, about the same as their payroll tax (for Social Security/Medicare) of 7.65 percent. It is common for millions of ordinary citizens to pay a higher payroll tax than a federal income tax. Finally, their income is reduced by state and local taxes on property, income, and sales that combine to total 8.1 percent. This figure is somewhat lower than the nationwide average of 8.8 percent.[30] This family pays about 24 percent of its income in taxes, a rate higher than that of many rich persons and families but typical at this income level. On that basis, the Martinezes have a net monthly income of about $4,000 from which they must pay their living expenses.

In order to ease comparison with a similar table to be presented in Chapter 10, the monthly living expenses depicted in Table 9.4 are divided between those for food and nonfood. Note, however, the cost of food (purchased both at home and away) has been combined with the cost of personal supplies people normally buy in a grocery store, such as toothbrushes, vitamins, toilet paper, and the like. As sketched in the table, Margarita and Alberto Martinez have relatively fixed expenses totaling almost

TABLE 9.4 Income and Expenses for a Hypothetical Working-Class Family (Two Adults, Two Children)

INCOME

Gross Income from Husband's Job	$42,000
Gross Income from Wife's Job	28,000
Total Gross Income	70,000

Minus Expenses Taken Before Taxes

Employee share of cost of Medical Insurance	−2,000
Employee share of Retirement Contribution[a]	−5,000
Total Taxable Income	$63,000

Minus Taxes on $60,400

Income tax at 8%[b]	−5,000
Social Security/Medicare tax at 7.65%	−4,800
State & Local Taxes at 8.1%[c]	−5,100
All Taxes = 23.75%, Yielding Net Yearly Income	$48,100
Net Monthly Income (48,100 ÷ 12)	$4,000

MONTHLY LIVING EXPENSES[d]

Total Food (home & away, plus personal supplies)	$ 900
Mortgage Payment	$ 600
Utilities (including family cell phone)	350
Transportation (car payment, insurance, public trans.)	500
Life Insurance	50
Health Care (deductibles, noninsured expenses)	200
Church Contribution	100
Education (for children's expenses)	50
Entertainment	200
Tobacco & Alcohol	100
Saving for children's college education	300
Nonallocated	650
Total Nonfood	$3,100
Total Monthly Living Expenses (total food + total nonfood)	$4,000

[a]$3000 for him, $2000 for her, see United States Bureau of Labor Statistics (2006d).

[b]Assumes normal deductions for a family of four. All income is from wages.

[c]Assumes couple lives in Pennsylvania. Includes sales, property, and state/local income taxes. The nationwide average for a couple like this would be 8.8%. See Institute on Taxation and Economic Policy (2003).

[d]These figures are illustrations based on United States Bureau of Labor Statistics (2006d).

two-thirds of their take-home income: mortgage, utilities, transportation, life insurance, and health care not covered by insurance. This leaves about one-third for expenses and purchases of the sort that every family makes. Even so, note that this budget contains no provision for credit card debt, a new transmission for the car, dental work, or shoes for their children (endorsed by a popular athlete, of course), to name some obvious unallocated but plausible expenses. Nor does it take into account expenses for holidays, birthdays, or vacations. All in all, then, a family like this gets by. Although it is not poor, the fear of poverty is always there: What happens when Alberto gets laid off? As mentioned earlier, this is very likely for insulators working in the construction industry. Because he has only recently joined the union, Alberto has little seniority. Like many other minority persons, he will get the axe before others do and remain unemployed for a longer time.

When he loses his job, the family's income is cut by 60 percent. Although Alberto is eligible for unemployment benefits (not everyone is), this supplement is time limited and only covers a portion of lost pay. Hence, the Martinezes' first task is to cut back on expenses. The family will retain medical insurance because they get it through Margarita's employer, but she will stop contributing to her retirement fund (as will Alberto, of course, since he is not working). Church contributions, holidays, entertainment, and optional purchases (dentist?) are also eliminated. Selling the car is a possibility, especially in Philadelphia, but it limits Alberto's work options because jobs are increasingly located in suburban areas that are difficult to commute to via mass transit. This would be much more of a problem, of course, for a family living in a city without good public transportation. If Alberto's unemployment persists, the basic elements of the family's lifestyle will be affected: the car is sold, heat is set lower, and the like.

The second task is to generate new resources. Like many working-class men, Alberto has a variety of skills and is resourceful; when unemployed, he works off-the-books whenever possible to generate income. But the pay at these kinds of jobs is nearly always at or near the minimum wage. In addition, the modest funds in Alberto's and Margarita's retirement funds can be tapped, albeit with a tax penalty. Of course, that strategy means a leaner old age. Finally, when they become truly desperate, they can obtain a small amount of financial help from kin or have one of the children leave high school and enter the labor force. Although none of these strategies will be effective for very long, they do tide families like this over (remember, the sketch here is hypothetical). The single most important priority in cutting expenses and generating resources is to continue paying the mortgage. "We could be on the street"; it is the primordial fear that rises in working-class families when unemployment occurs.[31]

If, however, the period without work is short-term, a few weeks or months (at most), families like the Martinezes can often recover their lifestyle. If, however, it persists for very long, the consequences are catastrophic. Here is an empirical generalization that expresses the relationship between unemployment and economic deprivation: *The longer the duration of unemployment, the greater the economic deprivation and the more likely impoverishment.* And homelessness.

Furthermore, remember that unemployment does not happen gradually. Rather, a person is suddenly laid off or fired, just before the mortgage payment is due, just before a holiday, just before—something—there is no convenient time. And most unemployment, it will be recalled, occurs among working-class people, precisely those who have the least amount of money in savings, the least economic flexibility. The suffering that results can permanently erode people's sense of self-worth and confidence in the world, and often causes familial disruption.

Psychological Stress

Although, as indicated earlier, research on the human consequences of unemployment is rather sparse, some work has been done. For example, studies undertaken during and after the depression of the 1930s showed consistently that men who are thrown out of work, who are forced to be idle because no jobs are available, interpret this experience as a threat to their self-worth.[32] More recent literature indicates that this finding remains accurate.[33] It shows that the economic deprivation, loss of social support, abrupt changes in daily routine, and the disruption of long-term financial plans that accompany unemployment lead individuals to suffer depression, anxiety, and physical ailments. Ethnographic studies of working-class families portray these results vividly.[34]

In effect, people without jobs feel small. They speak of their insignificance, their impotence, their boredom, of their inability to control their own lives.[35]

> I've been lost in the general scheme of things. . . . I don't even know what I'm doing, you know? I'm just what they call 'free falling.' There's not plans or anything. I used to try to make plans; there's no concentration. I feel like I'm in a fog. I have been called a vegetable. I don't read the newspaper. I try. It's just that I can't really concentrate. I used to.

"I can't really concentrate . . . " This statement is a sign of depression, something that often accompanies unemployment.[36] What happens is that most people in the United States are socialized (or taught) by parents, teachers, and clergy that the work ethic is a fundamental value. (You should recall here the four principles of socialization presented in Chapter 1.) This value becomes part of their sense of self, of who and what they are. When people who have internalized the work ethic as part of their sense of self and who have been steadily employed all their lives suddenly find that they can no longer be active, productive members of the society, they lose confidence in themselves and display other indications of stress. This argument can be summarized as a simple empirical generalization: *Individuals who are or have been unemployed display more psychological stress than those who have not.* One manifestation is depression. Another is excessive drug use, especially alcohol. These results can be long-lasting.

Familial Disruption

Although the available evidence is scant, it appears that individuals who experience unemployment also endure family disruption. The phrase "family disruption" refers not only to unhappiness and divorce but also spouse abuse and child abuse.

In a context where families are dealing with economic deprivation and the unemployed person is trying to cope with his or her own stress, then disruption becomes likely. Ethnographic studies, for example, report that working-class men not only had financial problems when they were unemployed, but also drank excessively and displayed more tense marital relationships.[37] What happens, apparently, is that unemployed people—especially men—experience economic deprivation and stress, which leads them to become more irritable, tense, and hostile. Such feelings are acted out on those immediately around them: children and spouses. So the discipline of children becomes more arbitrary, punitive, and violent.[38] Marital relations also suffer, with spouse abuse and divorce more likely.[39] This argument can be expressed as a simple, albeit hard to demonstrate, hypothesis: *Families in which one of the spouses is or has been unemployed have a higher probability of familial disruption than those who have not.*

This hypothesis is hard to demonstrate because the relationship between unemployment and familial disruption is probably not a simple causal connection.[40] Thus, the overall strength of the marriage, the personality characteristics of the spouses, and previous experience with unemployment and income loss are all probably related to the degree of and form of familial disruption. For example, a couple in which the spouses are nurturing and supportive of one another and emotionally stable is probably going to have less familial disruption as it adjusts to economic deprivation and job loss than one in which the spouses are consistently critical of one another and display emotional instability. It is likely that these characteristics are class related.

In sum, one premise underlying the *Embourgeoisement Hypothesis* is that the working class has become as affluent as the middle class. Unfortunately, those doing blue-collar work not only earn less money, they have less job security than those doing white-collar work. Their lifestyles are not secure.

SOCIAL CLASS, LIFE CHANCES, AND LIFESTYLE

The *Embourgeoisement Hypothesis* also presumes that working- and middle-class people have essentially similar lifestyles. **Lifestyle,** you might recall, refers to people's way of living, as indicated by their consumption habits, use of leisure, and fundamental choices and values. One easy indicator of how consumption differs by class is the kind of clothes people wear, both on the job (work clothes vs. suits, for example) and at play. Other examples are the type of car or truck owned, leisure-time activities, furniture purchased, magazines subscribed to, mail order catalogues bought from, even the sweetness of drinks. All give fairly obvious clues about people's social class and way of living.[41] Moreover, there is an enormous amount of pretension inherent in lifestyle— at all class levels. One result of such hubris (or undue pride) is that people act to protect their way of life by discriminating against others whom they consider inferior or, at least, different, a complex way of referring to class conflict.

Housing provides an important way of illustrating the differences in lifestyle displayed by the working and middle classes. Some of these differences are subtle, but easily noticed. For example, house color, lawn decorations, number of pets running loose, and many other external features. Moreover, the interior of people's houses provides countless clues to their occupants' class identity and, hence, their lifestyle. For example, it appears that the television often occupies the central place in working-class living rooms.[42] Patterns of interaction vary as well. For example, working-class persons appear to evaluate middle-class neighborhoods as too impersonal, since people nearby do not interact much and may not even know one another. Conversely, middle-class people are often suspicious of working-class neighborhoods precisely because there is so much street life. People become familiar with and develop an emotional affinity for a particular kind of neighborhood, and they make negative judgments of other areas in terms such as these. These alternative value judgments reflect the lifestyle of each class.

These differences in lifestyle, of course, reflect taste and skill combined with economic necessity—another way of talking about life chances. As described in Chapter 2, most American cities are divided into neighborhoods by class, race, and ethnicity, and residents accurately perceive these differences. When they are asked by researchers to identify how neighborhoods differ, most persons refer to the relative income characteristics of people living in different sections of town or, in suburban areas, entire communities. Thus, particular areas will be seen as poor, working class, middle class, or rich, by observing their housing characteristics and imputing income.

When respondents mention income to interviewers asking about housing location and neighborhood, however, it may serve as a convenient proxy for invidious judgments they make but are reluctant to talk about openly and, sometimes, are only partly aware of. For example, working-class neighborhoods are characterized by higher housing density, more garages converted into extra rooms, and more cars being repaired in driveways or on the street. While people recognize these differences, they are not the first thoughts that come to mind when asked to compare neighborhoods.

People's housing, whether a home or an apartment, is usually their biggest single expenditure and it symbolizes their share of the distribution of resources in the society. As such, it has positive consequences for individuals and families.[43] For example, it leads to preferential tax treatment (recall the discussion of tax expenditures in Chapter 8) and wealth accumulation. Homeowners have greater ties to the community and their children often do better in school. But differences exist among homeowners, differences that call the *Embourgeoisement Hypothesis* into question.

As most observers know intuitively, the quality of housing differs by social class. In order to illustrate some of these differences, Table 9.5 uses a few easily quantifiable indicators to compare the housing of families at three income levels: That between $40,000 to $59,000 is typical of a working-class household (note that it is just below that of the hypothetical Martinez family), while the other two are typical middle-class income levels (see Table 8.2).

Table 9.5 displays data for households who own their homes. It shows that working-class families usually live in older houses, which means that repair costs are higher. At some point, the roof begins leaking or the water heater stops functioning. Yet the budget for working-class families is usually stretched pretty thin. Table 9.4, for example, does not include the cost of replacing a leaky water heater. Where is the money going to come from? Newer homes are less likely to have these kinds of problems, which means that middle-class people do not have to use resources for them. Given different income levels, it follows that working-class people own homes that are less expensive than those of middle-class people. But in order to obtain housing, working-class people must pay a higher proportion of their income for it. Thus, the table shows that families with incomes around $50,000 who own their homes spend about 20 percent of their incomes for housing, compared to 16 percent and 13 percent for families with higher incomes. Although data for renters is not shown, the pattern displayed in Table 9.5 is the same. Hence, these differences can be expressed as an empirical generalization that applies to both: *The lower the social class, then the older the housing, the lower the value of housing, and the higher the proportion of income spent on housing.*

TABLE 9.5   Social Class and Housing: Owner-Occupied Units

Housing Characteristics	HOUSEHOLD INCOME		
	40,000–59,000	80,000–99,000	120,000 +
Housing Age			
Median Year Built	1973	1977	1980
Housing Cost			
Median Value of Home	$146,000	$214,000	>$300,000
Monthly Costs as % of Income	20%	16%	13%
Housing Amenities			
Median Square Footage	1,700	2,000	>2,500
Percent with 2+ Baths	58%	71%	85%

Source: United States Bureau of the Census (2006e:165–73).

This empirical generalization has important implications for life chances. The relatively high proportion of income spent on housing means there is less money available to working-class families for other things that bring pleasure and express lifestyle: going bowling or to the opera, buying a pickup truck or a car, contributing to a church or a political campaign, and saving for children's college education. It also means that since the value of their house is often less, when working-class people sell late in life, as at retirement, they have less money (and, hence, fewer choices) to take them through old age. Finally, the houses themselves have fewer amenities and, perhaps, depending on one's point of view, do not look as nice.

The bottom portion of Table 9.5 displays selected differences in housing amenities, another way of assessing the quality of housing. As indicated above, some things people do to their homes indicate their taste: color of paint, kind of yard decorations, and the like. Class differences in things like this reflect varying values as well as relative economic situation. The table, however, displays some "big bucks" amenities, fundamental choices people make in purchasing and renting their homes, and in each case, working-class families are significantly less well off. Thus, on the average, families with lower incomes have significantly less square footage available to them: an average of 1,700 square feet in the working class, compared to 2,000 and 2,500 in the middle class. Each 300 to 400 increase in square footage means the house is about one room larger. Similarly, only 58 percent of owners in the $50,000 range have homes with two or more baths, compared to 71 percent and 85 percent at higher income levels. Again, the pattern is the same for renters, although the square footage and percentages are lower in each case. Such variations are expressed in the following empirical generalization: *The lower the social class, then the fewer amenities built into housing.*

Items like those used in the table are significant because they indicate families' level of physical comfort and convenience. Not shown in the table are differences in the availability of air conditioning, quality of insulation, and other factors that decisively influence comfort and convenience. But the square footage and bathrooms are important in another way as well, for they indicate the degree of crowding that occurs. Part of this is "just" daily hassle: getting into and out of the bathroom each morning as family members prepare for work and school is much easier if more bathrooms are available. In addition, however, crowding has more serious implications. Smaller houses (or apartments) make daily life more difficult because people have less privacy. A couple's sex life is more restricted, there is less space for children to do homework, and there is less ability to get away from each other when someone is angry, among many other problems. Recall that unemployment leads to stress and family disruption; crowded living conditions exacerbate these problems. Ultimately, it does not matter whether these variations in amenities reflect comparative cost, which means in every case that the working class is less well off, or simply taste. As Max Weber emphasized, people make subjective invidious judgments of others based on their sense of sharing a common way of life. The working class is different from the middle class.

ON THE WORKING CLASS

The *Embourgeoisement Hypothesis* does not accurately describe the condition of the working class in the United States. As you may recall, this argument has been used as a pedagogical device, an example of hypothesis testing in the social sciences. Thus, the available evidence shows that working-class people labor at inferior occupational settings that carry with them lower incomes and less job security. Furthermore, the life chances and lifestyles of the working and middle classes differ. Thus, based on the empirical data, the *Embourgeoisement Hypothesis* should be rejected because its premise is incorrect.

For contemporary Marxists, however, the *Embourgeoisement Hypothesis* implies a rather different kind of analysis. Karl Marx saw capitalist society as divided into two great classes: the bourgeoisie, consisting of a small group of capitalists who own the means of production, and the proletariat, consisting of the vast majority of people who own nothing and must sell their labor power to survive. The relationship between the two was inherently exploitive, Marx believed, and he predicted that over the long run an impoverished proletariat would rebel and usher in a new society. The problem for contemporary Marxists is to explain why this scenario has not occurred.

For this reason, the size, composition, and political orientation of the working class is a matter of some controversy.[44] Although the circumlocutions (or excessive words) become very complex in Marxist writings, a typical strategy is to downplay the differences between the working and middle class and argue, in some form or another, that the vast majority of people are still essentially proletarians who have been temporarily bought off by the bourgeoisie. Thus, it is asserted, engineers, accountants, real estate agents, electricians, and police officers are "really" proletarians because they possess few assets and have nothing to sell but their labor power.[45] Ultimately, contemporary Marxists are still presuming that all those who do not own capital will eventually disregard their middle- or working-class status, recognize their true interests, unite, and overthrow a repressive regime.[46] The *Embourgeoisement Hypothesis* implies this type of analysis. Thus, contemporary Marxists remain committed to an evolutionary interpretation of history: A communist revolution and the destruction of capitalism are historically inevitable. This position is as much a leap of faith today as it was in 1848, when the *Communist Manifesto* was published.

Yet even if a Marxist explanation is rejected, the question remains: Why are working-class people in the United States not politically radical? In Western Europe, working-class persons have organized socialist and labor political parties, some of which are quite radical, to represent their interests. This has not happened in the United States. Part of the reason, as shown in Chapter 6, is that working-class persons in the United States do not have the political resources comparable to their counterparts in Western Europe and participate in politics at a much lower rate than do middle-class and rich persons. Furthermore, Americans consistently say they do not want economic equality.[47]

While the reasons for these attitudes are unclear, a few suggestions can be made.[48] The transformative impact of the Protestant Reformation (especially Puritanism) was much greater in the United States than in other nations, mainly because of the absence of a feudal tradition in the new world. Moreover, the existence of the frontier probably served as a sort of safety valve, diluting class conflict and allowing opportunity.[49] Further, as seen in Chapter 3, the very real possibility of upward mobility over the past century has buttressed the dream of success through hard work. The result is a unique emphasis on individual rather than collective action. Finally, the half-century conflict between the former Soviet Union and the United States made the "American Dream," with its emphasis on individual responsibility, into an ideology, relatively impervious to contradictory facts. While the impact of these phenomena cannot be demonstrated empirically, they constitute plausible reasons for the lack of working-class radicalism in the United States.

SUMMARY

This chapter used the *Embourgeoisement Hypothesis* as a pedagogical vehicle for sketching some of the characteristics of the working class in the United States. About 40 percent of the population does blue-collar work, with somewhat higher percentages among minorities (Table 9.1). Coupled with the class identification question in Chapter 2, this figure provides an approximate estimate of the size of the working class in the United States.

The occupational setting in which working-class people labor is often dangerous due to heat and cold, noise, noxious and toxic fumes, risky machines, and other factors. The level of danger is revealed by high rates of work-related injuries and fatalities (Table 9.2). Working-class people also endure very close supervision, petty work rules, and intense production pressures as employers attempt to regulate the rate and rhythm of work.

As shown in Chapter 8, working-class people have lower incomes, on the average, than do middle-class people and less job security (Table 9.3). Most people without jobs do not leave them voluntarily. The human consequences of unemployment include economic deprivation (Table 9.4), lowered self-concept, and increased familial disruption.

The lifestyles of working- and middle-class people are quite different, as illustrated by the characteristics of housing (Table 9.5). Working-class persons own houses at lower rates, own less expensive houses, and spend a higher proportion of their incomes paying for housing than do middle-class people. Furthermore, the houses working-class people live in have fewer amenities, such as extra bedrooms and bathrooms. The chapter concluded by describing some possible reasons why the working class in the United States is not radical.

NOTES

1. Goldthorpe (1969). For the best critique, see van den Berg (1993).
2. Bell (1976).
3. Lenski (1984).
4. Zweig argues that the working class is the majority of the population (2000; 2004).
5. Rubin (1994:41).
6. Rubin (1994:26).
7. Armstrong et al. (1999), Orr (2000), Brown (2003).
8. Here are a few among many possible examples: Reardon (1993), Hertzberg et al. (2002), Liang et al. (2006), Liao et al. (2006), Naidoo et al. (2006), Harris (2006).
9. Again, here are only a few examples: Personick and Harthun (1992), Kitsantas (2000), Johansen et al. (2002), Pegula (2005), Taylor et al. (2002), Meyer and Pegula (2006).
10. Sygnatur (1998), Bell and Helmkamp (2003).
11. United States Bureau of Labor Statistics (2005b).
12. Orr (2000), Brown (2003).
13. Webster (1999), Grimsrud et al. (2002), Sygnatur (1998).
14. United States Bureau of Labor Statistics (2005b).
15. Case and Deaton (2005).
16. Barstow and Bergman (2003; 2003a; 2003b), Nordheimer (1996).
17. Barstow and Bergman (2003a).
18. Barstow and Bergman (2003a).
19. Barstow (2003; 2003a; 2003b).
20. Gordon (1996).
21. United States Bureau of Labor Statistics (2006b).
22. United States Bureau of Labor Statistics (2006b).
23. United States Bureau of Labor Statistics (2006c).
24. Weber (1968 [1920]).
25. General Social Survey (2004).
26. Ehrenreich (1990:137–38).
27. LeMasters (1976:26).
28. Rubin (1994:104).
29. United States Bureau of Labor Statistics (2006d).
30. Institute on Taxation and Economic Policy (2003).
31. Rubin (1994:114).
32. Bakke (1940), Komarovsky (1940).
33. Glyptis (1989), Feather (1990; 1992), Breslin and Mustard (2001), Uchitelle (2006).
34. LeMasters (1976), Rubin (1994).
35. Cottle (1994:78), Murphy and Athanasou (1999), Uchitelle (2006).
36. Rubin (1994), Khan et al. (2002).
37. LeMasters (1976), Rubin (1994), Dooley and Prause (1998), Gallo et al. (2001).
38. Lenton (1990), Elder et al. (1992), Catalano et al. (2002).
39. Gelles (1990), Sander (1992), Rubin (1994), Uchitelle (2006).
40. Liker and Elder (1983), Rubin (1994).
41. Fussell (1983).
42. Rubin (1994).
43. Green and White (1997), DiPasquale and Glaeser (1999), Aaronson (2000).
44. van den Berg (1993).
45. Wright (1997).
46. Gagliani (1981).
47. Hochschild (1981), General Social Survey (2004).
48. Lipset (1977).
49. Turner (1920).

THE POOR

We are two nations. One of them is familiar. It comprises the vast majority of the population—working-class and middle-class people who earn a decent living and enjoy the fruits of their labor. Although their level of affluence varies considerably, previous chapters have shown that they usually possess the resources necessary to deal with personal crises. Thus, when faced with a failed marriage, a pregnant daughter, a needed auto repair, a cavity, or any of the other tribulations and difficulties of modern life, they have a range of effective choices. The other nation is unfamiliar. Yet hand-lettered signs, "Will work for food," announce it. So does being accosted by a panhandler: "Can you spare some change?" So do those who walk the street: the drunk, the mentally ill, possessed by their peculiar demons. Such behavior suggests they have become so poor and so desperate that they are willing to debase themselves in public. This response is inexplicable to most people. But not every member of this unfamiliar nation displays extreme behavior. Many work, often full-time. Many are aged. Many are children. All live poorly in America. Recall the *Class Structure Hypothesis* from Chapter 1: "*The poor have fewer choices and find it harder to solve their personal dilemmas compared to members of other social classes.*" Coping is often the best they can do.

Felicia Dorsey, 33, mother of two children aged four and five, worked as an assistant manager at a convenience store in Waldorf, Maryland, a bedroom community most of whose residents commute to work in Washington, DC.[1] She had lived in an apartment for about four years and walked to work each day. Her supervisor at the convenience store described her as a dependable employee, always on time. She was evicted from the apartment, however, after falling behind on the rent. She had a job to keep and nowhere to live. Her options were few: She was priced out of most apartments. There was no space in the local homeless shelter. Housing vouchers, which would subsidize rent, were unavailable; the waiting list held more than 2,500 people. Ms. Dorsey's solution was to rent a six-by-twelve foot self-storage shed at a cost of $75 per month, which included a 24-hour access card. She and her children lived there for about a week before the manager of the storage facility heard the children talking inside the unit. Ms. Dorsey had locked the children within it while she was at work. The police came, broke the lock, and found the children—who were clean and in good health. Ms. Dorsey was arrested and charged with child endangerment and leaving a child unattended. The children were placed in foster care.

It is easy to view this decision harshly. And the harshness with which the non-poor judge the poor ought to alert you to the fact that they inhabit an unfamiliar nation. In fact, Ms. Dorsey's decision does not appear irrational—given her options. Using a storage shed as a temporary abode is more common than you might think.[2] While the result was not tragic in this case, it could have been. Nationwide, parents report leaving more than three million children under the age of 13 (some as young as Ms. Dorsey's children) unattended on a regular basis each week. The motive is often to go to work.[3] On the one hand, they are clearly endangering their children. On the other hand, they also need to go to work in order to feed their children. The poor frequently find themselves in extreme situations. For them, coping with problems requires a degree of wisdom and heroism that few possess, and even these traits often do not help.

The example also illustrates the dilemma faced by those who would assist the poor.[4] When physicians diagnose an illness, they confront not only a medical problem but poverty. When teachers send work home or want a conference with parents, they confront not only education but poverty. When counselors deal with a drug abuser, they confront not only self-destructive behavior but poverty. It affects every dimension of life, often with a cascading effect. When would-be helpers are unfamiliar with the reality of poverty, they often fail to recognize the extent to which problems are interconnected.

In order to consider such connections, a definition is necessary. Definitions of poverty are of two types: absolute and relative.[5] **Absolute definitions** refer to a standard below which basic needs cannot be met. **Relative definitions** compare a person's or family's economic position to that of the rest of the population, often using the distribution of income as the metric. In the United States, an absolute definition is employed. Thus, **poverty** refers to a minimum income level below which individuals or families find it difficult to subsist. The word subsist should be taken literally. As you will see in a few moments, it is hard for poor people to obtain food, shelter, and medical treatment. Felicia Dorsey and her children provide an example. Other Western nations employ relative definitions. Although the European Union does not have an official poverty line, the indicator for eligibility for minimal social benefits is 60 percent of the median income and that cutoff serves as a de facto threshold.[6] Most scholars doing cross-national research use some proportion of the median income (usually either 50% or 60%) as the indicator of poverty.

DIMENSIONS OF POVERTY

An initial step toward making the poor seem more familiar is to count them. How many people live in poverty? And how poor are they? It turns out, however, that counting the poor requires a series of subjective decisions in order to produce a realistic figure.

Poverty in the United States

Standards of living change over time, which makes assessing the long-term trend in the poverty rate tricky.[7] In 1900, only 1 percent of all families owned an automobile, which meant it had no impact on people's economic circumstances because social life was organized without requiring ownership of high-speed transportation.[8] Today, those without a car find it difficult (sometimes impossible) to get to and from work. Similarly, only 12 percent of the population had running water in their homes in 1900, which meant that most people used outhouses to relieve themselves. Although this practice exposed people to disease and, hence, had negative health consequences, it was free. Today, it is impossible to use an outhouse in any city, where most people now live. The poor must pay—with cash—for water, heat, electricity, and all other items necessary for living.

One way to resolve the problem of changes in the standard of living is to ask a simple question that stems from the definition offered earlier: What proportion of the population has difficulty subsisting? The answer provides an estimate that takes into account the changes mentioned above. These data are presented in Figure 10.1.

The figure shows that about 45 percent of the population was poor during the latter part of the nineteenth century. This percentage, however, is squishy. A review of estimates for this period shows that they range between 40 percent and 60 percent.[9] Hence, selecting a relatively low estimate in this range avoids overstating the level of impoverishment during the late 1800s. The poverty rate began dropping around the turn of the century, primarily because of industrialization and other changes to be discussed. In assessing the long-term trend, ignore the spikes caused by World Wars I and II, and the Depression. Immediately after World War II, the poverty rate probably stood around 30 percent, with a much narrower range of error. By 1960, it had declined to about 22 percent, then to 11 to 12 percent during the 1970s. This is the lowest level ever attained, at least in the United States. The poverty rate rose during the later 1970s and 1980s to about 14 to 15 percent and remained at that level for about two decades. It dropped briefly at the turn of the century but then rose again to its current level, 13 percent. Note that the data for the last 46 years reflect the official poverty line adopted by the government. They comprise the most accurate information available—assuming you agree that the poverty line provides a realistic measure. As will become clear, the key word is "realistic," not "valid" or "objective" or "correct."

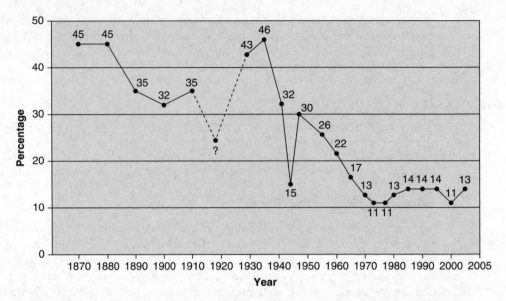

FIGURE 10.1   Poverty Estimates in the United States, Selected Years, 1870–2005

Note: There are no data for World War I (but see Plotnick et al [1998]). The dashed line is designed to suggest that the poverty rate probably fell around 1918.

Sources: 1870–1910 (Hartley, 1969:19), for 1929–44 (Ornati, 1966:158), for 1947–55 (Council of Economic Advisors [1969:154]), 1960–2005 (United States Bureau of the Census [2006d]).

The historical data presented in Figure 10.1 reveal that a long-term decline in poverty occurred in the United States. These data, however, need to be supplemented with information from other nations in order to place the American poverty problem in perspective.

Poverty in Cross-National Perspective

As described earlier, most other nations employ relative definitions of poverty, usually some proportion of the median income. The most frequent one defines as poor all those earning less than 50 percent of the median. Selected results are shown below.[10]

United States	17%
United Kingdom	12
Canada	11
Germany	8
Netherlands	7
Sweden	7

No matter how it is measured, poverty has declined in all Western nations over the last century and a half. Yet these cross-national data show that the American rate remains much higher compared to other nations. Moreover, because these nations provide more in-kind (noncash) benefits for all citizens, regardless of ability to pay, being poor is not nearly as onerous as in the United States. For example, access to medical treatment is regarded as a right of citizenship in all these nations, which means that women, like Felicia Dorsey, can obtain treatment for their children at no cost. In this country, by contrast, most people obtain medical insurance through their employer, with the result that many lack insurance and, hence, access to treatment when they need it. These differences suggest that, unlike the United States, most Western nations apply notions of fairness to society's victims, to those least able to cope with life's crises. These differences also suggest that public policies can be devised which place fewer people in situations like Felicia Dorsey. Modern societies are not helpless in the face of problems. The United States, however, chooses to maintain a rather large impoverished population and to live with the consequences—in this case, higher rates of homelessness, hunger, and other problems.

But is the American poverty line realistic? Do those living below it find it hard to subsist? The answer to a question like this inevitably involves issues of measurement and the limits of the social sciences.

The Measurement of Poverty

The official poverty line for a family of four in 2005 was \$19,971.[11] Because most people still think in terms of the stereotypical family of four, this figure is the most commonly recognized poverty threshold. The cut-off varies, however, by family size, being lower for a two-person family and higher for a six- to seven-person family. The line also varies depending on the age of the head of the household, being slightly lower if the head is over 65 and higher if less than 65. The poverty threshold does not vary by region or rural–urban residence, mainly because the methodological problems are great. As mentioned, taking all these permutations into account, about 13 percent of the United States population lived in poverty in 2005: 34 million people. Of this total, approximately 13 million were children. Thus, about one in seven young persons in the United States lives in poverty. It would be wise to consider the long-term consequences, both for them and the society.

Right now, however, the issue is the logic underlying the poverty line. Developed in the 1960s, the poverty line embodies a series of arbitrary decisions.[12] First, it is based on the cost of a standard market basket of goods, using the U.S. Department of Agriculture's Thrifty Food Plan. Second, a point to remember, it assumes that poor persons spend one-third of their income on food and two-thirds on everything else (rent, utilities, medical treatment, etc.). Third, the threshold is adjusted each year in light of changing prices, using the Consumer Price Index. Finally, the poverty line refers to cash income before taxes from any source, such as a job, alimony, social security, or public aid. Again, all of these decisions are arbitrary and subjective, and this was true at the time the line was adopted.[13]

The most common criticisms of the poverty line are that the food plan does not provide a nutritionally adequate diet over the long run, the ratio between food and nonfood expenses is wrong, the focus on before-tax income fails to account for the (lesser) amount of money really available to families (after sales and other regressive taxes), and it does not include the value of in-kind benefits, such as Medicaid or Food Stamps, which improve the lives of recipients. By dealing with these criticisms, policy makers could define a smaller or larger population as poor.

And there lies the rub. If, for example, the ratio between food and nonfood costs was changed to reflect the actual percentage of income spent on food, then more people would be labeled poor. Alternatively, if in-kind income (such as the value of food stamps) was counted as income, then fewer people would be labeled poor because they would then have higher "incomes." The Census Bureau has experimented with alternative poverty lines, most of which would increase the number of people defined as poor.[14] The point to remember, however, is that either result—raising or lowering the number of impoverished persons—carries political implications.

Because any decision about the poverty line would be a political one, the search for a "more accurate," more "valid," or "more scientific" threshold is fruitless.[15] It is, nonetheless, a perennial siren song for social scientists, often involving logic traps.[16] For example, it is argued that the benefits of various public assistance programs lift people out of poverty. Thus, Food Stamps allow (some) poor people to purchase more food than they could otherwise. Medicaid allows (some) of the poor to obtain medical treatment. Housing subsidies allow (some) of the poor to rent apartments. And cash programs, such as Temporary Assistance for Needy Families (TANF) and the Earned Income Tax Credit provide extra cash for (some) poor families. Impoverished people who receive such benefits are indeed better off as a result. But they remain poor. This assertion is correct substantively, as an analysis of their budget will show. It is also correct logically. Because these programs are means tested, people must become poor in order to be eligible for them and stay poor in order to keep receiving benefits. It is an illusion to think that a family so destitute that it receives TANF or Food Stamps or a housing subsidy or Medicaid is not poor.[17] A scientifically accurate poverty line is a contradiction in terms. Recall for a moment the limits of the social sciences discussed in Chapter 1 (in the section on Max Weber's work). These disciplines can discover the facts, explain them, and describe the implications that follow. The most important question about the poverty line is not whether it is accurate, but whether it is realistic.

Are the Poor Really Poor?

In order to illustrate the difficulties impoverished people face trying to survive, Table 10.1 presents a budget for a hypothetical family of four living at the poverty line.[18] Before proceeding, however, you should understand that any family (or household) used as a point of reference is inevitably arbitrary. For example, the needs of a family composed of two parents and two small children will differ from the needs of a family composed of one parent and two teenagers. Also, families will have different needs depending on where they live. For example, the cost of living in Alaska and Hawaii is significantly higher than in the 48 contiguous states. Similarly, costs vary in rural Florida compared to New York City. So in considering the vignette that follows, make mental adjustments for families with different characteristics and situations. No matter what variations are considered, however, any analysis of family budgets at or near the poverty line will show they have limited lifestyles and life chances compared to other citizens. They are poor.

In order to illustrate this fact, please recall the Smith family. A vignette about them was used in Chapter 5 to show how people in their situation cope, thus affecting the status-attainment process. Since we last saw them, however, Edward Smith has lost his job because the food processing plant in which he worked closed. He now stays home to care for his two children and maintain the household. Jane Smith continues working 40 hours a week, 52 weeks per year in the textile mill. Contrary to common-sense assumptions, there are no two-week paid vacations, paid time-off, or holidays at this economic level. Those who do not show up for work do not get paid. If, for example, they must go to the welfare office to get certified for Food Stamps, or take a child to the doctor, or go to the dentist, they lose time at work—and income. As shown in Table 10.1, Mrs. Smith earns $9.50 per hour or $19,700 annually, before taxes. This places the family just below the poverty threshold of $19,971. While her income may seem relatively high, setting it at the minimum wage would leave the family far below the poverty line.

The income and expenses shown in the table involve several assumptions. It is assumed, for the moment, that Edward Smith earns no money informally and that Jane Smith is employed on the books and must have Social Security taxes taken from her paycheck. But she is smart and has no income tax withheld. Although the Smiths are eligible for the Earned Income Tax Credit, this fact will be dealt with later; for now, the table assumes they do not receive that or any other form of public aid. It is assumed that the Smiths live in Florida (this was established in the vignette in Chapter 5), which relies on regressive taxes to fund state government. Thus, the family must not only pay social security tax but also a variety of sales and other taxes; these total 14.4 percent—higher than a similar family living in other states would pay. Finally, following from the way the poverty line is defined, it is assumed that the Smiths spend one-third of their income for food. On this basis, the table outlines typical monthly expenses for a family living at this income level.

For comparison purposes, the format of Table 10.1 makes it easy to contrast the Smiths' budget with that of the Martinez family described in Chapter 9 (Table 9.4). Such a comparison will suggest how constricted the lifestyle of a poor family is compared to a working-class family. In their new circumstances, the issue for the Smiths is no longer whether they can purchase a computer for the children or send them to camp; the issue is survival. Can they subsist on $19,700? After all, it seems like a lot of money.

The food budget of $430 translates into $3.58 per person per day, assuming a 30-day month. It will be slightly more in February (because it has only 28 days) and the Smiths will fast one day in each month that has 31 days. This last is sarcasm, of course, but with a serious message: The Smiths cannot obtain a nutritionally adequate diet on $3.58 per day. (Actually, you cannot even go to Burger King and get a Whopper meal on that amount.) Moreover, poor persons nearly always pay more for food (and other essentials) because nearby markets are either mom-and-pop operations or franchised small stores. Large supermarkets with low prices rarely serve impoverished areas, especially impoverished areas with a high proportion of African-American residents.[19] This amount is not enough to cover their food costs, so the Smiths cannot remain within their food budget. They are, however, eligible for Food Stamps. The formulas for determining how much they receive are very complex, depending not only on their income but their assets and other factors. Let us assume they would receive $300 per month in coupons, $2.50 per person each day. If they actually obtain the coupons (no easy task for a family like them), they now have the equivalent of $6.08 per person per day for food. (They can afford a Whopper Meal, except that the coupons cannot be used in restaurants. The coupons are like money, but not the same

TABLE 10.1   Income and Expenses for a Hypothetical Poor Family (Two Adults, Two Children)

INCOME

Gross Income from Husband's Job[a]	0
Gross Income from Wife's Job	19,700
Total Gross Income[b]	19,700

Minus Expenses Taken Before Taxes

Employee share of cost of Medical Insurance	−0
Employee share of Retirement Contribution	−0
Total Taxable Income	19,700

Minus Taxes on $19,700

Income tax	−0
Social Security/Medicare tax at 7.65%	−1,400
State & Local Taxes at 14.4%[c]	−2,800
All Taxes = 22.5%, Yielding Net Yearly Income	15,500
Net Monthly Income (15,500 ÷ 12)	1,300

MONTHLY LIVING EXPENSES[d]

Total Food (home & away, plus personal supplies)[e]	430
Housing Payment (usually rent)	500
Utilities (including cell phone)	200
Transportation (car payment, insurance, public trans.)	300
Life Insurance	0
Health Care (deductibles, noninsured spending)	150
Church Contribution	50
Education (for children's expenses)	30
Entertainment	70
Tobacco & Alcohol	70
Saving for children's education	0
Nonallocated	0
Total Nonfood	1,370
Total Monthly Living Expenses (food + total nonfood)	1,800
Monthly Balance (income − living expenses)	−500

[a] Assumes the husband receives no off-the-books income.

[b] Assumes the family receives no public assistance income.

[c] Assumes couple lives in Florida. Includes sales, excise, property, but no income taxes. If they lived in Pennsylvania (as in Table 9.4) the tax rate would be 11.4%. The nationwide average for a couple like this also would be 11.4%. See Institute on Taxation and Economic Policy (2003).

[d] These figures are roughly typical of a family at this income level, see United States Bureau of Labor Statistics (2006d).

[e] Assumes one-third of net income is spent on food.

as money.) But even with this supplement the Smiths still find it hard to eat nutrition-ally. The benefit of Food Stamps does not change their basic situation: The Smiths cannot remain within their food budget, they must use part of their nonfood budget in order to eat.

A sidebar: Assuming the Smiths receive Food Stamps (many poor families do not) their total value would be the equivalent of $3,600 per year. If the coupons are seen as like money, their "income" is now above the poverty line. Does it make sense to argue, either substantively or logically, that this family is no longer poor? Since the program is means tested (requiring low income and few resources as a condition for receiving benefits), is it not more accurate to say that their poverty makes them eligi-ble for aid?

The Smiths' nonfood budget is not adequate to cover their living expenses either, even if none of it is used for food. Table 10.1 shows a very modest nonfood budget of $1,370 per month to cover the cost of rent, utilities, automobile use and maintenance, medical and dental bills, clothing, educational expenses for children, and everything else necessary for living in the United States. Although the table pre-sents living expenses that are more or less typical of low-income families, it is hard for many people to secure housing for the amount shown: $500 per month. Given this budget, the specter of homelessness arises constantly. Utility expenses refer to the price of gas, electricity, and a cell phone. The figure used in the table, $200 per month may not cover their costs in some months because homes, apartments, and trailers in which the poor live are often badly insulated. Finally, transportation costs are about $300. This figure can be less in large cities, assuming a person's house and job are both near public transportation stops. The vast majority must rely on their cars. What hap-pens when the brakes go out?

The Smiths' nonfood budget now has $370 left each month to pay for medical and dental bills, clothing, purchases necessary for a school-age child, entertainment, and everything else. Even purchasing birth control pills is difficult. And if Jane Smith becomes pregnant the family's finances fall apart completely. Again, the poor usually pay more for goods and services because major suppliers have relocated to suburban areas.[20] Although none of the amounts in the nonfood budget are very high and much variation occurs from one location and family to another, no matter how they are manipulated, it is clear that the Smiths probably cannot stay within the nonfood budget for very long. New and unexpected expenses always occur. Yet, as noted above, this family cannot stay within its food budget either. In fact, as shown at the bottom of Table 10.1, the typically modest living expenses incurred by a poor family put it in the hole by $500 each month.

The example used in Table 10.1 has been for a family living just below the poverty line and assumes Mrs. Smith works 40 hours per week, 52 weeks a year—hardly realistic. Even a cursory analysis of the income and expenses of poor families reveals that they face a conundrum: They must often choose between paying for utilities and food, or housing and food, or medical treatment and food. It should not be surprising, then, that hunger and homelessness occur among the poor. Recall that about 13 per-cent of the population lived below it in 2005. The average poor family had a cash income $7,600 below the cutoff.[21] Thus, imagine the problems a household of four would have with an income of $13,400. Yet millions of people do just that. Thus, it seems reasonable to assert that the 34 million persons living below the poverty line, of which 13 million are children, are really poor and that the official threshold provides a realistic indicator of the extent of poverty in the United States today.

Another sidebar: A partial solution to the Smiths' conundrum exists. They filed federal income tax forms and received Earned Income Tax and Child Credits of $3,960. These are tax expenditures, as described in Chapter 8 (see Tables 8.4 and 8.5). Let us say that they used the money to pay two months' back rent of $650 and old medical bills of $800. They also spent $300 on new clothes and shoes for the children and themselves, and $180 on tires for the car. The remaining $2,030 they set aside for emergencies. As the analysis of the income and expenses shown in Table 10.1 reveals, these are perfectly plausible uses of this money. And as that analysis also reveals, the money set aside will not last very long because the Smiths' monthly expenses exceed their income. This family simply does not have enough money to meet its expenses.

Now let us add the value of Food Stamps (treating them as equivalent to cash) and the two tax credits to the Smith's earned income:

Net Income	$19,700
Food Stamps	3,600
EIT/Child Credits	3,960
	$27,260

Based on this amount, it can be argued that the Smiths are no longer poor. After all, their "income" is above the poverty line. But once again: Does this argument make sense, either substantively or logically? Since both public assistance programs are means tested, is it not more accurate to say that their poverty makes them eligible for aid?

As the situation in which the Smiths find themselves illustrates, the millions of families living at the poverty line are not simply short of cash, a problem everyone has sometimes. Such families are desperate. They do not, on their own, have enough money to meet the basic expenses necessary for living in a modern economy. This fact can be summarized by the *Class Structure Hypothesis* presented in Chapter 1: *The lower the social class, the fewer choices people have and the less effective they are in solving personal problems.* People who have few options often must turn to public assistance in order to survive.

PUBLIC ASSISTANCE AND POVERTY

Because people are poor, public assistance alleviates some of the problems inherent to living poorly in America but does not change people's station in life. In fact, it can be argued that public assistance programs provide as many (if not more) benefits to those who are not poor as to those who are poor. In order to see why this paradox is possible, it is necessary to understand how the programs are organized and what actually happens to the money.

The Characteristics of Public Assistance Programs

There are two types of public assistance programs: those providing cash to recipients, such as Temporary Assistance to Needy Families (TANF) and Supplementary

Security Income (SSI), and those providing noncash benefits, such as Food Stamps and Medicaid. These are the four programs reviewed here.

Temporary Assistance to Needy Families.   This program originated with passage of the Personal Responsibility and Work Opportunity Reconciliation Act of 1996. All states were required to replace Aid to Families with Dependent Children (AFDC) with TANF by July 1, 1997. TANF is financed by block grants from the federal government to the states and by state-appropriated funds. States have a great deal of discretion in how they use federal money to implement the goals of the program.

Although the details of the TANF program are devilishly complex, among its most important elements are the following: All "needy" families with children are eligible to receive aid, but each state determines the definition of "needy." A parent (typically a woman) must assist in identifying the other parent (typically a man) and sign over any child and spousal support she gets to the state. There is a five-year lifetime limit on eligibility, regardless of work effort or earned income. Parents must work after two years of receiving aid, but states can choose to require work prior to that time (even immediately). "Work" is defined as having a job, obtaining on-the-job-training, actively looking for a job, being in a vocational training program, attending school, or engaged in community service. Under complicated criteria, states can exempt certain parents from the work requirement. Nonetheless, states must encourage employment by disregarding some earnings in calculating benefits. How this goal is accomplished, however, is left to their discretion. At state option, limits can be set on receipt of Medicaid during the "transition" from public assistance to work. States must subsidize childcare, but have discretion as to the amount and duration. States may allow recipients to establish "individual development accounts" in order to save money (for example, children's college education). Finally, states must set a minimum level of resources a family may possess (mainly checking and savings account balances, but also other economically valuable assets) and benefit levels. This resource limit combined with income constitutes the means test.

As implied by these requirements and its name, the primary goal of Temporary Assistance to Needy Families is to reduce the number of people receiving assistance by encouraging them to work. Indeed, the Department of Health and Human Services claims that this program is a "success because more families are working and entering the economic mainstream."[22] Nationwide, receipt of TANF benefits declined by 73 percent between 1996 and 2005, to about 1.2 million families or 4.2 million persons.[23] This decline suggests that many people are not being encouraged, but pushed off the rolls. Leaving public assistance, however, is not the same as entering the economic mainstream or even getting out of poverty. It is possible, of course, that some unknown number of these people obtained jobs and are no longer poor. Thus, it can be argued that the strength of the economy (as indicated by the relatively low level of unemployment) led to the temporary decline in the poverty rate in 2000 (recall Figure 10.1) before it rebounded to higher levels. But many, if not most, of those no longer on the welfare rolls do not do very well.[24] In Wisconsin, for example, about two-thirds of former recipients had lower incomes after losing public assistance. In Milwaukee (Wisconsin's largest city), 86 percent of those who lost public assistance had incomes below the poverty line. The major barriers to employment are the availability of jobs, the lack of child care, and transportation. As will be shown in a few moments, the structure of the economy means that there are not enough jobs for either current or former public aid recipients.

While receiving TANF benefits, the program regulates people's lives (and lifestyles) in rather detailed ways. As mentioned above, each state has a great deal of latitude in setting requirements. Table 10.2 illustrates how the program might operate for a family of three.

Panel A of Table 10.2 displays some typical program provisions that recipients must satisfy in Pennsylvania. Recall that these will vary considerably by state. In this illustration, the family can have assets worth no more than $1,000. This amount refers mainly to bank accounts and other financial resources. In reality, few recipients have any money at all. The applicant must begin working immediately—in the sense noted above (be employed, in school, looking for a job, etc.). The only exemption would be if the applicant has an infant less than one year old. Although states can exempt some recipients from work, there are funding penalties if they do so too often. In this example, the reward for employment is that the state will allow a family to retain 50 percent of the TANF grant for every dollar earned. This state will not allow recipients to save some money, even for educational purposes. During the first year of employment, the state will provide both Medicaid coverage and a child care subsidy. After that time, however, the family is on its own. This fact is important because in the example, the family is at the end of its first year on the program.

Panel B of Table 10.2 illustrates the benefits from TANF and other programs that a family of three might receive at various income levels in Pennsylvania. As a point of comparison, the poverty line for a three-person family (one adult, two children) was $15,735 in 2005. In Example (1), the family resources of $9,200 are only 58 percent of the poverty line. It is hard to survive on this amount of money. Example (2) shows how employment is encouraged, since the family gets to keep half of its TANF grant as well as the Earned Income Tax credit. Hence, the available benefits (assuming Food Stamps are counted as equivalent to cash) push the family closer to the poverty line. Note, however, that Medicaid benefits and the child care subsidy are expiring. It is not clear how the mother will be able to continue working under these conditions. If a three-person family budget were calculated similar to that in Table 10.1, it would be shown that this family faces precisely the same difficult choices as shown there. In this regard, Example (3) is most interesting. It posits that a recipient worked for nearly a year at the minimum wage and still retains some TANF benefits plus those from other programs. Observers arguing that public aid programs get people out of poverty, point to people in categories like this one. In this case, the family's income and benefits place them about $2,000 above the poverty line. Substantively, of course, the family remains poor, as a budget calculation will show. Logically, since the programs require that the family continues to have almost no assets, it must stay poor to remain eligible. Finally, the unstable job market for those earning the minimum wage combined with their limited resources mean that the odds are low of a family staying above the poverty line, especially as Medicaid and child care subsidies are withdrawn. What will happen to this family if it hits the lifetime limit?

In thinking about the implications of this example, note that the TANF benefits it posits are about average for the nation as a whole. Nationwide, the average for a family

TABLE 10.2   Temporary Assistance to Needy Families (TANF): Illustrative Program Provisions and Public Aid Benefits at Three Earnings Levels for a Family of Three

PANEL A: ILLUSTRATIVE TANF PROGRAM PROVISIONS

Assets Allowed:	$1,000 (excluding a car)
Must Begin Working:	Immediately on receiving TANF
Work Exemption:	If child is less than 12 months old (1 time)
Earnings Disregard:	50%
Medicaid:	Yes, for 12 months
Child Care Subsidy:	Yes, 20% of earnings for 12 months
Individual Development Account:	No
Five-Year Lifetime Limit:	Yes, no benefits to children after limit reached

PANEL B: ILLUSTRATIVE PUBLIC AID BENEFITS AT THREE EARNINGS LEVELS, FAMILY OF THREE

Earnings (+ Benefits, − Taxes)	Example (1)	Example (2)	Example (3)
Earnings	$ 0	$7,000	$11,000
+ Earned Income Tax (EIT)	0	2,800	3,600
+ TANF	4,800	2,700	1,500
+ Food Stamps	4,400	2,700	2,500
− Social Security Taxes	0	500	800
	$9,200	$14,700	$17,800

Notes: Program provisions in Panel A are common among states. Receipt of EIT (shown in Panel B) is not automatic. The EIT in (2) and (3) is not easy to calculate; take these amounts as reasonable guesses. In (1) TANF benefits from the state of Pennsylvania are used and Food Stamp benefits are calculated based on reasonable assumptions. Sales and other regressive taxes are significant but excluded. The TANF benefit in (2) was obtained as shown below. The amount in (3) was obtained in a similar manner.

$7,000 (earnings)	$4,800 (maximum TANF)
− 3,500 (50% earnings disregard)	− 2,100 (net earnings)
− 1,400 (20% child care subsidy)	$2,700 (TANF benefit)
$2,100 (net earnings)	

Source: United States Department of Health & Human Services (2004:chapter 12).

of three is $4,776, just below that used in Example (1). Moreover, there is great variability by state, as shown in Table 10.3. At the lowest are the southern twins, Alabama and Mississippi, with maximum TANF benefits of $1,998 and $2,040 yearly, respectively. At the other end, California and Massachusetts seem positively generous, with maximum benefits of $8,148 and $7,596 yearly, respectively. This "generosity" vanishes, of course, when families must meet their living expenses. These data suggest that the lifestyle (and life chances) of an impoverished family receiving assistance varies a great deal depending on where they live. Whether such variations should be allowed is, of course, a political question. Some might argue that the cost of living is less in Alabama than in California.

TABLE 10.3   Maximum Yearly TANF Benefit Levels in Least Generous and Most Generous States

LEAST GENEROUS		MOST GENEROUS	
State	*Yearly Maximum*	*State*	*Yearly Maximum*
Alabama	$1,998	California	$8,148
Mississippi	2,040	Massachusetts	7,596
Tennessee	2,220	Vermont	7,548
South Carolina	2,448	Wisconsin	7,476
Arkansas	2,448	New Hampshire	7,200
Texas	2,496	New York	6,924
Louisiana	2,880	Rhode Island	6,648
Nationwide Average:	$4,776		

Note: "Most generous" refers only to the continental United States. Both Alaska and Hawaii have significantly higher benefit levels because of the very high cost of living.

Source: United States Department of Health & Human Services (2004:Table 12.2).

Perhaps. But is there an Alabama brand of shoes or pampers or cereal? Do manufacturers give TANF recipients in Alabama a 10 percent discount?

Supplementary Security Income.   Unlike TANF, which is administered by the states and displays considerable variability in benefit levels as a result, Supplementary Security Income (SSI) provides a minimum monthly income for poor aged, blind, and disabled persons that is relatively uniform throughout the nation. There were about 6.8 million recipients in 2005. They received a maximum benefit of $7,236 yearly if they were single, living independently, and had no other income, and $10,848 yearly if they were a couple and living independently.[25] Both individuals and couples who qualify for SSI are automatically eligible for Food Stamps in small amounts that vary by state. (Do SSI recipients living in Alabama get a discount on cereal?) As the title of the program suggests, recipients can have a low income from other sources, such as Social Security or wages, and use SSI benefits to supplement it. In addition, 44 states provide small additional stipends to the basic SSI grant. The result, however, still leaves most recipients below the poverty line. In addition to being poor and aged, blind, or disabled, eligibility requirements for SSI dictate that beneficiaries must satisfy a means test; which is to say that they must become destitute and stay that way. Thus, their assets (again, everything they own) must be less than $2,000 for single persons and $3,000 for couples, excluding a car.[26] Like TANF, then, recipients must become poor and remain so in order to remain eligible for SSI.

Medicaid.   Although the Medicaid program is the nation's primary mechanism for insuring that the poor obtain medical treatment, many Americans go without. The Medicaid program only pays for treatment for about 41 percent of the poor. Among the poor, those covered vary by age, as shown below:[27]

AGE	% OF POOR WITH MEDICAID
0–5	69%
6–10	62
11–18	54
19–44	27
45–64	31
65+	29

Those not covered are left to fend for themselves, which usually means not obtaining treatment or begging for it at an emergency room. Among those covered, states are required to offer the following services: hospital (inpatient and outpatient), laboratory and x-ray, family planning (including supplies), physician and nursing treatment, and what is called "early and periodic screening, diagnosis, and treatment" for children.[28] This last is the only form of preventive treatment paid for by Medicaid. Beyond this minimum, the scope of health problems covered varies sharply from state to state.[29] Although TANF recipients are not automatically eligible for Medicaid coverage, most states provide it, usually for one year. Although impoverished persons who do not receive TANF qualify for the program, many do not receive benefits. For example, in some states, poor children who cannot see clearly may or may not be examined by a doctor and get glasses. Similarly, in some states, poor children who need antibiotics may or may not get them. In some states, poor children who need psychological services because they have been abused or for some other reason, probably will not get them. Whether these limits are wise is a political question.

Food Stamps. Poor persons may not get enough to eat, either. The U.S. Department of Agriculture states that the Food Stamp program is "America's first line of defense against hunger" because "it enables low-income families to buy nutritious food."[30] As with all other public assistance programs, eligibility for Food Stamps requires that recipients satisfy a means test; that is, they must use up all their assets and earn little or no income. Thus, while TANF and SSI recipients are automatically eligible for food stamps, all other persons receiving them can retain resources worth less than $2,000, not counting a car.[31] All adults without dependent children must work (defined, more or less, the same way as in the TANF program). But whether employed or not, benefit levels are very low. For example, as illustrated in Table 10.2, a family of three in Pennsylvania with no income receives only $4,400 in coupons per year, about $4.02 per person per day. If they are treated as a form of cash and combined with TANF benefits the total of $9,200 is only about 58 percent of the poverty line. Nationwide, Food Stamps provide an average benefit of $93.30 per person per month, about $3.11 per day.[32] But a significant proportion of those who are eligible for Food Stamps do not receive them. Although about 25.7 million people received coupons in 2005, about 34 million people were officially impoverished in that year and, presumably, eligible.[33] As will be discussed in a few moments, this fact implies that many people go hungry—at least sometimes—with malnourishment following.

They do so because significant barriers exist to obtaining food stamps in many states.[34] (1) The application forms are often very long. Nationwide, the average length is 12 pages. In two states (Minnesota and West Virginia) they are more than 30 pages long. By comparison, when middle-class people apply for federally guaranteed home mortgages of several hundred thousand dollars, the average length is four pages. When people apply to carry a firearm, the average application is one page long. (2) The applications in many states are complex and employ bureaucratic terminology that is difficult for many people to understand, especially those with low levels of formal education. (3) The applications ask nonessential and threatening questions. (4) The process of obtaining the necessary interviews is complex and filled with pitfalls designed to prevent applicants from obtaining benefits.

In one study, researchers simply wrote to request a food stamp application in California.[35] It is 13 pages long and asks questions like the following: "If you are a noncitizen applying for Medi-Cal and you are not (a) LPR (an alien who is a lawful permanent resident of the U.S.), (b) an amnesty alien with a valid and current I-688, or (c) PRUCOL (an alien permanently residing in the U.S. under color of law), please do not fill in the shaded box for 'Birthplace.'" Near the end of the application, just above the required signature, is the following statement: I understand that "if I do not follow food stamp rules . . . I may be fined up to $250,000 and/or sent to jail/prison for 20 years." A comforting thought for anyone nervous about the process. Once the application is completed, people are scheduled for interviews. In many states, an appointment date and time is mailed to applicants without regard to work or family considerations. In California, a sheet accompanying the application describes "What to Expect When You Come In For Your Intake Interview." It includes the following instructions: "At 7:25 AM report to window 8 to check in." "At 7:30 AM an orientation will begin that reviews your rights and responsibilities." "At 7:31 AM you are late for this appointment and you will be rescheduled for another day." "Please be prepared to spend **several hours (noon or longer)** completing the intake process" (emphasis in original).

Imagine a single parent, working at the minimum wage trying to support and feed two children. This is what she must go through to obtain food stamps. Similar bureaucratic processes exist for those applying for Temporary Assistance for Needy Families, Medicaid, and other programs. The problem of obtaining food stamps provides an example of what the *Class Structure Hypothesis* means: *No matter what the task, the lower the social class, the fewer the choices people have and the less effective they are in solving problems.*

The Paradox of Public Assistance

Once it is recognized that public aid programs provide help while requiring that the poor remain poor, their paradoxical impact becomes clear. On the one hand, they help the poor with income support and in-kind benefits. The result alleviates some of the problems they face. The word "alleviate" is important; it means to relieve pain, to make suffering more bearable. This is what public assistance programs do by reducing the level of deprivation. It is all they do. As a result, however, they function to maintain the economic status quo because people must remain poor in order to stay eligible for benefits. The mechanism for achieving this result is the means test, which stipulates that if recipients obtain additional income or assets above specified levels they become ineligible for public assistance. What happens is that recipients receive aid and it is immediately returned to the taxpayers, either by the beneficiaries themselves when they use TANF and SSI to pay bills or purchase necessities, or by the government when it reimburses providers of noncash benefits.

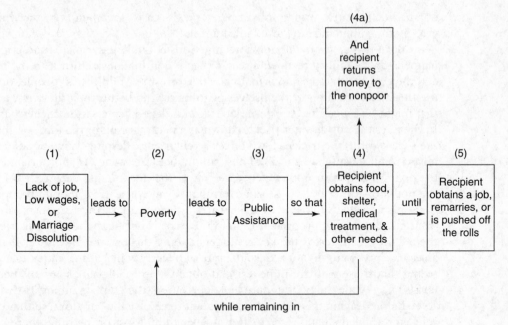

FIGURE 10.2   A Model of the Cycle of Poverty and Public Assistance

As an aside, while there is nothing wrong with using a means test or asking people to remain poor in order to continue receiving benefits, the implication of so doing is that grandiose notions about America's generosity toward the poor are misbegotten. Despite much rhetoric, the programs described in the previous section are not "antipoverty programs." The cycle of poverty and public assistance programs shown in Figure 10.2 suggests this fact.

Box (1) of the figure anticipates the discussion in the next section by showing that the main causes of a family's entry onto the public assistance rolls are lack of a job, low wages, or marital dissolution. As the Smith and Martinez vignettes illustrate, job loss is always a potential problem for working-class people, whose employment responds to economic fluctuations (recall Chapter 9). Thus, when a factory closes down or reduces its workforce, the persons laid off first and for the longest time are those in blue-collar occupations. Further, for many intact families, their receipt of public aid—especially Food Stamps and Medicaid—reflects low wages rather than lack of work. As indicated previously, a family in which the head earns the minimum wage lives well below the poverty line. Millions of jobs pay at or near this level. Finally, for many women with children, marital dissolution because of divorce or separation forces them to turn to public assistance.

Boxes (2) to (4) depict the obvious functions of public assistance. They describe what happens to recipients each month when they receive aid: For reasons noted above, they become (2) poor enough to satisfy the means test, which leads (3) to the use of public assistance, so that (4) they obtain needed benefits. As indicated by the feedback loop, this sequence repeats itself each month while they remain in poverty. In this way, then, public assistance helps the poor to survive by alleviating some of their problems. The sequence does not stop until, as indicated in Box (5), recipients obtain an adequately paying job, remarry (in the case of women), or exceed the five-year lifetime limit and are kicked off the rolls.

Box (4a) depicts the nonobvious functions of public assistance. It describes what happens to the money recipients receive each month: They return it to the nonpoor and the economic status quo is maintained as a result. Middle-class people, of course, use this money to support themselves or to invest and better their lifestyles, a process that might be called the "trickle-up effect" in order to denote its artificial character.[36] In the physical world, water trickles down as a natural result of the force of gravity. In the social world, the trickle-down effect rarely occurs, despite claims by some economists (recall Chapters 6 and 7). Thus, simply because money is appropriated to help the poor, does not mean they get to keep it or that income has been redistributed by the nonpoor to the poor. Just as governments can construct elaborate pumping stations and aqueducts in order to make water flow upward, so they can (far more easily) insure that money appropriated to help the poor is not permanently redistributed to them. The means test is the key to understanding this paradox. It insures that public assistance programs do not reduce the rate of poverty while, at the same time, guaranteeing that those who are impoverished obtain help to alleviate some of their problems. Thus, while the poor endure less deprivation, they remain impoverished.

Before leaving this topic, it is important to resolve the paradox. Neither conspiracies nor accidents happen very often in social life. Most of the time, there are relatively straightforward explanations for social arrangements, if observers care to look. Put simply, the paradox of public assistance results from who has power in this country. As the *Political Power Hypothesis* suggests: *The higher the social class, the greater the influence over the distribution of resources in the society.*

The nonpoor, especially the rich and middle class, who dominate the political process in the United States, control poverty policy. Through their representatives, they enact public assistance programs. This fact means that the organization of these programs reflects the economic interests of the nonpoor. It is why the means test insures that only the very poor receive assistance and that the money is returned immediately to the nonpoor. The significance of the means test can be seen in its selective use. The many income transfer programs going to the middle class and rich are never called public assistance (or welfare), and none include a means test as a condition for aid (recall Chapter 7). Another problem remains. If public assistance requires people to remain poor and a large class of impoverished people persists, who benefits? And what implication follows?

The Benefits of Poverty

The implication is that the nonpoor, including readers of this book, benefit from the misery and deprivation of others. This result is common. Whenever harmful conditions persist over time, it usually means that some segment of the population is benefiting.[37]

First, poverty benefits the nonpoor by making a class of low-skill workers available who can and will perform vital tasks that others do not wish to do. Such jobs come easily to mind: making cloth and clothes, picking crops, cooking and serving food, cleaning buildings and streets, and all the other dirty, menial, dangerous, low-paying, and short-term occupations that must be performed in an industrial society.[38]

Thus, the persistence of a high rate of poverty ensures that many people in the United States have so few options that they must fill positions no one else wants. This situation benefits the nonpoor.

An unexpected implication of this point of view is a recognition of the dual impact of the public schools on the status-attainment process (described in Chapter 5). On the one hand, schools facilitate achievement. On the other hand, they also weed out a sufficient number of individuals who become available for dead-end jobs. Thus, even though education can be a vehicle for upward mobility on the part of some individuals, by systematically failing to educate a certain proportion of students, the schools help to create and perpetuate a class of poor people who make up the cadre of low-skill workers our society needs. The irony here is that this process really is at least partly unintended, for it occurs despite the efforts of dedicated teachers.

Second, poverty benefits the nonpoor by keeping prices down. Because its members have no alternative to working for low wages, the existence of an indigent class subsidizes the consumption activities of the more affluent. Thus, clothes are cheaper, food is less expensive, mortgages are reduced, and taxes are kept low. What this interpretation means is that the lifestyle of the middle class and rich in American society depends on the existence of a low-paid workforce.

The unexpected implication of this point of view is that nonpoor people have an economic stake in preventing the majority of hardworking poor persons—whose jobs include picking produce in the hot sun, making clothes in sweat shops, and picking up garbage in the streets—from obtaining education or job skills and thereby earning higher wages. It is easy to dismiss such people as low-skill workers and, hence, deserving of low wages. But they perform vital tasks, and if they were paid livable wages, the lifestyle of nonpoor people would suffer.

Third, poverty benefits the nonpoor by creating jobs and income for persons who would regulate, serve, or exploit those who are less fortunate. For example, people who cannot obtain work sometimes resort to illegal drugs and street crime to sustain themselves, thereby guaranteeing jobs for police officers, lawyers, judges, probation officers, and everyone else connected with the criminal justice system. By the way, this fact is not an apologia, merely a recognition that such illegal activities benefit the nonpoor population (which is least victimized). In addition, dependence on public aid guarantees jobs for social workers, clerks, and administrators employed in social service departments of government at all levels. This is because people who publicly declare their inability to provide for themselves and thereby receive aid from the state must be regulated by the nonpoor.[39] Less obviously, but just as importantly, the existence of a class of poor persons provides work for grocers, clerks, liquor store dealers, pawnshop owners, doctors, nurses, pharmacists, and many other individuals. Finally, there exist academicians who get huge grants to study the poor, write books about them, obtain tenure, and make money thanks to mass poverty. Thus, the jobs of millions of affluent people are dependent directly or indirectly, on the existence of a high rate of poverty.

An unexpected implication of the fact that poverty creates jobs and income for the nonpoor is the existence of the trickle-up effect associated with public assistance. As indicated earlier, this process occurs in two ways. On the one hand, public assistance programs require hordes of bureaucrats to administer them, social workers to regulate the recipients, physicians to provide medical treatment, pharmacists to supply medicine, computer programmers to keep track of the funds, and so forth. In this way, the government gives public assistance money directly to middle-class people. On the other hand, the trickle-up effect occurs as poor persons spend their "welfare" checks and stamp allotments. This money also ends up in the hands of the nonpoor: grocers, gasoline station operators, utility companies, landlords, and so forth.

Fourth, poverty benefits the nonpoor because destitute persons purchase goods and services more affluent people do not want. Indigents have so few alternatives that they must buy deteriorating or ill-constructed merchandise, patronize second-hand stores, and thereby give new life to old products, and provide a market for stolen goods of all sorts (if they wish any amenities of modern life). In addition, poverty forces people to obtain services from badly trained or malevolent professionals who cannot make a living from middle-class customers. It should be emphasized that this argument is not just a repetition of the assertion above that poverty creates jobs and income; rather, the point here is that the poor are exploited more and have less legal protection than any other segment of the population.

The unexpected implication of a recognition that poor people purchase goods and services others do not want is that perverse consequences result when they try to plan ahead. Thus, by purchasing discount (that is, shoddy) or aging merchandise, indigent people are trying to save money, be frugal, and plan ahead for other expenses; they are, in short, trying to live by dominant values characteristic of the United States. And what they often learn from this attempt is that such efforts do not pay off, since what they buy is so frequently either useless or does not last. While it is easy to indict impoverished people for not being willing to plan ahead, to delay gratification, the experience of many low income persons is that such strategies are fruitless. As a caveat, it should be recognized that some highly qualified persons do choose to serve or work for the poor, our most vulnerable citizens. Thus, the irony is that while impoverished people can be readily exploited, and this benefits the nonpoor, they also constitute an outlet for those with a more altruistic orientation, and this also benefits the nonpoor.

Finally, the poor are made to absorb the costs of economic policies. For example, whenever inflation has been high over the past 50 years the federal government pursued fiscal and monetary policies that produced increasing unemployment. Such policies did reduce inflation, but at terrible cost to those who, through no fault of their own, were thrown out of work. Similarly, whenever reducing the federal budget deficit has become an issue, the programs suffering the greatest cuts were those designed to aid the poor. Put bluntly, this interpretation means that the existence of mass poverty provides a class of people who can be exploited by the rest of the population—at least so long as they do not protest in some way or become unruly.

The unexpected implication of this point of view is the possibility that the political system in the United States is not really open to everyone, especially the poor. As consistent victims, perhaps they are kept from participating, except by disruptive or unruly behavior (recall Chapter 6). For now, however, the next two sections discuss the causes of poverty from two different angles, each of which provides a different kind of information. Thus, one way to understand the causes of poverty is to ask why individuals (like the Smiths) become poor. This line of analysis applies a basic sociological orientation to understanding impoverishment: Individuals act on and react to the situations in which they find themselves. In addition, another way to understand the causes of poverty is to ask how the social structure produces such a large class of impoverished persons. This question applies the notion that the social structure decisively influences rates of events to the study of poverty. Taken together, these angles of vision lower the possibility for self-deception and provide a clear, if cynical, view of American society. They make the unfamiliar familiar.

THE INDIVIDUAL AND POVERTY

Poor persons in the United States are unfamiliar because they live on the margin in a land of plenty. They do not share in its material abundance. Given the exposition here and in previous chapters, the characteristics of those who are poor are just those you might expect.

Age

Children are more likely to be poor than people at any other stage of the life cycle. Thus, about 18 percent of American children are poor, compared to 11 percent between the ages 18 to 64 and 10 percent of those over age 65.[40] One reason so many children are poor is that they are born of children and young adults, persons who have not acquired education or job skills, as illustrated by the vignette about the Smith family and their children in Chapter 5. It is a stereotype but nonetheless true that as people mature into adulthood and obtain job skills, the probability of poverty declines. Thus, even though it is usually unwise for young persons to marry or establish households independently of their parents, they sometimes try to do so—a fact that suggests how restricted their choices are. For example, one factor leading to this decision is pregnancy. Yet the United States makes it relatively difficult for young persons to obtain contraception and, thereby, prevent pregnancy.[41] This difficulty affects the poor most of all. In addition, sometimes girls become sexually active and pregnant as a reaction to an abusive home life or other deprivations.[42] In effect, they respond by confusing sexual intercourse with love, and by conceiving a child as evidence of their humanity, their adulthood. Boys from impoverished backgrounds often react in similar ways. They make someone pregnant under the delusion that this result indicates their manhood.[43] Still another factor leading young persons to establish their own households is the desire to escape an impoverished home life.[44] Hence, young persons make unwise decisions in specific contexts in which their choices are limited and their experiences teach them (often falsely) that they will be better off forming their own families.

Race and Ethnicity

Whites are less likely to be poor than any other racial or ethnic group, as indicated by the data below.[45]

African Americans	25%
Hispanic Americans	22%
Asian Americans	11%
White Americans	8%

You should note, however, that the pattern differs when absolute numbers are shown. Thus, the percentages refer to about 16 million white Americans, 9 million African Americans, 9 million Hispanic Americans, and 1 million Asian Americans. Hence, more Whites are poor than any other group. The reason a higher proportion of minorities endure poverty is discrimination (recall Chapter 2).

Family Characteristics

Divorce, separation, or abandonment often leads to poverty for mothers and children: *Single parent families are more likely to be poor than two-parent families.* Thus, 31 percent of female-headed and 13 percent of male-headed single-parent families are poor, compared to only 6 percent of two-parent families.[46] In considering the importance of a two-parent (hence, two-earner) family, let us return again to the Smiths. Recall from Chapter 5 that before Edward Smith lost his job, the family had a low but steady income, around $43,000 per year. They managed the stresses inherent to their economic situation. Since losing his job, however, Edward has battled feelings of meaningless and a sense of helplessness because he cannot provide for his family. Fights between Jane and Edward have increased. This is partly because Edward feels so bad and partly because money has become so tight. It will take courage for this family to remain together. Millions of couples find themselves in situations like this. Some break apart. And when this happens women usually get custody of the children.[47] As a result, more than half of all poor families are headed by women.[48]

Low-Wage Job Skills

The fewer the job skills people possess, the greater the likelihood of poverty. Thus, people with higher education—such as those who write well, speak a foreign language, learn the law, and fill prescriptions—have job skills. They rarely become impoverished. People without higher education—such as those who type, serve food, operate cash registers, and repair cars—also have job skills. But they are more prone to poverty. In modern societies, skills are traded for wages. One of the most important indicators of skill is education. Listed below are poverty rates among individuals aged 25 years and older by educational attainment.[49]

Less than High School Diploma	22%
High School Diploma	12%
College Diploma	4%

Work Experience

People who work less are more likely to be poor. Thus, among the poor population aged 25 to 54 (the prime earning years), 54 percent were not employed during the previous year. Some observers take this fact as indicating laziness. Another point of view, however, is that some people get beaten down by poverty. (This argument will be considered in a few moments.) For now, think about these data in the context of those presented above. Work experience often leaves people impoverished because their wages are so low.

Put simply: A lot of employed people are poor. As mentioned in constructing the family budget, Jane Smith, for example, earns $9.50 per hour, a wage that places her family just below the poverty line even though she works full-time all year long. Of course, the Smiths constitute a hypothetical example. But they represent millions of people. Among the poor population aged 25 to 54 years, 29 percent work part of the year and 17 percent work full-time all year long.[50]

Poverty is thus a transformative event. In Chapter 1, **socialization** was defined as the lifelong process by which individuals learn norms and values, internalize motivations and needs, develop intellectual and social skills, and enact roles as they participate in society. Children whose parents go through the experiences described here learn quickly that life is neither predictable nor controllable. Such events can be defining episodes in people's lives. Not all of them suffer hunger and malnutrition, but many do. Not all of them endure homelessness, but some do. Not all of them withdraw into drug abuse or join gangs and express their rage, but a few do. All of them, however, even those whose families remain stable, go through hardship and deprivation.

Now the usual, common sense approach to understanding poverty is to blame individual deficiencies: If only they would work harder, it is said, they could escape impoverishment. And there is truth to this adage, albeit partial truth. Some economists adopt the common sense approach by seeing poverty as resulting from lack of **human capital.** As described in Chapter 3, the term refers to job skills or education, which can be converted into skills that produce income. From this angle, people who are poor because they do not earn enough should simply augment their human capital so as to make their services more valuable and increase their income. At the very least, they should look for a job. And it is true, as common sense would have it, that individuals without a high school degree can often find a job if they look hard enough. A few vacancies exist even in central cities, despite declining employment opportunities in these areas. Yet, if successful, this strategy will only solve an individual's problem. It will not reduce the high rate of poverty. The reason is simple: There are not enough jobs. Thus, if a large proportion of those out of work sought all the jobs available, they would overwhelm the vacancies at the lower skill levels.[51] This fact means that advocating self-help strategies to eliminate poverty—whether as common sense or dressed up on academic jargon—is not very practical. Such proposals affirm dominant values without increasing understanding. The latter occurs when structural questions are asked.

SOCIAL STRUCTURE AND POVERTY

A fundamental transformation has occurred in modern societies. For the first time in human history, poverty has declined—not only in the United States but in every Western society (Figure 10.1). At the same time, however, data also reveal that the American poverty rate is higher than in comparable nations. This fact suggests that our country chooses to maintain a larger population of impoverished persons. This section deals with these two issues. First, why did a long-term fall in the rate of poverty occur? Second, why is the American level so much higher than in other societies? The answers illustrate the anomic character of modern societies.

The Long-Term Fall in the Poverty Rate

Common sense, American style, dictates that people avoid poverty by working hard. Regardless of social class, people learn from an early age that hard work will produce success. This is a restatement, of course, of the American Dream. Failure consists in giving up. From this point of view, it is easy for those who achieve some success to attribute it to their work ethic. After all, they sacrificed while training, found a job, and labored for years to achieve some modicum of economic success. Their lives confirm the American Dream. By extrapolation, then, the conventional explanation assumes that in "a social context where plenty of opportunity exists," those who have worked hard have been successful and those who are poor must not have worked very hard.

Students, of course, develop a similar work ethic. They learn that a correlation exists between hard work and success in the form of grades and college matriculation. Thus, those whose good grades enable them to attend Outstanding Private University assume that anyone can get in if they work hard. Similarly, those whose good grades enable them to attend the state-supported Flagship University assume that anyone can get in if they work hard. Finally, those attending Community College assume that anyone can go if they work hard. Thus, in both everyday life and higher education, people believe that hard work explains their success.

It does. People who succeed occupationally and economically have worked hard. But, even so, this explanation is too facile. This is partly because it ignores the impact of family background on the status-attainment process. As shown in Chapters 5 and 7, where you start from makes a huge difference in your eventual level of success. In addition, the explanation is too facile because it assumes "a social context where plenty of opportunity exists." The phrase was placed in quotes to alert you that this context has not always existed. It is, in fact, rather recent.

Throughout most of history, human beings lived at the mercy of nature. Productivity was low, based on muscle power. Nearly everyone scratched the soil for subsistence. The few amenities (goods that make life pleasant) were monopolized by an elite group. Life was short. Mobility was limited and most people's position in society was based primarily on ascription. Nearly everyone was poor. During the past century or two, however, this situation changed radically (recall Figure 1.1). This change leads to a structural question: What factors produced a new historical context, one in which opportunity increased and hard work could pay off for many people? The hypothesis presented here is this: *The long-term fall in the poverty rate reflects (1) industrialization, (2) the emergence of science, (3) the rise of capitalism, (4) the appearance of democracy and democratic ideology, (5) the emphasis on the rule of law, and (6) the development of the culture of capitalism.* These phenomena each appeared over the last few centuries and display, as Max Weber pointed out, an elective affinity for one another. Modern societies have been transformed. As mentioned in Chapter 1, they are like Prometheus unbound, released from the chains of the past. Productivity is now high, based on nonliving sources of energy. Amenities are spread throughout the population. Life is long. Mobility rates are relatively high and few people are poor.

Industrialization.   As you may recall, **industrialization** refers to the transformation of the economy as new forms of energy were substituted for muscle power, leading to huge advances in productivity. Although this process is harsh in its early years, bringing with it dislocation and misery, in a relatively short time industrialized nations became wealthy and healthy compared to the past. In the process, and in order to take advantage of new technology, the occupational structure changed in fundamental ways: leading first to the rise of blue-collar jobs (and a working class) and later to the dominance of white-collar jobs (and a middle class). For example, as shown in Table 5.4 (in Chapter 5), the white-collar workforce rose from 18 percent to 61 percent between 1900 and 2005. In contrast, the farm workforce fell from 38 percent to 1 percent. The new job slots at the top of the class structure were, in effect, a vacuum that had to be filled. Over time, people who worked hard were "pulled" upward, out of poverty. This is because an industrial society requires millions of people to fill the newly created and highly skilled white-collar occupations. Most people work today in jobs that simply did not exist two centuries ago. These positions must be filled based on merit and achievement, not ascription, which implies both political freedom (democracy) and individual competition. Poverty rates fell as the majority of the population rose above subsistence levels, actually well above subsistence levels. But industrialization could not have occurred in historical isolation from other changes that also affected the poverty rate.

Emergence of Science. **Science** refers to the systematic use of observation and reason to understand and explain natural and social life. Scientific knowledge provides the mechanism for rapid technological change that drives industrialization. Without a methodical, empirically based approach to problems of productivity, industrialization would have been impossible. In addition, a scientific ethos underlies capitalism and permeates everyday life in modern societies. This spirit reflects a long-term historical process that Max Weber called **rationalization:** All aspects of social life become methodically organized based on the use of reason and observation. Thus, in the traditional societies of the past, custom, often religiously sanctified, regulated social interaction. In this context, opportunity was limited as positions were filled the way they always had been, which is to say, by ascription. The rise of science as a way of understanding stimulates a change to what Weber called "instrumentally rational action": Means and ends are increasingly related to each other based on empirical knowledge. In this context—when science combines with technological advance and fuels industrialization—achievement became increasingly important, opportunity expanded, and the poverty rate fell.

Rise of Capitalism. In a context where productivity is high, some mechanism must be available for distributing the newly available goods and services. In a mass market economy, capitalism provides the most efficient distributive mechanism. In capitalist societies, goods and services are produced in an open market for the purpose of making a profit. Supply and demand determines the price of goods, services, and labor. The means of production are privately owned. As the great economist Adam Smith first recognized in *Wealth of Nations* (first published in 1776, the same year as the Declaration of Independence), capitalist societies are economically dynamic because individuals act in their own self-interest to provide goods and services that others want at a price they are willing to pay.[52] One result of this competitive process is that, in a context where, based on scientific advance, industrialization is occurring and productivity is expanding, more opportunity became available. Poverty rates fell.

Democracy and Democratic Ideology.   As mentioned in earlier chapters, power and authority in democratic societies are based on the "will of the people" as citizens elect their representatives and hold them accountable for their policy decisions. In such contexts, personal freedom and the innate dignity of every individual become fundamental values. These orientations fit with capitalism, which also requires that people compete in pursuit of their self-interest.[53] As was described in Chapter 2, democracy has become one of the standards by which societies are judged. In this context, democratic ideology was used to reduce discrimination against minority groups and women. The logic, of course, is that everyone ought to be free to compete for success. Although the democratic process is imperfect, as emphasized in Chapter 6, governments act to protect the common good. In conjunction with the other factors discussed here, the poverty rate fell in all democratic nations.

Rule of Law.   Democratic societies emphasize the use of written laws adopted via established procedures that outline the nature and extent of authority, especially government authority. Moreover, those who make and enforce laws are also bound to obey them. The rule of law results not only in a long-term decline in interpersonal violence as a mechanism for solving disputes, it also increases predictability in human interaction. These characteristics not only allow capitalism to flourish in an industrialized context, they also make democratic decision making possible.[54] The poverty rate fell.

Culture of Capitalism.   Finally, while a great deal of variation exists, all modern societies display some sort of **culture of capitalism**, a set of values that emphasize occupational achievement, individualism, universalism (being evaluated based on merit), rationality (dealing with issues methodically), activism (taking direct action to obtain a goal), and making money.[55] Such sentiments lead to a work ethic that everyone learns. People are taught at home and at school that hard work is a practical and moral imperative, the foundation of the American Dream. But individuals do not learn this peculiar orientation by chance. According to Max Weber, it emerged as an unintended consequence of the Protestant Reformation. The culture of capitalism and the work ethic it stimulates fits with the other variables described here, leading to a decline in the poverty rate in all modern societies.

Now it remains true that most individuals only succeed by hard work combined with ability and a little luck. The structural variables outlined here are important, however, because they provided a historical context in which these attributes could pay off. A little counterfactual thought experiment suggests their impact. Three centuries ago, the vast majority of people worked on farms using muscle power to produce goods. Nearly all were poor. Many were malnourished. If the occupational structure had not changed, based on the development of science and combined with the rise of capitalism, democracy, the rule of law, and the culture of capitalism, then these people and their descendants (most of you) would be impoverished hardworking farmers today. In the real world, however, people's options did change. Although no one was forced to be upwardly mobile, both the jobs and the people to fill them existed. These facts had nothing to do with each individual's motives or abilities. In Emile Durkheim's phrase, they reflected a change "in the nature of society itself."[56] The result has been a decline in the proportion of poor people in all industrial nations, more so in Western Europe than the United States.

The American Poverty Rate Today

The falling poverty rate, however, carries with it an inherent irony: Not everyone can succeed. The jargon term for this state of affairs is **anomie,** a disconnection between value placed on success and the ability to achieve it in legitimate ways.[57] Although every modern capitalist society is anomic, it can be argued that the United States is especially so. One indicator is that this country maintains a higher rate of poverty than do other Western nations. This difference can be accounted for in structural terms.[58] *The rate of poverty in the United States reflects (1) the reproduction of the class structure, (2) the vicious circle of poverty, (3) macroeconomic policy, (4) the structure of elections, (5) the structure of the economy, and (6) institutionalized discrimination.*

The Reproduction of the Class Structure.   In the United States, as in all societies, the class structure is stable over time. The game of Monopoly can be used as a metaphor to illustrate how the class structure is reproduced and some of the implications of this process.[59] In the game as it is actually played, each participant starts with an equal amount of money, $1,500. By combining luck (symbolized by the roll of the dice) and hard work (symbolized by purchase and auction decisions), competitors seek economic success. The point to remember about the game is that everyone begins with the same chance of winning. After all, a game is only fair under such conditions and no one wants to participate in a contest in which some of the players have an unfair advantage at the beginning.

Although many people believe that life is like a game of Monopoly and that their occupational achievement represents their reward for hard work, this attitude is self-deceptive; the real world is rather different in that some people are born with more advantages than others and the result of their hard work varies accordingly. This is, of course, another way of describing an anomic society. A fictional version of Monopoly follows, one that is more analogous to the real world. Begin by imagining that four groups of people are participating and that they compete both as individuals against all other individuals and, in certain situations, as members of their respective groups. They are like the social classes described in earlier chapters.

Group One is very small; in fact, its members are statistically insignificant. They are almost never included in sample surveys. But they are relatively advantaged at the start of the game, for they own some property and possess lots of Monopoly money, say, $5,000 each. In addition, the members of this group take care of the bank and, because of their enormous responsibility, get two rolls of the dice each turn. They view this benefit as justified because they see themselves as living according to dominant cultural values. They believe they embody the American Dream. Thus, while these people are statistically insignificant, they are of great substantive importance.

Group Two is very large but its members have considerably fewer advantages with which to begin the game. They have no property and about $2,000 each. Nonetheless, they believe in the cultural values characteristic of all capitalist societies and think that everyone else playing the game can be like Bill Gates and move into Group One if they work hard enough.

Group Three is also very large but its members are even more disadvantaged at the beginning of the game. They have no property and only about $1,000 each.

Nonetheless, they also believe in hard work, individualism, and all the other elements of the American Dream.

Group Four is smaller but still significant in size. Its members, however, are the most disadvantaged of all. They not only own no property and have very little money, about $500 each; they also do not know all the rules of the game. Perhaps as a result, they often (more or less randomly) lose a turn and frequently pay more than list price for properties and fines. Even so, they also aspire to the American Dream.

One final point about this game: No one can stop competing; no one can quit striving for success. Any players who run out of money or go to jail are required to beg for more cash, pay their penalties, and continue playing—indefinitely.

In this context, then, the competition begins. Now Monopoly is a game played by individuals and it would be easy to measure the process by which each participant acquired income and property, and thereby found a place in the game. This would be the Monopoly equivalent of status attainment, of course. While such an analysis would be useful in order to understand precisely how individuals in the various groups behave, it would be misleading to extrapolate an explanation of the game as a whole based only on the analysis of the experiences of individuals. This is because the players were divided into groups with unequal advantages when the game began. An interpretation that does not recognize this fact, which does not ascertain the game's structure of stratification, has to be misleading.

If, however, one takes a structural view, it becomes possible to sketch the results of the game in a plausible way. The members of Group One, the rich, will generally remain well off unless they are very unlucky or unwise (in fact, downright stupid). This is because they began competing with many built-in advantages and share some of them; for example, they pool their "get out of jail free" cards. Furthermore, given their responsibility for taking care of the bank, a few of them illegally "borrow" money occasionally while other players are not looking. When caught, of course, they are (sometimes) forced to pay back what they stole.

Similarly, the members of Group Two, the middle class, will usually maintain their positions. Although upward mobility into Group One and downward mobility into Group Three will occasionally occur, most movement will be within Group Two itself and of relatively short distance. These people generally ignore the fact that few of them actually move into Group One and take satisfaction in being better off than less advantaged persons. They attribute this fact to their hard work and ability rather than the advantages with which they began. They live in nice neighborhoods (the Monopoly equivalent of, say, Marvin Gardens) and think they have obtained the American Dream.

The members of Groups Three and Four, the working class and poor, are obviously in the most precarious positions. While some upward mobility into Group Two does take place, most movement will be short distance, usually within or between the lower-level groups. Security is always uncertain for these participants in the game, mainly because the resources available to them are so minimal that it is difficult, on their own, to make much headway. Nonetheless, nearly everyone in these two groups works hard and learns to live with their precarious position in the game.

Some members of Groups Three and Four, however, become **alienated**; that is, their personal experiences lead them to believe they are powerless to influence their own lives. Alienated people find that the American Dream is hopelessly remote, even meaningless. Adhering to these values does not (indeed, cannot, lead to success). They recognize, albeit in an inchoate way, that the social structure in modern societies is **anomic;** that is, regardless of the values they have internalized, their ability to succeed is very limited. As a result, some readjust their goals and only play by going through the motions. Others, however, get high and just sit at the game board passively while their tokens are moved for them. Still others (surprisingly few) pull out guns and use them to alter their economic situation. But given spatial arrangements separating the various groups, their victims are usually other members of Groups Three and Four. When caught, these people are sent to jail for long periods.

With apologies to the many dedicated scholars working in the field, this fictional vignette reflects the major findings in the study of social mobility as reviewed in Chapter 5: While a great deal of mobility occurs, most of it short distance, the class structure is reproduced over time because occupational inheritance predominates. The emphasis here is on the poor: No matter how hard they work, most individuals who begin their lives at or near the bottom of the class structure remain there.

The Vicious Circle of Poverty. Sometimes impoverishment that would ordinarily be temporary combines with other difficulties, like a vicious circle. These multiple difficulties snare a significant number of people into long-term poverty.

One way people become trapped occurs when their efforts at escaping poverty are thwarted and they become so discouraged they give up. Consider the Smiths, and remember they represent lots of families. As you may recall, they live in Cedar Key, Florida. Although it has been a rural backwater for many years, it has always been a pleasant place to live. The climate is pleasant and little crime occurs (okay, a few locals run drugs up and down the coast . . .). But very few legitimate jobs exist and many residents are poor. In the last few years, however, a significant number of artists have moved there and it has become something of a tourist haven. Thus, Edward Smith decided to try to take advantage of a context where opportunity exists. He set up a kiosk next to the town dock and began selling locally made "art" (junk, but the tourists don't know that). The result was transformative. He started shaving every day and stopped drinking. He now brought income into the family, which desperately needed it. Alas, after protests to the police by the Chamber of Commerce, Edward was forced to stop because a city ordinance limits the number of street venders. So Edward tried another strategy to earn money: He cleaned up his car and started using it to take people staying in condominiums to the dock area at $3.00 per person. But after protests by the local Cab Company, he was again forced to stop because, as before, a city ordinance limits the number of cabs that can operate. Nonetheless, like other Americans, Edward believes in the American Dream that hard work leads to success.

These imaginative illustrations are not exaggerated. Edward Smith was participating in the **informal economy.**[60] The term refers to that portion of the overall economy existing in every society in which employers and individual entrepreneurs engage in legal but unregulated activities to produce goods and services. It is cash-based and does not comply with standard business practices, tax law, record keeping, or other kinds of regulations. When people work "under the table" or on their own, without either the regulations or protections of government, they are participating in the informal economy. Although informal economic activities tend to be small scale, low-income operations, they often provide a vital means of support for families on limited budgets (as implied by Table 10:1).

In many cities and towns, lots of opportunities exist—cab drivers, jitney van operators, cosmetologists, and street vendors, to name a few—that do not require much capital or education. They require, instead, entrepreneurship. But such individual initiative is often thwarted. For example, limits are placed on the number of jobs in any one sector of the economy. In New York City, for example, a few years ago, licenses allowed exactly 12,187 taxis, 4,000 food vendors, and 1,700 merchandise peddlers to operate legally.[61] Every city and town grants a few licenses to individuals or companies, allowing them to engage in activities like these. In addition, extensive training is required that has little relevance to public safety.[62] In order to protect the public safety, doctors, dentists, and lawyers must be licensed; that is, they must have a minimum level of education and pass competency examinations. But what about hairstylists or barbers, audio and video equipment operators, librarians, beekeepers, or auto body repairers? These are just a few of the hundreds of jobs for which one must have a license. In New York, for example, one needs 900 hours of training to become a licensed cosmetologist, compared to 116 hours to become an emergency medical technician and 47 hours to become a security guard (with a gun).[63]

In every city in the United States, thousands of bootstrap entrepreneurs work illegally in the informal economy. They function on the economic margin, unable to expand their businesses, always subject to being shut down. Even so, they believe in the American Dream: One is supposed to keep trying, work hard, and eventually succeed. Most people, in fact, keep on trying, whether in the formal or informal economy, even after being repeatedly thwarted. Some, remarkably few, give up.

Another way people become trapped in poverty occurs when people must choose between a job and Medicaid coverage. Let us suppose that one of Edward Smith's friends works at a company where a janitorial position opens up and he gets the job (most jobs are obtained by word of mouth). He now earns $5.50 per hour, or $11,440 per year. (This assumes he works 40 hours per week for 52 weeks, including Christmas, and is never sick.) Alas, a major problem follows: The children have become ineligible for Medicaid because Edward and Mary Smith's combined income of $29,640 is so high(!). The Smiths must choose between work and health insurance for their children. This is a *Catch-22* phenomenon.[64] In the novel of that title by Joseph Heller, if Captain Youssarian was crazy he could get out of the war. But since he saw that the war itself was crazy, he was clearly sane. Hence, he could not get discharged. In the real world, people like Edward Smith sometimes choose not to accept formal employment. Are people like him lazy? Yet the long-term impact can snare such persons into poverty.

Assume for a moment that Edward turns down the job in order to maintain Medicaid coverage for the children. Their problems are not over. Young Samuel develops an earache. The nearest Medicaid provider is 90 miles away in Gainesville. Out-of-pocket expenses for gas and lunch while at the emergency room of the teaching hospital there will be at least $30. So the Smiths decide to wait and see if their son recovers. And he seems to. Although this is a reasonable strategy, since some medical problems improve over time without treatment, it has unfortunate results. Sam had *otitis medea*, a common childhood ailment, easily diagnosed and treated. Left untreated, however, it results in hearing loss, even deafness. Thus, this little child has a long-term disability, one that increases the odds of him doing poorly in school and ending up trapped in poverty himself as an adult. This is the social context in which the Smiths and millions of real people must act.

The Smith vignettes suggest how factors associated with poverty can sometimes form a vicious circle trapping people. Remember: Laws regulating small businesses, determining eligibility for welfare, and making health insurance dependent on formal employment (instead of being universally available) reflect policy choices made by middle-class and rich people. So do macroeconomic decisions.

Macroeconomic Policy.   **Macroeconomic policy** refers to the way government regulates the economy, especially inflation and unemployment. Ideally, there would be minimal amounts of both. In practice, however, a trade-off usually occurs such that one is higher than the other.[65] Although the government can regulate the economy in many ways, the most well-known mechanism is interest rates as set by the Federal Reserve Board. In principle, when the Fed (as it is known) increases interest rates, it raises the cost of borrowing money for both businesses and consumers. This leads to deferred spending, slower economic growth, and lower inflation; it also leads to greater unemployment and poverty. In contrast, again in principle, when the Fed decreases interest rates, the reverse effects occur: greater spending, economic growth, and higher inflation, which in turn lower unemployment and poverty. The qualifier "in principle" should alert you to the fact that applying macroeconomic tenets to real world problems remains a very imprecise process.

Even so, every few months the Federal Reserve Board meets and tries to do just that. In considering the impact of changing interest rates, you should understand that all economic problems are political problems. There is no politically painless way to decide whether to emphasize low inflation or unemployment. No matter what choice is made, someone's interests must be harmed while others benefit. In general, unemployment hurts the poor more than inflation. For example, a 1 percent increase in the unemployment rate increases the poverty rate by an almost identical .97 percent (note the decimal point). In comparison, a 1 percent increase in inflation increases the poverty rate by only .12 percent.[66] Thus, unless the situation is atypical, when macroeconomic policy decisions are made, the poor benefit by keeping unemployment low.

Since World War II, however, American policy has focused primarily on keeping inflation in check.[67] It has sought (not always successfully) lower levels of inflation, 2 to 3 percent, in exchange for higher levels of unemployment, 5 to 6 percent. This emphasis has practical consequences: It influences the level of poverty. Put crudely, when macroeconomic policy is effective (which is not always the case), the United States seeks a higher rate of unemployment and poverty.

The American emphasis on keeping inflation down reflects the political priorities of middle-class and rich persons. They generally do not worry about unemployment and do not suffer its consequences. Rather, they see the value of their salaries and return on investments fall due to inflation, even if it is only moderate. Therefore, their representatives act to prevent it.

The Structure of Elections. The phrase "their representatives" is deliberately provocative. It is meant to suggest that public officials usually make choices reflecting the interests of the most powerful segments of a society. The fact that public policy in the United States creates more poverty than in other nations indicates the political dominance of middle-class and rich people. Quite simply, they participate in the political process (either by voting or contributing money) at a much higher rate than the working class and poor.

This fact means, as shown in Chapter 6, that the poor are relatively incapable of protecting their interests. Recall, for example, that holding elections on working days (rather than weekends or holidays) limits the ability of working-class and poor persons to vote. Those who overcome this handicap most easily have jobs that are less physically tiring, enjoy personal leave time as a job perquisite, have child care available, own a car, and live in safe neighborhoods. In addition, registration requirements limit the ability of the poor to vote. Those who overcome this handicap most easily are middle class and rich, who are more aware of and able to deal with election laws. Finally, of course, people also participate by contributing money to campaigns. Rich persons always have an advantage here, and they gain access to decision makers as a result. It is not accidental that laws often favor their interests. As one example, macroeconomic and public aid policies reflect the interests of the nonpoor. In this context, the structure of the economy must also be recognized.

The Structure of the Economy. Hard work often does not prevent poverty, mainly because of the structure of the economy. The pay attached to many jobs is low, as indicated earlier by the fact that 17 percent of the poor population aged 25 to 54 work full-time all year long. Such persons, like Jane Smith, are motivated, responsible, and have jobs. What they do not have is an income high enough to live on.

But those with employment are lucky. They earn something. Recall that the nation's main public assistance program, Temporary Aid to Needy Families, posits that families will move from welfare to work. But where are the jobs? Whenever this crucial question is asked, it is like the sound system goes out. Projections of the availability of low-skill jobs indicate that former public aid recipients alone (that is, not counting impoverished persons who are not on the rolls) will outnumber the new jobs by about two to one.[68] And the problem is worst in those states with the highest public aid caseloads. This phenomenon is not new. Adults earning the minimum wage tend to get trapped in those jobs.[69] Disregarding this fact, the TANF program is organized (by the nonpoor) on the assumption that public aid is temporary, that the poor will find work on their own.

The phrase "low-skill jobs" in the above paragraph refers to occupations in such industries as cleaning and building service, food preparation, and textiles and apparel—jobs that require little formal education and limited on-the-job training. These jobs are not likely to carry high wages. It has been estimated that the odds of one of these low-skill jobs paying a poverty-level wage for a family of three are about 22 to one.[70] The odds of such a job paying a wage at 150 percent of the poverty line are about 64 to one. And the odds of such a job paying a "livable wage" (arbitrarily set at about $25,000 for a family of four) are about 97 to one. "These numbers probably represent the most realistic estimate of the odds that a typical target of welfare reform will escape poverty through employment," and these results are consistent with other studies.[71]

The structural problem, however, is not only the availability of any jobs at all, but the location of those jobs that do exist. A mismatch exists between the location of jobs and people.[72] In the past, cities were centers for the manufacture and distribution of goods, which meant that people (immigrants, for example) without much formal education could find work. Since about 1970, however, cities have lost hundreds of thousands of manufacturing jobs. Many are now located in suburban areas. Getting to them requires a long and expensive commute. In New York City, for example, more than 18,000 household workers endure daily commutes of 90 minutes or more for jobs that pay less than $25,000 per year.[73] This job mismatch has especially affected minority groups, who are less able to live in suburban areas because of housing discrimination. Observers can only speculate about why these jobs have moved. One reason is probably cheaper land and easier access to transportation (interstate highways and airports). Another possibility is corporate aversion to African-American workers.[74] Regardless of the reason, the result is massive unemployment in central cities, concentrated among minority people.

Thus, the structure of the economy insures that millions of people will be poor no matter how hard they work, no matter what their skills, no matter how much they try. This fact exists independently of their individual efforts. Institutionalized discrimination exacerbates this problem.

Institutionalized Discrimination.   It was mentioned earlier that members of minority groups suffered from overt and legal forms of institutionalized discrimination in the past. As a result, they were unfairly confined to low-wage, blue-collar jobs. Thus, one cause of a high rate of poverty among minorities today is their historical class of origin, not current discrimination.

Yet, as discussed in Chapter 2, discrimination still exists, only now it is covert and illegal. In its institutionalized form, discrimination is sometimes not intended. For example, African Americans, Hispanics, Asians, Native Americans, and Whites usually participate in different social networks. Thus, Whites work at different jobs, their children go to different schools, they live in different neighborhoods, and they attend different churches. In effect, these forms of segregation identify the boundaries of the social networks in which members of each group participate. Such boundaries indicate how the class structure affects interaction patterns, housing choice, educational attainment, occupational attainment, and virtually every other aspect of life. The fact of segregation, of participating in different social networks, often produces discrimination, even when no individual intends to do so. One result is a higher rate of poverty among minority groups.

It was also noted earlier that traditional gender norms meant, until recently, that women were systematically denied the opportunity to work outside the home, prevented from competing with men when they did, and kept economically, politically, and psychologically dependent on men. Although this situation has improved considerably in recent years, Chapter 3 shows that many people still govern their lives by such rules. Moreover, they teach their children, male and female, that such norms still provide guides for living. One result is that women are less successful occupationally, economically, and politically.

We are two nations: one poor, one not poor. It is often the case that, when presented with ethnographic accounts of poverty or the details of poor people's lives in some other way, nonpoor persons react with sympathy and understanding. When discussing "the poor," however, without specifics, these same persons revert to stereotypes about "deservedness." The structural analysis presented here should alert you to the fact that poor individuals acting in their own self-interest cannot reduce the level of poverty. No amount of moralizing about the importance of self-reliance and individual initiative will change that blunt fact.

CONCLUDING COMMENTS

Some individuals believe that suffering brings purification, that through suffering one achieves nobility. Perhaps. It seems more likely, however, that suffering mutilates people. It twists the spirit, sometimes breaking it. As stress piles on stress, some people lose hope. In sociological jargon, they become **alienated.** That is, they believe they have little control over their lives. For people living in poverty, this perception is often very realistic. It is easy for the nonpoor to convince themselves that they would behave differently, heroically, if placed in the situations in which the poor find themselves. Reality is usually far different. The poor have fewer and less effective choices than do members of other social classes. In order to illustrate this fact, this chapter concludes with a brief look at hunger and homelessness.

Although the United States does not display starvation like that occurring in some third world nations, many Americans go hungry for significant periods of time and suffer malnutrition as a result. The term **hunger** refers to the chronic under-consumption of nutrients. The most reasonable estimate is that 28 million people live in "food insecure" households in this country.[75] This figure makes sense in light of the family budget described earlier. For some, hunger occurs at the end of the month when food stamps run out and the cupboards are empty. For others, unable to obtain coupons, it is a pervasive, every day affair. The presence of food distribution centers in every city suggests that the nutritional needs of many people go unmet. According to one study, such centers feed about 25 million people each year.[76] Of those fed, about one-third are employed adults, about 40 percent are children. These data suggest that hunger is widespread among the poor, that the Food Stamp program does not solve the problem.

The long-term consequences of hunger are catastrophic, especially for children. They display slow growth and mental deficiencies as a result of malnutrition. A six year old can look (and act) three years old. Many children, hence, become stupid because they have not had enough food to eat during the first years of life. They do not recover. Ever. Lack of nourishment makes people more susceptible to disease and less capable of recovering. This is important because many common illnesses have a long-term impact. For example, if strep throat, a typical childhood disease, is not treated with antibiotics it leads to heart and kidney damage. The result is a sickly adult who cannot be a productive person. A nutritious diet can help prevent strep.

Yet obtaining a nutritious diet requires difficult choices.[77] About 42 percent of clients at food distribution centers report they must choose between paying for food and paying for utilities. About 35 percent must choose between food and rent. And about 32 percent must choose between food and medicine or medical treatment. Forcing people to make these sorts of choices does not bring nobility. It does, however, provide a practical example of alienation. Moreover, the long-term impact redounds (overflows) to affect the entire society.

So does **homelessness.** The term refers to the lack of access to a conventional dwelling: a house, apartment, mobile home, or rented room. Those without housing sleep in places not intended for these activities: cars, scrap-metal shacks, and public areas (such as bus stations or fire grates outside buildings). Some also sleep in shelters. Although counting the homeless is difficult, a reasonable estimate is that at least 3.5 million people, of whom 1.4 million are children, experience homelessness each year.[78]

In surveys, it appears that most of those who are homeless are men, with many reporting they are veterans. A significant minority report problems with drug addiction, mental illness, or both. The fastest growing segment of the homeless population, however, comprises families with children.[79] One night in January, a reporter went looking for homeless people near the White House. Within a few minutes he found "an African-American woman, eight months pregnant, sleeping on the lawn of the Justice Department" and "five veterans, sleeping on a heat grate for warmth." If he had gone to a nearby shelter, he would have found people like twenty-six-year-old Martha Harris and her two children.[80] After an abusive childhood, she fled a husband who beat her regularly. Her five-month-old daughter, Sara, is listless and underweight. She cannot hold down food or grasp a rattle. Her fifteen-month-old son, Matthew, does not speak, has trouble sleeping, and often refuses to eat. These examples are designed to remind you that real people underlie quantitative data, people whose range of choices is so restricted that they cannot even obtain a place to live.

The impact of homelessness is most obvious in families with children. For example, homeless women and their children are less able to obtain preventive medical services.[81] So the odds of bearing low birth weight babies, with all the human tragedy and costs they entail, become much higher. Children in shelters or on the streets are more likely to be abused or neglected. They display chronic medical and psychological problems. They do not attend school or do so irregularly. The McKinney-Vento Act, by the way, requires school districts to provide extra educational help for homeless children. The logic, of course, is that such assistance can avoid long-term problems, misery, and societal costs. It is my impression, however, that most districts really wish homeless children would just go away.[82] And they do.

They live in grief and on grates. Such experiences do not produce nobility of soul. Without a home, they lack stability and nurturance. They lack friends, family, faith group, schools, and regular medical treatment. The consequences are catastrophic and, like hunger, redound to affect the entire society.

The high rate of poverty in the United States means that central cities, especially the largest ones, have the aesthetic flavor of some third world nations: Teams of homeless people wander around. Large areas are disorganized and dangerous. Drug abusers appear everywhere. People live amidst the rubble of empty buildings. An air of hopelessness pervades the streets. And this situation affects not only the unfortunate souls inhabiting these areas but everyone who is not poor as well. Yet it is not inevitable. As the cross-national data show clearly, the level of poverty in this country could be far lower. If so, its negative consequences would be less severe. One has to wonder why it is allowed to continue.

If we wish to reduce the rate of poverty and endure fewer of its results the direction public policy should take is clear: The United States needs to redistribute money, benefits, training, and—above all—jobs. By benefits, here, the reference is to programs that prevent poverty over the long-term. Access to birth control, for example, will allow poor women to prevent unwanted pregnancy. Access to medical treatment will prevent illness from becoming chronic, especially if the emphasis is on prevention. Access to housing will help prevent trauma to children and family break-up. There are other types of programs that should be considered, but these suggest the direction this country should take if it wishes to cut the poverty rate. But such programs imply an expansion of what is sometimes called the "welfare state."

When confronted with this possibility, however, we Americans tend to throw up our hands in despair. There exists a pervasive fear that government creates problems, it does not solve them. But this is self-deceptive. Middle-class and rich people do not hesitate to use government. They seek tax breaks, contracts, and services. They protest mightily, and often effectively, when these benefits are taken away. Only when the issue is sharing benefits with the poor do questions about the deservedness of the recipients arise. Only when the issue is protecting all our children does the public resist.

Americans persist in believing that we can take income support from the poor and they will be able to get jobs and support themselves. That we can take training programs from the poor and they will somehow train themselves. That we can take child care from the poor and they will be able to go to work. That we can prevent the poor from accessing medical treatment and they will be healthy. That we can prevent the poor from accessing drug treatment programs and they will get off drugs. That we can limit access to birth control and abortion, and they will have fewer children. That we can reduce the amount of affordable rental housing and they will still find places to live. That schools can be underfunded yet kids will learn. Is this wise? Should we divide ourselves into two nations?

SUMMARY

The poor remain unfamiliar to nonpoor persons. Poverty refers to a minimum income level below which individuals or families find it difficult to subsist.

Although living standards have changed considerably over time, it appears that at least 45 percent of the population was poor during the last part of the nineteenth century. Ignoring declines during World Wars I and II, and a huge increase during the Depression, a long-term fall in the poverty rate occurred (Figure 10.1). It dropped to a low of about 11 percent in the 1970s, jumped to 14 to 15 percent during the 1980s and 1990s, and declined slightly in 2000 before rising again. The level of poverty in the United States is significantly higher than in other Western societies. The measurement of poverty is an arbitrary process. The question is not whether a "scientifically accurate" measure exists, but whether the line is realistic or not. Preparing a budget for a family near the cut-off shows that those living below it are desperate (Table 10.1). They have difficulty obtaining food, shelter, medical treatment, and other necessities.

Public assistance programs alleviate some of the problems poor people face, but do not eliminate poverty. This is because the means test requires that people become poor and remain poor in order to stay eligible (Figure 10.2). TANF provides very low cash benefits (Table 10.2) that vary greatly by state (Table 10.3) to people who must not have any assets. SSI provides low cash benefits to poor aged, blind, and disabled people, who must also be devoid of all assets. Food Stamps provides coupons for small amounts of food purchases, coupled with a means test. And Medicaid provides medical treatment for the poor, also coupled with a means test. Public assistance programs reflect the political priorities of the nonpoor population. It can be shown that the nonpoor benefit from a high rate of poverty: An impoverished population constitutes a class of low-skill workers who perform jobs others avoid. They subsidize consumption by the more affluent. They create jobs for nonpoor persons who regulate, serve, and exploit the less fortunate. They are exploited and have less legal protection than other segments of society. And they absorb the costs of change. These are practical examples of alienation, an inability to control one's own life.

Young persons display a greater likelihood of poverty. Whites are less likely to be poor than members of other racial and ethnic groups. Female-headed families are especially likely to be poor. Individuals with low-wage job skills are more likely to be poor, even if they are employed.

The long-term fall in the poverty rate reflects the impact of industrialization, the emergence of science, the rise of capitalism, the appearance of democracy and democratic ideology, the emphasis on the rule of law, and the development of the culture of capitalism. The poverty rate today reflects the impact of the reproduction of the class structure, the vicious circle of poverty, macroeconomic policy, the structure of elections, the structure of the economy, and institutionalized discrimination. The reproduction of the class structure occurs because of the tendency for occupational inheritance. Poverty can be seen as a vicious circle that traps people, as indicated by the problems of obtaining work while on public aid and seeking medical treatment. Macroeconomic policy in the United States generally trades higher unemployment (hence, poverty) for lower inflation. The poor participate less in elections because they are held on working days and require advanced registration. The economy does not provide enough high wage jobs, located in areas where the poor live. Finally, institutionalized discrimination continues to prevent women and minorities from achieving.

A major implication of poverty is that it twists the spirit; people become alienated. This response reflects people's experience with hunger, homelessness, and violence. Yet modern societies like the United States determine how much poverty exists.

NOTES

1. Snyder (2004), Kinzie and Partlow (2004), Stockwell (2004).
2. Kinzie and Partlow (2004).
3. Child Trends (2003).
4. Shipler (2005).
5. Iceland (2006).
6. Eurostat (2000), Atkinson et al. (2002), Smeeding (2005). Iceland reviews this issue (2006).
7. Fisher (1997), Iceland (2006).
8. United States Bureau of the Census (1975:717).
9. Patterson (2000). Plotnick et al. estimated poverty rates back to 1914 (1998). They show a pattern similar to that in Figure 10.1, but the

percentages are higher: 70% prior to World War I, more than 30% after World War II. As they suggest, the former seems unreasonably high. What you should learn is that such estimates are tricky and involve a large amount of guessing and a large error term. For a recent review, see Iceland (2006).
10. Smeeding (2005).
11. United States Bureau of the Census (2006d).
12. Orshansky (1965), Citro and Michael (1995), Fisher (1998), Garner et al. (1998), Bernstein (2001), Smeeding (2005), Iceland (2006).
13. Orshansky (1965).

14. United States Bureau of the Census (2002c: 13–19). See also Citro and Michael (1995).
15. Beeghley (1984).
16. Citro and Michael (1995), Bernstein (2001).
17. Beeghley (1984).
18. Ehrenreich (2001), Barnes (2005), and Wong (2006; 2006a; 2006b; 2006c) all show how difficult it is for the poor to subsist.
19. Barnes (2005). See also Fellowes (2006).
20. Barnes (2005).
21. United States Bureau of the Census (2006d).
22. United States Department of Health & Human Services (2006).
23. United States Bureau of the Census (2006:372), United States Office of Family Assistance (2006).
24. Children's Defense Fund (1998; 1998a).
25. Social Security Administration (2006a:7).
26. Social Security Administration (2006a:7).
27. Committee on Ways and Means (2004:15–19).
28. Committee on Ways and Means (2004:15–20).
29. Committee on Ways and Means (2004:15–22).
30. United States Department of Agriculture (2006).
31. Committee on Ways and Means (2004:15–19).
32. United States Department of Agriculture (2006a).
33. United States Department of Agriculture (2006a).
34. America's Second Harvest (2003).
35. America's Second Harvest (2003:2–3).
36. Beeghley (1983).
37. See the classic article by Herbert Gans, "The Positive Functions of Poverty" (1972). See also Galbraith (1992).
38. Ehrenreich (2001), Barnes (2005), Wong (2006; 2006a; 2006b; 2006c).
39. Piven and Cloward (1971).
40. United States Bureau of the Census (2006d:52).
41. Luker (1996).
42. Dash (1989).
43. Marsiglio (1993).
44. Rubin (1994).
45. United States Bureau of the Census (2006d:46).
46. United States Bureau of the Census (2006c: table pov02).
47. Beeghley (1996).
48. United States Bureau of the Census (2006c: table pov02).
49. United States Bureau of the Census (2006c: table pov29).
50. United States Bureau of the Census (2006:474).
51. Kasarda (1995).
52. Smith (1976 [1776]). On the revolutionary impact of capitalism, see Berger (1986), Easterbrook (2003).
53. Berger (1986) argues that capitalism and democracy are linked in that economic development leads to pressure for personal freedom and vice versa.
54. See Beeghley (2003) on Max Weber and the significance of the rule of law.
55. Weber (1958 [1905]). See also Turner, Beeghley, and Powers (2006).
56. Durkheim (1982 [1895]:128).
57. Merton (1968a).
58. Beeghley (1983; 1989).
59. The name of the game, Monopoly, is the trademark of Parker Brothers for its Real Estate Trading Game (Beverly, MA: Parker Brothers Division of General Mills Fun Group, Inc., 1935, 1946, 1961). An earlier version of this vignette appeared in my *Living Poorly in America* (Beeghley, 1983).
60. Portes et al. (1989). Edgcomb and Thetford (2004).
61. Mellor (1996).
62. Kleiner (2006). For a state-by-state list of occupations covered by licensing requirements, see http://www.acinet.org/acinet/licensedoccupations.
63. Mellor (1996).
64. Heller (1961).
65. Heilbroner and Thurow (1982).
66. Blank and Blinder (1986:187).
67. Hibbs (1977).
68. Weisbrot (1998).
69. Boushey (2005).
70. Weisbrot (1998). See also Boushey (2005).
71. Weisbrot (1998:8). See also Danziger and Lehman (1997), Meyer and Cancian (1996), Burtless (1998).
72. Kasarda (1990; 1995; 2000), Glaeser et al. (2004).
73. Berger (2004).
74. Williams (1987), Aguirre and Turner (2004).
75. United States Department of Agriculture (2005:6).
76. America's Second Harvest (2006), United States Conference of Mayors (2006). For a case study, see DiFazio (2006).
77. America's Second Harvest (2006).
78. National Coalition for the Homeless (2006).
79. National Coalition for the Homeless (2006a).
80. DeParle (1993), Bassuk (1991).
81. Bassuk (1991), Lewis et al. (2003).
82. National Coalition for the Homeless (2006b).

CHAPTER ELEVEN

THE UNITED STATES IN GLOBAL CONTEXT

POVERTY AND INEQUALITY IN THE
UNITED STATES AND DEVELOPING
NATIONS

EXPLANATIONS OF POVERTY AND
INEQUALITY AROUND THE WORLD

INEQUALITY IN THE UNITED STATES
AND WESTERN NATIONS

All societies display stratification. But the arrangement of classes, of course, and the overall level of inequality within and between them can vary a great deal. As a result, life chances vary as well. In order to think about these issues in a global context, consider the following hypothetical societies:

In the first, everyone makes a living by fishing. People's incomes in this society will not be equal, of course, since some individuals are willing to work harder than others and some have more ability than others. Hence, over time a set of classes will develop and valued resources will be distributed unequally. In the process, however, the main criterion by which people are evaluated is achievement: how much fish they catch. Although people's life chances will vary by social class, it is likely that the level of inequality between the rich and poor will be low. In this context, most people will see the structure of stratification as fair. A nation like this one is likely to be democratic (in some form) and stable. There will probably be little need for the use of force (especially military force) to control the population.

In the second, everyone makes a living by gold prospecting. As above, people's incomes will not be equal, since a few will have discovered or simply seized mother lodes and become wealthy. Some may have found small deposits of ore and do reasonably well. Most, however, will not locate much and will end up with little to show for their efforts even though they work hard. As above, a set of classes will develop over time. In this case, however, distribution of valued resources will be very unequal and so will people's life chances. Of course, some of this inequality will reflect ability (since some individuals may have greater skill at spotting signs of gold) and some will be willing to spend more hours prospecting than others. For the most part, however, the stratification structure will reflect luck combined with rapaciousness. Over time, this result means that the main criterion by which people are evaluated will be ascription, nonperformance-related characteristics. This is because no matter how much ability they have or how hard they work, most prospectors will end up poor. In this context,

287

many people will see the structure of stratification as unfair. A nation like this one is likely to be undemocratic and, hence, it will sometimes be necessary to rely on force to control the population.[1]

These are, of course, hypothetical societies. They can be seen as ideal types, to use a phrase of Max Weber's, benchmarks against which our own and other real nations can be compared. Previous chapters have shown that inequality in the United States has increased over the past few years. The distribution of valued resources and the life chances that follow are more unequal than ever before. Thus, one can argue that the United States now resembles the gold-prospecting society more than the fishing society. And to the extent true, this result should be cause for concern because, as mentioned in Chapter 6, people's dissatisfaction may erupt in violence or some other form of unruliness. But just how unequal is the United States compared to other nations? Does the United States really resemble the gold-prospecting society? As it turns out, the answer to this question depends on the angle of vision from which it is asked.

In order to place the structure of stratification in the United States in a global context, the focus will be on income inequality (although other points of comparison will be made as well), mainly because worldwide observations are available. In certain respects, however, such observations are difficult to assess.[2] (1) Although the data presented in this chapter are the most recent available, they are gathered in different years. This fact means they reflect different economic and social conditions—both within each nation and between them. (2) The definition of income varies. For example, it may be before or after taxes. The latter is a measure of disposable income (and, hence, probably better). In addition, "income" may include transfer payments. As should be clear from Chapter 8 (the middle class) and 10 (the poor), transfers can significantly alter people's lifestyles. (3) The reporting unit varies. It can refer to individuals, families, or households. If households constitute the unit of analysis, which is most common, then it is usually assumed that income sharing occurs. But this is not always so. (4) The purchasing power of money varies. And (5), translating local currencies into dollar values is a very imperfect business. These difficulties mean that complete comparability is not possible, even with countries like Canada and the United States or the United Kingdom and the United States. Nonetheless, as suggested in previous chapters, comparability is a matter of degree and it is possible to reach an acceptable and meaningful level. Scholars do what they can, knowing the pitfalls.

POVERTY AND INEQUALITY IN THE UNITED STATES AND DEVELOPING NATIONS

Historically, industrialization in Western Europe and the United States lead to increasing global inequality. Toward the end of the twentieth century, however, industrialization began spreading around the world and inequality between nations around the globe began declining.[3] Cross-national poverty rates provide an illustration. The World Bank defines **extreme poverty** as living on less than $1 per day and **moderate poverty** as living on less than $2 per day.[4] These thresholds are arbitrary, of course. As one observer points out, all "poverty lines are as much political as scientific constructions."[5] Even so, these lines have rhetorical appeal because they are easy to understand

and obviously qualify as impoverished living standards when compared to those enjoyed in the United States and other economically developed nations.

Table 11.1 illustrates how the world's poorest people fared during the last years of the twentieth century. Using the extreme standard, Panel A of the table shows that the number of impoverished individuals declined from about 1.5 billion to about 1.1 billion in just twenty years. Panel B shows that extreme poverty within the developing world fell almost in half, from 40 percent of the population in those regions to 21 percent.

TABLE 11.1 Poverty Rates by Region, 1981 and 2001, Using Two Standards

PANEL A: NUMBER IN POVERTY (IN MILLIONS)

REGION	LESS THAN $1 PER DAY		LESS THAN $2 PER DAY	
	1981	*2001*	*1981*	*2001*
East Asia (China)	796 (634)	271 (212)	1,170 (876)	864 (594)
East. Europe & Cent. Asia	3	17	20	93
S. America & Caribbean	36	50	99	128
Mid. East & N. Africa	9	7	52	70
South Asia (India)	475 (382)	431 (359)	821 (630)	1,064 (826)
Sub-Saharan Africa	164	313	288	516
Total	1,482	1,089	2,450	2,735

PANEL B: PERCENT IN POVERTY WITHIN EACH REGION AND AS A PERCENT OF WORLD POPULATION

	LESS THAN $1 PER DAY		LESS THAN $2 PER DAY	
	1981	*2001*	*1981*	*2001*
Percent within each Region				
East Asia	58%	15%	85%	47%
China	64	17	88	47
Rest of East Asia	42	34	76	49
East. Europe & Central Asia	1	4	5	20
S. America & Caribbean	10	10	27	25
Mid. East & N. Africa	5	2	29	23
South Asia	52	31	89	77
India	54	35	90	80
Rest of South Asia	42	21	87	69
Sub-Saharan Africa	41	46	73	77
Average in these Regions only	40	21	67	53
Average excluding China	32	22	59	55
Percent of World Population	33	18	54	45

Source: Chen and Ravillion (2004)

Finally, the proportion of the world's population living in extreme poverty dropped from 33 percent to 18 percent. Although these falling rates of extreme poverty are significant, much of the world's population remains poor—often desperately poor. In fact, both the number and proportion of persons living on $1 per day rose in sub-Saharan Africa and stayed stable in South America and the Caribbean. By comparison, the proportion of people living in extreme poverty in the United States and Western Europe is zero, which is why these regions are not included in the table.

Using the moderate standard, Table 11.1 reveals a more ambiguous pattern. Panel A shows that the overall number of persons living on $2 per day rose between 1981 and 2001, from 2.5 billion to about 2.7 billion. Thus, as has been true throughout history, much of the world's population remains desperately poor. But within the developing world, as seen in Panel B, the proportion of the population living in moderate poverty fell from 67 percent to 53 percent. And the world's population living in moderate poverty declined from 54 percent to 45 percent. As above, the proportion of people living in moderate poverty in the United States and Western Europe is zero.

Regardless of which threshold is used, Table 11.1 also suggests that the declining rate of poverty has not occurred evenly around the world. Much of the improvement in living standards—and thus the overall decline in between-nation inequality—took place in China, the rest of East Asia, and India. Other parts of the world continue to fare much less well. In order to illustrate this variability and to make more systematic comparisons to the United States, the remainder of this section looks at six nations from around the world: China, India, Brazil, Mexico, Kenya, and Mozambique. They are chosen arbitrarily, but not accidentally. China, India, and to a lesser extent, Brazil, represent what are called "semiperipheral societies." That is, they display relatively diversified economies that appear to be in the process of industrialization—see them as more or less in a middle stage of economic development. Mexico, Kenya, and Mozambique represent what are called "peripheral societies." That is, they display a much lower level of economic development—see them as on the edge. The reason for these labels will become clear in a few moments.

The rate of extreme poverty varies significantly among these five nations, as shown below.[6]

% LIVING ON LESS THAN $1 PER DAY
Mexico (1996)	5%
Brazil (2003)	8
China (2001)	17
Kenya (1997)	23
India (2000)	35
Mozambique (1997)	38

The nation with the dubious honor of having the highest percentage of its population living on less than $1 per day is Zambia, at 76 percent. As you can see, while much variability exists, all these nations are much poorer than the United States.

But what does it mean to live on $1 per day, $365 per year? Can people really do this? The answer is yes, for three reasons. First, many staple foods around the world are much cheaper than in the United States. For example, sorghum is a mainstay of the diet in much of Africa, Central America, and South Asia. It is relatively easy to produce because it is drought-resistant and heat-tolerant. It is fed to cattle in the

United States. Similarly, millet is a traditionally important grain used in much of Africa and India. In India, it is often combined with sorghum to make flat bread. It is used as bird feed in the United States. Rice, of course, is a staple food in impoverished Asia, where it is much less expensive to produce and consume. Second, estimates of calorie intake suggest that the average poor person around the world eats significantly less than the average poor person in this country. And third, the economy is simpler in many less developed nations because production consists of unprocessed farm goods that are either directly consumed or sold or bartered in open-air markets.[7]

This simpler economy also suggests how poor many nations are compared to the United States. For example, the Gross Domestic Product (GDP) per capita describes the value of all the goods produced in a society, as divided by the total population.[8] It is $10,000 in Mexico, $8,200 in Brazil, $6,600 in China, $3,500 in India, and $1,200 in Kenya. The nation with the lowest GDP per capita in the world is Tanzania: $720. Zambia's is $950. By comparison, the American rate is $42,000. All of these nations are extremely poor compared to the United States.

This high rate of poverty in developing nations translates into restricted life chances for their citizens. The infant mortality rate provides one indicator of just how restricted people's lives are because it reflects their overall living standards. You should recall that the infant mortality rate is defined as the number of live babies who die in the first year of life. The rate is 122 per 1,000 in Mozambique, 52 in Kenya, 49 in India, 25 in Brazil, 19 in China, and 18 in Mexico.[9] The nations with the highest number of children dying are concentrated in Africa: Tanzania's is 101 and Zambia's is 102 per 1,000. These rates are similar to those seen in the United States during the nineteenth century. The current American rate is 6, and this is high by Western standards.

Their high level of poverty and restricted life chances imply that many developing nations exhibit a very unequal income distribution. In fact, while inequality between nations has declined somewhat in recent years (as mentioned above), inequality within nations around the world has increased.[10]

Let us begin with the "semiperipheral" nations, China, Brazil, and India. One overall way of assessing income inequality is to look at the Gini Coefficient. As you may recall from Chapter 8, the Gini Coefficient is a standard index in which zero would mean complete equality (every household has the same income) and 1.00 would mean complete inequality (one household has all the income). In the United States, for example, the distribution of household income produces a Gini Coefficient of .46, which (as shown in Chapter 8) is substantially higher than in the past. In comparison, the Gini for Brazil is .59, indicating greater inequality in the distribution of income, while it is .33 in India and .45 in China, indicating less inequality. The main reason for these differences occurs at the extremes of the income distribution. Displayed below are the shares of income going to the poorest and richest 20 percent of the population in these three nations and the United States:[11]

	INCOME SHARE TO THE	
	POOREST 20%	RICHEST 20%
Brazil (2001)	2%	63%
United States (2000)	5	46
China (2001)	5	50
India (1997)	9	43

Thus, Brazil has a more unequal income distribution than the United States, mainly because the richest fifth of the population takes 63 percent of all the income. In comparison, India is less unequal than the United States, at least in terms of income distribution. The poorest fifth of Indian households receives about 9 percent of the nation's income, compared to 5 percent in the United States. A similar difference exists at the other end of the distribution: The richest fifth of all households receives 43 percent of the income in India, compared to 46 percent in the United States. But this relatively equal income distribution in India does not obviate the fact that it remains a very poor nation: As pointed out earlier, 35 percent of its population lives in extreme poverty and 80 percent in moderate poverty (see Table 11.1). Moreover, its infant mortality rate is 49 per 1,000.

The "peripheral" nations also vary a great deal in terms of income distribution. Mexico, for example, displays a Gini Coefficient of .55, while Mozambique's is .40 and Kenya's is .43. The most unequal nation in the world, by the way, is Namibia. In that sad country, the Gini Coefficient is .71 with the poorest 20 percent of the population receiving only 1 percent of the income.[12]

Although these data may understate the degree of income inequality in some nations, such as India and Brazil, they imply that the United States resembles the fishing society more than the gold-prospecting society. This conclusion, however, depends on the question asked. It is useful to ask a different question, one that goes beyond simply comparing poverty and inequality in developing nations and the United States: Why is there so much poverty and inequality around the world?

EXPLANATIONS OF POVERTY AND INEQUALITY AROUND THE WORLD

One way of answering this question requires a change in the unit of analysis such that the focus becomes the worldwide circumstances in which poverty and inequality occur. In sociological terms, the unit of analysis must change from the nation-state to a world system. This orientation is useful because developing nations today must confront the already developed nations, like the United States, which have interests to protect. Thus, it can be argued that economic and distributive processes that appear to be internal to them—to Brazil or Mozambique, let us say—are actually affected by their location in the world system. When this change in the unit of analysis takes place, then the United States and other Western nations are viewed in a different way.

In the world system, nations can be seen as like classes, competing for scarce resources.[13] Envision, if you will, a three-tiered global stratification structure.

The "core societies" are analogous to the rich: comprising the industrialized countries such as the United States, Sweden, Germany, France, and most of the other Western European nations. They control most of the world's wealth, military force, technology, and financial services. Their economies are diversified, with a focus on manufacturing and—increasingly—service industries. They do not export unfinished raw materials. These nations tend to be democratic, stable, and powerful.

The "semiperipheral" societies are analogous to the middle class. Such nations are industrializing, or trying to. But achieving this goal is difficult because they are so dependent on the core societies. For example, developing nations often provide skilled labor to companies based in core nations, as when computer programmers and engineers from India work for American-based corporations. Or, to take another example, developing nations are exploited due to their low labor costs: American-based companies manufacture products or parts of products destined to be exported back to the United States and to other Western nations, such as when an automobile plant is located in Brazil. Although some of these societies are democratic, like Brazil and India, they remain unstable. They have little military power compared to the United States and other Western nations.

The "peripheral" societies are analogous to the poor. Like the poor, these nations are relatively "unskilled" in the sense that their economies are simple (and sometimes so disorganized that they are unable to take advantage of their resources). Hence, they depend on the "core" nations for financial aid, technology, and for markets for their raw materials (for example, coffee from Brazil). Economic development is difficult in this context because decisions are made in terms of the interests of corporations based in core nations and their governments' foreign policy. Moreover, elites in peripheral societies (sometimes called compradors) are dependent for their wealth on these same foreign corporations and, hence, function as their agents against the nation's interests. Such nations are usually not democratic; they rely on military force (whose soldiers are often trained by core nations) to control their populations.

According to Immanuel Wallerstein in his now classic book, *The Modern World System*, the reason there is so much poverty and inequality in developing nations is because Western industrial nations like the United States exploit them.[14] The "semiperipheral" and "peripheral" societies provide the cheap labor and raw materials that enrich the rich nations. From this point of view, the Western industrial nations (the so-called "core societies") have an interest in keeping developing nations undeveloped; they have an interest in keeping them poor. In short, from this point of view, poverty and inequality around the world reflect the impact of Western imperialism.

This chapter opened with a comparison between a hypothetical fishing and gold-prospecting society. When nations of the world are compared in terms of this ideal type, then the United States appears to resemble the former more than the latter. But when the world system becomes the unit of analysis, the global stratification structure seems to resemble a single giant gold-prospecting society. From this point of view, the United States and other Western nations are the successful (and rapacious) prospectors.

Although western exploitation provides one answer to the question of poverty and inequality around the world, and it is useful, it is not the only answer. Another response involves looking at the developing nations themselves. This angle of vision requires shifting the unit of analysis from the world system back to nation-states.

It was mentioned earlier that most people in most developing societies are poor. But this is not always so. Some nations, such as Japan and South Korea, have successfully pursued economic development over the past half-century even though they were clearly economically and politically dependent on the United States. This fact has important implications, not only for understanding how development occurs but also for their levels of poverty and inequality.

Unlike Brazil and the other nations described earlier, there is very little poverty in either Japan or South Korea. As used before, one indicator of living standards is the infant mortality rate.[15] It is 6 per 1,000 live births in South Korea (the same as in the United States) and 3 in Japan—the lowest in the world. Japan, in fact, has become the healthiest nation in the world. (Remember that the infant mortality rate is 31 per 1,000 in Brazil, 58 in India.) Another indicator of economic development and its impact on poverty and inequality is the Gross Domestic Product per capita.[16] In Japan, it is $31,000, while in South Korea it is $21,900. Although both are less than in the United States, $42,000, they resemble that in other Western nations: Sweden's is $31,400. And both are much higher than in China, Brazil, India, Kenya, and Mozambique.

The overall level of inequality in Japan and Korea also resembles that displayed in Western nations. The Gini Coefficient summarizing the income distribution among households is .25 in Japan and .32 in South Korea, both of which are much lower than in the United States.[17] The income distribution in these nations reflects this development, as shown below by the proportion going to the bottom and top 20 percent, respectively:[18]

	INCOME SHARE TO THE	
	POOREST 20%	RICHEST 20%
Japan (1993)	11%	36%
South Korea (1998)	8%	39%

Yet both Japan and South Korea were devastated in the aftermath of war, World War II and the Korean War, respectively. It is hard to imagine two nations more dependent on the United States. But both pursued aggressive policies designed to produce economic development, with considerable success.[19] The revised *Kuznets Hypothesis* describes what happened. As you may recall from Chapter 7, the argument is that *inequality of wealth and income increases during the early phases of economic growth when the transition from preindustrial to industrial society is most rapid, stabilizes for awhile, and then becomes subject to negotiation.* What apparently occurs is that the early stages of economic development require large-scale capital formation. Since only the (relatively few) who are rich have sufficient wealth to invest, they reap greater rewards initially and the level of inequality increases. Over time, however, as the economy is transformed the combination of demographic factors (the rich do not reproduce themselves) and government regulation of the market results in a reduced level of inequality, or at least the issue becomes open to political intervention. There is logic to this explanation. This is why the *Kuznets Hypothesis* was used in Chapter 7 to explain the historical pattern of inequality in the United States. The experience of both Japan and South Korea appears to conform to that predicted by the hypothesis. Today, neither would be called a developing nation.

According to Peter Berger in *The Capitalist Revolution*, there are lessons to be learned from the experiences of Japan and South Korea.[20] He argues that what these nations did—in rather different ways—was to pursue an aggressive form of capitalism (what Berger describes as "a growth-oriented private enterprise" strategy) with some attention to land ownership among the poor, attracting investment in labor-intensive projects that increased the wages of ordinary people and fostered industrialization, and removing legal and social barriers to opportunity. Obviously the specific form of this strategy would vary from one society to another. But over time, Berger hypothesizes, *the more a developing nation is included in the world capitalist system* (by these and other strategies), *the greater its economic development.* And the impact of economic development will be, over the long run, to reduce poverty and inequality—as has happened in the West and in Japan and South Korea.

But nothing resembling this process has occurred in most countries around the world. To varying degrees, many developing nations can be described as "a Sweden superimposed on an India." That is, they display a relatively modern, technologically based, and (small) affluent sector of the population coexisting with masses who live in extreme poverty.[21] Those who have traveled to, say, Brazil, know that deviating only a little way from a rather narrow range of airports, modern hotels, and tourist venues will lead a person into areas of abject poverty. Such experiences are even more common in other nations. From this angle of vision, then, perhaps wealthy elites and the governments they control are the problem in developing nations. They are like the lucky and rapacious gold prospectors in the hypothetical society described at the beginning of this chapter.

Apart from the metaphor, one guess is that any explanation of poverty and inequality in developing nations will have to take into account both a world system and a nation-state explanation. In other words, it is probably true that Western industrial nations have exploited developing nations and it is also probably true that many of these nations have adopted policies that mainly benefit their own elites (keeping the masses impoverished). But the overall interest in this book is somewhat different than that developed in the above excursus: an understanding of the structure of stratification in the United States. Even though the distribution of valued resources in the United States has become more unequal in recent years, it seems less harsh when compared to that in developing nations. The level of poverty in this country, bad as it is, is far less than in many nations in the world. And the consequences of poverty, in the form of infant mortality (other indicators could have been used) are less widespread. But whether such comparisons are meaningful is unclear. The economic, political, and cultural differences are so great that it is hard to know whether the contrasts are useful for understanding. People who are poor or working class in the United States do not compare their situations to people in Brazil or India. Hence, another perhaps more useful way to look at the structure of stratification in this country is to compare it to that among Western European nations. These nations are similar to the United States economically, politically, and culturally.

INEQUALITY IN THE UNITED STATES AND WESTERN NATIONS

The United States and other Western nations also display similar structures of stratification. In Chapter 4, for example, it was shown that an empirical generalization exists: *Hierarchies of occupational prestige are similar across all Western industrial nations.* This stable finding means that the social standing of the jobs people have is nearly the same in, say, the United Kingdom, France, and the United States. A physician and a lawyer, an automobile mechanic and a sales clerk, will all be similarly ranked. In Chapter 5, it was shown that, while some variability exists, all Western nations display relatively high rates of occupational mobility. The United States's levels of mobility are neither the highest nor the lowest. Finally, it was also shown in Chapter 5 that the variables affecting status attainment are similar in all these nations, a combination of ascribed factors (family background) and achieved factors (education), with increasing emphasis on the latter. These similarities suggest the degree to which all Western industrial societies resemble the fishing village described at the beginning of the chapter.

But there are differences as well, and they are significant. Chapter 6 showed that voting rates are much lower in this country. And these differences are class based: Those who participate at lower levels are primarily working class and poor. In America, the middle class dominates voting. And in America, the rich dominate by contributing money to political campaigns, which allows them access to decision makers. Ultimately, it can be argued that these differences result in greater income and wealth inequality in the United States. One aspect of the overall income distribution is the greater number of poor persons in this country. Chapter 10 showed that the poverty rate in the United States is significantly higher than in other Western nations.

It follows that the United States displays much more inequality in the income distribution than does any other Western industrial nation. Gini Coefficients for the nations that have been compared to the United States in previous chapters are below:[22]

Sweden (2000)	.25
Germany (2000)	.28
Netherlands (1999)	.31
Canada (1998)	.33
France (1995)	.33
United Kingdom (1999)	.39
United States (2001)	.46

Nearly all the difference in the income distribution occurs at the bottom and top. For example, as mentioned previously, the bottom 20 percent of the U.S. population receives about 6 percent of the total income, while the top 20 percent takes 44 percent. In comparison, in Sweden, the most egalitarian of these nations, the bottom 20 percent gets 9 percent and the top gets 37 percent. The other nations shown above are in between. By the way, there tends to be a division among Western European nations such that those in southern Europe exhibit somewhat greater income inequality.[23] Even so, none of these nations approach the level found in the United States.

The result is that people have more restricted life chances in this country, as indicated by the infant mortality rates (per 1,000 live births) shown below for 2004:[24]

Japan	3.3
Sweden	4.0
Germany	4.2
France	4.3
Canada	4.8
Netherlands	5.1
United Kingdom	5.2
United States	6.6

These data imply that the United States resembles the gold-prospecting society more than the fishing society. But the metaphor is not to be taken too literally. Looked at as a whole, this chapter leads to several conclusions. First, most people in most developing nations are much poorer than in the United States.[25] Second, many developing nations exhibit both more poverty and more income inequality than the United States. Third, some developing nations endure more poverty but similar or even less income inequality. Fourth, among economically developed nations, the United States displays much more inequality. This last point is revealing: It suggests the extent to which recent increases in inequality in the United States reflect political choice. Choices made can be unmade.

SUMMARY

When the United States is compared to developing nations, such as China, India, Brazil, Kenya, and Mozambique, it becomes clear that they are much poorer. Many developing nations, but not all, also display greater income inequality.

Two explanations for these differences were discussed. In the first, the world system becomes the unit of analysis, with various nations being seen as analogous to classes. The "core nations" are like the rich. The "semiperipheral nations" are like the middle class. The "peripheral nations" are like the poor. The argument is that both "semiperipheral" and "peripheral" nations are exploited and kept dependent by the "core" nations. The second explanation shifts the unit of analysis back to nation-states and focuses on the elites and governments in developing nations. Japan and South Korea constitute examples of how economic development can occur, thereby reducing poverty and inequality.

When the United States is compared to other Western nations, it becomes clear that all have similar structures of stratification. It also becomes clear that the United States exhibits much more inequality than any other economically developed country.

NOTES

1. I have adapted the description of these hypothetical societies from Krugman (1995).
2. See Firebaugh (2003:33–68), Chen and Ravillion (2004), Deaton (2004; 2006).
3. Firebaugh (2003). See also Bardhan (2006).
4. World Bank (2006).
5. The observer is Angus Deaton, quoted in Krueger (2005).
6. World Bank (2006:290–91).
7. Firebaugh (2003:46–48).
8. World Bank (2006:288–89).
9. United States Bureau of the Census (2006:868).
10. Firebaugh (2003).
11. World Bank (2006a).
12. World Bank (2006a).
13. Wallerstein (1974), Chirot (1986).
14. Wallerstein (1974). See also Chirot (1986).
15. United States Bureau of the Census (2006:868).
16. World Bank (2006:288–89).
17. World Bank (2006a).
18. World Bank (2006a).
19. Berger (1986).
20. Berger (1986:138).
21. Berger (1986:132).
22. World Bank (2006a).
23. Atkinson (1996).
24. United States Bureau of the Census (2006:868).
25. For some practical steps that can be taken to reduce worldwide poverty, see Sachs (2005; 2006).

■ ■ ■ ■ ■ ■

CHAPTER TWELVE

REFLECTIONS ON THE STUDY OF SOCIAL STRATIFICATION

OBJECTIVITY IN THE STUDY
  OF STRATIFICATION
RESEARCH METHODS IN THE STUDY
  OF STRATIFICATION

PARADOX IN THE STUDY
  OF STRATIFICATION

Sociology systematically attempts to see social life as clearly as possible, to understand its various dimensions and their interrelationships, and to do so without being swayed by personal hopes and fears.[1] This book has attempted to illustrate the possibilities inherent to sociology by focusing on a specific aspect of social life, the structure of stratification, explaining it on different levels (individual and structural), and summarizing the relevant research results. In this last chapter, it is time to reflect on some implications that follow from this orientation. Although the comments to follow will emphasize the study of social stratification, the topics are of general significance to all areas of sociological inquiry. The first issue is the problem of objectivity, because it is required if sociologists are to see the world clearly. The second is the problem of research methods, because they provide the key to understanding the dimensions of social life. The final issue is the paradoxical nature of sociological analyses, because this characteristic highlights people's hopes and fears about the future.

OBJECTIVITY IN THE STUDY OF STRATIFICATION

In order to see any aspect of social life clearly, such as stratification, a specific orientation is necessary, one not required of ordinary persons: Bias must be eliminated as much as possible. This goal is far more difficult to achieve in the social sciences than in other disciplines because observers are embedded in their subject. Thus those interested in the study of stratification also occupy a specific location in the class structure; they earn an income, they have a job with its level of occupational prestige, they own property, they are married and have children, and the like. These facts mean that a researcher's personal experiences, values, and economic interests can easily bias the analysis.

The reduction of bias requires that sociologists try to adhere to the norms of science, regardless of their personal experiences, values, or economic interests. These rules direct researchers to report findings without regard to their motives for undertaking the study. They require researchers to use the most systematic evidence available and to make logical deductions. And they adjure researchers to make their own values explicit so that others may assess whether bias enters the analysis. Such rules provide those studying stratification with a way of looking at the world that is decisively different from daily life. Moreover, two additional norms exist that influence the community of scholars who examine social scientific findings. Thus, researchers are directed to critically evaluate others' work. This injunction also applies to students. It means, for example, that readers should ask themselves whether the author's personal values might have distorted the presentation in earlier chapters. Finally, researchers are taught to try to refute previous work. When these efforts fail and findings are replicated, especially if different types of data or methods produce similar results, then the probability of their being accurate reflections of reality goes up. Over the long run, these norms insure that objective, scientific findings about the structure of stratification will be produced. They help us to see social life as clearly as possible.

This orientation is why the importance of hypothesis testing has been emphasized throughout the book. Thus some intuitively plausible ideas, such as the *Job Perquisite Hypothesis* (Chapter 8) or the *Kuznets Hypothesis* (Chapters 7 and 11), must remain tentative statements because either adequate data do not exist or testing has not yet occurred. Such hesitance is useful because some very good ideas, like the *Embourgeoisement Hypothesis* (Chapter 9), turn out to be false when systematically examined. Moreover, even empirical generalizations must be continually evaluated and sometimes modified, as with the finding that the prestige hierarchy is similar across Western industrial societies (Chapter 2). But over the long run, empirical generalizations emerge. These stable research findings constitute statements of fact. Although they are not immutable, since times change, they do indicate how the benefits of a stress on objectivity and the elimination of bias lead to knowledge.

RESEARCH METHODS IN THE STUDY OF STRATIFICATION

Research methods, C. Wright Mills asserted in *The Sociological Imagination*, comprise the procedures sociologists use to apprehend social life in all its aspects.[2] No matter how objective research is, no matter how free of bias, if the procedures sociologists use do not take into account the various dimensions of stratification, then a full and accurate depiction of this topic becomes impossible. As it turns out, an understanding of each level of social life requires rather different procedures.

One dimension of social life involves the study of individuals and the way in which they act on and react to the situations in which they find themselves. As indicated in Chapter 1, most researchers, at least in the United States, are prone to focus on individuals when studying stratification. Thus, a great deal of work exists that identifies the reasons why people move upward or downward occupationally, become poor, vote or participate in politics in other ways, and endure gender or racial inequality. The empirical generalizations summarizing these relationships are among the most significant results in sociology. Such studies typically involve survey data, statistical analyses, and quantitatively precise findings. An exclusive focus on individuals, however, is limiting because it omits the existence of other aspects of social life which, although less often studied, provide additional insight into stratification.

Yet sociologists in the United States tend to avoid asking any questions that cannot be answered in quantitative terms. In practice, this orientation means that "research" is usually defined as the analysis of survey data. Underlying this choice of methodology is a dominant value orientation shared by all American citizens, regardless of class: a preference for seeing individuals as both cause and solution to social problems. Sociologists are no different from other people. They believe in and benefit from individual initiative, competition, and the rewards that ensue. This background leads many of them to adopt a nominalist methodological stance, which means that society is considered to be nothing more than the sum of its parts—individuals.[3] If this were true, then quantitative analyses of survey data ought to identify the true causes of the high mobility rate, the poverty rate, the rate of political participation, and the level of gender and racial and ethnic inequality. In fact, however, they do not, primarily because such an orientation excludes the structural dimension of social life from consideration.

In public policy terms, this preference for focusing on individuals is why the United States lost the war on poverty in the 1960s. Virtually all the antipoverty programs developed at that time emphasized job training and education so that poor individuals could better themselves. While there is nothing particularly wrong with such programs, they did not and could not reduce the poverty rate in this country because individual characteristics are not responsible for the large number of impoverished people. Rather, as shown in Chapter 10, the high American rate of poverty results from the reproduction of the class system, macroeconomic policy, and other structural factors. What is needed is a way of seeing the structural aspect of social life as clearly as possible. This alternative approach does not substitute for the study of individuals; rather, it complements such analyses and leads to greater insight into social stratification.

It was argued in Chapter 1 that the social structure determines rates of events and that this orientation can be seen in the work of sociologists as different as Marx, Durkheim, and Merton. The hypothesis offered there was that lower-class people have fewer and less effective choices in comparison to upper-class persons, with the result that rates of behavior are decisively effected. In subsequent chapters, this idea was applied to the analysis of mobility rates, poverty rates, political participation rates, levels of gender inequality, and levels of racial and ethnic inequality. In each chapter, the account followed a similar pattern and none of the proposed explanatory factors dealt with individuals.

As shown in Chapter 5, for example, in order to explain the rate of mobility, variables like industrialization, class differences in fertility rates, immigration, institutionalized gender discrimination, and institutionalized racial and ethnic discrimination are necessary. Note that the rate of mobility is accounted for in terms of other rates, not individual characteristics. Thanks to the explosion of research on status attainment over the past twenty-five years, it is clear in this case more than any of the others that the factors affecting individual mobility (the status-attainment process) are different than those influencing the rate of mobility.

An important but little recognized implication follows from the fact that rates of events must be explained by rates of other events. To use Durkheim's language, social facts (rates) are things and they must be explained by other social facts.[4] Methodologically, this injunction usually means that survey research or other analogous modes of data analysis often cannot be used. Although the topics dealt with in this book are amenable to quantitative methods in principle, the aggregate survey data needed for their analysis do not exist. Instead, it was necessary in each case to perform a mental experiment similar to Max Weber's in *The Protestant Ethic and the Spirit of Capitalism*.[5] Weber's research strategy involved the construction of a set of logically interrelated variables, which he called "ideal types," and the empirical assessment of how actual cases deviated from a purely logical formulation.[6] The analyses in this book proceeded in a similar way, that is, by identifying a set of structural factors, such as the rate of mobility, poverty, etc., and hypothesizing the manner in which they are affected by other structural variables. In each case, an implicit counterfactual hypothesis posited that if the proposed explanatory variables had different configurations, then the rate of mobility and the like would be far different. The argument is that this methodological procedure provides observers with a way to confront many significant issues for which survey data cannot be used.

In practice, this research strategy reflects a process Willer and Webster call abduction; that is, it attempts to identify, based on theory and empirical observation, those variables affecting the phenomenon of interest.[7] This procedure invites creativity, which is useful in any analysis. In this book, the process involved looking at how the major institutions—economy, family, education, and government—interact with the stratification structure. The resulting explanation did not identify new variables; it was, rather, synthetic: showing how well-known forces (many of which appear unrelated to one another) produce a high rate of some phenomenon, placing these factors into a coherent theoretical context, and systematically following through the implications of the analysis. In so doing, the way explanations focusing on individuals and structures complement one another became clear. For example, when the process of status attainment and the causes of a high rate of mobility are considered together, then much more is known about stratification in the United States than if either angle of vision is ignored.

Yet structural analyses such as those presented in this book appear unscientific to many sociologists because the results seem unmeasurable quantitatively and, hence, imprecise. The assumption that quantitative precision makes an analysis scientific constitutes a frequent mistake by researchers in the so-called "soft" sciences. In all disciplines, significant questions exist that cannot be measured directly and, as indicated earlier, it becomes necessary to perform a mental experiment. In so doing, however, it is often convenient to think in multivariate statistical terms. Thus, in accounting for the level of impoverishment in the United States, the dependent variable (Y in a regression equation) is the rate of poverty, and the independent variables (the Xs in a regression equation) comprise a set of structural factors: the reproduction of the class system, macroeconomic policies, and so forth. The advantage of thinking in this way is that each of the variables must be clearly specified and related to one another. The major difference, of course, is that the data are manipulated logically rather than computationally. Now there is no special reason why mathematical values could not be assigned to each of the variables used in explaining the rate of, say, poverty, and numerical results produced. For example, armed with a set of plausible assumptions, one could show that if inflation averages X percent higher and unemployment X percent lower, then the rate of poverty will be reduced by Y percent. Having performed this exercise, however, the result would be neither more precise nor more scientific than before.

A similar judgment could be made about most econometric models, such as forecasts of next year's inflation rate; they constitute mental experiments in quantitative form and the numbers should be translated to mean "a lot" or "a little." So too with mental experiments in other disciplines. For example, Sagan calculated that 10,400 thermonuclear explosions with a total yield of 5,000 megatons of which 20 percent explode over cities may produce so much dust and soot in the atmosphere that the average July temperature at mid-latitudes would decline to −9 degrees Fahrenheit within a few weeks.[8] Subsequently, Thompson and Schneider, using a different model of the atmosphere and making somewhat different assumptions, found that the average temperature might decline to between 60 and 70 degrees Fahrenheit.[9] It is important to recognize that in both cases these rather precise numbers are illusions. In reality, Sagan showed that one result of a thermonuclear war might be that the temperature will decline "a lot" as a result of "nuclear winter," while Thompson and Schneider showed that the temperature may decline "a little" due to "nuclear fall." Now this research is imaginative and substantively important; it is good science. It is also a mental experiment, no different in logic from that occurring in many other fields, including those performed in this book. Of course, the effects of one variable on another should be empirically measured whenever possible. But observers should not let either a fetish for measurement or a shortsighted view of what science is get in the way of research. Economists do not. Physicists do not. Neither should sociologists.

Nonetheless, both the procedures described here and the structural analyses described in this book often seem alien because they are so unfamiliar, especially in the United States.[10] The emphasis on individuals runs deep. But sociology, Emile Durkheim said, should cause people to see things in a different way than the ordinary, "for the purpose of any science is to make discoveries and all such discoveries more or less upset accepted opinions."[11] A structural approach such as that used in this book is one (but not the only) way of performing this task. The consequences, however, are paradoxical.

PARADOX IN THE STUDY OF STRATIFICATION

If sociologists are indeed able to see social life clearly and to understand its dimensions and their interrelationships, the results have implications for people's hopes and fears about the future. Paradox follows. Sociological analyses, including those presented in earlier chapters, often seem to be contradictory; they appear politically radical yet also conservative, liberating for the individual yet also constraining. This paradox, Peter Berger has suggested, is inherent to sociological inquiry.[12]

On the one hand, almost any sound analysis of the topics covered in this book can suggest ways in which to improve our society or aspects of it. This fact constitutes people's hope for progress in the future. What happens is that knowledge liberates people by opening up the possibility for change. This is especially true of structural descriptions because they often reveal hidden or nonobvious facets of a phenomenon. As a result, those proposing radical departures from the status quo can point to alienation, exploitation, inequality, and inequity. Yet sociological analyses also show that improvement does not always follow from change, a fact that has conservative implications. Disorder, at least for a short time, often does. This fact makes people fear the future, which constrains them. Thus, most individuals are enmeshed in structures of norms and roles with which they are both familiar and comfortable. Few persons dislike everything about their lives, which means they want to preserve what is good, maintain their traditions, and retain a sense of orderliness and continuity from one generation to another. This orientation militates against radical change.

The result of these contradictory impulses, as Professor Berger comments, is that sociology often produces a paradoxical, but by no means irrational, stance on the part of its practitioners and others exposed to it: that of a person who thinks daringly but acts prudently. Put differently, there are no easy answers to the problems revealed in this book. All solutions carry with them both benefits and liabilities, and it is best to be as clear as possible about each.

NOTES

1. Berger (1977).
2. Mills (1959).
3. Bryant (1985).
4. Durkheim (1982 [1895]).
5. Weber (1958 [1905]).
6. See Turner, Beeghley, and Powers (2006).
7. Willer and Webster (1970).
8. Sagan (1984).
9. Thompson and Schneider (1986).
10. Much more complex structural orientations exist, as shown by Turner (1984) and by the readings in Blau (1975), Blau and Merton (1981). Unfortunately, most of them are impractical for understanding such real-world issues as social mobility, poverty, political participation, gender inequality, or racial and ethnic inequality.
11. Durkheim (1982 [1895]:31).
12. Berger (1977).

REFERENCES

Aaronson, Daniel. (2000). A note on the benefits of homeownership. *Journal of Urban Economics*, 47, 356–369.

Acemoglu, Daron, and James A. Robinson. (2000). Why did the West extend the franchise? Democracy, inequality, and growth in historical perspective. *Quarterly Journal of Economics*, 115, 1167–1199.

Acker, Joan. (1973). Women and social stratification: A case of intellectual sexism. *American Journal of Sociology*, 78, 936–946.

Acuña, Rodolfo. (1987). *Occupied America: A history of Chicanos, 3rd Edition*. New York: Pearson Education.

Adams, James Thuslow. (1931). *The epic of America*. New York: Blue Ribbon Books.

Adler, Jeffrey. (2006). *First in violence, deepest in dirt: Homicide in Chicago, 1875–1920*. Cambridge, MA: Harvard University Press.

Aeschylus. (1975). *Prometheus bound*. New York: Oxford University Press.

Aguirre, Adalberto, Jr., and Jonathan H. Turner. (2004). *American ethnicity, 4th edition*. New York: McGraw-Hill.

Alexander, Karl L., Bruce K. Eckland, and Larry J. Griffin. (1975). The Wisconsin model of socio-economic achievement: A replication. *American Journal of Sociology*, 81, 324–342.

Allen, H.W., and K.W. Allen. (1981). Vote fraud and data validity. pp. 153–193 in J.M. Chubb, W.H. Flanigan, and N.H. Zingale (eds.), *Analyzing electoral history*. Beverly Hills, CA: Sage.

Allen, James, Hilton Als, John Lewis, and Leon F. Litwack. (2000). *Without sanctuary: Lynching photography in America*. Santa Fe, NM: Twin Palms Press.

Allen, Michael Patrick. (1990). *The founding fortunes: A new anatomy of the super-rich families in America*. New York: E.P. Dutton.

Allitt, Patrick. (2005). *I'm the teacher, you're the student*. Philadelphia: University of Pennsylvania Press.

Allport, Gordon W. (1954). *The nature of prejudice*. Cambridge, MA: Addison-Wesley.

Amato, Paul R., and Shelley Irving. (2006). Historical trends in divorce in the United States. pp. 41–58 in Mark A. Fine and John H. Harvey (eds.), *Handbook of divorce and relationship dissolution*. Mahwah, NJ: Lawrence Erlbaum.

America's Second Harvest. (2003). *The red tape divide state-by-state review of food stamp applications*. Washington, DC: America's Second Harvest.

———. (2006). *Hunger in America*. Washington, DC: America's Second Harvest.

American Political Science Association. (2004). *American democracy in an age of rising inequality*. Washington, DC: American Political Science Association.

Anderson, Eiljah. (1994). The code of the streets. *The Atlantic Monthly*, 273(May), 80–110.

———. (1999). *The code of the street: Decency, violence, and the moral life of the inner city*. New York: W.W. Norton.

Anker, R., H. Malkas, and A. Korten. (2003). Gender-based occupational segregation in the 1990s. Working Paper 16. Geneva: International Labour Office.

Ansolabehere, Stephen, and Shanto Iyengar. (1995). *Going negative: How attack ads shrink and polarize the electorate*. New York: Free Press.

Archer, Melanie, and Judith R. Blau. (1993). Class formation in nineteenth-century America: The case of the middle class. *Annual Review of Sociology, Vol 19*. New York: Annual Reviews, Inc.

Argersinger, Peter H. (1986). New perspectives on election fraud in the gilded age. *Political Science Quarterly*, 100, 669–689.

Armstrong, T., J. Foulke, C. Bir, et al. (1999). Muscle responses to simulated torque reactions of hand-held power tools. *Ergonomics*, 42, 146–149.

Arneson, Ben A. (1925). Non-voting in a typical Ohio community. *American Political Science Review*, 19, 816–825.

Arsenault, Raymond. (2006). *Freedom riders: 1961 and the struggle for racial justice*. New York: Oxford University Press.

Association of Community Organizations for Reform Now. (2005). *The high cost of credit: Disparities in high-priced refinance loans to minority homeowners in 125 American cities*. Washington, DC: Association of Community Organizations for Reform Now.

Atkinson, Anthony B. (1996). Income distribution in Europe and the United States. *Oxford Review of Economic Policy*, 12, 15–28.

Atkinson, Anthony B., Bea Cantillon, Eric Marlier, et al. (2002). *Social indicators: The EU and social inclusion*. Oxford: Oxford University Press.

Bakke, Edward W. (1940). *The unemployed worker*. New Haven, CT: Yale University Press.

Balkovic, Brian. (2006). High-income tax returns for 2003. *SOI Bulletin*, 25(Spring), 8–58.

Baltzell, E. Digby. (1958). *Philadelphia gentlemen: The making of a national upper class*. New York: Free Press.

———. (1964). *The protestant establishment: Aristocracy and caste in America*. New York: Vintage.

Bamshad, Michael J., and Steve E. Olson. (2003). Does race exist? *Scientific American*, 289(December), 78–85.

Bamshad, Michael J., Stephen Wooding, Benjamin Salisbury, et al. (2004). Deconstructing the relationship between genetics and race. *Nature Reviews Genetics*, 5, 598–609.

Bannerjee, Neela. (2006). Clergywomen find hard path to bigger pulpit. *New York Times*, National Edition. August 26, A1.

Bardhan, Pranab. (2006). Does globalization help or hurt the world's poor? *Scientific American*, 294 (April), 84–91.

Barlett, Donald L., and James B. Steele. (1994). *America: Who really pays the taxes*. New York: Simon & Schuster.

Barnes, Sandra L. (2005). *The cost of being poor*. Albany, NY: State University of New York Press.

Barstow, David. (2003). A trench caves in; A young worker is dead. Is it a crime? *New York Times*, National Edition. December 21, 1.

———. (2003a). U.S. rarely seeks charges for deaths in the workplace. *New York Times*, National Edition. December 22, 1.

———. (2003b). California leads in making employer pay for job deaths. *New York Times*, National Edition. December 23, 1.

Barstow, David, and Lowell Bergman. (2003). At a Texas foundry, an indifference to life. *New York Times*, National Edition. January 8, 1 & 15.

———. (2003a). Family's profits, wrung from blood and sweat. *New York Times*, National Edition. January 9, 1 & 14.

———. (2003b). Deaths on the job, slaps on the wrist. *New York Times*, National Edition. January 10, 1 & 15.

Bassuk, Ellen L. (1991). Homeless families. *Scientific American*, 265(December), 66–74.

Baunach, Dawn Michelle. (2002). Trends in occupational sex segregation and inequality. *Social Science Research*, 31, 77–98.

Bebchuk, Lucian A., and Robert J. Jackson. (2005). Executive pensions. Working Paper 11907. Cambridge, MA: National Bureau of Economic Research.

Becker, Howard. (1967). Whose side are we on? *Social Problems, 14*, 239–247.

Beeghley, Leonard. (1983). *Living poorly in America*. New York: Praeger.

———. (1984). Illusion and reality in the measurement of poverty. *Social Problems, 31*, 312–324.

———. (1986). Social class and political participation: A review and an explanation. *Sociological Forum, 1*, 496–513.

———. (1989). Individual versus structural explanations of poverty. *Population Research and Policy Review, 8*, 201–222.

———. (1992). Social structure and voting in the United States: A historical and comparative analysis. *Perspectives on Social Problems, 3*, 265–287.

———. (1996). *What does your wife do: Gender and the transformation of family life*. Boulder, CO: Westview.

———. (1999). *Angles of vision: How to understand social problems*. Boulder, CO: Westview.

———. (2003). *Homicide: A sociological explanation*. Boulder, CO: Rowman & Littlefield.

Beeghley, Leonard, and Debra Van Ausdale. (1990). The status of women faculty in graduate departments of sociology: 1973 and 1988. *Footnotes, 18*(December), 3–4.

Beeghley, Leonard, and John C. Cochran. (1988). Class identification and gender role norms among employed married women. *Journal of Marriage and Family, 50*, 719–729.

Beeghley, Leonard, and Denise Donnelly. (1989). The consequences of family crowding: A theoretical synthesis. *Lifestyles: Family and Economic Issues, 10*, 83–102.

Beeghley, Leonard, Ellen Van Velsor, and E. Wilbur Bock. (1981). The correlates of religiosity among black and white Americans. *Sociological Quarterly, 22*, 403–412.

Bendix, Reinhard. (1974). Inequality and social structure: A comparison of Marx and Weber. *American Sociological Review, 38*, 149–161.

Bell, Daniel. (1976). *The coming of post-industrial society*. New York: Basic Books.

Bell, Jennifer L., and James C. Helmkamp. (2003). Non-fatal injuries in the West Virginia logging industry. *American Journal of Industrial Medicine, 44*, 502–509.

Bellow, Adam. (2003). *In praise of nepotism: A natural history*. New York: Doubleday.

Berger, Joseph. (2004). 4-hour trek across New York for 4 hours of work, and $28. *New York Times*, National Edition. May 6, p. A1.

Berger, Peter M. (1977). Sociology and freedom. pp. 10–19 in P.L. Berger, *Facing up to modernity*. New York: Basic Books.

———. (1986). *The capitalist revolution*. New York: Basic Books.

Berlin, Ira. (2003). *Generations of captivity: A history of African-American slaves*. Cambridge, MA: Harvard University Press.

Berlin, Ira, and Leslie M. Harris. (2006). *Slavery in New York*. New York: New York Historical Society.

Bernstein, Jared. (2001). Let the war on the poverty line commence. *Working Paper Series*. New York: Foundation for Child Development.

Bernstein, Patricia. (2005). *The first Waco horror: The lynching of Jesse Washington and the rise of the N.A.A.C.P.* College Station, TX: Texas A & M Press.

Biblarz, Timothy, Vern L. Bengtson, and Alexander Bucur. (1996). Social mobility across generations. *Journal of marriage and the family, 58*, 188–200.

Bird, Carolyn. (1968). *Born female: The high cost of keeping women down*. New York: Van Rees Press.

Blais, André. (2006). What affects voter turnout? *Annual Review of Political Science, 9*, 111–125.

Blakeslee, Nate. (2005). *Tulia: Race, cocaine, and corruption in a small Texas town*. New York: Public Affairs Press.

Blank, Rebecca M., and Alan S. Blinder. (1986). Macroeconomics, income distribution, and poverty. pp. 180–208 in S. H. Danziger and D. H. Weinberg (eds.), *Fighting poverty: What works and what doesn't*. Cambridge, MA: Harvard University Press.

Blau, Francine D., and Lawrence M. Kahn. (2000). Gender differences in pay. Working Paper 7732. Cambridge, MA: National Bureau of Economic Research.

Blau, Peter M. (ed.). (1975). *Approaches to the study of social structure*. New York: Basic Books.

Blau, Peter M., and Otis Dudley Duncan. (1967). *The American occupational structure*. New York: Wiley.

Blau, Peter M., and Robert K. Merton. (1981). *Continuities in structural inquiry*. Beverly Hills, CA: Sage.

Bledstein, Burton J., and Robert D. Johnston (eds.). (2001). *The middling sorts: Explorations in the history of the American middle class*. New York: Routledge.

Blumin, Stuart. (1989). *The emergence of the middle class*. New York: Cambridge University Press.

Bobo, Lawrence D. (2001). Racial attitudes and relations at the close of the twentieth century. pp. 264–301 in Neil Smelser, William Julius Wilson, and Faith Mitchell (eds.), *America becoming: Racial trends and their consequences*, Volume I. Washington, DC: National Academy Press.

Bourdieu, Pierre. (1986). The forms of capital. pp. 241–258 in John G. Richardson (ed.). *Handbook of theory and research for the sociology of education*. New York: Greenwood Press.

———. (1987). *Distinction: A social critique of the judgement of taste*. Cambridge, MA: Harvard University Press.

Boushey, Heather. (2005). No way out: How prime-age workers get trapped in minimum wage jobs. *WorkUSA: The Journal of Labor and Society, 8*, 659–670.

Bowler, Mary. (1999). Women's earnings: An overview. *Monthly Labor Review, 130*(December), 13–21.

Boyer, Debra, and David Fine. (1992). Sexual abuse as a factor in adolescent pregnancy and child maltreatment. *Family Planning Perspectives, 24*, 4–11.

Boyle, Paul, Thomas J. Cooke, Keith Halfacree, et al. (2001). A cross-national comparison of the impact of family migration on women's employment status. *Demography, 38*, 201–218.

Bradsher, Greg. (2006). A founding father in dissent. *Prologue, 38*(Spring), 30–35.

Bramel, Dana. (2004). The strange career of the contact hypothesis. pp. 49–67 in Lee, Yuch-Ting, Clark McCauley, Fathali Moghaddam, et al. (eds.), *The psychology of ethnic conflict*. New York: Praeger.

Branch, Taylor. (2006). *At Canaan's edge: America in the King years, 1965–1968*. New York: Simon & Schuster.

Breen, Richard (ed.). (2004). *Social mobility in Europe*. New York: Oxford University Press.

Breen, Richard, and Jan O. Jonsson. (2005). Inequality of opportunity in comparative perspective: Recent research on educational attainment and social mobility. *Annual Review of Sociology, 31*, 223–243.

Brennan, John, and Edward W. Hill. (1999). *Where are the jobs?: Cities, suburbs, and the competition for employment*. Washington, DC: Brookings Institution.

Breslin, F. Curtis, and Charles Mustard. (2001). A longitudinal study examining the effects of unemployment on adults. *American Journal of Epidemiology, 153*(Supplement), S235.

Brewer, N. B., and S. L. Gaertner. (2001). Toward a reduction in prejudice: Intergroup contact and social categorization. pp. 451–472 in A. Tessor (ed.), *Blackwell handbook of social psychology, vol. 3: Intergroup processes*. Oxford: Basil Blackwell.

Bridges, J.S. (1989). Sex differences in occupational values. *Sex Roles, 20*, 205–211.

Brim, Orville G. (1966). Socialization through the life-cycle. pp. 1–49 in O.G. Brim and S. Wheeler, *Socialization after childhood*. New York: Wiley.

Brown, Jeffery D. (2003). Amputations: A continuing workplace hazard. *Compensation and working conditions online*. Bureau of Labor Statistics: www.bls.gov.

Brownlee, W. Elliot. (2000). Historical perspectives on U.S. tax policy toward the rich. pp. 29–73 in J. Slemrod (ed.), *Does Atlas shrug? The economic consequences of taxing the rich*. New York: Russell Sage Foundation.

Brownmiller, Susan. (1975). *Against our will*. New York: Simon & Schuster.

Brundage, W. Fitzhugh. (1997). Introduction. pp. 1–23 in W.F. Brundage (ed.), *Under sentence of death: Lynching in the South*. Chapel Hill, NC: University of North Carolina Press.

Brush, Michael. (2006). "Superperks" sweeten executives' pay. www.moneycentral.msn.com.

Bryant, Christopher A. G. (1985). *Positivism in social theory and research*. New York: St. Martin's Press.

Budig, Michelle J., and Paula England. (2001). The wage penalty for motherhood. *American Sociological Review, 66*, 204–225.

Buijs, Frank J., and Jan Rath. (2002). Muslims in Europe: The state of research. New York: Russell Sage Foundation.

Burnham, Walter Dean. (1980). The disappearance of the American voter. pp. 35–73 in Richard Rose (ed.), *Electoral participation*. Beverly Hills, CA: Sage.

Burtless, Gary. (1998). Can the labor market absorb three million welfare recipients? *Focus, 19* (Summer/Fall), 1–6.

Burtless, Gary. (2001). Has widening inequality promoted or retarded U.S. growth? Washington, DC: Brookings Institution.

Butterfield, Fox. (1996). *All God's children: The Bosket family and the American tradition of violence*. New York: Avon Books.

Caltech/MIT. (2001). *Voting: What is, what could be*. Pasadena, CA: California Institute of Technology & Massachusetts Institute of Technology.

Camarillo, Albert M., and Frank Bonilla. (2001). Hispanics in a multicultural society: A new American dilemma? pp. 103–134 in Neil Smelser, William Julius Wilson, and Faith Mitchell (eds.), *America becoming: Racial trends and their consequences, Volume I*. Washington, DC: National Academy Press.

Caplow, Theodore. (1982). *Middletown families: Fifty years of change and continuity*. Minneapolis, MN: University of Minnesota Press.

Carney, Judith A. (2001). *Black rice: The African origins of rice cultivation in the Americas*. Cambridge, MA: Harvard University Press.

Carrigan, William D. (2004). *The making of a lynching culture: violence and vigilantism in central Texas, 1836–1916*. Urbana, IL: University of Illinois Press.

Case, Anne, and Angus Deaton. (2005). Broken down by work and sex: How our health declines. pp. 185–205 in David Wise (ed.), *Analyses in the economics of aging*. Chicago: University of Chicago Press.

Cassidy, John. (1997). The return of Karl Marx. *The New Yorker*, October 20 & 27, 248–259.

Catalano, Ralph, Raymond W. Novaco, and William McConnell. (2002). Layoffs and violence revisited. *Aggressive Behavior, 28*, 233–248.

Catalyst. (2003). 2002 catalyst census of women corporate officers and top earners in the Fortune 500. www.catalystwomen.org.

Cavilli-Sforza, Luca, Paolo Menozzi, and Alberto Piazza. (1995). *The history and geography of human genes*. Princeton, NJ: Princeton University Press.

Center for Media and Democracy. (2006). Earmarks. www.sourcewatch.org/index.

Centers for Disease Control. (2000). Youth risk behavior surveillance—United States, 1999. *Morbidity & Mortality Weekly Report* June 9, 1–96.

Centers, Richard. (1949). *The psychology of social classes: A study of class consciousness*. Princeton, NJ: Princeton University Press.

Century Foundation. (1999). *The basics: Tax reform*. New York: Century Foundation Press.

Charles, Maria, and David B. Grusky. (2004). *Occupational ghettos: The world wide segregation of women and men*. Stanford, CA: Stanford University Press.

Chen, Shaohua, and Martin Ravallion. (2004). How have the world's poorest fared since the early 1980's? World Bank Policy Research Working Paper 3341. Washington, DC: World Bank.

Cherlin, Andrew J. (1992). *Marriage, divorce, and remarriage*, revised and enlarged edition. Cambridge, MA: Harvard University Press.

Child Trends. (2003). Left unsupervised: A look at the most vulnerable children. *Child Trends Research Brief*. Washington, DC: Child Trends.

Children's Defense Fund. (1998). *New studies look at the status of former welfare recipients*. Washington, DC: Children's Defense Fund.

———. (1998a). *Welfare to what: Early findings on family hardship and well-being*. Washington, DC: Children's Defense Fund.

Chinhui, Juhn, and Kevin M. Murphy. (1997). Wage inequality and family labor supply. *Journal of Labor Economics, 15*, 72–97.

Chirot, Daniel. (1986). *Social change in the modern era*. New York: Harcourt Brace Jovanovich.

Choldin, Harvey M. (2005). Chicago Housing Authority. *The Electronic Encyclopedia of Chicago*. www.encyclopedia.chicagohistory.org.

Citizens for Tax Justice. (2006). The Bush tax cuts enacted through 2006: The latest CTJ data. www.ctj.org.

Citro, Constance F., and Robert T. Michael (eds.). (1995). *Measuring poverty: A new approach*. Washington, DC: National Academy Press.

Clark, Rodney, Norman B. Anderson, Vernessa R. Clark, et al. (1999). Racism as a stressor for African Americans: A biosocial model. *American Psychologist, 54*, 805–816.

Cohen, Mark A. (2001). *Final report on racial impact of NMAC's finance charge markup policy*. Nashville, TN: Owen Graduate School of Management, Vanderbilt University.

Commission on Wartime Relocation and Internment of Civilians. (1982). *Personal justice denied*. Washington, D.C.: United States Government Printing Office.

Committee on Ways and Means. (2004). *2004 Green book: Background material and data on programs within the jurisdiction of the Committee on Ways and Means*. Washington, DC: U.S. Government Printing Office.

Coleman, James S. (1966). *Equality of educational opportunity*. Washington, DC: U.S. Government Printing Office.

Collins, William J., and Melissa A. Thomasson. (2002). Exploring the racial gap in infant mortality rates, 1920–1970. Working Paper 8836. Cambridge, MA: National Bureau of Economic Research.

Conger, Rand, Katherine Conger, and Glen Elder. (1997). Family economic hardship and adolescent adjustment: Mediating and moderating processes. pp. 288–310 in G. Duncan and J. Brooks-Gunn (eds.), *Consequences of growing up poor*. New York: Russell Sage.

Congressional Budget Office. (2004). *Accounting for employee stock options*. Washington, DC: Congressional Budget Office.

Conway, M. Margaret. (2000). *Political participation in the United States, 3rd edition*. Washington, DC: Congressional Quarterly Press.

Converse, Philip E. (1972). Change in the American electorate. pp. 263–338 in Angus Campbell and Philip E. Converse (eds.), *The human meaning of social change*. New York: Russell Sage.

Correspondents of the New York Times. (2005). *Class matters*. New York: Henry Holt.

Coser, Lewis A. (1956). *The functions of social conflict*. New York: Free Press.

———. (1967). Some social functions of violence. pp. 73–92 in his *Continuities in the study of social conflict*. New York: Free Press.

Costo, Stephanie L. (2006). Trends in retirement plan coverage over the last decade. *Monthly Labor Review*, 137(February), 58–64.

Cott, Nancy. (1987). *The grounding of modern feminism*. New Haven, CT: Yale University Press.

Cottle, Thomas J. (1994). When you stop, you die: The human toll of unemployment. pp. 75–82 in J.H. Skolnick and E. Currie (eds.), *Crisis in American institutions, Ninth Edition*. New York: HarperCollins Publishers.

Crook, Clive. (2006). The height of inequality. *The Atlantic*, September, 36–37.

Cutler, David M., and Edward L. Glaeser. (2006). Why do Europeans smoke more than Americans? Working Paper 12124. Cambridge, MA: National Bureau of Economic Research.

Dahl, Robert A. (1967). *Pluralist democracy in the United States: Conflict and consent*. Chicago: Rand McNally.

Dahrendorf, Ralf. (1959). *Class and class conflict in industrial society*. Stanford, CA: Stanford University Press.

Dansky, Bonnie. (1997). The National Women's Study: Relationship of victimization and post-traumatic stress disorder to Bulimia Nervosa. *International Journal of Eating Disorders*, 21, 213–228.

Danziger, Sheldon, and Robert Plotnick. (1977). Demographic change, government transfers, and income distribution. *Monthly Labor Review*, 100(April), 7–11.

Danziger, Sheldon, Robert Haveman, and Robert Plotnick. (1981). How income transfer programs affect work, savings, and the income distribution. *Journal of Economic Literature*, 19, 975–1026.

Danziger, Sheldon, and Jeffrey Lehman. (1997). How will welfare recipients fare in the labor markets. *Challenge*, 39(March/April), 8–15.

Dash, Leon. (1989). *When children want children: The urban crisis of teenage childbearing*. New York: William Morrow.

Davis, Kingsley, and Wilbert Moore. (1945). Some principles of stratification. *American Sociological Review*, 7, 242–249.

Davis, Theodore J. (1997). The occupational mobility of black males revisited: Does race matter? *Social Science Journal*, 32, 121–136.

de la Garza, Rodolfo. (1992). *Latino voices: Mexican, Puerto Rican, and Cuban perspectives on American politics*. Boulder, CO: Westview Press.

Deaton, Angus. (2004). Measuring poverty. Research Program in Development Studies. Princeton, NJ: Princeton University.

———. (2006). Purchasing power parity exchange rates for the poor: Using household surveys to construct PPPs. Research Program in Development Studies. Princeton, NJ: Princeton University.

Degler, Carl N. (1980). *At odds: Women and the family in America from the Revolution to the present*. New York: Oxford University Press.

Delgado, Richard. (1997). *The coming race war? And other apocalyptic tales of America after affirmative action and welfare*. New York: New York University Press.

Dellinger, Kirsten, and Christine L. Williams. (2005). The locker room and the dorm room: Workplace norms and the boundaries of sexual harassment in magazine editing.

pp. 109–131 in Claire M. Renzetti and Raquel Kennedy Bergen (eds.), *Violence against women*. Lanham, MD: Rowman & Littlefield.

DeParle, Jason. (1993). Secretary of housing's intentions on homeless raise questions. *New York Times*, National Edition. January 30, 1.

Deutsch, Morton, and M. E. Collins. (1951). *Interracial housing: A psychological evaluation of a social experiment*. Minneapolis, MN: University of Minnesota Press.

DiFazio, William. (2006). *Ordinary poverty: A little food and cold storage*. Philadelphia: Temple University Press.

DiMaggio, Paul. (1979). Review essay on Pierre Bourdieu. *American Journal of Sociology*, 84, 1460–1474.

DiNatale, Marisa, and Stephanie Boraas. (2002). The labor force experiences of women from "Generation X." *Monthly Labor Review*, 133(March), 3–15.

DiPasquale, Denise, and Edward L. Glaeser. (1999). Incentives and social capital: Are homeowners better citizens? *Journal of Urban Economics*, 45, 354–384.

DiPrete, Thomas A., and K. Lynn Nonnemaker. (1997). Structural change, labor market turbulence, and labor market outcomes. *American Sociological Review*, 62, 386–404.

Djilas, Milovan. (1965). *The new class*. New York: Praeger.

Dobash, Russell P., R. Emerson Dobash, Margo Wilson, et al. (2005). The myth of sexual symmetry in marital violence. pp. 31–55 in Claire M. Renzetti and Raquel Kennedy Bergen (eds.), *Violence against women*. Lanham, MD: Rowman & Littlefield.

Dooley, David, and Joann Prause. (1998). Underemployment and alcohol misuse in the national longitudinal survey of youth. *Journal of Studies on Alcohol*, 59, 669–671.

Duncan, Greg J., W. Jean Yeung, Jeanne Brooks-Gunn, et al. (1998). How much does childhood poverty affect the life chances of children? *American Sociological Review*, 63, 406–423.

Duncan, Greg J., Johanne Boisjoly, Dan M. Levy, et al. (2003). Empathy or antipathy? The consequences of racially and socially diverse peers on attitudes and behaviors. Working Paper 326, Joint Center for Poverty Research. Evanston, IL: Northwestern University.

Durkheim, Emile. (1951 [1897]). *Suicide*. New York: Free Press.

———. (1982 [1895]). *The rules of the sociological method*. New York: Free Press.

Duverger, Maurice. (1954). *Political parties: Their organization and activity in the modern state*. New York: John Wiley.

Easterbrook, Gregg. (2003). *The progress paradox*. New York: Random House.

Easton, Barbara. (1976). Industrialization and femininity: a case study of 19th century New England. *Social Problems*, 23, 389–401.

Echenique, Federico, and Roland G. Fryer, Jr. (2005). On the measurement of segregation. Working Paper 11258. Cambridge, MA: National Bureau of Economic Research.

Edgcomb, Elaine L., and Maria Medrano Armington. (2003). *The informal economy: Latino enterprises at the margins*. Washington, DC: Aspen Institute.

Edgcomb, Elaine L., and Tamra Thetford. (2004). *The informal economy: Making it in rural America*. Washington, DC: Aspen Institute.

Edlund, Jonas. (2003). The influence of class situations of husbands and wives on class identity, party preference and attitudes toward redistribution: Sweden, Germany, and the United States. *Acta Sociologica*, 46, 195–214.

Ehrenreich, Barbara. (1990). *Fear of falling: The inner life of the middle class*. New York: HarperCollins Publishers.

———. (2001). *Nickel and dimed: On (not) getting by in America*. New York: Henry Holt & Co.

Election Assistance Commission. (2005). *The impact of the National Voter Registration Act, 2003–2004.* Washington, DC; U.S. Government Printing Office.

Electionline.org. (2006). Holding form: Voter registration 2006. www.electionline.org.

Elder, Glen, Robert Conger, Elizabeth Foster, et al. (1992). Unemployment and alcohol disorder in 1910 and 1990: Drift vs. social causation. *Journal of Occupational and Organizational Psychology, 5,* 277–290.

Elias, Norbert. (1978). *The civilizing process: The development of manners; changes in the code of conduct and feeling in early modern times.* New York: Urizen Books.

Elliott, Jane. (2005). Comparing occupational segregation in Great Britain and the United States. *Work, Employment and Society, 9,* 153–174.

Ely, Melvin Patrick. (2005). *Israel on the Appomattox: A Southern experiment in black freedom.* New York: Random House.

Engelberg, Stephen, and Deborah Sontag. (1994). Behind one agency's walls: Misbehaving and moving up. *New York Times,* National Edition. December 21, A1.

England, Paula. (1982). The failure of human capital theory to explain occupational sex segregation. *Journal of Human Resources, 17,* 358–370.

———. (1992). *Comparable worth: Theories and evidence.* New York: Aldine de Gruyter.

Erikson, Robert, and John H. Goldthorpe. (1993). *The constant flux: A study of class mobility in industrial societies.* New York: Oxford University Press.

———. (2002). Intergenerational inequality: A sociological perspective. *Journal of Economic Perspectives, 16,* 31–44.

Eurostat. (2000). Recommendations of the task force on statistics on social exclusion and poverty. Luxembourg: European Statistical Office.

———. (2005). EU labour force survey, principle results 2004. *Statistics in Focus.* Brussels: Eurostat.

Farley, Reynolds, and William H. Frey. (1994). Changes in the segregation of Whites from Blacks during the 1980s: Small steps toward a more integrated society. *American Sociological Review, 59,* 23–45.

Feather, Norman T. (1990). *The psychological impact of unemployment.* Ann Arbor, MI: Edwards Brothers.

———. (1992). Expectancy-value theory and unemployment effects. *Journal of Occupational and Organizational Psychology, 65,* 315–330.

Featherman, David L., and Robert M. Hauser. (1978). *Opportunity and change.* New York: Academic Press.

Federal Election Commission. (2006). Frequently asked questions about election day. www.fec.gov.

Feinstein, Leon. (2003). Inequality in the early cognitive development of British children in the 1970 cohort. *Economica, 70,* 73–97.

Fellowes, Matt. (2006). From poverty, opportunity: Putting the market to work for low income families. Washington, DC: Brookings Institution.

Felson, Marcus, and David Knoke. (1974). Social status and the married woman. *Journal of Marriage and Family, 36,* 63–70.

Fernandez, Roberto M., and Marie Louise Mors. (2005). Competing for jobs: Queues and gender sorting in the hiring process. Paper presented at the Annual Meetings of the American Sociological Association.

Fernandez, Roberto M., and M. Lourdes Sosa. (2005). Gendering the job: Networks and recruitment at a call center. *American Journal of Sociology, 111,* 859–904.

Ferree, Myru Marx, and Beth B. Hess. (2000). *Controversy and coalition: The new feminist movement.* New York: Routledge.

Ferrie, Joseph. (2005). The end of American exceptionalism? Mobility in the U.S. since 1850. Working Paper 11324. Cambridge, MA: National Bureau of Economic Research.

Fifield, Adam. (2001). Shopping while Black. *Good Housekeeping Magazine.* November, pp. 128–138.

Financial Markets Center. (2000). Employee stock options. *Background report: A publication of the financial markets center.* April. www.fmcenter.org.

Firebaugh, Glenn. (2003). *The new geography of global income inequality.* Cambridge, MA: Harvard University Press.

Fischer, David Hackett. (1978). *Growing old in America.* New York: Oxford University Press.

———. (1989). *Albion's seed: Four British folkways in America.* New York: Oxford University Press.

———. (1994). *Paul Revere's ride.* New York: Oxford University Press.

Fisher, Gordon M. (1997). From Hunter to Orshansky: An overview of (unofficial) poverty lines in the United States from 1904 to 1965. Poverty Measurement Working Paper, U.S. Census Bureau. Washington, DC: U.S. Government Printing Office.

———. (1998). Setting American standards of poverty: A look back. *Focus, 19*(Spring), 47–53.

Fitzgerald, F. Scott. (1954). The rich boy. pp. 317–349 in Fitzgerald, *The short stories of F. Scott Fitzgerald.* New York: Charles Scribner's Sons.

Foner, Eric. (1988). *Reconstruction, 1863–1877.* New York: Harper & Row.

———. (2005). *Forever free: The story of emancipation and reconstruction.* New York: Knopf.

Forbes, Hugh D. (1997). *Ethnic conflict: Commerce, culture, and the contact hypothesis.* New Haven, CT: Yale University Press.

———. (2004). Ethnic conflict and the contact hypothesis. pp. 69–88 in Lee, Yuch-Ting, Clark McCauley, Fathali Moghaddam, et al. (eds.), *The psychology of ethnic conflict.* New York: Praeger.

Foster, Eugene A., M.A. Jobling, P.G. Taylor, et al. (1998). Jefferson fathered slave's last child. *Nature, 396* (November 3), 27–28.

Fosu, Augustin Kwasi. (1997). Occupational gains of black women since the 1964 Civil Rights Act: Long-term or episodic? *American Economic Review, 87,* 311–315.

Fountain, John W. (2002). Team leaves white league in silence instead of cheers. *New York Times,* National Edition, p. A1.

Frank, Robert. (2004). New luxury goods set super-wealthy apart from pack. *Wall Street Journal.* December 14, p. 1.

Franklin, Benjamin. (1961). *The autobiography and other writings.* New York: New American Library.

Freeman, Richard B. (2003). What, me vote? Working Paper 9896. Cambridge, MA: National Bureau of Economic Research.

Freedman, Samuel G. (2006). Bleak housing: Alexander Polikoff describes his long legal battle to integrate Chicago's slums [review of Polikoff, 2006]. *New York Times Book Review.* March 19, p. 25.

Friedan, Betty. (1963). *The feminine mystique.* New York: Norton.

Frost-Knappman, Elizabeth, and Kathryn Cullen-DuPont (eds.). (1997). *Women's rights on trial: 101 historic trials from Anne Hutchinson to the Virginia Military Institute cadets.* Detroit: Gale.

Fryer, Bronwyn. (1999). Executive privilege: The perk that big shots don't want you to talk about. *Worth Guide to Benefits, Compensation, and Perks. 8*(Winter), 71–72.

Fussell, Paul. (1983). *Class: A guide through the American status system.* New York: Ballantine.

Gagliani, Giorgio. (1981). How many working classes? *American Journal of Sociology, 87,* 259–285.

Galbraith, John Kenneth. (1992). *The culture of contentment.* New York: Houghton Mifflin.

Gallman, Robert E. (1969). Trends in the size distribution of wealth in the 19th century. In Lee Soltow (ed.), *Six papers on the size distribution of wealth and income.* New York: Columbia University Press.

Gallo, William T., Elizabeth H. Bradley, Michelle Siegel, et al. (2001). The impact of involuntary job loss on subsequent alcohol consumption by older workers. *The Journals of Gerontology, Series B 56*, S3–10.

Gallup Poll. (1994). *The Gallup poll: Public opinion 1993*. Wilmington, DE: Scholarly Resources.

———. (1997). Black/white relations in the U.S. http://www.gallup.com.

———. (2001). *The nine weeks of election 2000*. Wilmington, DE: Scholarly Resources.

Galster, George, and Erin Godfrey. (2005). By word and deeds: Racial steering by real estate agents in the U.S. in 2000. *Journal of the American Planning Association, 71*, 251–268.

Gamson, William A. (1975). *The strategy of protest*. Homewood, IL: Dorsey Press.

Gans, Herbert. (1972). The positive functions of poverty. *American Journal of Sociology, 78*, 275–289.

———. (2006). Race as class. *Contacts, 4*, 17–21.

Garland, Hamlin. (1917). *A son of the middle border*. New York: Macmillan.

———. (1995). *The main travelled roads*. Lincoln, NE: University of Nebraska Press.

Garner, Thesia I., Kathleen Short, Stephanie Shipp, et al. (1998). Experimental poverty measurement for the 1990s. *Monthly Labor Review, 121*(March), 39–45.

Garrow, David. (1986). *Bearing the cross: Martin Luther King, Jr., and the Southern Christian Leadership Congress*. New York: William Morrow.

Gatrell, V.A.C. (1994). *The hanging tree: Executions and the English people, 1770–1868*. New York: Oxford University Press.

Gelles, Richard. (1990). *Intimate violence in families*. Newbury Park, CA: Sage.

General Social Survey. (2004). *GSS 1972–2004 cumulative datafile*. Chicago: National Opinion Research Corporation.

Glaeser, Edward L., Eric A. Hanashek, and John M. Quigley. (2004). Opportunities, race, and urban location: The influence of John Kain. NBER Working Paper 10312. Cambridge, MA: National Bureau of Economic Research.

Glick, Peter. (1995). Images of occupations: Components of gender and status in occupational stereotypes. *Sex Roles, 32*, 565–583.

Glyptis, Sue. (1989). *Leisure and unemployment*. Philadelphia: Open University Press.

Golden, Daniel. *The price of admission: How America's ruling class buys its way into elite colleges—and who gets left outside the gates*. New York: Crown Publishers.

Goldin, Claudia. (1990). *Understanding the gender gap: An economic history of American women*. New York: Oxford University Press.

———. (2004). From the valley to the summit: The quiet revolution that transformed women's work. Working Paper 10335. Cambridge, MA: National Bureau of Economic Research.

Goldin, Claudia, and Cecilia Rouse. (2000). Orchestrating impartiality: The impact of "blind" auditions on female musicians. *American Economic Review, 90*, 715–742.

Goldthorpe, John. *The affluent worker in the class structure*. New York: Cambridge University Press.

Goode, William J. (1973). Functionalism: The empty castle. pp. 64–96 in W.J. Goode, *Explorations in social theory*. New York: Oxford University Press.

Gordon, David M. (1996). *Fat and mean: The corporate squeeze of working Americans and the myth of managerial "downsizing."* New York: Free Press.

Gordon-Reed, Annette. (1997). *Thomas Jefferson and Sally Hemings: An American controversy*. Charlottesville, VA: University Press of Virginia.

Gosnell, Harold F. (1927). *Getting out the vote: An experiment in the stimulation of voting*. Chicago: University of Chicago Press.

Gottschalk, Peter, Björn Gustafsson, and Edward Palmer. (1997). What's behind the increase in inequality? pp. 1–11 in P. Gottschalk, B. Gustafsson, and E. Palmer (eds.), *Changing patterns in the distribution of economic welfare*. Cambridge: Cambridge University Press.

Graetz, Michael J., and Ian Shapiro. (2005). *Death by a thousand cuts: The fight over taxing inherited wealth*. Princeton, NJ: Princeton University Press.

Graham, Lawrence Otis. (1995). *Member of the club*. New York: Harper & Row.

Granovetter, Mark. (1995). *Getting a job: A study in contacts and careers, 2nd edition*. Chicago: University of Chicago Press.

Graybill, Wilson H., Clyde V. Kiser, and Pascal K. Whelpton. (1958). *The fertility of American women*. New York: Wiley.

Green, John, Paul Hermson, Lynda Powell, et al. (1998). Individual Congressional campaign contributors: Wealthy, conservative, and reform minded. www.opensecrets.org.

Green, Richard K., and Michelle White. (1997). Measuring the benefits of homeownership: The effects on children. *Journal of Urban Economics, 41*, 441–461.

Greenstein, Theodore N., and Shannon N. Davis. (2006). Cross-national variations in divorce: Effects of women's power, prestige, and dependence. *Journal of Comparative Family Studies, 37*, 253–273.

Greven, Philip. (1991). *Spare the child: The religious roots of punishment and the psychological impact of physical abuse*. New York: Knopf.

Grimsrud, Tom K., Steiner R. Berge, Tor Haldorsen, et al. (2002). Exposure to different forms of nickel and risk of lung cancer. *American Journal of Epidemiology, 156*, 12–13.

Gross, Daniel. (2006). Painting for profit: Is art a good investment? *Slate Magazine*. June 21. www.slate.com.

Grusky, David B., and Jesper B. Sørensen. (1998). Can class analysis be salvaged? *American Journal of Sociology, 103*, 1187–1234.

Grusky, David B., and Kim A. Weeden. (2001). Decomposition without death: A research agenda for a new class analysis. *Acta Sociologica, 44*, 201–218.

Hacker, Andrew. (1992). *Two nations: Black and white, separate, hostile, unequal*. New York: Scribners.

Hagedorn, John. (1998). *The business of drug dealing in Milwaukee*. Titusville, WI: Wisconsin Policy Research Institute.

Hale, Edward Everett. (1903). Old age pensions. *Cosmopolitan, 35*, 168–169.

Harms, Robert. (2001). *The diligent: A voyage through the worlds of the slave trade*. New York: Basic Books.

Harper, Shannon, and Barbara Reskin. (2005). Affirmative action at school and on the job. *Annual Review of Sociology, 31*, 357–379.

Harris, Patrick M. (2006). Nonfatal occupational injuries involving the eyes, 2004. *Compensation and Working Conditions Online*. Bureau of Labor Statistics: www.bls.gov.

Hauser, Robert M. (1975). Structural changes in occupational mobility: Evidence for men in the United States. *American Sociological Review, 40*, 585–598.

Haveman, Robert, and Barbara Wolfe. (1995). The determinants of children's attainments: A review of methods and findings. *Journal of Economic Literature, 33*, 1829–1878.

Hayes, Sam. W., and Christopher Morris (eds.). (1997). *Manifest Destiny and empire: American antebellum expansionism*. College Station, TX: Texas A & M Press.

Heath, Anthony, and Clive Payne. (2000). Social mobility. pp. 254–278 in A. H. Halsey and Josephine Webb (eds.), *Twentieth century British social trends*. New York: St. Martin's Press.

Heffetz, Ori. (2005). Who sees what? Demographics and the visibility of consumer expenditures. Unpublished Working Paper. Ithaca New York: Department of Economics, Cornell University.

Heilbroner, Robert L., and Lester C. Thurow. (1982). *Economics explained*. Englewood Cliffs, NJ: Prentice Hall.

Helgeson, Baird, and Mary Shedden. (2005). Wal-Mart accused of racism. *Tampa Tribune*. December 3, p. A-1.

Heller, Joseph. (1961). *Catch-22: A novel*. New York: Simon & Schuster.

Herbert, Bob. (1998). Mounting a war on bias. *New York Times*, National Edition. January 18, p. A-21.

———. (2005). A new Civil Rights Movement. *New York Times*, National Edition. December 26, p. A-20.

Herman, Judith Lewis. (1981). *Father-daughter incest*. Cambridge, MA: Harvard University Press.

———. (1989). Wife beating. *Harvard Mental Health Newsletter. 5*(April), 4–6.

———. (1992). *Trauma and recovery*. New York: Basic Books.

Hertz, Tom. (2005). Rags, riches, and race: The intergenerational mobility of black and white families in the United States. pp. 165–192 in Samuel Bowles, Herbert Gintis, and Melissa Osborne Groves (eds.), *Unequal chances: Family background and economic success*. New York: Russell Sage.

Hertzberg, Vicki S., Kenneth D. Rosenman, Mary Jo Reilly, et al. (2002). Effect of occupational sillica exposure on pulmonary function. *Chest, 122*, 721–729

Hibbs, Douglas A. (1977). Political parties and macroeconomic policy. *American Political Science Review, 71*, 1467–1487.

Higley, Stephen Richard. (1995). *Privilege, power, and place: The geography of the American upper class*. Lanham, MD: Rowman & Littlefield.

Hill, Catherine, and Elena Silva. (2005). *Drawing the line: Sexual harassment on campus*. Washington, DC: American Association of University Women.

Hiro, Dilip. (1991). *Black British, White British: A history of race relations in Britain*. London: Grafton.

Hirsch, Arnold R. (1983). *Making the second ghetto: Race and housing in Chicago, 1940–1960*. New York: Cambridge University Press.

Hochschild, Jennifer. (1981). *What's fair? American beliefs about distributive justice*. Cambridge, MA: Harvard University Press.

———. (1995). *Facing up to the American dream*. Princeton, NJ: Princeton University Press.

Holmes, William F. (1969). Whitecapping: Agrarian violence in Mississippi, 1902–1906. *Journal of Southern History, 35*, 165–185.

———. (1973). Whitecapping in Mississippi: Agrarian violence in the populist era. *Mid-America, 55*, 134–148.

Holzer, Harry, and David Neumark. (2000). Assessing affirmative action, *Journal of Economic Literature, 38*, 483–568.

Hout, Michael. (1988). More universalism, less structural mobility: The American occupational structure in the 1980s. *American Journal of Sociology, 93*, 1358–1400.

Hout, Michael, and William R. Morgan. (1975). Race and sex variations in the causes of the expected attainments of high school seniors. *American Journal of Sociology, 81*, 364–394.

Hyman, Herbert. (1942). The psychology of status. *Archives of Psychology*, No. 269.

Iceland, John. (2006). *Poverty in America: A handbook, 2nd Edition*. Berkeley, CA: University of California Press.

Inland Revenue. (2003). Personal wealth [in the United Kingdom]. www.inlandrevenue.gov.uk/stats/personal_wealth/dopw_t04.

Inniss, Leslie. (1992). The black "underclass" ideology in race relations analysis. *Social Justice, 16*, 13–34.

Institute on Taxation and Economic Policy. (2003). *Who pays? A distributional analysis of the tax systems in all 50 states, 2nd edition*. www.itepnet.org.

———. (2005). *Tax expenditures: Spending by another name*. Policy Brief #4. Washington, DC: Institute for Tax Policy.

———. (2006). *Tax principles: Building blocks of a sound tax system*. Policy Brief #9. Washington, DC: Institute for Tax Policy.

Internal Revenue Service. (2006). *2006 Federal tax rate schedule*. www.irs.gov.

International Institute for Democracy and Electoral Assistance. (2005). *Electoral system design: The new IDEA handbook*. Stockholm: International Institute for Democracy and Electoral Assistance.

———. (2006). www.idea.int/vt/country_view.cfm.

International Labour Office. (2004). *Breaking through the glass ceiling: Women in management*. Geneva: International Labour Office.

Jackman, Mary R., and Robert W. Jackman. (1983). *Class awareness in the United States*. Berkeley, CA: University of California Press.

Jacobs, Janet Liebman. (1994). *Victimized daughters: Incest and the development of the female self*. New York: Routledge.

Jacobs, Jerry A. (1990). *Revolving doors: Sex segregation and women's careers*. Stanford, CA: Stanford University Press.

Jacobs, David, and Katherine Wood. (1999). Interracial conflict and interracial homicide: Do political and economic rivalries explain white killings of blacks or black killings of whites? *American Journal of Sociology, 105*, 157–190.

Jaffe, A. J. (1940). Differential fertility in the white population in early America. *Journal of Heredity, 31*, 407–411.

Jaimes, Annette M. (1992). Federal Indian identification policy: A usurpation of indigenous sovereignty in North America. pp. 113–135 in Fremont Lyden and Lyman Legters (eds.), *Native Americans and public policy*. Pittsburgh: University of Pittsburgh Press.

Jaynes, Gerald David, and Robin M. Williams. (1989). *A common destiny: Blacks and American society*. Washington, DC: National Academy Press.

Jefferson, Thomas. (1999). *Notes on the state of Virginia*. New York: Penguin Books.

Jencks, Christopher S. (1979). *Who gets ahead: The determinants of economic success in America*. New York: Basic Books.

Johansen, Christoffer, Maria Feychting, Mogens Moller, et al. (2002). Risk of severe cardiac arrhythmia in male utility workers. *American Journal of Epidemiology, 156*, 857–862.

Johnson, Barry W., and Brian G. Raub. (2006). Personal wealth, 2001. *SOI Bulletin 26*, 120–146.

Johnston, David Cay. (2003). *Perfectly legal: The covert campaign to rig our tax system to benefit the super rich—and cheat everybody else*. New York: Penguin.

Joint Committee on Taxation. (2006). *Estimates of Federal tax expenditures for fiscal years 2006–2010*. Washington, DC: U.S. Government Printing Office.

Justice Policy Institute. (2004). *Cellblocks or classrooms?: The funding of higher education and corrections and its impact on African American men*. Washington, DC: Justice Policy Institute.

Kain, John F. (1968). Housing segregation, Negro employment, and metropolitan decentralization. *Quarterly Journal of Economics, 82*, 165–197.

Kanter, Rosabeth Moss. (1978). Some effects of proportion on group life: Skewed sex ratios and responses to token women. *American Journal of Sociology, 82*, 965–990.

Kasarda, John. (1990). Structural factors affecting the location and timing of urban underclass growth. *Urban Geography, 11*, 234–264.

———. (1995). Industrial restructuring and the changing location of jobs. pp. 215–265 in Reynolds Farley (ed.), *State of the Union: America in the 1990s*. New York: Russell Sage.

———. (2000). Urban underclass. pp. 345–355 in *Encyclopedia of sociology*. New York: Macmillan.

Katt, Peter. (1997). A reality check: Do you need to buy long-term care insurance? *AAII Journal 19*(November), 2–4.

Katznelson, Ira. (2005). *When affirmative action was white*. New York: W.W. Norton.

Kaufman, Gayle, and Peter Uhlenberg. (2000). The influence of parenthood on the work effort of married men and women. *Social Forces, 78*, 931–951.

Kavanagh, Brian. (2005). *Ten years later: A promise unfulfilled. The National Voter Registration Act in public assistance agencies, 1995–2005*. New York: Demos: A Network for Ideas and Action.

Keister, Lisa A. (2005). *Getting rich: America's new rich and how they got that way*. New York: Cambridge University Press.

Keister, Lisa A., and Stephanie Moller. (2000). Wealth inequality in the United States. *Annual Review of Sociology, 26*, 63–81.

Kendall, Diana. (2006). Class in the United States: Not only alive but reproducing. *Research in Stratification and Mobility, 24*, 89–104.

Kennedy, Stetson. (1995). *After Appomattox: How the South won the war*. Gainesville, FL: University Press of Florida.

Kennickell, Arthur B. (2003). A rolling tide: Changes in the distribution of wealth in the U.S., 1989–2001. Washington, DC: Federal Reserve Board.

Kenworthy, Lane. (1995). Equality and efficiency: The illusory tradeoff. *European Journal of Political Research, 27*, 225–254.

Key, V.O. (1949). *Southern politics in state and nation*. New York: Vintage Books.

Keyssar, Alexander. (2000). *The right to vote: The contested history of democracy in the United States*. New York: Basic Books.

Khan, Shaila, Robert P. Murray, and Gordon E. Barnes. (2002). A structural equation model of the effect of poverty and unemployment on alcohol abuse. *Addictive Behaviors, 27*, 405–423.

King, Mary C. (1992). Occupational segregation by race and sex, 1940–1988. *Monthly Labor Review, 115*(April), 30–36.

Kingston, Paul W. (2000). *The classless society*. Stanford, CA: Stanford University Press.

Kinzie, Susan, and Joshua Partlow. (2004). Storage unit as shelter not unique, workers say: Girls found in Md. shed spotlight housing woes. *Washington Post*, November 24, p. A-1.

Kitsantas, Panagiora, Anastasia Kitsantas, and H. Richard Travis. (2000). Occupational exposures and associated health effects among sanitation landfill employees. *Journal of Environmental Health, 63*, 17–23.

Klebanov, Pamela K., Jeanne Brooks-Gunn, Cecelia McCarton, et al. (1998). The contribution of neighborhood and family income to developmental test scores over the first three years of life. *Child Development, 69*, 1420–1436.

Kleiner, Morris M. (2006). *Licensing occupations: Ensuring quality or restricting competition?* Kalamazoo, MI: W.E. Upjohn Institute.

Kohn, Melvin. (1987). Cross-national research as an analytic strategy. *American Sociological Review, 52*, 713–731.

Kolko, Gabriel. (1962). *Wealth and power in America*. New York: Praeger.

Komarovsky, Mira. (1940). *The unemployed man and his family*. New York: Octagon Books.

Korupp, Sylvia E., Karin Sanders, and Harry B.G. Ganzeboom. (2002). The intergenerational transmission of occupational status and sex-typing at children's labour market entry. *European Journal of Women's Studies, 9*, 7–29.

Kozol, Jonathan. (2005). *The shame of the nation: The restoration of apartheid schooling*. New York: Crown.

Krueger, Alan. (2005). The U.N. aims to cut poverty in half, even as the experts wonder how to measure it. *New York Times*, National Edition. February 3, p. C2.

Krugman, Paul. (1995). What the public doesn't know can't hurt us. *Washington Monthly, 27*(October), 8–12.

———. (2003). Still blowing bubbles. *New York Times*, National Edition. June 20, A-18.

Krymkowski, Daniel H. (1991). The process of status attainment in Poland, the U.S., and West Germany. *American Sociological Review 56*, 46–59.

Krysan, Maria. (2002). *Recent trends in racial attitudes: A 2002 update for the 1997 book, racial attitudes in America*. http://tigger.cc.uic.edu.

Kumar, Krishan. (1988). *The rise of modern society*. New York: Blackwell.

Kuznets, Simon. (1955). Economic growth and income inequality. *American Economic Review, 45*, 1–28.

Lake, Celinda, and Robert L. Borosage. (2000). Voters and donors agree: In Washington big business' clout is growing. *The Nation*. August 21, p. 29.

Lareau, Annette. (1989). *Home advantage: Social class and parental education in elementary education*. Philadephia: Falmer Press.

Lazarsfeld, Paul, and Robert K. Merton. (1954). Friendship as a social process: A substantive and methodological analysis. pp. 18–66 in Morroe Berger, Theodore Abel, and Charles H. Page (eds.), *Freedom and control in modern society*. New York: Van Nostrand.

Lee, David J., William LeBlanc, Lora Fleming, et al. (2004). Trends in U.S. smoking rates in occupational groups: The national health interview survey, 1987–1994. *Journal of Occupational and Environmental Medicine, 46*, 538–548.

Lemann, Nicholas. (1992). *The Promised land: The great black migration and how it changed America*. New York: Vintage.

———. (2006). *Redemption: The last battle of the civil war*. New York: Farrar, Straus & Giroux.

LeMasters, E.E. (1976). *Blue collar aristocrats*. Madison, WI: University of Wisconsin Press.

Lenski, Gerhard. (1984). *Power and privilege*. Chapel Hill, NC: University of North Carolina Press.

Lenton, Robert L. (1990). Techniques of child discipline and abuse by parents. *Canadian Review of Sociology and Anthropology, 27*, 157–185.

Leonhardt, David. (2006). Political clout in the age of outsourcing. *New York Times*, National Edition. April 19, p.B-1.

Levitt, Steven D., and Sudhir Alladi Vankatesh. (2000). An economic analysis of a drug-selling gang's finances. *Quarterly Journal of Economics, 115*, 755–775.

Levy, Andrew. (2005). *The first emancipator: The forgotten story of Robert Carter, the founding father who freed his slaves*. New York: Random House.

Levy, Frank, Ari Goelman, and Kyoung-Hee Yu. (2006). Paging Dr. Gupta: Radiology as a case study in sending skilled jobs offshore. *The Milken Institute Review, 8*(June), 64–72.

Levy, Frank, and Richard J. Murnane. (1992). U.S. earnings levels and earnings inequality: A review of recent trends and proposed explanations. *Journal of Economic Literature, 30*, 1333–1381.

Lewis, Anthony. (2006). Uneasy allies [review of *At Canaan's edge*, by Taylor Branch]. *New York Times Book Review*. February 5, p. 1.

Lewis, Joy H., Ronald M. Andersen, and Lillian Gelberg. (2003). Health care for homeless women: Unmet needs and barriers to care. *Journal of General Internal Medicine, 18*, 921–928.

Liang, H.W., S.T. Hsieh, T.J. Cheng, et al. (2006). Reduced epidermal nerve density among hand-transmitted vibration-exposed workers. *Journal of Occupational and Environmental Medicine, 48*, 549–555.

Liao, Y.H., L.C. Hwang, J.S. Kao, et al. (2006). Lipid peroxidation in workers exposed to aluminum, galium, indium, arsenic, and antimony in the optoelectric industry. *Journal of Occupational and Environmental Medicine, 48*, 789–793.

Library of America. (2003). *Reporting Civil Rights*. New York: Library of America.

Lieberson, Stanley. (1980). *A piece of the pie: Blacks and white immigrants since 1880*. Berkeley, CA: University of California Press.

———. (1992). Einstein, Renoir, and Greeley: Some thoughts about evidence in sociology. *American Sociological Review, 57*, 1–15.

Lijphart, Arend. (1997). Unequal participation: Democracy's unresolved dilemma. *American Political Science Review, 91*, 1–14.

Liker, Jeffrey K., and Glen H. Elder, Jr. (1983). Economic hardship and marital relations in the 1930s. *American Sociological Review, 48*, 343–359.

Limerick, Patricia Nelson. (1995). Turnerians all: The dream of a helpful history in an intelligible world. *American Historical Review, 100*, 697–717.

Lin, Nan. (1999). Social networks and status attainment. *Annual Review of Sociology, 25*, 467–487.

————. 2000. Inequality of social capital. *Contemporary Sociology*, 29, 785–795.

Lipset, Seymour Martin. (1963). *The first new nation: The United States in historical and comparative perspective*. New York: Basic Books.

————. (1977). Why no socialism in the United States? pp. 31–149 in S. Bialer and S. Sluzar (eds.), *Sources of contemporary radicalism*. New York: Westview Press.

Lloyd, Susan. (1998). Domestic violence and women's employment. *NU policy research: An electronic journal of the institute for policy research at Northwestern University*. http:www.nwu.edu/ipr/publications 3(Spring), 1–10.

Loewen, James W. (2005). *Sundown towns: A hidden dimension of American racism*. New York: New Press.

Long, Jason, and Joseph Ferrie. (2005). A tale of two labor markets: Intergenerational occupational mobility in Britain and the U.S. since 1850. Working Paper 11253. Cambridge, MA: National Bureau of Economic Research.

Losby, Jan L., Marcia E. Kingslow, and John F. Else. (2003). *The informal economy: Experiences of African Americans*. Washington, DC: Institute for Social and Economic Development Solutions.

Loughlin, Sean, and Robert Yoon. (2003). Millionaires populate U.S. Senate. CNN.Com/Inside Politics. June 13. www.cnn.com.

Loury, Glenn C. (2002). *The anatomy of racial inequality*. Cambridge, MA: Harvard University Press.

Lovell, Vicky. (2004). No time to be sick: Why everyone suffers when workers don't have paid sick leave. *IWPR Publication #B242p*. Washington, DC: Institute for Women's Policy Research.

Lowenstein, Roger. (2005). We regret to inform you that you no longer have a pension. *New York Times Magazine*, October 30, 56–88.

Lueck, Thomas J. (1999). New York's cabbies show how multicolored racism can be. *New York Times*, National Edition. November 7, p. C-3.

Luker, Kristin. (1984). *Abortion and the politics of motherhood*. Berkeley, CA: University of California Press.

————. (1996). *Dubious conceptions: The politics of teenage pregnancy*. Cambridge, MA: Harvard University Press.

Lynd, Robert S. (1929). *Middletown: A study in contemporary American culture*. New York: Harcourt, Brace, and Company.

Lynd, Robert S., and Helen Merrill Lynd. (1937). *Middletown in transition: A study in cultural conflicts*. New York: Harcourt, Brace, and Company.

MacKinnon, Catherine. (1979). *Sexual harassment of working women: A case of sex discrimination*. New Haven, CT: Yale University Press.

MacKinnon, Neil J., and Tom Langford. (1994). The meaning of occupational prestige scores. *Sociological Quarterly*, 35, 215–245.

Mahler, Vincent A. (2002). Exploring the subnational dimension of income inequality: An analysis of the relationship between inequality and electoral turnout in the developed countries. *International Studies Quarterly*, 46, 117–142.

Maier, Pauline. (1997). *American scripture: Making the Declaration of Independence*. New York: Knopf.

Main, Jackson Turner. (1965). *Social structure in revolutionary America*. Princeton, NJ: Princeton University Press.

Mann, Charles C. (2002). 1491. *The Atlantic Monthly* March, 41–53.

————. (2005). *1491: New revelations of the Americas before Columbus*. New York: Knopf.

Marquis, Don. (1989). Why abortion is immoral. *Journal of Philosophy*, 86, 183–202.

Marsiglio, William. (1993). Adolescent male's orientation toward paternity and contraception. *Family Planning Perspectives*, 25(January/February), 22–31.

Marston, Cicely, and John Cleland. (2003). Relationships between contraception and abortion: A review of the evidence. *International Family Planning Perspectives*, 29, 6–13.

Martinez, Michael D., and David Hill. (1999). Did motor voter work? *American Politics Quarterly*, 27, 296–315.

Marx, Karl. (1956 [1875]). Critique of the Gotha Program. pp. 9–30 in Karl Marx and Friedrich Engels, *Selected works, Volume III*. Moscow: Progress Publishers.

————. (1967 [1867]). *Capital*. New York: International.

————. (1978 [1843]). A contribution to the critique of Hegel's philosophy of right. pp. 53–66 in Robert C. Tucker (ed.), *The Marx-Engels reader*. New York: Norton.

Marx, Karl, and Friedrich Engels. (1971 [1848]). The communist manifesto. pp. 85–126 in Dirk Struik (ed.), *The birth of the communist manifesto*. New York: International.

Massey, Douglas S. (1995). Getting away with murder: Segregation and violent crime in urban America. *University of Pennsylvania Law Review*, 143, 1203–1232.

————. (2001). Residential segregation and neighborhood conditions in U.S. metropolitan areas. pp. 391–434 in Neil Smelser, William Julius Wilson, and Faith Mitchell (eds.), *America becoming: Racial trends and their consequences, Volume I*. Washington, DC: National Academy Press.

Massey, Douglas S., and Nancy A. Denton. (1993). *American apartheid: Segregation and the making of the underclass*. Cambridge, MA: Harvard University Press.

Massey, Douglas S., and Mary J. Fischer. (2000). How segregation concentrates poverty. *Ethnic and Racial Studies*, 23, 670–691.

Mauer, Marc, and Tushar Kansal. (2005). *Barred for life: Voting rights restoration in permanent disenfranchisement states*. Washington, DC: The Sentencing Project.

Mayer, Susan E. (1997). *What money can't buy: Family income and children's life chances*. Cambridge, MA: Harvard University Press.

————. (2001). How did the increase in economic inequality between 1970 and 1990 affect children's educational attainment? *American Journal of Sociology*, 107, 1–32.

Mayer, Susan E., and Paul E. Peterson (eds.). (1999). *Earning and learning: How schools matter*. New York: Russell Sage Foundation.

McBrier, Debra Branch, and George Wilson. (2004). Going down? Race and downward occupational mobility for white-collar workers in the 1990s. *Work and Occupations*, 31, 283–322.

McIntosh, Peggy. (2000). White privilege and male privilege: A personal account of coming to see correspondences through work in women's studies. pp. 30–38 in Anne Minas (ed.), *Gender basics, 2nd Edition*. Belmont, CA: Wadsworth.

McNamee, Stephen J., and Robert K. Miller, Jr. (2004). *The meritocracy myth*. Lanham, MD: Rowman & Littlefield.

McNeil, Donald G., Jr. (2004). Real men don't clean bathrooms. *New York Times*, National Edition. September 19, p. wk-3.

McPherson, Michael S., and Morton Owen Schapiro. (1998). *The student aid game: Meeting need and rewarding talent in American higher education*. Princeton, NJ: Princeton University Press.

McPherson, Miller, Lynn Smith-Lovin, and James M. Cook. (2001). Birds of a feather: Homophily in social networks. *Annual Review of Sociology*, 27, 415–444.

McRae, Courtney. (2006). More states move to automatically restore ex-felon voting rights. *Election Line Weekly* August 3. www.electionline.org.

McWhorter, Diane. (2001). *Carry me home: Birmingham, Alabama: The climactic battle of the Civil Rights revolution*. New York: Simon & Schuster.

Medley, Keith Weldon. (2005). *We as freemen: Plessey v. Ferguson*. Gretna, LA: Pelican.

Meeks, Kenneth. (2000). *Driving while black: Highways, shopping malls, taxicabs, and sidewalks*. New York: Broadway Books.

Mei/Moses Fine Art Index. (2006). New Mei/Moses annual art index vs. total return S & P 500 since 1954. www.meimosesfineartindex.org.

Mellon, Andrew W. (1924). *Taxation: The people's business*. New York: Macmillan.

Mellor, William H. (1996). No jobs, no work: Local restrictions block the exits from welfare. *New York Times*, National Edition. August 31, p. A-12.

Mencken, F. Carson, and Idee Winfield. (2000). Job search and sex segregation. *Sex Roles, 31*, 847–862.

Merton, Robert K. (1968). *Social theory and social structure*. New York: Free Press.

———. (1968a). Social structure and anomie. pp. 185–214 in R.K. Merton, *Social theory and social structure*. New York: Free Press.

Merton, Robert K., and Alice S. Rossi. (1968). Contributions to the theory of reference group behavior. pp. 279–334 in R.K. Merton, *Social theory and social structure*. New York: Free Press.

Meyer, D.R., and Maria Cancian. (1996). The economic well-being of women and children following an exit from AFDC. *Discussion Paper 1101–1196*. Madison, WI: Institute for Research on Poverty.

Meyer, Samuel W., and Stephen M. Pegula. (2006). Injuries, illnesses, and fatalities in construction, 2004. *Compensation and working conditions online*. Bureau of Labor Statistics: www.bls.gov.

Miller, Arthur. (1996). *Death of a salesman*. New York: Penguin Books.

Miller, N. (2002). Personalization and the promise of contact theory. *Journal of Social Issues, 58*, 387–410.

Mills, C. Wright. (1951). *White collar*. New York: Oxford University Press.

———. (1959). *The Sociological Imagination*. New York: Oxford University Press.

Minnite, Lori, and David Callahan. (2003). *Securing the vote: An analysis of election fraud*. New York: Demos—A Network for Ideas and Action.

Mitchell, Alison. (1998). A new form of lobbying puts public face on private interest. *New York Times*, National Edition. September 30, 1.

Mitchell, Daniel J. B. (1992). "Employers" welfare work: A 1913 BLS report. *Monthly Labor Review, 115*(February), 52–55.

Mohr, John, and Paul DiMaggio. (1995). The intergenerational transmission of cultural capital. *Research in Social Stratification, 14*, 167–199.

Molnar, Beth E., Stephen L. Buka, and Ronald C. Kessler. (2001). Child sexual abuse and subsequent psychopathology. *American Journal of Public Health 91*, 753–783.

Monmonier, Mark. (2001). *Bushmanders and Bullwinkles: How politicians manipulate electronic maps and census data to win elections*. Chicago: University of Chicago Press.

Morgan, Dan. (2006). Farm program pays $1.3 billion to people who don't farm. *Washington Post*, July 2, p. A-1.

Morgan, Philip D. (1998). *Slave counterpoint: Black culture in the eighteenth century Chesapeake and low country*. Chapel Hill, NC: University of North Carolina Press.

Morgenson, Gretchen. (2002). Pipeline to a point man: A friend on Main St., or Wall St.? *New York Times*, National Edition. November 3, p. C-1.

Moskovitz, Marina. (2004). *Standard of living: The measure of the middle class in modern America*. Baltimore, MD: Johns Hopkins University Press.

Mouw, Ted. (2000). Job relocation and the racial gap in unemployment in Detroit and Chicago, 1980 to 1990. *American Sociological Review, 65*, 730–753.

Murphy, Gregory C., and James A. Athanasou. (1999). The effect of unemployment on mental health. *Journal of Occupational and Organizational Psychology, 72*, 83–85.

Myrdal, Gunnar. (1944). *An American dilemma*. New York: Harper & Row.

Naidoo, Rajen N., Thomas G. Robins, Noah Seixas, et al. (2006). Respirable coal dust exposure and respiratory symptoms in South-African coal miners: A comparison of current and ex-miners. *Journal of Occupational and Environmental Medicine, 48*, 581–590.

Nakanishi, Don T. (2001). Political trends and electoral issues of the Asian Pacific American population. pp. 170–199 in Neil Smelser, William Julius Wilson, and Faith Mitchell (eds.), *America becoming: Racial trends and their consequences, Volume I*. Washington, DC: National Academy Press.

Nakao, Keiko, and Judith Treas. (1994). Updating occupational prestige and socioeconomic scores: How the new measures measure up. pp. 1–72 in Peter V. Marsden (ed.), *Sociological methodology*. Washington, DC: American Sociological Association.

National Center for Health Statistics. (2005). *Health United States, 2005*. Washington, D.C.: U.S. Government Printing Office. Hyattsville, MD: Centers for Disease Control.

———. (2005a). Deaths: Leading causes for 2002. *National Vital Statistics Reports, 53*, Number 17. Hyattsville, MD: Centers for Disease Control.

National Center for Victims of Crime. (1992). *Rape in America: A report to the nation*. Washington, DC: National Center for Victims of Crime.

National Coalition for the Homeless. (2006). *How many people experience homelessness?* Washington, DC: National Coalition for the Homeless.

———. (2006a). *Who is homeless?* Washington, DC: National Coalition for the Homeless.

———. (2006b). *The McKinney-Vento Act*. Washington, DC: National Coalition for the Homeless.

National Institute of Justice. (2000). *Extent, nature, and consequences of intimate partner violence*. Washington, DC: U.S. Government Printing Office.

———. (2006). Extent, nature, and consequences of rape victimization: Findings from the National Violence Against Women Survey. *NIJ Special Report*, January. Washington, DC: U.S. Government Printing Office.

National Research Council. (2004). *Measuring racial discrimination*. Washington, D.C.: National Academies Press.

Neumark, David M., Roy J. Bank, and Kyle D. Van Nort. (1996). Sex discrimination in restaurant hiring: An audit study. *Quarterly Journal of Economics, 111*, 915–941.

Niebuhr, Gustave. (1998). Southern Baptists declare wife should "submit" to her husband. *New York Times*, National Edition. June 10, p. 1.

Nielsen, François, and Arthur S. Alderson. (1997). The Kuznets Curve and the Great U-Turn: Income inequality in U.S. counties, 1970 to 1990. *American Sociological Review, 62*, 12–33.

Niemi, Richard. (1989). *Trends in public opinion: A compendium of survey data*. New York: Greenwood Press.

Norden, Lawrence, Jeremy M. Creelan, David Kimball, et al. (2006). *The machinery of democracy: Usability of voting systems*. New York: Brennan Center for Justice at NYU School of Law.

Nordheimer, Jon. (1996). One day's death toll on the job. *New York Times*, National Edition. December 22, 3–1.

Oakes, Jeannie. (1985). *Keeping track: How schools structure inequality*. New Haven, CT: Yale University Press.

O'Brien, Timothy L. (2006). Fortune's fools: Why the rich go broke. *New York Times*, National Edition. September 17, p. A-1.

Office of National Statistics. (2005). *Annual Labour Force Survey, 2001/2002*. www.statistics.gov.uk.

———. (2005a). *UK 2005: The official yearbook of the United Kingdom*. London: Office of National Statistics.

Okun, Arthur M. (1975). *Equality and efficiency: The big tradeoff*. Washington, DC: Brookings Institution.

Ondich, Jan, Stephen Ross, and John Yinger. (2003). Now you see it, now you don't: Why do real estate agents withhold available houses from black customers? *Review of Economics and Statistics, 85*, 854–873.

O'Neill, William L. (1972). *Women at work, including "The long day: The story of a New York working girl, by Dorothy Richardson."* Chicago: Quadrangle Books.

Open Secrets. (2006). *The big picture, 2004.* www.opensecrets.org.

Orfield, Gary. (2001). *Schools more separate: Consequences of a decade of resegregation.* Cambridge, MA: The Civil Rights Project, Harvard University.

Ornstein, Norman. (2006). Vote—or else. *New York Times,* National Edition. August 10, p. A-23.

Orr, Tamra B. (2000). Avoiding job-related injuries. *Current Health, 26*, 28–33.

Orshansky, Mollie. (1965). Counting the poor: Another look at the poverty profile. *Social Security Bulletin, 28*, 3–29.

Oshinsky, David M. (1996). *Worse than slavery: Parchman farm and the ordeal of Jim Crow justice.* New York: Free Press.

Padavic, Irene and Barbara Reskin. (2002). *Women and men at work, 2nd edition.* Thousand Oaks, CA: Pine Forge Press.

Page, Benjamin I. (1983). *Who gets what from government.* Berkeley, CA: University of California Press.

Palmer, Phyllis M. (1989). *Domesticity and dirt: Housewives and domestic servants in the United States, 1920–1945.* Philadelphia: Temple University Press.

Parisi, Michael, and Michael Strudler. (2003). The 400 individual income tax returns reporting the highest adjusted gross incomes each year, 1992–2000. *SOI Bulletin, 25*, 7–9.

Parsons, Talcott. (1951). *The social system.* NY: Free Press.

———. (1954). A revised analytical approach to the theory of social stratification. pp. 386–439 in T. Parsons, *Essays in sociological theory, Revised Edition.* New York: Free Press.

Passell, Peter. (1998). Benefits dwindle along with wages for the unskilled. *New York Times,* National Edition. June 14, A-1.

Patterson, James T. (2000). *America's struggle against poverty in the twentieth century.* Cambridge, MA: Harvard University Press.

Patterson, Orlando. (1997). *The ordeal of integration: Progress and resentment in America's racial crisis.* New York: Civitas.

———. (2006). A poverty of the mind. *New York Times,* National Edition. March 26, p. A-22.

Pegula, Stephen M. (2005). Occupational injuries among groundskeepers, 1992–2002. *Compensation and Working Conditions Online.* Bureau of Labor Statistics: www.bls.gov.

Perrin, Emily. (1904). On the contingency betwen occupation in the case of fathers and sons. *Biometrika, 3*, 467–469.

Persell, Caroline Hodges, and Peter W. Cookson, Jr. (1985). Chartering and bartering: Elite education and social reproduction. *Social Problems, 33*, 114–129.

Personick, Martin E., and Laura A. Harthun. (1992). Job safety and health in soft drink manufacturing. *Monthly Labor Review, 15*(April), 12–18.

Pessen, Edward. (1971). The egalitarian myth and American social reality: Wealth, mobility, and equality in the "era of the common man." *American Historical Review, 76*, 989–1034.

———. (1973). *Riches, class, and power before the Civil War.* Lexington, MA: D.C. Heath & Co.

Petersen, Trond, and Ishak Saporta. (2004). The opportunity structure for discrimination. *American Journal of Sociology, 109*, 852–901.

Peterson, Richard A. (1996). A re-evaluation of the economic consequences of divorce. *American Sociological Review, 61*, 528–566.

Pettigrew, T. F., and L. R. Tropp. (2000). Does intergroup contact reduce prejudice? Recent meta-analytic findings. pp. 93–114 in S. Oskamp (ed.), *Reducing prejudice and discrimination: social psychological perspectives.* Mahwah, NJ: Lawrence Erlbaum.

Phillips, Kevin. (2002). *Wealth and democracy.* New York: Broadway Books.

Piketty, Thomas, and Emmanuel Saez. (2003). Income inequality in the United States, 1913–1998. *Quarterly Journal of Economics, 118*, 1–39.

———. (2006). The evolution of top incomes: A historical and international perspective. *American Economic Review, Papers and Proceedings, 96*, 200–205.

Pillay, Anthony L., and Susan Schouben-Hesk. (2001). Depression, anxiety, and hopelessness in sexually abused adolescent girls. *Psychological Reports, 88*, 727–730.

Piven, Frances Fox, and Richard A. Cloward. (1971). *Regulating the poor.* New York: Vintage Books.

———. (1977). *Poor people's movements.* New York: Pantheon.

———. (1988). *Why Americans don't vote.* New York: Pantheon.

Plotnick, Robert D., Eugene Smolensky, Eirik Evenhouse, et al. (1998). Inequality and poverty in the United States: The twentieth-century record. *Focus, 19*, 7–14.

Polikoff, Alexander. (2006). *Waiting for Gautreaux: A story of segregation, housing, and the black ghetto.* Evanston, IL: Northwestern University Press.

Portes, Alejandro, Manuel Castells, and Lauren A. Benton. (1989). *The informal economy: Studies in advanced and less developed countries.* Baltimore, MD: Johns Hopkins University Press.

Powell, G. Bingham. (1982). *Contemporary democracies: Participation, stability, and violence.* Cambridge, MA: Harvard University Press.

———. (1987). American voter turnout in comparative perspective. *American Political Science Review, 37*, 391–414.

Public Campaign. (2002). The evil of access. *Ouch! A regular bulletin on how money in politics hurts you. #106*(October 18): www.publiccampaign.org.

———. (2003). *State of the Union: Congress meets Wall Street.* www.publiccampaign.org.

Purdum, Todd. (2006). Go ahead, try to stop K Street. *New York Times,* National Edition. January 8, p. wk-1.

Reagan, Leslie. (1997). *When abortion was a crime: Women, medicine and the law in the United States.* Berkeley, CA: University of California Press.

Reardon, Jack. (1993). Injuries and illnesses among bituminous and lignite coal miners. *Monthly Labor Review, 115*(October), 49–55.

Reed, James. (1978). *From private vice to public virtue: The birth control movement and American society since 1830.* New York: Basic Books.

Reuter, Peter, Robert MacCoun, and Patrick Murphy. (1990). *Money from crime: A study of the economics of drug dealing in Washington, D.C.* Santa Monica, CA: Rand Corporation.

Revell, Janice. (2003). CEO pensions: The latest way to hide millions. *Fortune,* April 28, 68–70.

Reynolds, Morgan, and Eugene Smolensky. (1977). *Public expenditures, taxes, and the distribution of income: The United States, 1950, 1961, 1970.* New York: Academic Press.

Rhoden, William C. (2002). Oregon likes visibility on Broadway. *New York Times,* National Edition. July 25, p. C-10.

Ritter, Kathleen, and Lowell L. Hargens. (1975). Occupational positions and class identification: A test of the Asymmetry Hypothesis. *American Journal of Sociology, 80*, 934–948.

Rodriguez, Ned, Hendrika V. Kemp, Susan W. Ryan, et al. (1997). Post-traumatic stress disorder in adult female survivors of childhood sexual abuse. *Journal of Consulting and Clinical Psychology, 65*, 53–60.

Rose, Stephen J., and Heidi J. Hartmann. (2004). Still a man's labor market: The long-term earnings gap. Washington, DC: Institute for Women's Policy Research.

Rosen, Sherwin. (1981). The economics of superstars. *American Economic Review 71*, 845–858.

Rosenstone, Steven, and John Mark Hansen. (1993). *Mobilization, participation, and democracy in America.* New York: Macmillan.

Rosenthal, Robert, and Lenore Jacobson. (1968). *Pygmalion in the classroom: Teacher expectations and pupils' intellectual development.* New York: Holt, Rinehart, and Winston.

Roth, Guenther. (1968). Introduction. pp. 27–104 in Max Weber, *Economy and society: An outline of interpretive sociology*. New York: Bedminster Press.

Rothenberg, Paula S. (2004). *White privilege*. New York: Worth Publishers.

Rothman, Ellen K. (1984). *Hands and hearts: A history of courtship in America*. New York: Basic Books.

Royster, Deirdre. (2003). *Race and the invisible hand: How white networks exclude black men from blue-collar jobs*. Berkeley, CA: University of California Press.

Rubin, Lillian. (1994). *Families on the fault line*. New York: HarperCollins Publishers.

Rusk, David. (2001). *The "Segregation Tax:" The cost of racial segregation to black homeowners*. Washington, DC: Brookings Institution.

Rusk, Jerrold. (1970). The effect of the Australian ballet reform on split ticket voting: 1876–1908. *American Political Science Review*, 72, 22–45.

Russell, Diane E. H., and Rebecca M. Bolen. (2000). *The epidemic of rape and child sexual abuse in the United States*. Thousand Oaks, CA: Sage.

Ryscavage, Paul. (1999). *Income inequality in America: An analysis of trends*. New York: M.E. Sharpe.

Rytina, Steven. (2000). Is occupational mobility declining in the U.S.? *Social Forces*, 78, 1227–1276.

Sachs, Jeffrey. (2005). *The end of poverty: Economic possibilities for our time*. New York: Penguin Books.

———. (2006). Can extreme poverty be eliminated? *Scientific American*, 293(September), 55–65.

Saez, Emmanuel. (2006). Income and wealth concentration in a historical and international perspective. pp. 221–259 in Alan J. Auerbach, David Card, and John M. Quigley (eds.), *Public policy and income redistribution*. New York: Russell Sage.

Sagan, Carl. (1984). Nuclear war and climatic catastrophe. *Foreign Affairs*, 62, 257–292.

Sander, William. (1992). Unemployment and marital status in Great Britain. *Social Biology*, 39, 299–305.

Sanderson, Warren. (1979). Quantitative aspects of marriage, fertility, and family limitation in nineteenth-century America. *Demography*, 16, 339–358.

Sawhill, Isabel V. (2000). Opportunity in the United States: Myth or reality? pp. 22–35 in N. Birdsall and C. Graham (eds.), *New markets, new opportunities?: Economic and social mobility in a changing world*. Washington, DC: Brookings Institution.

Sawinski, Zbigniew, and Henryk Domanski. (1991). Stability of prestige hierarchies in the face of social changes: Poland, 1958–1987. *International Sociology*, 6, 227–242.

Sayer, Liana C. (2006). Economic aspects of divorce and relationship dissolution. pp. 385–408 in Mark A. Fine and John H. Harvey (eds.), *Handbook of divorce and relationship dissolution*. Mahwah, NJ: Lawrence Erlbaum.

Sayer, Liana C., and Susanne M. Bianchi. (2000). Women's economic independence and the probability of divorce. *Journal of Family Issues*, 21, 906–943.

Schoen, Robert, Nan Marie Astone, Kendra Rothert, et al. (2002). Women's employment, marital happiness, and divorce. *Social Forces*, 81, 643–662.

Scofea, Laura A. (1994). The development and growth of employer-provided health insurance. *Monthly Labor Review*, 117(March), 3–10.

Scott, John. (2001). *Power*. New York: Cambridge University Press.

Scully, Diana, and Joseph Marolla. (2005). "Riding the bull at Gilley's": Convicted rapists describe the rewards of rape. pp. 15–30 in Claire M. Renzetti and Raquel Kennedy Bergen (eds.), *Violence against women*. Lanham, MD: Rowman & Littlefield.

Sewell, William H., Archibald O. Haller, and George W. Ohlendorf. (1970). The educational and early occupational attainment process: Replication and revisions. *American Sociological Review*, 35, 1014–1027.

Sewell, William H., and Vimal P. Shah. (1968a). Social class, parental encouragement, and educational aspirations. *American Journal of Sociology*, 73, 559–572.

———. (1968b). Parent's education and children's educational aspirations and achievements. *American Sociological Review*, 35, 1014–1027.

Shafer, Byron E. (1999). American exceptionalism. *Annual Review of Political Science*. 2, 445–463.

Shakespeare, William. (1989). *Romeo and Juliet*. London: Metheun Drama.

———. (1991). *Measure for measure*. New York: Cambridge University Press.

Shapiro, Isaac. (2005). New IRS data show income inequality is again on the rise. Washington, DC: Center on Budget and Policy Priorities.

Shaw, George Bernard. (1957). *Pygmalion*. New York: Penguin.

Shehan, Constance. (2003). *Marriages and Families, 2nd Edition*. Boston: Allyn & Bacon.

Shipler, David. (1993). Jefferson is America—and America is Jefferson. *New York Times*, National Edition. April 12, p. A-12.

———. (2005). *The working poor: Invisible In America*, with a new epilogue. New York: Vintage.

Sibley, Elbridge. (1942). Some demographic clues to stratification. *American Sociological Review*, 7, 315–325.

Simmel, Georg. (1908). Conflict. pp. 1–20 in G. Simmel, *Conflict and the web of group affiliations*. New York: Free Press, 1954.

Simon, Scott. (2002). *Jackie Robinson and the integration of baseball*. New York: John Wiley & Sons.

Sims, Calvin. (2006). An arm in the air for that cab ride home. *New York Times*, National Edition. October 15, wk3.

Sixma, H., and W.C. Ultee (1984). An occupational scale for the Netherlands in the eighties. pp. 101–115 in B.F. Bakker (ed.), *Social stratification and mobility in the Netherlands*. Amsterdam: SISWO.

Skellington, Richard. (1992). *Race in Britain today*. London: Sage.

Slemrod, Joel, and Jon Bakija. (2004). *Taxing ourselves: A citizen's guide to the great debate over taxes, 3rd Edition*. Cambridge, MA: MIT Press.

Smeeding, Timothy. (2005). Poor people in rich nations: The United States in comparative perspective. Luxembourg Income Study Working Paper No. 419. Syracuse, NY: Maxwell School of Citizenship and Public Affairs.

Smith, Adam. (1976 [1776]). *An inquiry into the nature and causes of the wealth of nations*. Oxford: Clarendon.

Smith, J. Owens. (1987). *The politics of racial inequality*. NY: Greenwood Press.

Smock, Pamela J., Wendy D. Manning, and Sanjiv Gupta. (1999). The effect of marriage and divorce on women's economic well-being. *American Sociological Review*, 64, 794–812.

Snyder, David. (2004). Mother accused of locking 2 in shed is released on bond. *Washington Post*. November 21, p. A-1.

Social Security Administration. (2006). *What are the tax, benefit, and earning amounts for 2006?* www.ssa.gov.

———. (2006a) *Annual Report of the Supplemental Security Income Program*. Washington, DC: U.S. Government Printing Office.

Solon, Gary. (1992). Cross-country differences in intergenerational earnings mobility. *Journal of Economic Perspectives*, 16, 59–66.

Soltow, Lee. (1975). The wealth, income, and social class of men in large northern cities in 1860. pp. 233–276 in James D. Smith (ed.), *The personal distribution of income and wealth*. New York: National Bureau of Economic Research.

Sorokin, Pitirim. (1927). *Social and cultural mobility*. New York: Free Press, 1959.

Special Advisor to the Board of Police Commissioners on the Civil Disorders in Los Angeles. (1994). *City in crisis*. Los

Angeles: Special Advisor to the Board of Police Commissioners.

Squires, Gregory D., and Sally O'Conner. (2001). *Color and money: Politics and prospects for community reinvestment in urban America*. Albany, NY: State University of New York Press.

Stack, Carol B. (1974). *All our kin: Strategies for survival in a black community*. New York: Harper & Row.

Stanley, Thomas J., and William D. Danko. (1998). *The millionaire next door*. New York: Pocket Books.

Staples, Brent. (2003). Just walk on by: A black man ponders his power to alter public space. pp. 130–133 in Donald M. McQuade and Robert Atwan (eds.), *The writer's presence*. Boston: St. Martin's Press.

Starr, Paul. (1982). *The transformation of American medicine*. New York: Basic Books.

Statistics Netherlands. (2005). *Statistical yearbook of the Netherlands, 2005*. The Hague: Statistics Netherlands.

Statistics Sweden. (2005). *Statistical yearbook of Sweden, 2005*. Örebro, Sweden: Statistics Sweden.

Steelwater, Eliza. (2003). *The hangman's knot: Lynching, legal execution, and America's struggle with the death penalty*. Boulder, CO: Westview Press.

Stevenson, Betsy, and Justin Wolfers. (2003). *Bargaining in the shadow of the law: Divorce laws and family distress*. NBER Working Paper No. 10175. Cambridge, MA: National Bureau of Economic Research.

Stock, Jacqueline L. (1997). Adolescent pregnancy and sexual risk-taking among sexually abused girls. *Family Planning Perspectives, 29*, 200–203.

Stockwell, Jamie. (2004). Mother saw shed as only option. *Washington Post*, November 22, p. A-1.

Strathlee, S.A., R. Ikeda, N. Shah, et al. (2001). Childhood sexual abuse independently predicts early initiation of injection drug use. *American Journal of Epidemiology, 153*, 179–190.

Stratmann, Thomas. (1995). Campaign contributions and congressional voting: Does the timing of contributions matter? *Review of Economics and Statistics, 77*, 127–137.

Sullivan, Harry Stack. (1940). *Conceptions of modern psychiatry*. Washington, DC: William A. White Foundation.

Swain, Carol M. (2001). Affirmative action: Legislative history, judicial interpretations, public consensus. pp. 318–347 in Neil Smelser, William Julius Wilson, and Faith Mitchell (eds.), *America becoming: Racial trends and their consequences, Volume I*. Washington, DC: National Academy Press.

Swarns, Rachel L. (2004). "African American" becomes a term for debate. *New York Times*, National Edition. August 29, p. A-1.

Sygnatur, Eric F. (1998). Logging is perilous work. *Compensation and Working Conditions, 4*(Winter), 3–7.

Takaki, Ronald. (1989). *Strangers from a different shore: A history of Asian Americans*. New York: Penguin Books.

Taylor, A.J., G. McGwin, F. Valent, et al. (2002). Fatal occupational electrocutions in the United States. *Injury Prevention, 8*, 306–313.

Teachman, Jay, Lucky Tedrow, and Matthew Hall. (2006). The demographic future of divorce and dissolution. pp. 59–84 in Mark A. Fine and John H. Harvey (eds.), *Handbook of divorce and relationship dissolution*. Mahwah, NJ: Lawrence Erlbaum.

Teixeira, Ruy A. (1992). *The disappearing American voter*. Washington, DC: Brookings Institution.

Thernstrom, Abigail, and Stephan Thernstrom (eds.). (2002). *Beyond the color line: New perspectives on race and ethnicity in America*. Stanford, CA: Hoover Institution Press.

Thernstrom, Stephan, and Abigail Thernstrom. (1997). *America in black and white: One nation indivisible*. New York: Simon & Schuster.

Thompson, Starley, and Stephen H. Schneider. (1986). Nuclear winter reappraised. *Foreign Affairs, 64*, 981–1005.

Thornton, Russell. (1987). *American Indian holocaust and survival: A population history since 1492*. Norman, OK: University of Oklahoma Press.

———. (2001). Trends among American Indians in the United States. pp. 135–169 in Neil Smelser, William Julius Wilson, and Faith Mitchell (eds.), *America becoming: Racial trends and their consequences, Volume I*. Washington, DC: National Academy Press.

Tierney, John. (2006). Your page, M'Lord. *New York Times*, National Edition, October 3, p. A-23.

Tobias, Sarah, and David Callahan. (2002). *Expanding the vote: The practice and promise of election day registration*. New York: Demos—A Network for Ideas and Action.

Tocqueville, Alexis de. (1954 [1835]). *Democracy in America*. New York: New American Library.

Tolnay, Stewart E., and E.M. Beck. (1995). *A festival of violence: An analysis of Southern lynchings, 1882–1930*. Urbana, IL: University of Illinois Press.

Tolnay, Stewart E., E.M. Beck, and James L. Massey. (1992). Black competition and white vengence: Legal execution of blacks as social control in the American South. *Social Science Quarterly, 73*, 627–644.

Toobin, Jeffrey. (2003). The great election grab. *The New Yorker*. December 8, 63–80.

Treiman, Donald J. (1977). *Occupational prestige in comparative perspective*. New York: Academic Press.

———. (2000). Occupations, stratification, and mobility. pp. 297–313 in Judith R. Blau (ed.), *The Blackwell companion of sociology*. Malden, MA: Blackwell Publishers.

Treiman, Donald J., and Harry B.G. Ganzeboom. (1990). Cross-national status attainment research. *Research in Social Stratification and Mobility, 9*, 105–130.

Treiman, Donald J., and Kam-Bor Yip. (1989). Educational and occupational attainment in 21 countries. pp. 373–394 in M.L. Kohn (ed.), *Cross-national research in sociology*. Newbury Park, CA: Sage.

Trelease, Allen W. (1971). *White terror: The Ku Klux Klan conspiracy and Southern reconstruction*. New York: Harper & Row.

Tumin, Melvin M. (ed.). (1970). *Readings in social stratification*. Englewood Cliffs, NJ: Prentice-Hall.

Turner, Frederick Jackson. (1920). *The significance of the frontier in American history*. New York: Henry Holt.

Turner, Jonathan H. (1984). *Societal stratification*. New York: Columbia University Press.

———. (2003). *The structure of sociological theory*, 7th Edition Belmont, CA: Wadsworth Publishing Co.

Turner, Jonathan H., Leonard Beeghley, and Charles Powers. (2006). *The emergence of sociological theory*, 6th Edition. Belmont, CA: Wadsworth Publishing Co.

Turner, Margery Austin, Stephen L. Ross, George C. Galster, et al. (2002). *Discrimination in metropolitan housing markets: National results from phase 1—African Americans and Hispanic Americans*. Washington, DC: United States Department of Housing and Urban Development.

Turner, Margery Austin, and Stephen L. Ross. (2003a). *Discrimination in metropolitan housing markets: Phase 2—Asians and Pacific Islanders*. Washington, DC: United States Department of Housing and Urban Development.

Turner, Margery Austin, and Stephen L. Ross. (2003b). *Discrimination in metropolitan housing markets: Phase 3—Native Americans*. Washington, DC: United States Department of Housing and Urban Development.

Twain, Mark. (1963). *Roughing it, Vol. 2*. Hartford, CT: American Publishing Company.

Uchitelle, Louis. (2006). *The disposable American: Layoffs and their consequences*. New York: Knopf.

Ueda, Reed (ed.). (2006). *A companion to American immigration*. New York: Blackwell.

Ueda, Reed. (1994). *Postwar immigrant America: A social history*. Boston: St. Martin's Press.

Uggen, Christopher, and Jeff Manza. (2002). Democratic contraction? Political consequences of felon disenfranchisement in the United States. *American Sociological Review*, 67, 777–803.

Uggen, Christopher, and Amy Blackstone. (2004). Sexual harassment as a gendered expression of power. *American Sociological Review*, 69, 64–92.

United Nations. (2005). *United Nations 2005 Development Programme Report*. New York: United Nations.

United States Bureau of the Census. (1975). *Historical statistics of the United States: Colonial times to 1970*. Washington, DC: U.S. Government Printing Office.

———. (1994). Tracking the American Dream—Fifty years of housing history. *Current Population Reports*, Series H121/94–1. Washington, DC: U.S. Government Printing Office.

———. (2001). The 65 years and over population: 2000. *Census 2000 Brief*. Washington, DC: U.S. Government Printing Office.

———. (2002a). Racial and ethnic residential segregation in the United States, 1980–2000. *Current Population Reports*, censr-3. Washington, DC: U.S. Government Printing Office.

———. (2002b). Voting and registration in the election of November 2000. *Current Population Reports*, pp. 20–542. Washington, DC: U.S. Government Printing Office.

———. (2002c). Poverty in the United States, 2001. *Current Population Reports*, pp. 60–219. Washington, DC: U.S. Government Printing Office.

———. (2003). Custodial mothers and fathers and their child support: 2001. *Current Population Reports*, pp. 60–225. Washington, DC: U.S. Government Printing Office.

———. (2005). Income, poverty, and health insurance coverage in the United States: 2004. *Current Population Reports*, pp. 60–229. Washington, DC: U.S. Government Printing Office.

———. (2006). *Statistical abstract of the United States*. Washington, DC: U.S. Government Printing Office.

———. (2006a). Asian and Pacific Islander population in the United States: March, 2002. *Current Population Reports*, pp. 20–540. Washington, DC: U.S. Government Printing Office.

———. (2006b). Voting and registration in the election of November 2004. *Current Population Reports*, pp. 20–556. Washington, DC: U.S. Government Printing Office.

———. (2006c). *Annual demographic survey, March Supplement*. www.census.gov.

———. (2006d). Income, poverty, and health insurance coverage in the United States: 2005. *Current Population Reports*, pp. 60–231. Washington, DC: U.S. Government Printing Office.

United States Bureau of Labor Statistics. (2004). Time-use survey—First results announced by BLS. *News: United States Department of Labor*. Washington, DC: U.S. Government Printing Office.

———. (2005). *Employment and earnings, vol. 52* (January). Washington, DC: U.S. Government Printing Office.

———. (2005a). *Women in the labor force: A databook*. Washington, DC: U.S. Government Printing Office.

———. (2005b). Lost-worktime injuries and illnesses: Characteristics and resulting days away from work, 2004. *News: Bureau of Labor Statistics*. Washington, DC: U.S. Government Printing Office.

———. (2006). *Employment and earnings, vol. 53* (January). Washington, DC: U.S. Government Printing Office.

———. (2006a). National census of fatal occupational injuries in 2005. *News: United States Department of Labor*. Washington, DC: U.S. Government Printing Office.

———. (2006b). The employment situation. *News: United States Department of Labor*. Washington, DC: U.S. Government Printing Office.

———. (2006c). *Insulation workers*. www.bls.gov.

———. (2006d). Consumer expenditures in 2004. *Report 992*. Washington, DC: U.S. Government Printing Office.

United States Conference of Mayors. (2006). *A status report on hunger and homelessness in America's cities: 2005*. Washington, DC: United States Conference of Mayors.

United States Department of Agriculture. (2002). *Agriculture fact book*. Washington, DC: U.S. Government Printing Office.

———. (2005). Household food security in the United States, 2004. *Food Assistance and Nutrition Report*, Number 42. Washington, DC: U.S. Government Printing Office.

———. (2006). *Food Stamp Program*. www.fns.usda.gov/fspmain.

———. (2006a). *Program data: Food Stamp Program*. www.fns.usda.gov.fspmain.

United States Department of Health and Human Services. (2002). *Child maltreatment 2000*. Washington, DC: U.S. Government Printing Office.

———. (2006). Welfare reform reauthorized. *News Release*, February 8.

United States Department of Labor. (2006). *National Compensation Survey: Employee benefits in private industry in the United States*. Washington, DC: U.S. Government Printing Office.

United States Office of Family Assistance. (2006). *Temporary Assistance for Needy Families*. www.acf.hhs.gov.

Useem, Jerry. (2003). Have they no shame? Their performance stank last year, yet most CEOs got paid more than ever. Here's how they're getting away with it. *Fortune*, April 28, 56–64.

Valian, Virginia. (1998). *Why so slow? The advancement of women*. Cambridge, MA: The MIT Press.

van den Berg, Axel. (1993). Creeping embourgeoisement? Some comments on the Marxist discovery of the new middle class. *Research in Stratification*, 12, 295–328.

Van Velsor, Ellen, and Leonard Beeghley. (1979). Class identification among employed married women. *Journal of Marriage and the Family*, 41, 771–779.

Vandal, Gilles. (2000). *Rethinking Southern violence: Homicide in post-Civil War Louisiana, 1866–1884*. Columbus, OH: Ohio State University Press.

Vanneman, Reeve, and Fred C. Pampel. (1977). The American perception of class and status. *American Sociological Review*, 42, 422–437.

Veblen, Thorstein. (1979 (1899)). *The theory of the leisure class*. New York: Penguin Books.

Vernon, Amelia Wallace. (1993). *African Americans at Mars Bluff, South Carolina*. Baton Rouge, LA: Louisiana State University Press.

Voslenski, Michael. (1985). *Nomenklatura: The Soviet ruling class*. New York: Doubleday.

Wakin, Daniel J. (2005). In violin sections, women make their presence heard. *New York Times*, National Edition. July 23, p. A-16.

Waldinger, Roger. (1995). The "other side" of embeddedness: A case study of the interplay between economy and ethnicity. *Ethnic and Racial Studies*, 18, 555–580.

Wallace, James. (1993). *Hard drive: Bill Gates and the making of the Microsoft empire*. New York: HarperCollins Publishers.

Wallace, Michael. (1997). Revisiting Broom and Cushing's "modest test of an immodest theory," In *Research in Social Stratification and Mobility*, 17, 239–254.

Wallerstein, Immanuel. (1974). *The modern world system*. New York: Academic Press.

Warner, Judith. (2005). *Perfect madness: Motherhood in the age of anxiety*. New York: Riverhead Books.

Warren, John Robert, Robert M. Hauser, and Jennifer T. Sheridan. (2002). Occupational stratification across the life course: Evidence from the Wisconsin Longitudinal Study. *American Sociological Review*, 67, 432–455.

Warren, Maryanne. (1996). On the moral and legal status of abortion. pp. 434–440 in T.A. Mappes and D. DeGrazia (eds.), *Biomedical ethics, 4th edition*. Boston: McGraw-Hill.

Weber, Max. (1946a [1920]). Science as a vocation. pp. 129–158 in *From Max Weber: Essays in sociology*. New York: Oxford University Press.

———. (1946b [1920]). Politics as a vocation. pp. 77–128 in *From Max Weber: Essays in sociology*. New York: Oxford University Press.

———. (1949 [1904]). Objectivity in social science and social policy. In *The methodology of the social sciences*. New York: Free Press.

———. (1951 [1913]). *Religion of China*. New York: Free Press.

———. (1952 [1917]). *Religion of India*. New York: Free Press.

———. (1958 [1905]). *The Protestant ethic and the spirit of capitalism*. New York: Scribners.

———. (1968 [1920]). *Economy and society: An outline of interpretive sociology*. New York: Bedminster Press.

Webster, Timothy. (1999). Work-related injuries, illnesses, and fatalities in manufacturing and construction. *Compensation and Working Conditions, 5* (Fall), 34–38.

Weeden, Kim. A. (2002). Why do some occupations pay more than others? Social closure and earnings inequality in the United States. *American Journal of Sociology, 108*, 55–101.

———. (2004). Profiles of change: Sex segregation in the United States, 1910–2000. pp. 131–178 in Maria Charles and David B. Grusky (eds.), *Occupational ghettos: The worldwide segregation of men and women*. Stanford, CA: Stanford University Press.

Weeden, Kim A., and David H. Grusky. (2005). The case for a new class map. *American Journal of Sociology, 111*, 141–212.

Weinberg, Albert K. (1935). *Manifest Destiny: A study of nationalist expansionism in American history*. Baltimore: Johns Hopkins University Press.

Weisbrot, Mark. (1998). *Welfare reform: The jobs aren't there*. Washington, DC: Preamble Center for Public Policy.

Welsh, Sandy. (1999). Gender and sexual harassment. *Annual Review of Sociology, Vol. 25*. New York: Annual Reviews, Inc.

Westoff, Charles F. (1988). Contraceptive paths toward a reduction of unintended pregnancy and abortion. *Family Planning Perspectives, 20*, 4–13.

Whelpton, Pascal K. (1928). Industrial development and population growth. *Social Forces, 6*, 458–467.

Wilkerson, Isabel. (2005). Angela Whitaker's climb. pp. 202–233 in Correspondents of the New York Times. *Class Matters*. New York: Henry Holt.

Willer, David, and Murray Webster. (1970). Theoretical concepts and observables. *American Sociological Review, 35*, 748–756.

Williams, Bruce B. (1987). *Black workers in an industrial suburb: The struggle against discrimination*. New Brunswick, NJ: Rutgers University Press.

Williams, Lou Falkner. (1996). *The great South Carolina Ku Klux Klan trials, 1871–1872*. Athens, GA: University of Georgia Press.

Williamson, Jeffrey G., and Peter H. Lindert. (1980). *American inequality: A macroeconomic history*. New York: Academic Press.

Wilson, Fiona, and Paul Thompson. (2001). Sexual harassment as an exercise of power. *Gender, Work, and Organization, 8*, 61–83.

Wilson, George. (1997). Pathways to power: Racial differences in the determinants of job authority. *Social Problems, 44*, 38–54.

Wilson, George, Ian Sakura-Lemessy, Jonathan P. West. (1999). Reaching the top: Racial differences in mobility paths to upper-tier occupations. *Work and Occupations, 26*, 165–186.

Wilson, William J. (1996). *When work disappears: The world of the new urban poor*. New York: Knopf.

Winship, Christopher. (1992). Race, poverty, and "the American occupational structure." *Contemporary Sociology, 21*, 639–643.

Wolfe, Alan. (1998). Climbing the mountain: The second volume of Taylor Branch's study of Martin Luther King Jr. runs from the March on Washington to Selma. *New York Times Book Review*, January *18*, 12.

Wolfe, Jessica, Erica Sharkansky, Jennifer P. Read, et al. (1998). Sexual harassment and assault as predictors of PTSD symptomatology among U.S. female Persian Gulf War military personnel. *Journal of Interpersonal Violence, 13*, 40–58.

Wolff, Edward N. (2002). *Top heavy: The increasing inequality of wealth in America and what can be done about it*. New York: The New Press.

Woodward, C. Vann. (1966). *The strange career of Jim Crow*. New York: Oxford University Press.

Wong, Jan. (2006). Maid for a month, part I: Coming clean. *Toronto Globe and Mail*, April 1, p. A-1.

———. (2006a). Maid for a month, part II: The rules: No radio, no eating, no talking, no laughing, and never use a client's washroom. *Toronto Globe and Mail*, April 8, p. A-1.

———. (2006b). Maid for a month, part III: Cinder Sam and Benderalla. *Toronto Globe and Mail*, April 15, p. A-1.

———. (2006c). Maid for a month, part IV: Maggie and Me. *Toronto Globe and Mail*, April 28, p. A-1.

Wordes, Madeline, and Michell Nunez. (2002). *Our vulnerable teenagers: Their victimization, its consequences, and directions for prevention and intervention*. Washington, DC: National Center for Victims of Crime.

World Bank. (2006). *World Development Report, 2007*. Washington, DC: World Bank.

———. (2006a). *World Development Indicators*. www.devdata.worldbank.org.

World Health Organization. (2006). *Abortion rates, 1980–2000*. www.euro.who.int.

Wright, Erik Olin. (1997). *Classes*. New York: Verso.

Wyatt, Ian D., and Daniel E. Hecker. (2006). Occupational changes during the 20th century. *Monthly Labor Review, 129* (March), 35–57.

Xu, Wu, and Ann Leffler. (1992). Gender and race effects on occupational prestige, segregation, and earnings. *Gender & Society, 6*, 376–392.

Yamaguchi, Kazuo, and Vantao Wang. (2002). Class identification of married employed women and men in America. *American Journal of Sociology, 108*, 440–475.

Yaqub, Reshma Memon. (1999). Perking right along: The trends in benefits and goodies. *Worth Guide to Benefits, Compensation, and Perks, 8* (Winter), 14–21.

Yinger, John. (1997). Cash in your face: The cost of racial and ethnic discrimination in housing. *Journal of Urban Economics, 42*, 339–365.

Zangrando, Robert L. (1980). *The NAACP crusade against lynching, 1909–1950*. Philadelphia: Temple University Press.

Zax, Jeffrey S., and John F. Kain. (1996). Moving to the suburbs: Do relocating companies leave their black employees behind? *Journal of Labor Economics, 14*, 472–504.

Zelizer, Viviana A. (1994). *The social meaning of money*. New York: Basic.

Zhou, Xueguang. (2005). The institutional logic of occupational prestige ranking: Reconceptualization and reanalyses. *American Journal of Sociology, 111*, 90–140.

Zipp, John F., and Eric Plutzer. (2000). From housework to paid work: The implications of women's labor force experiences on class identity. *Social Science Quarterly, 81*, 538–554.

Zweig, Michael. (2000). *The working class majority: America's best kept secret*. Ithaca, NY: ILR Press.

———. (2004). *What's class got to do with it? American society in the Twenty-first century*. Ithaca, NY: ILR Press.

INDEX